Magic Lies
The Art of W.O. Mitchell

As the author of one of Canada's all-time best-selling novels, *Who Has Seen the Wind*, W.O. Mitchell presents an unusual challenge to those who consider Canadian popular culture a contradiction in terms. *Magic Lies* celebrates the range of this versatile author, whose writing bridges the border between serious art and mass culture. It is the first book to take a comprehensive look at the sixty-year career of this important Canadian writer and how he has transformed the role of the community storyteller into that of national mythologizer.

The first section in *Magic Lies* examines Mitchell's fiction; the second, his writings for radio, television, and theatre; and the third is composed of interviews and personal recollections. Contributors include literary scholars, novelists, theatre and television directors, an actor, and a popular radio host and journalist. Together their essays invite further creative readings and critical dialogue, and deepen our understanding of a writer whose sense of community and locality has influenced a national literary tradition.

Given the broad appeal of Mitchell's work and the interdisciplinary nature of this collection, *Magic Lies* will interest both general readers and scholars in the areas of English literature, drama, broadcasting, Canadian studies, and popular culture.

SHEILA LATHAM is a librarian and has completed a dissertation on Mitchell at the University of Leeds.

DAVID LATHAM teaches Canadian and English literature at York University.

Magic Lies

The Art of
W.O. Mitchell

Edited by
Sheila Latham and David Latham

University of Toronto Press
Toronto Buffalo London

Canadian Cataloguing in Publication Data

Main entry under title:

Magic lies : the art of W.O. Mitchell

Includes bibliographical references and index.
ISBN 0-8020-0967-0 (bound)   ISBN 0-8020-7930-X (pbk.)

1. Mitchell, W.O. (William Ormond). 1914–   – Criticism
and interpretation.   I. Latham,
Sheila.   II. Latham, David William, 1951–   .

PS8526.I9765Z78 1997   C813'.54   C97-930514-4
PR9199.3.M57Z78 1997

University of Toronto Press acknowledges the assistance to its publishing program of the Canada Council and the Ontario Arts Council

Contents

Preface

As a study of academic literature and popular culture, *Magic Lies* is the first collection of essays that investigates the unusual versatility of W.O. Mitchell. He began his career at the forefront of popular culture in Canada, turning his literary skills from university quarterlies to family magazines and radio shows. As a 'liar hunter' exploring the popular art of the people, he has contended that a country's richest ore is its folklore, the self-creating 'magic lies' by which we write ourselves into existence. These critical essays are meant to be magic lies as well, inviting and provoking further creative readings and critical dialogue which may thereby contribute to the popularizing of an otherwise academic literary culture. Mitchell describes this dialogical experience between writer and reader as a creative partnership wherein the reader detonates the repressed implications of the writer's text: 'If the artist allows a creative partner to complete the art experience, that is where the real magic happens. The writer deals in provocative cues to character or to people; it's as though the writer mines his piece of art with triggers, and the explosion takes place within the creative partner... *That's* the creative magic; that's when it gets away from these funny artificial symbols of words on white paper, and it becomes creation' (qtd. in Cameron 53–54).

The collection redresses the imbalanced attention to Mitchell's earlier work by presenting the first extended analysis of his later work. From 1947 to 1980 Mitchell published four books of fiction;

since 1980 he has published seven books of fiction and one book of plays. Previous criticism was fixed on the early work; the recent prolific period received virtually nothing more than brief book reviews. Though some might argue that academics were marginalizing Mitchell, it is more important to emphasize that all of these eight recent books have been best sellers. Mitchell is here analyzed for the artistry of his literary texts and for the mass appeal of his productions for popular culture.

In various interviews over the years, Mitchell has discussed the dichotomy between his responsibility as a serious novelist and his reputation as a popular entertainer. *Magic Lies* celebrates the range of a writer who has managed to transcend the alleged border between serious art and popular culture. The transcendence could not have been accomplished easily for a writer growing up in a country that has long remained unsure of itself, with too many of its artists left relegated to the margins of a culture dominated by the interests of foreign markets.

What makes this collection of essays unique is the diverse approaches of its contributors. In addition to the academic scholars, the contributors include two theatre directors; a television director and actor; two fiction writers – one a contemporary, the other a former student who discusses Mitchell's role as a teacher; and a popular radio host and journalist who followed Mitchell as an editor of *Maclean's*. Their essays demonstrate the complexity of his rural prairie novels and his Livingstone University novels, his short stories and his radio scripts, his stage plays and his television scripts. The index directs the reader to the different discussions of his work in a variety of media, including each of his books: *Who Has Seen the Wind* (1947), *Jake and the Kid* (1961), *The Kite* as a novel (1962), *The Black Bonspiel of Wullie MacCrimmon* as a novella (1964), *The Devil's Instrument* (1973), *The Vanishing Point* (1973), *How I Spent My Summer Holidays* (1981), *Dramatic W.O. Mitchell* (1982, containing the stage plays *Back to Beulah*, *The Black Bonspiel of Wullie MacCrimmon*, *The Devil's Instrument*, *For Those in Peril on the Sea*, and *The Kite*), *Since Daisy Creek* (1984), *Ladybug, Ladybug ...* (1988), *According to Jake and the Kid* (1989), *Roses Are*

Difficult Here (1990), and *For Art's Sake* (1992), and *The Black Bonspiel of Wullie MacCrimmon* as a novel (1993).

This first major book on W.O. Mitchell is thus intended to serve a wide audience of scholars, students, and general readers with its variety of critical approaches to Mitchell's literature and the personal insights of novelists, journalists, directors, and actors regarding his contributions to popular culture.

The young writer at his typewriter in 1946. Courtesy of the W.O. Mitchell Papers, University of Calgary Libraries

Mitchell near his High River home in 1946, posing on the prairie for the photograph included on the original dust jacket for *Who Has Seen the Wind*. Courtesy of Macmillan Canada

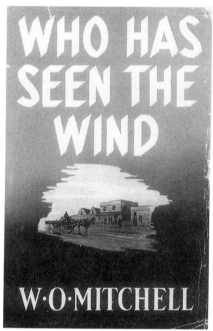
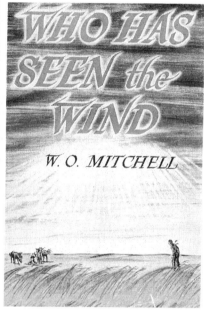

The dust jackets for (top) the Macmillan (Toronto) and (bottom) the Atlantic-Little, Brown (Boston) editions of *Who Has Seen the Wind*, published in February 1947

Murray Westgate as Jake and Rex Hagon as the Kid in the 'You Gotta Teeter' episode of the *Jake and the Kid* CBC television series, broadcast on 25 July 1961. Directed by David Gardner. Photo by Albert Crookshank, courtesy of the Canadian Broadcasting Corporation

Ben Campbell as the Kid and Shaun Johnston as Jake in the 'Prairie Lawyer' episode of the *Jake and the Kid* Nelvana series, broadcast on Global Television 20 January 1996. Directed by Otta Hanus. Photo by Robert Van Schaik, courtesy of Nelvana Ltd

Les Barringer as Keith, John Vernon as David, and Jack Creley as Daddy Sherry in the CBC television production of 'The Kite' for *Show of the Week*, broadcast on 26 April 1965. Directed by David Gardner. Photo by Dale Barnes, courtesy of the Canadian Broadcasting Corporation

Roger Dunn as Pipe-Fitting Charlie, Stephen Russell as the Devil, and David Glyn-Jones as Wullie in the Theatre Aquarius's stage production of *The Black Bonspiel of Wullie MacCrimmon*, 27 October–13 November 1993. Directed by Peter Mandia. Photo by Barry Gray, courtesy of the Hamilton *Spectator*

Mitchell in 1988. Photo by Ed Ellis for the dust jacket of *Ladybug, Ladybug...*
Courtesy of McClelland and Stewart

Magic Lies

W.O. Mitchell: An Introduction

DAVID LATHAM AND SHEILA LATHAM

'Who is the reader? He is another part of myself. That's why I read
aloud to myself.' (qtd. in Adachi, M3)

'The art experience is not private; it is a bridging, or at least the illusion of bridging, between two creative partners; the artist and
his reader.' (*Free-fall*, i)

The popularity of W.O. Mitchell as a literary figure who has
bridged the divide between academic art and popular culture is a
remarkable phenomenon. It refutes such contemporary presump-
tions as Gore Vidal's complaint that the phrase 'famous novelist'
has become about as oxymoronic as 'famous ceramicist.' Through
the power of his prose and the charisma of his personality,
Mitchell has managed to transform the role of the community
story-teller into that of a national mythologizer for a country of
disparate regions that stubbornly resist shared experiences. *Who
Has Seen the Wind* is among the all-time best-selling novels in
Canada. *How I Spent My Summer Holidays* is considered to be comparable to Mark Twain's *Huckleberry Finn*, both novels being the
darker companion to each author's first novel. With *Jake and the
Kid* Mitchell moved to the forefront of popular culture as he
experimented with the new genres of the broadcasting media. He
wrote the *Jake* stories first for family magazines in the 1940s, next
as weekly radio scripts in the 1950s, then for a television series in

the 1960s, and they are now loosely adapted as hour-long television dramas in the 1990s.

A key to his success may be found in his contention that 'the basis of all literature is oral performance' (qtd. in Kirchhoff, C3). Indeed, elements of performance appear central to Mitchell's work in various ways. He has always read aloud drafts of his work-in-progress to his wife Merna, his lifelong editor. Remembering Mitchell's years as fiction editor for *Maclean's* magazine (1948–51), Pierre Berton has described the Mitchells as resembling a vaudeville act, 'continually interrupting one another, correcting old, well-loved anecdotes, shouting, screaming, but clearly very much attached to one another' (Berton, 34). CBC radio producer Harry Boyle tells of Mitchell's early acting role as the whistling prairie gopher for *Jake and the Kid*, and of how the number of these incidental gopher whistles suddenly increased from one script to the next after Mitchell learned about the performance fee of $18 a squeak. His readings at public libraries are the dramatic performances of a solo act in the tradition of Dickens, Twain, and Leacock, delivered with the energy and timing of a professional entertainer, with his hair tousled, voice rising, and body gesturing.

The engaging personality of this consummate performer asserts itself most memorably in the fictional characters, dramatic incidents, and poetic descriptions through which he transcends the esoteric artistry that marginalizes other novelists. If challenged to cite a quintessential passage that typifies his writings, few of us would find ourselves at a loss for words. We might recall a haunting passage read from a novel, a colloquial dialogue heard on a radio broadcast, a dramatic incident seen on the stage, or a set comic piece we might have experienced in person during one of his public readings of his own work. For Terry Goldie it remains the haunting image that opens *Who Has Seen the Wind*: 'Here is the least common denominator of nature, the skeleton requirements simply of land and sky – Saskatchewan prairie.' For Peter Gzowski it is the parallel passage at the end – the last page and a half that Gzowski shares with others from this novel – that remains a part of his soul: as the 'wind wings on ... breathing up topsoil and tumbleweed skeletons to carry them on its spinning way over the prairie, out and out to the far line of the sky,' the young Brian experiences his most extended moment of fleeting vision that breaks 'the chain of darkness' with the 'ultimate meaning of the cycle of life.' For Timothy Findley the host of images includes the voices of John Drainie and Billie Mae Richards making Jake and the Kid as 'real and everlasting as neighbours – someone you can visit in your mind as if they lived up the road.'

Up the road for some may be that mythical prairie world of Crocus and Shelby where Willie MacCrimmon works at his cobbler's bench: 'He moved back to his last. The cobbling hammer took up its impatient crooked rhythm in the dim stillness rich with the soft smell of new harness, bitter with the tang of leather dye. Now and again his hammer fell silent as he filled his mouth with tacks' (*Black Bonspiel of Willie MacCrimmon* [1993] 19). The smell of the leather harness and sound of the rapping hammer bring to life the shop that epitomizes the village community culture in which the toil of work and the joy of craftsmanship are one and the same. The mouthful of tacks not only suggests the experienced concentration of the artist at work but also foreshadows the 'tactics' the world champion curling team must exploit to compete with the devil at the 'otherworldly' brier (128–29).

Up the road for others may be the contemporary urban world of Livingstone University, where Professor Colin Dobbs prepares himself for the annual transition of university life from summer to autumn:

Because Livingstone University had not adopted the trimester system, its activity and metabolic rhythm resembled that of certain snails and crabs, torpid and dormant under the heat and dryness of summer. Except for the six weeks of summer school, this academic aestivation lasted from June convocation to September registration, administration brain centres kept alight mostly by secretaries. Each fall students wakened the university with their corpuscular flow across the campus from building to building, through halls, cafeterias, and common rooms, to offices, labs, and classrooms. (*Since Daisy Creek* 56)

The metaphors of the intertidal life of snails and crabs and of the dormant campus drained lifeless without the flow of students through its concrete body utterly deromanticize the world of academia, rendering it as both a business concern whose factories fall fast asleep and as an aestivated crustacean, another kind of hibernating beast Professor Dobbs must confront. The imagery enforces the deconstruction by subverting any illusions of a heroic quest. This beast is neither a dragon nor a grizzly to be slain, but rather the professor's own academic sterility. The reversed order of growth 'from June convocation to September registration' and the flow 'from building to building, through halls, cafeterias, and common rooms, to offices, labs, and classrooms' suggest a bathetic flow from bustling social activity to stagnation in confined quarters.

For still others, up the road may be the marginalized world of the Paradise Valley Reserve, where the bridge between cultures can threaten to make the alien vanish. The Stoney Native Archie Nicotine subverts this threat with a deadpan gesture of grateful compliance: fined for indecent exposure after relieving himself in the alley behind a city beerhall, he overpays the fine, insisting that the court should keep the change for a credit on his account since, as Archie acknowledges, he 'sometime ... might want to ... fart – when I'm in this civilized city again' (*Vanishing Point* 248). Archie's self-confident contempt for the bureaucratic city is masterfully controlled, as his ironic discourse of compliance and gratitude is accompanied by the gesture of generosity so playfully disruptive to the judicial system which lacks the bureaucratic means to deal with credit.

What makes these passages so memorable is that they arise from the imaginative communities Mitchell has been creating for more than fifty years. In *Since Daisy Creek*, Colin Dobbs explains to his creative writing students at Livingstone University the key to creating these imaginative worlds of art: 'If you want to fool your reader, your poem or play or novel or short story must seem to be in the world of the many. They are illusions that can be smelled and tasted and heard and touched and seen ... That tells you that what you have written has bridged, has reached over to them (*Since Daisy Creek* 102). The universality of 'the world of the many' is derived from the concrete details of personal experience. These may be selected from the contemporary urban experience of the sophisticated façades of intellectual life in a university institution. Or they may be projected from the urban nostalgia for the simpler innocence of a frontier village recalled from the collective youth of our Canadian heritage. The nightmarish horror of the sophisticated university is counterbalanced by the dream of the rustic country. The innocence of the frontier rustic appeals to the memories of an older generation as it appeals to new immigrants curious about the mythical land of the West.

Willie MacCrimmon personifies the progression of our national history:

> Willie had been eighteen when the MacCrimmons had migrated to the new world. His parents settled in Toronto, where his father opened up a shop, but urban life was not for Willie ... His second year in the concrete jungle he put on hold his return to the land of his birth and decided to explore the west with its cowboys and Indians ... In the foothills he found again the bonny braes and banks and streams he'd loved and lost. He found work on fall threshing crews, graduated to hired man, then to roughnecking in the oilfields. His father was not prospering in Toronto; evidently city Canadians simply threw away their damaged shoes and bought new ones, and saddles and harnesses were not top items for many Torontonians. Willie persuaded his father to move west and set up shop in Shelby. Here for the next two years they were cobbling partners once more. (*Black Bonspiel of Willie MacCrimmon* [1993] 3–4)

The young immigrant drifts west to work as a thresher on farms like that of Brian O'Connal's Uncle Sean in the 1920s, graduates to hired man like Jake in the 1930s and 1940s, and then as an oil roughneck as late as the 1970s and 1980s. But the contrast between our city consumerism and the community values of the pastoral frontier ultimately leads Willie to pursue his flight from the present to the past by settling as a cobbler in a mythical pastoral village. Mitchell's villages, however, are never innocent. Here in Shelby, Willie may manage to outwit the devil at a curling brier, but with such satirical intrusions from the edge of town as Rory Napolean's honey-wagon (5) and Mame Harris's itinerant nieces (7), Mitchell reminds us that it is the pastoral dream that remains on the outskirts of reality.

Though Colin Dobbs has affixed to the wall of his university office the reminder that 'Life ain't Art,' Mitchell has conjured to life his mythical communities with details derived from his personal experiences in Weyburn and High River, at the universities of Windsor and Calgary, and at the Native communities of Carlyle Lake near Weyburn and the Eden Valley Reserve in the Alberta foothills. Born in 1914 in Weyburn, Saskatchewan, William Ormond Mitchell was the second of four sons to Maggie Mitchell (née McMurray), a nurse born in Clinton, Ontario, and Ormond Mitchell, a pharmacist and amateur elocutionist born in Waterdown, Ontario. Mitchell's childhood resembled that of several of his fictional characters, from Brian O'Connal of *Who Has Seen the Wind* and the Kid of *Jake and the Kid* to the later Kenneth Lyon of *Ladybug, Ladybug...* and Art Ireland of *For Art's Sake*. During his father's illness, he lived briefly on his uncle's farm; after his father and grandfather died in 1921, his grandmother moved to his home. To improve his tubercular wrist condition, his mother moved with him when he was thirteen to California and then to Florida, where he finished his school years before majoring in philosophy at the University of Manitoba. Before his graduation during the Depression of the 1930s he earned his way from Montreal to London by working as a galley boy aboard the Greek tramp steamer the *Onassapinellopi*, similar to the *Onassis Penelope* on which Art Ireland set off for Europe. His first publication, 'Panacea for Panhandlers,' a three-part series which appeared in the University of Manitoba's *'Toba* during 1933 and 1934, was based on letters written to his mother while hitchhiking across Europe. Upon his return he studied playwriting at the University of Washington, worked as a salesman for magazines and encyclopaedias, and then enrolled in the education program at the University of Alberta in 1940. Here he met and married Merna

Hirtle, whom he acknowledges to be his best editor. He met also at Alberta another important editor to whom he acknowledges a deep debt: Professor F.M. Salter. Mitchell sat in on Salter's creative writing class and, as requested, provided Salter with copies of everything he had written, including a short novel, some plays, and some loosely written work which Mitchell was later to call 'free-fall' writing. Salter took particular interest in a few rough pages describing a boy in a cemetery and asked Mitchell to develop the story. Such was the genesis of *Who Has Seen the Wind*, but its completion was as painstakingly slow as most first novels.

In his development as a writer, Mitchell found himself torn in two directions. While searching for and experimenting with suitable material for his first novel, he began writing a series of stories designed for the popular magazine market. 'You Gotta Teeter' and 'Elbow Room' appeared in the August and September 1942 issues of *Maclean's* as the first two *Jake and the Kid* stories. With the comical character of a farm-hand as his subject, the philosophy graduate was now putting on hold his ambition to become a serious novelist. For many years Mitchell would claim in interviews that the pressures to continue with the *Jake and the Kid* stories and scripts had distracted him from what he considered to be his more important work as a novelist. The consistent quality of the popular series, however, suggests otherwise: Mitchell appears to have shifted intentionally from high-brow literature to popular Canadian culture in a country where the latter is still widely considered to be a contradiction in terms. His dismissal of the importance of the *Jake* stories, however, was understandable. Journalists in search of the great Canadian novel wanted more than the two novels Mitchell produced between 1948 and 1980; editors discouraged him from maintaining Crocus as the fictional setting of the subsequent manuscripts he submitted, as though fearing that Crocus would become repetitive or reductive, despite such precedents as Wessex in England and Yoknapatawpha in America. Salter remained a solitary supporter, reminding Mitchell to treat his popular stories as seriously as Shakespeare treated his comedies.

The defensive attitude was a reaction to the failure of editors and reviewers to recognize the significance of Crocus. The perennial quest to discover the great Canadian novel was part of the larger preoccupation with the search for the Canadian identity. Mitchell has contributed much to this Canadian identity by creating the pastoral community of Crocus, which has become part of our popular mythology. Avonlea, Mariposa, and Crocus are the three mythical communities that rise most visibly above the flood of foreign mythologies that saturate popular culture in Canada. In joining the character of a tall-tale teller with description of the social issues that arise from a prairie farm and rural town, Mitchell has balanced sentiment and satire within the pastoral tradition prominent through two centuries of Canadian literature.

After the critical acclaim of *Who Has Seen the Wind* and the popular success of Jake and the Kid in magazines and on radio, Mitchell worked for several years on his third project, a self-consciously ambitious novel. Portions were serialized as 'The Alien' in *Maclean's* (September 1953–January 1954), but the manuscript grew unwieldy in plot and depressing in tone, until finally it was put aside. Initially bearing little more than the expression of the frustration experienced by the failed novelist David Lang of *The Kite* (1962), the manuscript was completely rewritten and eventually published as *The Vanishing Point* (1974). Indeed, the failed 'Alien' and the radio and television scripts of the 1940s and early 1950s have provided Mitchell with extensive sources for *The Kite, The Vanishing Point, According to Jake and the Kid, Roses Are Difficult Here,* and *The Black Bonspiel of Willie MacCrimmon.* This latter book typifies the complex relationships among his novels, plays, and broadcasting scripts. From *Wullie* to *Willie,* the text has undergone six transformations, from radio script (1951) to television script (1955), novella (1964), short story (1964), stage play (1980), and novel (1993).

Mitchell's career appears to be six-sided, moreover. One side of Mitchell is the author of rural prairie novels: *Who Has Seen the Wind, The Kite, The Vanishing Point, How I Spent My Summer Holidays, Roses Are Difficult Here,* and *The Black Bonspiel of Willie Mac-Crimmon.* These novels are set in a mythical village community torn between pastoral innocence and corrosive experience. A second side of Mitchell is the author of family magazine stories, and radio, television, and feature film scripts: the *Jake and the Kid* series, written for *Maclean's* and the CBC and published in book form as *Jake and the Kid* and *According to Jake and the Kid*; the *Foothill Fables* CBC series; and the screenplays for *Alien Thunder* (1974) and *Who Has Seen the Wind* (rewritten by Patricia Watson). While similar in content to the novels, these stories and scripts are technical experimentations with the emerging mass media genres of popular culture. A third side of Mitchell is the dramatist and author of stage plays: *The Devil's Instrument, The Black Bonspiel of Wullie MacCrimmon, Back to Beulah, For Those in Peril by the Sea,* and *The Kite* (all collected in *Dramatic W.O. Mitchell*), and *The Day Jake Made Her Rain,* the musical *Wild Rose,* and the collaborative *Centennial Play.* His chronological progression from the new genres of the mass media to the ancient genres of the traditional stage play might seem like a backward development except that most of these plays transcend the conventional division between high art and popular culture. A fourth side of Mitchell is the author of the Livingstone University urban novels: *Since Daisy Creek, Ladybug, Ladybug ...,* and *For Art's Sake.* In these novels he confronts the ominous reality of contemporary urban social problems endemic to what we allege to be our highest centres of learning. A fifth side of Mitchell is the teacher: beginning as a schoolteacher during the 1940s in New Dayton, Castor, and High River, Alberta, and later becoming a professor or a writer-in-residence at the universities of Calgary (1968–71), Alberta (1971–73), Toronto (1973–74), York University (1977–78), and the University of Windsor (1979–87), he continues to write from his office at the University of Calgary. A gifted teacher, he has passed on to two generations of students the same care and inspiration with which F.M. Salter initially provided him. Finally, a sixth side of Mitchell is the accomplished actor and raconteur, whose readings from his own works are inspired performances in the tradition of Dickens, Twain, and Leacock.

All six of these facets of his career are well represented by the diverse approaches of the contributors to *Magic Lies.* The first section focuses on Mitchell's fiction, with contextual surveys followed by analyses of specific texts. David Latham begins with an overview of the central metaphors concerning art and community, pursuing through the ten books of fiction Mitchell's demonstration of the role the artist plays in constructing our personal identity and social community. W.J. Keith proposes a provocative Leavisite challenge to confront the limitations of Mitchell's strengths and his alleged failure to match the breadth of vision achieved in *Who Has Seen the Wind* in subsequent works. Keith suggests that after this first novel Mitchell's 'country of the mind' declined to a sentimental 'country of the heart.' Dick Harrison analyses the various strategies Mitchell has developed in different novels to negotiate the borders of a sexuality repressed by a neo-Calvinist ideology, wherein sex is considered to be threatening rather than sensually beautiful. Muriel Whitaker explores the archetypal implications of this threat in *Who Has Seen the Wind* and *How I Spent My Summer Holidays*, and in William Kurelek's *A Prairie Boy's Winter* and *A Prairie Boy's Summer*. These discussions lead to her comparison of image and text in the illustrated editions of *Who Has Seen the Wind*. Terry Goldie pursues Eve Kosofsky Sedgwick's notions of homosocial issues in his discussion of *Who Has Seen the Wind* and *For Art's Sake*, in which male bonding ranges from the latent homoerotic to the blatant homophobic. Alexander Kizuk next extends to these male relationships a Lacanian reading of the psycholinguistic ground and the 'mental hole' of *Who Has Seen the Wind* and *How I Spent My Summer Holidays*.

O.S. Mitchell and Theresia Quigley shift our attention to *The Vanishing Point*. Orm Mitchell studies the gradual transformation of the ambitious 'Alien' manuscript into the successful *Vanishing Point*, a transformation that enables us to view the creative process at work as Mitchell turned his ideological interest in marginalized minorities into an artistic vision by creating the individual character of Archie Nicotine. Theresia Quigley provides a Jungian reading, through the lenses of Carol Pearson and Robert Bly, of Carlyle Sinclair's replacement of the colonizer's search for his lost Native lamb with a personal analysis of his own childhood.

Turning to *Since Daisy Creek,* Catherine McLay finds similar transformations, first in the novel's genesis as a radio play entitled 'The Trophy,' and second in the spiritual growth of Professor Colin Dobbs as he struggles to emerge from the academic sterility of his life. These personal quests for identity are complemented in *Roses Are Difficult Here* with the social quest for paradise, as Barbara Mitchell analyses this novel's exploration of the communal function of story-telling in all its various forms, focusing on W.O.'s interest in the relationships between truth and fiction and between the individual and the community. In the second Livingstone University novel, *Ladybug, Ladybug...,* Michael Peterman finds the self-constitutive search linked with the national myth, reading the story of Professor Lyon's effort to establish the thematic destination for his biography of Mark Twain as Mitchell's ambitious effort to place Canada within the literary genealogy of the North American continent.

The second section of *Magic Lies* focuses on Mitchell's work as a dramatist for radio, television, and the stage. Both Timothy Zeman and Alan Yates document the influence the popular *Jake and the Kid* radio series had on his later fiction and drama. Zeman discusses the radio plays as a fertile source and 'training ground' for later stories presented in different media. Yates discusses 'the collective chemistry' of radio production as providing a 'proving ground' through the instant reception of a mass public for a weekly radio broadcast. David Gardner discusses Mitchell's innovative experiments as a 'great purveyor of popular culture.' Gardner draws on his own experiences as an actor and director to provide a first-hand account of directing the *Jake and the Kid* television series and of acting in the motion picture adaptation of *Who Has Seen the Wind.*

Rick McNair and Guy Sprung discuss their personal experiences directing Mitchell's plays for the stage. McNair recounts his experience directing productions of *The Black Bonspiel of Wullie MacCrimmon, The Kite, Royalty Is Royalty,* and *For Those in Peril on the Sea,* citing Mitchell's popular appeal in a country traditionally unreceptive to new stage plays. Guy Sprung recounts his experience directing various productions of *Back to Beulah* and *The Black*

Bonspiel, emphasizing how different actors and actresses contributed to the personalities of the characters.

The third section of *Magic Lies* presents recollections and interviews with fellow writers and editors. Fellow novelist Timothy Findley reveals Mitchell not only as a consummate story-teller whose stories in print provide the kind of anecdotal past that establishes a formal literary tradition for other writers to work within, but also as a sincere friend who is always ready to provide the personal 'company' of an intimately welcoming literary community. That the creation of art matters for Mitchell is further confirmed by another fellow writer, Frances Itani, a former student and – as is expected with committed teachers – now a lifelong friend. She discusses the principles for creative writing that have inspired his students and that reveal much about his own creative process. *Magic Lies* ends with more of Mitchell's own words, conveyed in an interview with the journalist and broadcaster Peter Gzowski. Like Mitchell, Gzowski has worked as an editor of *Maclean's* magazine and is rivalled in the history of Canadian radio only by Foster Hewitt. The conversation between Gzowski and Mitchell epitomizes the notion of company, suggested by Findley, as having broadened the literary community across the country. The twenty essays of *Magic Lies* are intended to provoke the kind of debate that makes for the good company of a lively cultural community.

Good company returns us to the two epigraphs that introduce this Introduction. Mitchell is referring to the personal and the communal experience of art: in the first epigraph the reader is identified as 'another part of myself,' and in the second as the creative partner of the writer. Together the two epigraphs mark the range of company and community that Mitchell has envisioned and that his art has engaged. As prescriptions for both an inward and an outward exploration, they suggest his effort to build a bridge for establishing both identity and community. The context of the second epigraph is worth quoting in full for its succinct critique of the cooperative relationship between writer and reader, between the creative impulse and the critical response, as the creative reader assumes responsibility for con-

tributing to the construction or refashioning of the magic lies of
the text:

> The art experience is not private; it is a bridging, or at least the illu-
> sion of bridging, between two creative partners: the artist and his
> reader. If the artist has found fragments out of his past life, and
> then, built an illusion in which every single bit is the truth, and the
> whole thing is a more dramatic, more meaningful lie, there will be
> triggered off for his partner explosions of recognition, which the
> reader mistakenly attributes solely to the artist. Actually, the recog-
> nition belongs to both of them, and the reader's contribution comes
> out of *his* own subconscious notebook during the art experience. It
> is quite possibly the most intimate relationship between two
> humans, barring none.

PART I

The Fiction

Magic Lies and Bridges:
'A Story Better Told'

DAVID LATHAM

Since his first publication in 1933, W.O. Mitchell has been lying for more than sixty years. The range of his career extends from writing short stories, novels, and plays to writing scripts for radio, television, and feature film, and from occasional acting roles (as a whistling prairie gopher in his own *Jake and the Kid* radio series and a curmudgeon on the *Road to Avonlea* television series) to positions as a schoolteacher and university professor. A career so long and varied cannot be briefly introduced without reducing it to a few central aspects. The 'magic lie' serves here as a focus on his lifelong interest in the nature of art and the role of the artist as a mediator between the natural and social orders. Mitchell explores the relation between not only fact and fiction, but between social heritage and personal identity, and between the folklore of popular culture and the comic tradition of literature. Each of these relationships foregrounds the importance of community throughout Mitchell's works, an inclusive community constructed by what he calls bridge building. The following essay provides an overview of these central issues.

Different scenes spring to mind as illustrations of the range of meaning behind the 'magic lie,' the term Mitchell uses to explain the essence of art. One scene is from *Roses Are Difficult Here*. It concerns the origins of art, a subject that generally considers our need to 'sort out,' to render cosmos out of chaos, to construct illusions that transcend our own mortality. Matt Stanley is comparing his relinquished dream of writing the 'Great New World Novel' with his present condition as the small-town editor of the *Shelby Chinook* newspaper. His policy of 'considerate omission' (9) and reflecting 'only the best of all possible Shelbys' (11) limits him to reporting dull facts about mundane events. He knows that he is not even the sole source of information about the life of his community: 'What he did not present to public attention, many others did eagerly without press, ink or mailing list. With the quick swallow, the clucking tongue, the lifted eyebrow, they coloured and they embellished, distorting not so much out of malice as from relish in a story better told' (10). Mitchell thus links the origin of art with the desire for gossip. The 'magic lie' colours, embellishes, and distorts in order to relish 'a story better told.'

Another scene is from *Jake and the Kid*, from the chapter entitled 'The Liar Hunter.' This scene is a more fully elaborated dramatization of the magic lie. While travelling in a buckboard to a prairie farm, a young Eastern visitor explains to the old hired man how the overwhelming impact of the vast landscape 'is almost the catharsis of tragedy' (91). The hired man is thus prompted to remember that the visitor is 'one of them prefessors,' and asks if he has come for an archaeological dig:

> 'I dig,' Mr. Godfrey said, 'in a manner of speaking – but for folklore.'
> 'What kinda ore?'
> '... folklore – art – the common people ... I look for songs – ballads – that have – that express the life of the Old West ... But mostly stories ... tall tales.'
> 'Is that right?' Jake looked real pleased, and he cleared his throat the way he does before he starts to yarn.
> 'I'm looking for liars,' Mr. Godfrey said. (92)

Jake's sudden apprehension goes unnoticed as the young professor inquires about the father of the young woman whom he has come to visit. As a creative liar himself, Jake will only admit that Molly's father 'jist sorta deckerates thuh truth a bit' (92). As a 'liar hunter,' the professor should have explained his interests with more care, but Molly will no longer listen to him:

'Oh, no, Molly,' Mr. Godfrey said, 'You don't und –'

...

'I can explain what it is that –' Mr. Godfrey began.

...

'Will you let me explain?' (97)

The moment of epiphany is revealed artfully in that the professor's much-anticipated critical explanation is initially foregrounded but gradually marginalized while remaining the catalyst that precipitates the dramatically demonstrated epiphany. The story comes together as Molly emerges from an apparently incidental role to assume a significant influence on the Kid, who observes her actions as he narrates the story. The Kid's understanding evolves through glimpses of her inattentive responses to the shopkeeper's queries about her grocery list while she is overhearing the professor's explanation of liar hunting to Jake. ('What I do is important as history is important... Not the history of great and famous men... but of the lumberjacks and section men, hotelkeepers and teachers and ranchers and farmers. The people that really count... [whose] history is in the stories they tell – their tall tales' [100].) Moreover, as the professor makes his explanation, his very point is demonstrated by the simultaneous conversation between Molly and the shopkeeper that distractingly interrupts our concentration with the details of ordinary life: the ordering of ripe apples, nippy Ontario cheese, and a tin of blackstrap molasses at the counter of MacTaggart's general store by a young woman who is acquiring an understanding of not only her suitor but her own community – the cultural community of the prairie farmer.

'The Liar Hunter' is a 1945 short story which Mitchell later placed at the centre of the 1961 *Jake and the Kid* collection. It demonstrates Mitchell's conviction that a country's richest ore is its folklore, the self-creating 'magic lies' by which we write ourselves into existence. His fellow prairie writer Robert Kroetsch has expressed similar sentiments: 'In a sense, we haven't got an identity until somebody tells our story. The fiction makes us real' (*Creation* 63). The conclusion of 'The Liar Hunter' can be read in at least two different ways. After adding a postscript to his tall tale about a grasshopper the size of an airplane, Jake ends with an abrupt request: 'Han' me that there manure fork will yuh, Kid?' (104) Jake's final remark may be signalling the return from their imaginary flight through art to their physical reality deep in manure. Or, another reading may suggest that if Jake is equating the tall tale with bull manure, then the equation may be Mitchell's effort to subvert what he believes in most strongly, resorting to humour to veil a sermon on the function of art.

No reading should overlook the use of humour for deflecting and suppressing the convictions Mitchell articulates in his expository discourse. That the story of the 'magic lie' is central to Mitchell's personal ideology is made clear in his essays and interviews, where he explains his writing method: 'Put down whatever floats up from your unconsciousness. Put it all down. Every bit is the truth, but the whole thing, the final thing you create is a lie – a magic lie' (*Toronto Star*, 21 October 1989: J12; cf. *Vancouver Sun*, 9 November 1973: A36). The magic lie serves as a means for the writer to hide his intentions. As Mitchell has explained: 'The trick of the novelist is the balance and restraint. The very last thing you do after clearly thinking out your structure is to hide it, to hide your hammer marks, your saw marks, – to let the person reading it, the creative partner, think that he has read it into the actuality that just happened, the actuality that seemed to have no order' (Cowan 24).

This need for concealment is painfully demonstrated in the manuscript of 'The Alien,' with which Mitchell wrestled for so long after the publication of *Who Has Seen the Wind*, until he came to recognize that it was too serious, too bleak, and too self-conscious in its intentions to moralize. His minor revisions demonstrate a shift from the lush prose of *Who Has Seen the Wind* to the sparer prose that characterizes all of his subsequent writing. His major overhaul suggests a carefully deliberated decision to embrace the comic tradition.

In *Ladybug, Ladybug...*, the biographer of Samuel Clemens suggests the tradition within which Mitchell himself should be located: 'In the matter of literary genealogy, your [Clemens's] grampa is a Nova Scotia Canadian, Thomas Chandler Haliburton, the father of American humour. He left his mark first on Artemus Ward, then on you. Decent of both of you to have acknowledged this' (275). Clemens refers in a short story to that wise old owl from Nova Scotia, an allusion that again acknowledges the debt to Haliburton,[1] who was admired by Charles Dickens as well. In his conversation with Peter Gzowski, Mitchell acknowledges his lifelong admiration of Leacock. Hence, Haliburton, Dickens, Twain, Leacock, and Mitchell form a genealogical literary tradition that should legitimize Mitchell's place in popular culture. His discomfort with winning the Leacock award for humour arises from his experience with critics who fail to treat the comic tradition seriously. He explains his frustration to Gzowski in the interview which concludes the present volume by citing Shakespeare as one who typically marries the comic and tragic; Kenneth Lyon explains to young Rosemary that God never laughs 'because He wants to be taken seriously' (*Ladybug* 202); Matt Stanley insists to Canon Midford that 'I always take humour seriously' (*Roses* 119). The insistence is indicative of just how much Mitchell fears his humour has inadvertently invited his readers to misunderstand his serious intentions.

Even *Who Has Seen the Wind* is seldom studied with the care it deserves. This all-time best-selling novel in Canadian literature is seldom read as a whole, for all its reprintings other than the expensive illustrated edition published by McClelland and Stewart in 1991 have been reprints of the 1947 American Little, Brown edition, rather than the 1947 Canadian Macmillan edition. The original Canadian edition opens with a prefatory page identified as the 'Preface,' upon which an epigraph from Psalm 103 and Mitchell's summary counterpoint each other in the same manner as the opening two paragraphs of chapter 1. Indeed the two pages mirror each other. But in the close to a million reprintings from the American edition the preface is omitted leaving the psalm excerpt and Mitchell's summary on separate pages resembling two unrelated epigraphs. Moreover, the second paragraph of chapter 1 is omitted, the first of many paragraphs so treated.[2] These deletions disrupt the aesthetic unity, the foreshadowing motifs, and the thematic counterpointing.

Consider the opening two paragraphs:

> Here was the least common denominator of nature, the skeleton requirements simply, of land and sky – Saskatchewan prairie. It lay wide around the town, stretching tan to the far line of the sky, clumped with low buck brush and wild rose bushes, shimmering under the late June sun and waiting for the unfailing visitation of wind, gentle at first, barely stroking the long grasses and giving them life; later, a long, hot gusting that would lift the black top soil and pile it in barrow pits along the roads or in deep banks against the fences.
>
> But for now, it was as though a magnificent breath were being held; still puffs of cloud were high in the sky, retaining their shapes for hours on end, one of them near the horizon, presenting a profile view of blown cheeks and extended lips like the wind personification upon an old map. (Macmillan 1947, 1)

These two paragraphs work together like the octave and sestet of a sonnet. Three sentences are presented in two paragraphs. The first sentence expresses two analogies. The first analogy is arithmetical: a clean, reductive image of the prairie as 'the least common denominator of nature.' The second analogy is anatomical: the harsh reality of land and sky identified as the bare bones of nature. With neither rich vegetation nor forest, the land is but low brush and bush. The second sentence describes the relationship between the land and sky, a sky that is both mistress and master. As coy mistress, the sky woos the grass to life. But its gentle stroking turns to hot gusting: the wind that aroused the land to life next gusts it away and buries it, as the lowest common denominator reduces life to the bare absolutes of inspiration and expiration.

Whereas the first paragraph exemplifies the bleak absolutist sentiment of the epigraph from Psalm 103 ('As for man, his days are as grass: as a flower of the field, so he flourisheth. For the wind passeth over it, and it is gone; and the place thereof shall know it no more'), the second paragraph counters by exemplifying the humanist sentiment of Mitchell's own epigraph on the momentary breakthrough: 'the ultimate meaning ... revealed in moments of fleeting vision ... moments when an enquiring heart seeks finality, and the chain of darkness is broken. This is the story...' The terminology for this story of a boy who feels breathless moments of enlightenment is introduced in the long descriptive sentence comprising the second paragraph: 'But for now, it was as though a magnificent breath were being held; still puffs ... retaining their shapes for hours on end, ... a profile view of blown cheeks and extended lips.' It foreshadows with a concrete illustration the young Brian's recurring desire to sustain the incomprehensible feeling. During each fleeting occurrence, the feeling is accompanied 'with breathlessness and expectancy' (105), with 'an uncertain and breathless quality' (172), with 'breathless moments' (194), with 'a sudden breathlessness' (240).[3]

The second paragraph thus counters the bleak sentiment of the first paragraph with the momentary calm before the storm, the interval about which 'This is the story.' It locates the essence of life in the 'but for now,' the present interval poetically dependent upon 'a magnificent breath' held in suspension. But what the interval between the two absolutes is literally dependent upon is the 'magic lie' of the artist's simile. The shift from the first paragraph to the second is a shift from the absolute identity of the metaphor to the imagined analogy of the simile, the self-consciously contrived analogy. The self-referential personification – the clouds being 'like the wind personification upon an old map' – suspends the moment by foregrounding the relationship between art and reality, fiction and fact. Mitchell contrasts the romantic illusion with the physical reality, the peaceful serenity of the humanized map with the skeletal reality of the prairie about to be besieged by storms. The map is an artist's desktop notion of the land, an artefact, a cartoon, a personal illustration that stands in marked contrast to the bare denominator, the alien country that must be fictionalized to render it real to us, giving identity to it and to us. In this way the romantic illusion is not artificial, but becomes real.

The opening two paragraphs alert the reader to the two orders Mitchell will explore throughout the novel, indeed throughout his fiction: the natural order and the social order. The social order has as its foundation the same base cruelties of the natural order, but offers at its horizon a vision of individuals transcending their selfish human nature to join the cultural community of artists building bridges of communication.

The nature of art and the role of the artist as a mediator between the natural and social orders have remained pervasive issues in Mitchell's work for sixty years. In his exploration of the nature of art, Mitchell subverts the conventional codes of art and reality, of lies and truth. The pairs are reversed in their relationship as reality is corrupt with lies, while art provides the only truth worth knowing. The truth of conventional facts is useful only for establishing verisimilitude. In *How I Spent My Summer Holidays*, young Hugh practises the art of lying: 'The difficult skill I had to learn that summer was to walk a defensive high wire, using as much truth as possible for my balance pole. With no life net' (134). A modicum of truth is necessary as a balancing pole for maintaining the credibility of a story. Truth is a tool that contributes to the creation of the magic lie.

And once the fiction is created, it constructs identity by becoming more real than life. The fictional world of *Chums* made the 'misty moors' of the romanticized English countryside seem much more alive for Hugh than the mundane reality of the Canadian prairie (52). The manner in which fiction constructs identity is most obvious when the older Hugh recalls the ideology of propaganda in *Chums*: the superiority of the English over the Germans and of the upper-class public-school boys over the working-class townies (52). Even at the end of the dramatic summer that ended his youth Hugh does not choose 'How I Spent My Summer Holidays' as a topic to write about for his school assignment. Only years later, in retrospect, does the now fifty-year-old Hugh dare confront the topic, to 'have it sorted out' (224). Once sorted and shaped, his life assumes the epic proportions of art. Hugh can now identify his childhood 'as the age of Jason or of Ulysses or of Aeneas' (3), his prairie home as 'Greek; the grass sea around us was our Aegean' (3), and the ritual procession of his friends to the swimming hole as 'a true pilgrimage not to Canterbury so much as to Mecca' (6). 'It' recurs throughout *How I Spent My Summer*

Holidays, much like the fleeting 'feeling' that recurs throughout *Who Has Seen the Wind*. From the very first sentence of *Holidays* 'it' is again a fleeting moment, but whereas in *Who Has Seen the Wind* the feeling is something of an emotional enlightenment of the soul wherein the child feels at one with the world, in *How I Spent My Summer Holidays* 'it' is a revelation to the mind wherein the adult comprehends memories of experience he has suppressed. The vision of *Who Has Seen the Wind* is now the nightmare of *How I Spent My Summer Holidays*. 'It' is anticipated with apprehension: 'it' is not only the fleeting moment of inspiration but the aftermath of comprehended consequences, the 'memory resonance' not only of summer fun but of winter hardship (1), beautiful and ugly, innocent and sordid, good and evil, sane and insane, mystical and physical: 'The loss of my own innocence was not a simple event; it must have been an imperceptible corruption taking time' (4). The loss of faith in the possibility of throwing his voice, as illustrated in the 'Ventrillo' advertisement (4), and of carving 'a boomerang that would never come back to me' led to his 'growing cynicism' (5).

When another 'it' is identified as the crotch of a young schoolmate who consented 'to show it' – ' "it" had been quite disappointing and nothing at all to see' (3) – the humour eases the descent of childhood to disillusionment and cynicism, with the comical implication that the descent need not be permanent: what disappoints the child may later captivate the adult.

Each generation loses its youth and innocence, just as civilizations lose their monuments and creative energy. As in *Jake and the Kid*, Mitchell compares the artist to an archaeologist, this time searching to recover an 'extinct child society' that has left no inscriptions or monuments as tangible evidence of its life (16). The difficulty of discovering Hugh's buried childhood out on the prairie is illustrated by his attempt to sort out the significance of the day he and his friend painted themselves in white mud. He retraces their progression from assuming a clownish image of goofiness to a tearful image of sadness, then from a serpentine image of savagery to a skeletal image of death, and finally to the silent and vanishing image of a ghost (15). Still, Hugh remains unable to comprehend what he cannot 'hold in [his] hands to examine and to wonder about and to label' (16).

The artist as an archaeologist of knowledge and acrobat with truth are recurring metaphors in Mitchell's fiction and drama. They are connected with recollections that are personal, ancestral, and national. The tales of the pioneer 'prairie days' that Grandmother MacMurray tells Brian (*Wind* 271–72, 273–74) are the tales that Jake tells the Kid and Daddy Sherry tells Keith. These 'untrue' myths are the fictional creations by which we form our identity and heritage. Without them Grandmother MacMurray finds her life is 'just senseless' (273). In *The Kite*, journalist David Lang compares centenarian Daddy Sherry to Methuselah (71), but Daddy is more like Lazarus, bringing back to life the history of the ancestors of our homeland: not the heroes and heroines at the centre of power, but the daily experiences of pioneers overlooked by conventional history. Thus, though Daddy Sherry has forgotten much about the Red River and Riel Rebellion, he provides Lang with a 'wealth of sensuous detail; rough as [his notes of his interviews with Daddy] were, the prairie perfumed them; the foothills sun had warmed them; ever so faintly one could catch the gay and martial impudence of fife and drum; this was the sort of material to stain his narrative with immediacy. But it was difficult to bring to order' (124). 'And there's a lot – enough for a novel,' he adds, while confessing that he envies the talent of novelists: 'I'm just a journalist' (126). As Barbara Mitchell observes in her essay on *Roses Are Difficult Here*, 'most of Mitchell's novels are concerned with the rediscovery of the protagonist's creative energy.'

That *The Kite* documents the rediscovery of a jaded journalist's creative energy is aptly demonstrated as we come to recognize that David's magazine assignment develops into the very novel we are reading. David has consolidated and ordered his notes of young Keith's story into chapter 5, of Dr Richardson's story into chapter 7, of Title Jack's story into chapter 9, of Belva's story into chapter 14, and of Merton Spicer's story of this very morning into chapter 15. The shift from chapter 4 to chapter 5 is typical. Keith's conversation with David about Daddy's distaste for the grandmother's porridge at the end of chapter 4 turns in chapter 5 into the omniscient narration of the details and conse-quences of the porridge incident, followed by the return to David and Keith in the opening sentence of chapter 6: 'By the time the boy had told David why Daddy Sherry did not like his grand-mother, the April afternoon had lost most of its shallow warmth' (62). David is revealed as the author typing out this fictional re-creation of the townsfolk's stories. The typography of the chapter headings – in conventional typewriter face with broken under-lining – visually foregrounds David's role as the author of the novel we are reading.[4]

Such self-referential complexities as the following abound in Mitchell's fiction: 'The flood anecdote, of course, was Belva Louise Tinsley's, and it was from her that David got the rest of his story' (176). In this instance we can simplify the matter of who is narrating if we consider that the journalist is referring to himself in the third person, that he might otherwise have written 'it was from her that *I* got the rest of the story.' However, there are many other instances where the self-referential is a more insistent narra-tive device, too insistent to be glossed over. Consider these narra-tive intrusions from *Who Has Seen the Wind*: 'The Sunday that the Ben was received in to Knox congregation, was in a way a turning point in Brian O'Connal's spiritual life too' (103); 'Early in August,[5] the warp of the O'Connal family life was changed. It happened on a day when...' (195); 'That was the night that Mr. Powelly visited Digby' (210); 'Two weeks and five catalogue horses after the pig episode...' (219); 'It was just three days before his incarceration ended that the pencil-sharpening incident occurred' (267). All of these intrusions anticipate and foreshadow; moreover, they explicitly inscribe importance to narrative inci-dents as events being mythologized. As self-reflexive intrusions proclaiming their own importance, they also reveal the textuality of the plot, drawing attention to its episodic nature and to the identity of its narrator. Self-reflexivity begins before page 1 with the Preface: 'In this story I have tried to present... This is the story of a boy and the wind.' This is Brian's story, his recollection from adulthood. It is Brian's power of recollection which renders

Digby's exemplary empathy as a Berkeleyan extension of Brian's own life, which renders sense of his grandmother's life as providing the cultural heritage for his own identity.

We might expect this narrative technique to be more prominent in the rural prairie novels (with their emphasis on anecdotal story-tellers looking back to the past), but it is exploited as well in the urban Livingstone University novels (with their emphasis on contemporary issues and dialogue delivered in the present tense). In *Ladybug, Ladybug...*, we are told 'It was that night it happened' (28). In *For Art's Sake*, we are told 'It was after that incident that he stopped calling her by her proper name; now it was always "Ms Marble"' (130). In *Since Daisy Creek*, Colin Dobbs recognizes the significance of leaving an unfinished fishing fly clamped in the jaws of his fly-tying vice: 'That had been the night before he drove down to Shelby to meet Archie ... Now it was as though a vice pinched four months in its mouth, reminding him once more of the dreadful ellipsis that the grizzly sow had torn in his life' (46).

Roses Are Difficult Here exploits the same narrative device used in *The Kite* in that the author of each novel we are reading is meant to be the central character. Like journalist David Lang, newspaper editor Matt Stanley had felt defeated with regard to his lost destination as a novelist, resigning his destiny to the small outpost of Shelby. But just as David is encouraged by Helen to write *The Kite*, Matt is inspired by his predecessor, Uncle Ben Trotter, to write a paperback rebuttal to the sociologist's academic analysis of Matt's own community (324). Comparisons of Dr Melquist's analytical account (198–99) with Matt's newspaper reportage, and, of course, with Mitchell's metaphorical novel itself, amply demonstrate how the dead facts fail to illuminate the truth as the magic lie so readily does. As the metaphor of the toy top suggests, the whirling tune of the 'Gloria choral' is but a toy imitation, as if held in a net too coarse to hold the poetry of the earth. Dr Melquist's sociological statistics are similarly too coarse to convey the life of Shelby. Its life is conveyed in the novel through the poetry of each season, which sets four contexts for understanding the living community. Resembling four choruses, these poetic descriptions divide the novel into four parts.

Community is the essential issue with Mitchell. By placing the novel within the context of other media, Mitchell constructs a contextual cultural community wherein his stories investigate questions about art and community and their relationships with the natural and social orders. Community and media come demonstrably together in the 1993 novel version of *The Black Bonspiel of Willie MacCrimmon*. Its first four paragraphs begin with the non-fictional tone of a preface on the origins of curling. The qualifiers and disclaimers – 'might possibly,' 'also possible,' 'There are no documents to confirm or deny this story' – prepare us for the transition to the Mephistophelian tale in the fictional community of Shelby, a town mapped out with the charmingly general outline of romance. The novel ends by returning full circle to its beginning with an epilogue on the origins of curling, this time in the parodic form of a sports column. By disclaiming its own speculations as 'wild talk, the sort of thing no one would ever expect to see in print' (132), Mitchell manipulates our emergence from romance to the reality of 'one devil of a match' (135). Fact and fiction are blurred throughout Mitchell's work. He writes academic analyses and news accounts of his fictional characters. Millie writes a fantasy story for *This Is True* magazine (*Roses*). From the Kid's school scribbler to newspaper articles and editorials by Chet Lambert for the *Crocus Breeze* (*Jake*) and Matt Stanley for the *Shelby Chinook* (*Roses*), to magazine articles and sports columns like Bill Frayne's for *Maclean's* (*The Black Bonspiel of Willie MacCrimmon*), to academic books like June Melquist's sociological treatise (*Roses*), to news wires in *For Art's Sake*, a study is needed of the relationships among these different texts – their genres, their purposes, their prose styles, and their contribution to the artful development of the magic lie.

Mitchell's early move to the forefront of popular culture in Canada arose from his creation of a contextual cultural community through this experimentation with genres. Turning his literary skills from university quarterlies to family magazines and radio shows, he expressed his community interests through the appropriate media, from tall tales told, to family magazines read, to radio series heard. Since radio brought so many communities within reach, he was in a position to render some change to the nature of the community. When the *Jake and the Kid* radio series was first broadcast it raised controversial issues. Timothy Zeman quotes a 1952 letter from CBC director Peter Francis describing the reactions of Ottawa politicians as well as rural farmers to the radio show: '*Jake and the Kid* has become such an institution and a power in the land ... that almost anything said on the show seems to bring repercussions in high quarters ... Ten thousand farmers cheer and feel they have a voice ... The cause of tolerance has advanced several notches' [194].

The show, which was once considered political in its confrontation of controversial issues, is now, more than forty years later, considered quaint and charming and a successful example of what is too often considered as an oxymoron: popular Canadian culture.[6] With the recent publication of *According to Jake and the Kid* (1989), *Roses Are Difficult Here* (1990), and *The Black Bonspiel of Willie MacCrimmon* (1993), Mitchell is documenting an elegy of the old, elegizing the values of a community from the youth of a mythical, pastoral Canada. Despite such precedents as Hardy's Wessex and Faulkner's Yoknapatawpha, Mitchell's editors during the first thirty years of his career resisted his creation of a mythical community. Mitchell was merely adhering to the aesthetic principle that the universal must be rooted in the particular. Yet, however often the names were changed at the insistence of his editors, we can readily recognize the identity of the characters who play the same role whether they are called Repeat Godfrey or Repeat Golightly, Milt Palmer or Merton Spenser, and whether they live in Crocus, Kartoum, or Shelby; hence the mythical community emerges intact.

While Catherine McLay has called Mitchell's fictional community a 'country of the mind' and Muriel Whitaker has called it a 'landscape of the mind,' W.J. Keith has qualified it as a 'country of the heart,' finding it too sentimental for the mind. In his discussion of the different readerships Mitchell's earliest stories appeal to, Keith distinguishes between the popular and the academic: the popular meets our leisure-demand with charm and sentiment, while the academic demonstrates the rigour of art. Whether the distinction between popular culture and serious literature should remain hierarchical is a much-debated issue and beyond the scope of the discussion here. For now I shall address only the charge that the *Jake and the Kid* stories lack the double-edged balance of Leacock's *Sunshine Sketches*, that it is Mitchell's stories that lack the dark side. For shadows are by no means absent: each story invokes a different order of these shadows by inviting us to share the sentiments that replace them, to enjoy the charm of a fictional community where prejudice, hypocrisy, self-righteousness, or pretension is overcome by tolerance, integrity, humility, or charity. When read (or heard) within the context of popular culture, the *Jake and the Kid* stories are more subversively elegiac than sentimental, as the fictional world invokes a sense of loss suffered in the brazen, external world. In his preface to *According to Jake and the Kid*, Mitchell foregrounds this absence and loss with an elegy for the hired man whose disappearance is a Canadian metaphor for the rapid progression of time that leaves us with few things able 'to persist much beyond five decades' (ix). Like a serf doing other men's work, the hired man is also consistent with the ideology of self-sacrifice central to the national mythology of our culture. In American mythology, when Andrew Jackson stops the Indian fighter Davy Crockett from crossing a bridge to pursue his foe, Davy pushes Jackson aside with the explanation that a man has to do what he knows is right. In Canadian mythology, when the mounted policeman Sam Steele stops the crowd of greedy gold-rushers on the Klondike trail with the explanation that they will have to wait their turn because there are not enough supplies and services to accommodate them all, the crowd turns back in a spirit of cooperation. The Canadian faith in the act of self-sacrifice for the good of the community runs counter to the American faith in the self-assertion of the individual.

Mitchell updates this colonial mythology to our contemporary condition. The implication of his preface is that we are all doing other men's chores now, working on assembly lines to build other people's tractors. As times change, the hired man has not drifted far; only his influence has disappeared. Once akin to a nanny for the working class, the hired man is no longer central to the popular education of the farmer's children. He has lost his place in other people's families. The hired man once turned the nuclear family into a community; the tractor leaves the nuclear family in isolation.

Another dark shadow, lurking in the background of the *Jake and the Kid* stories but drawn to the foreground in many of Mitchell's novels, is the fatherless protagonist. As the community is assaulted by the alienation of urban sprawl, Mitchell's protagonists suffer the loss of the head of the initial unit of the community. These fatherless protagonists serve as metaphors in Mitchell's different works. They symbolize the condition of the new settlers of the western frontier, far removed from their ancestral home. In *Ladybug, Ladybug* ..., Kenneth Lyon compares his childhood on the frontier of the Canadian West with Samuel Clemens's childhood on the frontier of the American East (13). It is the same childhood as that of Brian O'Connal, who searches the prairie for the wind and its origins. The absence of the archetypal father leaves the protagonists epitomizing the condition of the modern state, adrift in a godless world, devoid of poetic justice. Like Colin Dobbs and Arthur Ireland of the other Livingstone University novels, they search for mentors amid an order of corrupt authority figures.

While the Crocus of *Jake and the Kid* is an idealized community where poetic justice inevitably prevails, Mitchell presents a more complicated world in his novels and dramas. The dichotomy between the natural order and the social order remains complex, with both orders possessing good and bad qualities. Nature is generally amoral, but society must work to avoid being maliciously immoral. As Digby and Milt Palmer realize, goodness takes thought (*Who Has Seen the Wind* 134); it arises from the social order. The Bens, on the other hand, are 'as naked of right and wrong as a coyote howling on a still, fall night, a plague of grasshoppers attacking every green thing, the sun cracking the face of the prairie itself' (81). The community must be the source of salvation from an amoral nature. The final paragraph of the penultimate chapter of *Who Has Seen the Wind* metaphorically conveys the death of Brian's grandmother. Its imagery of black boughs and white flakes is a refutation of Ezra Pound's 'In a Station of the Metro.' Mitchell turns the alienation image into an image of communal continuity, as the death of a family member is likened to a twig dropping from a growing tree (287). An affirmative faith in the community grows more strained and stubborn as corruption mounts in the novels that follow. In *The Kite*, the grayling fish, like the Indians who were seduced and exploited by the frontier fur traders (33–34), 'can't stand civilization very well' (39). In the comparison with Clemens referred to above in *Ladybug, Ladybug ...,* Kenneth Lyon 'and young Clemens smelled and tasted and touched and saw and heard a similar New World before man could badly scar your patch of the earth's skin' (13). Though Brian O'Connal had resisted Art's insistence that people are just like animals, mating 'just like dogs an' gophers an' – an' pigeons' (*Who Has Seen the Wind* 199), Hugh accepts the Swiftian evidence that people are worse than animals: 'Humans' [feces] had to be the worst smell of all' (*How I Spent My Summer Holidays* 152). Nor can Hugh find consolation in the community: 'The village of my prairie boyhood was not really one unified community.' Rather, it was alienated into four distinct societies – those of the children, the adults, the mental hospital, and the brothel: 'I cannot recall any great flow of understanding among them' (4). They are depicted as being as different as grasshoppers and ants, as different as the principal's parable of the grasshoppers and ants and King Motherwell's version of the parable, related only by the most metaphysical of connections. Connections become consequences as communication is reduced to intrusion, trespassing, and invasion. The children of underworld caves cannot escape the trespassing footprints of the upper-world adults (177), and the realm of summer innocence is invaded by winter knowledge in terms similar to Carlyle Sinclair's reference to Eve's Early Winter Knowledge in *The Vanishing Point* (185).

Sexual experience is a common metaphor for the rite of passage from innocence to maturity, and one which Mitchell uses to illustrate the principle that knowledge can be encountered too soon. As with reading Shakespeare's plays too early in youth, the profound beauty of the experience can be lost on the child.

Thus young Hugh finds the physical body of the 'other' sex 'all wrong,' with breasts dismissed as useless appendages (*How I Spent My Summer Holidays* 159). In *Roses Are Difficult Here*, Rory Napoleon's loss of control over the antler-decorated horses threatens to dispel the fantasy of Santa Claus's visit. The manuscript, in which Rory bellows through his Santa beard, 'Whoa, you cocksuckers!' was revised by the publisher to 'Whoa, you bay bastards!' (127). In *Who Has Seen the Wind*, the conversations between Brian and Digby raise the tragic implication that maturity marks the corrosive fall to experience when our various experiences become taken for granted. The child's sense of wonder, the joyful sense of 'splendour in the grass,' and the thirst for comprehending the mysteries of life are too often abandoned by the adult.

The adults who resist the corrosive nature of experience are generally defeated by the corrupt order of authority figures. When the Reverend Hislop is pressured to resign for his defence of the outcast Ramona, the pattern is set for Digby to be similarly pressured for his defence of the outcast young Ben. But with Miss MacDonald's replacement by Digby's ally Miss Thompson, Mitchell suggests that the corrupt order of the Mrs Abercrombies need not always prevail. In the Livingstone University novels, the corrupt authority figures are more prominent and dominant. They are less likely to be overcome; rather, as immovable fixtures, they must be worked around. With the depiction of psychotic characters like Slaughter produced by the corrupt system, *Since Daisy Creek* and *Ladybug, Ladybug...* expose the social order with the bleak vision normally controlled by Mitchell's reliance on comic relief. From the rural prairie novels to the Livingstone University novels, Mitchell pursues his investigation of the relationship between natural and social orders by moving from one extreme to the other: from the corrupt natural order of young children to the corrupt social order of higher education. In *Ladybug, Ladybug...* Dr Harbottle pinpoints the source of corruption in the university: 'Faculty. Leave just one letter – "c" – and what have you got?' (161). With a faulty faculty teaching future generations what is alleged to be the highest learning of our cultured society, the ivory tower is exposed as a faulty tower wherein the comic is replaced by the cruel, the petty, and the pathetic.

A corrupt ministry makes the church no better than the university. Apart from exceptions like Reverend Pringle of *The Black Bonspiel* and Canon Midford of *Roses Are Difficult Here*, Mitchell's ministers range from the rigid, like Reverend Powelly of *Who Has Seen the Wind* and the Preacher of *The Devil's Instrument*, who enforce conformity with the corrupt social order, to the criminal, like Heally Richards of *The Vanishing Point* and Elijah Matthews of *For Art's Sake*, who are frauds and molesters. Thus it comes as no surprise that heroes are killed for posing a threat to the corrupt social order. King Motherwell explains 'the way it is' to Hugh and Peter in *How I Spent My Summer Holidays*:

> 'If he can think of something the rest of them can't – makes him dangerous to the tribe.'
> 'Why?' Peter said.
> 'Breaks their rules – takes a different direction from all the others. General run of chiefs, kings, heroes, they're shit-disturbers, so – once the war's won – dragon's dead – treasure's dug up – girl's rescued – danger's past – time to kill him off.' (116)

But for a few mythical figures martyred in folklore, these outcasts are dismissed and forgotten in life. To redeem ourselves from our corrupt social order we must construct an inclusive community which accepts and understands and celebrates its outcasts. The community must be inclusive of all classes, as with the Bens and the Napoleons. It must be inclusive of all races, as with the 'China kids' – Tang and Vooie Wong, who suffer because Mariel Abercrombie is encouraged to continue her mother's agenda; as with Moses and Lazarus Lefthand, who have left their Blackfoot reserve to be 'one hundred percent altogether Canadian' (*Jake and the Kid* 161), and with Victoria Rider and Archie Nicotine, who negotiate their way through a complex relationship with the Stoney reserve and the Calgary community. For his construction of cultural bridges that enable us to envision the inclusive community, Mitchell is identified by Dick Harrison as the first writer of prairie fiction to explore the Native perspective (*Unnamed Country* 199).

Nietzsche may provide the best epigraph for Mitchell's philosophy: 'What is great about man is that he is not a purpose but a bridge' (*Also Sprach Zarathustra*). As Carlyle comes to understand in *The Vanishing Point*, people are 'accountable to each other,' they 'are responsible for each other ... Man lifted bridges between himself and other men so that he could walk from his own heart and into other hearts. That was the great and compensating distinction: man did – the jack rabbit, the badger, the kill-deer, the weasel, the undertaker beetle, did not' (385). Carlyle's stream of thought during the Prairie Chicken Dance is foregrounded fifteen years later in Kenneth Lyon's convocation speech at Livingstone University, as the epiphany is made public. Qualifying Socrates' academic opinion that the 'unexamined life is not worth living,' Professor Lyon adds this corollary:

> Man also does not live by reason alone; the simply *intellectual* life is not worth living. It is for this reason that humans build their bridges from lonely human self to lonely human self. This human need to bridge explains wives, mothers, brothers, sisters, regions, nations; these bridges cannot be built out of money, power, prestige – just love. We are the only animals who paint, sing, sculpt, compose, worship – all bridges.' (*Ladybug, Ladybug* ... 138–39)

Mitchell has conjured a variety of bridges, ranging from the recent image of rollicking fun derived from the 'good fellowship that curling folk tell you traditionally surrounds curling events' (*Black Bonspiel of Willie MacCrimmon* 134) back to the image of communal continuity derived from the haunting solitude of telephone wires that have magically come to life in the mind of a child 'following them from pole to pole to the prairie's rim. From each person stretched back a long line – hundreds and hundreds of years' (*Who Has Seen the Wind* 292). Such lines of communication bridge the abyss between ancestor and descendent, between the viewer and the vanishing point, between the forgotten experience of a common day and the magical stories whereby we construct our culture and thereby write ourselves into existence.

NOTES

1 In an interview Twain recalled from his boyhood purchasing with great pleasure Haliburton's 'Sam Slick' stories (Cyril Clemens, 'Unpublished Recollections,' *Mark Twain Quarterly,* 4 [Summer–Fall 1941]: 20, 23).

2 See Barbara Mitchell's discussion of these editorial revisions in 'The Long and the Short of It.'

3 Unless indicated otherwise, page references are to the 1982 Seal edition, reprinted since 1993 by Macmillan/Stoddart.

4 The conventional typewriter typography of the first edition was retained in the Laurentian Library paperback reprintings, but was eliminated in the Seal paperback edition.

5 The following clause appears in the 1947 Macmillan edition: 'Early in August, much as though long-continuing pressure of a foot upon a pedal of a loom had become suddenly final and the shift determining the pattern of weaving threads had become actual, the warp ...' (230).

6 His plays are among the most popular in Canada and may have influenced theatre from the West End to Broadway. David Gardner suggests that the pilot episode for the *Jake and the Kid* television series, 'Earn Money at Home,' anticipated the West End farce *No Sex Please, We're British. The Black Bonspiel,* first broadcast on CBC radio in 1951, may very well have been appropriated as the model for the Broadway musical *Damn Yankees.*

'The Litmus Years':
The Early Writings of W.O. Mitchell

W.J. KEITH

A myth has formed around the career of W.O. Mitchell. According to this myth, his first novel, *Who Has Seen the Wind*, was an outstanding popular and literary success, quickly establishing itself as a Canadian classic and bringing both fame and distinction to its author. Instead of going on to buttress his reputation, however, he is supposed to have deviated into radio and spent the next decade producing a series of amusing but sentimental radio scripts, a selection of which appeared in print as *Jake and the Kid* in 1961. A year later, a second novel, *The Kite*, appeared, but proved both less popular and less impressive than *Who Has Seen the Wind*. After another long silence, *The Vanishing Point* was published in 1973; this novel was treated respectfully as a serious and committed presentation of White/Indian relations, but once again lacked the popular appeal of the first novel. Since then, he has written plays and published more novels, but has not been fully successful in combining the serious and the popular.

That, as I say, is the W.O. Mitchell myth, and, like most myths, it contains a germ of truth. It is certainly true that his later novels, though commercially successful, have never rivalled the sales figures of *Who Has Seen the Wind*, and the academic commentators, possibly deterred by his reputation as a popular personality and entertainer, have not subjected his writing (with the exception of the first novel) to the detailed criticism they have lavished on the work of many of his contemporaries. But that is only part of the story – and in any case the myth is seriously marred by inaccuracy. First, Mitchell began publishing short stories, including many of the Jake and the Kid stories, in the better popular magazines years before the publication of *Who Has Seen the Wind*. Second (and this has been substantiated by his son, Orm Mitchell ['Invading Caves' 146]), far from sidestepping into the popular media he underwent a considerable personal crisis in the 1950s and early 1960s in an attempt to produce a second novel of equivalent quality. 'The Alien' was serialized in *Maclean's* in 1953–54, but Mitchell was dissatisfied with it and never published it in book form. Another manuscript of these years, *Roses Are Difficult Here*, failed to find sufficient publisher support, though it appeared in 1990 in what appears to be only a slightly revised version.

Opinions can differ drastically about the merits and/or weaknesses of his later work. Personally, I have always had a high regard for *The Kite*, though it is clearly a less ambitious novel than its predecessor. *The Vanishing Point*, often impressive and powerful, is seriously weakened, for me, by the unconvincing comic ending attached to a much darker and more serious main plot. As for the novels that have appeared in the 1980s and 1990s, they seem to me frustratingly unsatisfying, though I acknowledge that all contain vividly memorable scenes and that only a skilled writer could have produced them. But if, as seems clear, he has been at pains, in words he has applied to Mark Twain, to 'hit a serious balance of art and leisure-demand' (O'Rourke 159), it also seems clear that, since 1947, he has failed to achieve this self-imposed ideal. I suggest, however, that the reason for this (comparative) failure is likely to be found, not by painstakingly combing the later novels for merits and deficiencies, but by taking a closer look at Mitchell's earlier writings.

Mitchell himself has coined the phrase 'litmus years' to express the significance of early experiences. In *How I Spent My Summer Holidays*, the narrator, describing his return visit to the small town of his boyhood, writes as follows:

As I walked from Government Road towards the Little Souris, the wind and the grasshoppers and the very smell of the prairie itself –

grass cured under the August sun, with the subtle menthol of sage
– worked nostalgic magic on me ... Here was the melodramatic
part of the earth's skin that had stained me during my litmus years,
fixing my inner and outer perspective, dictating the terms of the
fragile identity I would have with my self for the rest of my life.
(9–10)

And in *Since Daisy Creek*, Colin Dobbs repeats the phrase while
giving advice to his creative-writing class: 'Most of what turns
out to be useful seems to come after a time lag. Often out of childhood. The early years of your life – the first ten – are the litmus
years, the ones that seem to stain us most vividly' (100). (It is
noteworthy, by the way, that the word 'stain' is employed in both
contexts.) I do not propose to go back quite as far as Dobbs rec-
ommends, though childhood is itself a preoccupation in his early
attempts at fiction; I am suggesting, however, that a chronological
examination of Mitchell's early published work will provide clues
that throw light upon his 'case.'

Before I proceed any further, however, there is one difficulty
that needs to be faced – namely, that the ordering of Mitchell's
first short stories is a subject of dispute. The bibliographical
record of publication is clear enough; Mitchell's first short story to
see the light of day was 'But As Yesterday,' which appeared in the
Summer 1942 issue of *Queen's Quarterly*. This was closely followed by the first of the Jake and the Kid stories, 'You Gotta Teeter,' published in *Maclean's* in the issue for 15 August 1942. An
editorial in this issue, however, informs us that, in the 'author's
own words,' the story represents 'my first magazine sale, article
or fiction, paid or unpaid for' ('In the Editor's Confidence' 2).
Which of these stories can claim temporal priority (who knows
how far behind schedule wartime issues of *Queen's Quarterly* may
have been?) is not perhaps of any particular importance. But the
matter is further complicated by a recent claim by Dick Harrison:
'The earliest acceptance ... was actually "[The] Owl and the Bens,"
a segment of *Who Has Seen the Wind* published in *Atlantic Monthly*,
though it did not appear until 1945' (199n2). This is contradicted,
however, by Barbara Mitchell, who offers the more likely accep-

tance date of 'late 1944' (9). These discrepancies are puzzling, but they do not seriously affect my argument. I gladly leave any resolution of this problem to subsequent archivists, literary historians, and bibliographers, and am content for the present purpose to follow the order of publication given by Sheila Latham in her annotated bibliography.

'But As Yesterday' tells the story of an understanding relationship established between a six-year-old boy and his eighty-year-old grandfather. It has never been reprinted, doubtless because its main components have since been incorporated into Mitchell's first two novels. With the substitution of grandmother for grandfather, the basic situation clearly develops into the well-known scene towards the end of *Who Has Seen the Wind*. Together the two make a top which the boy plays with at the conclusion of the story, and this looks forward to the two kite-making scenes at the beginning and end of the second novel. A defiance of the tyranny of clock-time is a common concern of the short story and both novels. In 'But As Yesterday,' the grandfather tells the boy a tall tale about Telesphore Toutant, a bear cub, and a saskatoon berry used as a glass eye – a tale repeated in the equivalent scene in *Who Has Seen the Wind* ('Yesterday' 136, *Wind* 274). The description of the falling snow at the time of death is virtually identical in the two narratives ('Yesterday' 138, *Wind* 287). Here, too, we find the beginnings of Mitchell's vigorous rustic speech conventions. 'It was enough to give a dog the heart-burn,' remarks the grandfather (133) – an early version of a saying, with 'gopher' replacing 'dog,' which becomes a Mitchell trademark. Indeed, the grandfather's speech in general looks forward to Jake Trumper's, to Saint Sammy's, and to Daddy Sherry's.

Above all, the atmosphere of the story, with its emphasis on basic human attitudes, is unabashedly sentimental. I do not mean this in any dismissive sense – the sentiment is genuine and moving – but it is clear that Mitchell is intent upon eliciting a warm emotional response from a wide range of readers. If we encounter the story after familiarity with Mitchell's subsequent work, we are immediately struck by the way in which it contains the essence of so much of the later fiction. Rapport between old and young is exploited not only in *Who Has Seen the Wind* and *The Kite* but in the Jake and the Kid stories as well – and, indeed, with certain variations (especially the relationship between aging father and young daughter or daughter-substitute) in most of his later work. To be sure, the story lacks several of the qualities that have become associated with vintage W.O. Mitchell. Most conspicuously, while a prairie background is implicit in the reference to the Indian and the saskatoon berry, there is no specific geographical detail, and the main characters even lack names. The intention, presumably, is to stress the universality of the relationship. 'But As Yesterday' appeared in an academic journal, and clearly aspires to literary significance, yet the situation obviously had much broader appeal. We might say that this story represents an auspicious beginning for a writer wishing to achieve 'a serious balance of art and leisure-demand.'

At about the same time, 'You Gotta Teeter,' destined to become the opening story in *Jake and the Kid*, appeared in *Maclean's* and heralded Mitchell's long association with that magazine. Here we meet for the first time not only the chief characters in the series – the ever-resourceful hired man Jake Trumper and the endearingly innocent and never-named Kid – but the town of Crocus and a number of its inhabitants who were to entertain a succession of magazine-readers, radio-listeners, and eventually television-viewers in the next two decades. The plot centres upon the Kid's speech at a school concert on behalf of a refugee fund, and the coincidental loss of his fox-terrier pup, cutely named Mr Churchill. Once again, we encounter a basic situation that Mitchell is to develop later, since the death of Brian O'Connal's dog will provide one of the climaxes in *Who Has Seen the Wind*. But the tone of these two scenes is notably different. Whereas in the novel this is one of a series of deaths, culminating in those of Brian's father and grandmother, that introduce Brian to the hard facts of mortality, in 'You Gotta Teeter' the theme is softened and disguised by a pleasant but essentially sentimental resolution: the Kid's spontaneous but effective speech causes the refugee campaign to be triumphantly successful, and not only is the Kid's lost dog replaced by an identical pup from the same litter but Violet, the refugee kid from England billeted down the road, is even promised 'Mr. Churchill's sister' ('Teeter' 30, *Jake* 14).

'You Gotta Teeter' caters to a very different readership from 'But As Yesterday,' though it would be wrong to discount totally the possibility of overlap. Here, however, 'leisure-demand' takes precedence over 'art.' *Maclean's* at this time was a magazine for family reading, intensely patriotic in its encouragement of the war effort, full of timely and thought-provoking articles on pressing topics of the day, but also providing fiction of broad popular appeal. This particular story was obviously designed to fit the needs of the moment, and the encouragement of the war effort is a conspicuous though not oppressive feature of the narrative. Moreover, we recognize in this story the first clear indications of Mitchell's warm, didactic, and essentially comic vision. The Kid makes a valiant effort to overcome his own grief in the interests of others, and ultimately all benefit. We soon realize that, in all the Jake and the Kid instalments, the basic decency represented by the two principal protagonists will eventually triumph. Thus, in 'A Voice for Christmas,' Jake is able to persuade the CBC team to broadcast from Crocus so that the Kid can speak with his father overseas; in 'Two Kinds of Sinner,' the Kid, with the help of his reluctant mother as well as Jake, wins the challenge of the horse-race; in 'The Golden Jubilee Citizen,' Jake Trumper, through the Kid's initiative and Miss Henchbaw's conversion, is officially honoured. As readers, we accept the comic – and popular and sentimental – convention that virtue, goodness, and human warmth will prevail.

The third Mitchell short story to appear in print, 'Elbow Room,' followed in September 1942. Another Jake and the Kid story, it wasn't collected until recently, when a somewhat revised version was published in *According to Jake and the Kid*. Here Mitchell inserts some early sentences announcing the death of the Kid's father in the last year of the war (13) – a fact which, though unrelated to the story itself, lends a piquancy to the whole effect. In the original, however, a combination of firm patriotism, generous attitudes self-consciously granted to the enemy, and a rather cloying sentiment reign supreme. Jake employs as stooker a passing stranger who turns out to be an escaped German prisoner-of-war. Eventually, after much soul-searching, he is turned in, but not before he has learned to appreciate the 'elbow room' of the Saskatchewan prairies, and to recognize that there is no place in Canada for 'dick-taters' ('Elbow' 20, *According* 21). On the way back to camp the prisoner spends part of his wages on buying the BB gun that the Kid has coveted throughout the story, and, via Jake, gives it to him as a parting gift. The Kid feels 'kind of sick' upon receiving it ('Elbow' 39, *According* 27), but Mitchell's readers are supposed to respond with a sense of liberal-minded satisfaction. The sentiment may have been admirable in the middle of the Second World War (though older readers will now be irresistibly, if somewhat ironically, reminded of Noel Coward's 'Don't Let's Be Beastly to the Germans'); to modern taste it seems syrupy and contrived as well as rather oppressively uplifting. In terms of Mitchell's literary development, however, it strengthens our sense of Crocus as a human community and introduces certain prairie images – gopher, meadowlark, coyote – that are going to become staples of Mitchell's local detail.

Half a dozen Jake and the Kid stories followed over the next two years. It is not necessary to consider each of these in detail; more important is a recognition of the comic-sentimental formula that Mitchell evolves at this time. Moreover, during this period he assembles a collection of Crocus inhabitants who have the makings of a coherent prairie society, some of them fated to become either recognizable character types or authentic individuals. Miss Henchbaw of Rabbit Hill School is quickly established as a firm and enterprising schoolteacher, even when seen through the eyes of one of her more obstinate students. Albert Ricky begins to emerge as a mean-minded and autocratic school-board chairman. Old Man Gatenby is as yet little more than a name, but he will eventually become a leading foil to the irrepressible Jake Trumper. In 'A Voice for Christmas,' there is even a single mention of a name to which, wise after the event, readers of *Who Has Seen the Wind* will immediately respond: Mrs Abercrombie. Much the same can be said of the settings of these stories – Crocus and its surroundings. We gradually become aware of the recurring geographical and architectural features. Crocus is the chief town in an area containing settlements called Tiger Lily, Conception, Brokenshell, Broomhead. Certain buildings are continually mentioned: the Royal Hotel, MacTaggart's store, the Maple Leaf Beer Parlour, Drew's Pool Hall, as well, of course, as the Rabbit Hill School.[1]

In April 1945 'The Owl and the Bens' was published in *Atlantic Monthly*, reminding us that, alongside the Crocus stories already discussed, Mitchell was working on the material that was later to come together as *Who Has Seen the Wind*. Another section of the novel, 'Saint Sammy,' duly appeared in the same journal some four months later. Both contributions contain material scattered through the final text of the novel which, as Catherine McLay has shown ('Novels' 87–88), was being written and laboriously revised at this time. Reading these extracts within the chronological order of publication of his other writings points up their tonal resemblance to the Jake and the Kid stories. Significantly, there is nothing here of the spiritual quest of Brian O'Connal. But the composite story of the Bens – the tall tale about the Young Ben's birth, the Old Ben's encounter with the apparent ghosts in the graveyard, the exploding still in the basement of the Baptist Church, the Young Ben's release from the prison of school – and the saga of Saint Sammy and Bent Candy are compatible with the morally simplistic world of Crocus, providing comforting parable-like fables concerning the centrality of liberty and the possibility of divine retribution. When such narratives form the centre of attention rather than acting as secondary elements within the fabric of *Who Has Seen the Wind*, they remain entertaining but pack far less power.

The human and physical connections between Crocus and the never-named town of *Who Has Seen the Wind* are inconspicuous but, when noticed, cumulatively impressive. It is not, perhaps, surprising that both towns should boast a Royal Hotel (*Jake* 9, *Wind* 64), but they also share a Hi-Art Theatre (*According* 65, *Wind* 130), Drew's Pool Hall (*Jake* 19, *Wind* 64), and the MacDougall Implement Company (*Jake* 163, *Wind* 50)). As far as the inhabitants are concerned, I have already mentioned Mrs Abercrombie as inhabiting both towns (*Jake* 41, *Wind* 23). This is also true of her bank-manager husband and their daughter Mariel (*According* 159, 166; *Wind* 41, 43). Also mentioned in *Who Has Seen the Wind* are Miss Henchbaw (265) and several Gatenbys (77, 152, 232).

If we conduct this kind of detailed analysis of the inhabitants and geographical locations of Mitchell's Crocus, we soon realize that it forms the matrix of all of his writings up to and including *How I Spent My Summer Holidays*. From it, connections branch out to establish links with the other books – curiously enough, even with those set in Shelby, supposedly located in the neighbouring province of Alberta and the setting for *The Kite, Roses Are Difficult Here*, occasional scenes in *The Vanishing Point*, and even by implication the unnamed setting of *How I Spent My Summer Holidays*. Mayor MacTaggart, who appears in so many of the Jake and the Kid stories, is also mayor of Shelby in *The Vanishing Point* (196). Mr Abercrombie (with a slight change of first name from Merton to Milton) turns up again as bank manager in *The Kite* (111). Malleable Brown's blacksmith shop is located not only in Crocus but in the Shelby of *Roses Are Difficult Here* (169). Chez Sadie's beauty parlour occurs in *The Kite* (202) as well as in *According to Jake and the Kid* (118). The Hanley reserve is in the vicinity of both Crocus (*According* 119) and Shelby (*Vanishing* 215). The barbers of the two towns have different names, but Repeat Golightly and Merton N. Spicer both display an interest in historical fiction and quote the identical passage from a historical romance (*Jake* 174, *Kite* 24). The *Crocus Breeze* reappears transparently as the *Shelby Chinook*. The Chinese-operated café appears under different names (Bluebird in *Who Has Seen the Wind, The Kite*, and *How I Spent My Summer Holidays*, the Sanitary Café in *Jake and the Kid*, the Palm Café in *Roses Are Difficult Here*), but Wing provides the uniforms for the local junior sports teams and sends hospital baskets in both *Jake* (176) and *Roses* (39, 222).[2]

The explanation for this apparent geographical confusion and conflation seems to be that Mitchell draws his inspiration not only from his childhood memories of Weyburn, Saskatchewan, but also from his later residence in the Alberta foothills at High River. One reviewer of *Jake and the Kid*, Dorothy Howarth, happened to share Mitchell's origins, and claimed to be able to link the characters in Crocus to 'the real townspeople of Weyburn' (Latham 357). It seems, moreover, that Mitchell, like Leacock before him, retained some of the actual names of his characters' originals. McLay lists the Tinchers, Mayor MacTaggart, and Old Man Gatenby ('Crocus' 337), and there is a hint in Donald Cameron's interview with Mitchell that Mrs Abercrombie may have derived from the same source (Cameron 50). In 'One Hour in High River, Alberta,' Peter Gzowski implies that Mitchell also based characters in the Jake and the Kid stories on actual people in High River, and Mitchell himself, speaking of *Who Has Seen the Wind*, is quoted as saying: 'Though it's prairie, a great deal of it depends on the mosaic of life that was High River in those days' (Gzowski 24). It was in High River that he worked on 'The Alien' and began to develop the character of Carlyle Sinclair, who was to become the protagonist of *The Vanishing Point*. We never learn directly where Carlyle grew up, but the childhood flashbacks are obviously set in Mitchell's 'Crocus' world. This did not become fully clear, however, until *How I Spent My Summer Holidays* appeared in 1981. There Hugh returns to the area of his childhood which is indisputably Crocus. 'Our town lay on the South Saskatchewan prairies,' we are told, and as he moves nostalgically down Government Road (6) we know that he must eventually pass the farm of Jake and the Kid. Other names – 'Brokenshell,' 'Manyberries' (6, 28) – echo those of the Crocus world. The connection with *The Vanishing Point* is clinched by the fact that Dr Sinclair, Carlyle's father, plays a minor role in *How I Spent My Summer Holidays*, and both novels introduce us to Sadie Rossdance's whorehouse (*Vanishing* 319, *How I Spent My Summer Holidays* 3).

For an informed literary-critical appraisal of Mitchell's work, it is important to realize that the Crocus of *Jake and the Kid* provides the imaginative foundation for his fictive world. Previous commentators have touched on this matter, though in general they have not given it the emphasis that it merits. Thus Michael Peterman has noted that 'the important relationships in *Who Has Seen the Wind* had their beginnings in the interaction of the Kid and

Jake Trumper' (10), and Catherine McLay observes that Jake, though 'a composite of as many as ten originals,' is partly modelled on Uncle Tom Mitchell, also the original of Uncle Sean in *Who Has Seen the Wind* ('Crocus' 341). Moreover, W.O. Mitchell himself told Patricia Barclay that, as he proceeded with the *Jake and the Kid* radio scripts, he 'wrote only one in five of the stories about the boy and the old man; other inhabitants of the mythical community of Crocus were created with the intention of providing "semi-polished material" from which he could draw future novels' (Barclay 54–55). An obvious instance is Daddy Sherry of *The Kite*, who begins as Daddy Johnston (or Johnson – the spelling varies in the Jake and the Kid stories; see *Jake* 176 and the uncollected 'How Crocus Got Its Seaway' 59), and appears under his later name in the revised versions published in *According to Jake and and the Kid* (216, 272, etc.).

While acknowledging the connections among all these fictions, however, we must be careful to make the necessary qualitative distinctions. Crocus may function as the *fons et origo* of Mitchell's later communities, but this does not mean that they are interchangeable. It is possible to exaggerate the significance of Crocus. Catherine McLay does so, I believe, in her thoroughly documented study when, under the subtitle 'A Country of the Mind,' she describes the town as 'a western Mariposa, a microcosm of the experience of many Canadians who had to leave their Mariposas in order to see them anew' ('Crocus' 355); and Mitchell's son goes even further in calling it 'a microcosm of the Canadian and world communities' ('Tall Tales' 18). Such remarks might reasonably be made of the unnamed town in *Who Has Seen the Wind*, but they are incongruous here. Crocus is a country of the heart rather than of the mind; it is indisputably 'innocent,' with only the faintest traces of any threatening shadows of the real world. In addition, it lacks the strain of salty abrasiveness that Leacock is careful to inject from time to time into his portrait of Mariposa. Part of the reason, of course, is that, in the original Jake and the Kid stories, the community is seen from the perspective of the Kid; in some of the radio scripts and in *According to Jake and the Kid*, the viewpoint varies from story to story between the Kid and Jake

Trumper, though the latter's world-view, if somewhat qualified by experience, is hardly subtle or complex. In neither do we gain the balanced and considered attitude of the narrator in *Who Has Seen the Wind*, who juxtaposes an adult perspective with that of Brian O'Connal.

In *Who Has Seen the Wind* alone, I would submit, does Mitchell achieve the all-important balance for which, in his best moments, he strove. And one of the main reasons for this seems to be that, in this case, to quote Barbara Mitchell, 'his mentor and second critical eye, Professor F.M. Salter, had edited every page of the manuscript before it was submitted' (9). Barbara Mitchell goes on to lay stress on 'the balancing of the dualities of light *and* dark, birth *and* death, caressing *and* avenging wind, human *and* prairie voices, insight *and* incomprehension' (13). This is precisely what we do *not* find in the presentation of Crocus. Although she admits that 'the tragic implications are undeveloped here,' McLay asserts that 'Gettin' Born' 'introduced the Kid to the problems of life and death' ('Crocus' 340), but there is nothing in the Crocus story of Brian's wonder at the birth of the pigeons or the pathos experienced when the baby pigeon dies in his hand. And Brian's dog, unlike the Kid's, is killed in his presence and is never replaced. There is no clear evocation of the 'heart of darkness' (*Wind* 212, 279) here, nothing to compare with the cruel boycotting of Tang Wong's birthday party. Miss Henchbaw, for all her attempts to curb the excessively imaginative attitudes of Jake over the Kid's mind, never resorts to the methods of Miss MacDonald, while Mrs Abercrombie and her daughter Mariel, as presented in Crocus, are the merest shadows of their domineering and oppressive selves.

But if, with the forceful encouragement of Salter, Mitchell achieved the all-important balance of opposites – including 'a serious balance of art and leisure-demand' – in *Who Has Seen the Wind*, he experienced great difficulty in maintaining the same standard in subsequent publications. That he tried desperately is not in question. He came closest, I believe, in *The Kite* and *The Vanishing Point*, but his own accounts of his struggles with these novels can be profoundly revealing. Here is what he tells David

O'Rourke abut the writing of *The Kite*: 'That novel *The Kite* was a dangerous novel. I have never been more deadly earnest in my life but, because the whole surface was exaggerated in caricature, slapstick, critics mistook it, didn't realize how serious it was. Jesus! What could you be more serious about than man's mortality?... That's a pretty goddam good novel' (154). It is possible to agree that contemporary reviewers and commentators underestimated the serious issues explored within *The Kite* while at the same time wondering about the discrepancy between 'deadly earnest' and 'slapstick.' It may not be wholly the fault of readers if a perilous balance between these qualities went unrecognized.

On *The Vanishing Point* he is even more revealing: 'When Victoria Rider takes [Carlyle's] hand in the Chicken Dance, and they climb into the bag together, I'm really saying that technology, religion, mysticism, myth won't work, but what will work – I'm embarrassed by saying it – but what will work is love' (156). He has a good reason to be embarrassed. Though he claims it to be 'a dreadfully serious novel, and very carefully thought out' (153), one wonders precisely what he means by 'love,' since elsewhere in the interview he had referred to Carlyle's hope that, 'under the influence of, first, the revival-meeting passion and, later, the Chicken Dance, he could *fuck* Victoria' (154). There is a linguistic as well as a philosophical and human gap between 'into the bag together' and 'love.' And the final comment, for all its self-styled superiority to the attitudes of the 'slob Romantic' (153), points towards Mitchell's ever-present sentimentality.

'That's a pretty goddam good novel'; 'they climb into the bag together.' The language here is surely close to the 'prairie-sod-buster slang' (Ricou, 'Notes' 13–14) of Jake Trumper himself. The point is not made lightly; indeed, it is crucial to my argument. W.O. Mitchell made the connection himself in a light-hearted article in *Canadian Broadcasting Times* in 1952 – 'Jake ... is entirely autobiographical' (see Latham 341) – but he is more forthcoming in the O'Rourke interview: 'Jake and what he does are pretty close to me: what I would call a life artist... – there's a lot of me in Jake, I guess. And then a lot of it is illusion so you hide your footprints and everything else. This may explain why so many people equate me with a folksy old Foothills fart and Jake, you know, which I ain't' (157).

To be sure, the man who won a gold medal in philosophy at the University of Manitoba is not to be confused with Crocus's number-one hired man, but language like 'folksy old Foothills fart' and 'I ain't,' even in the process of denying the identification, confirms a mask. And Mitchell's son has shrewdly observed: 'As a performer he has become very much like one of the first characters he created, Jake Trumper the "creative liar"' ('Tall Tales' 17). Mitchell may have played his part too successfully: his readers – even his sophisticated readers – are not altogether at fault for accepting the mask as the reality.

But to what extent is it a mask? That the persona of the 'folksy old Foothills fart' conceals a deeply committed and often agonized novelist may be granted, but the evidence I have assembled may also suggest that behind the serious artist lies a less sophisticated teller of tales, embracing the hilarious, the gutsy, and the sentimental, always yearning towards a popular reputation even at the cost of compromising his more permanent creative ambitions. In his more recent work, the desired 'balance' fails. True, he abandons the cloying 'innocence' of Crocus. In the 'age of permissiveness' he is quick to exploit the darker topics that had previously been taboo. Often this takes the form of adolescent toilet humour, but it also embraces homosexual relationships (in *How I Spent*), deception and perjury (in *Since Daisy Creek*), organized crime (in *For Art's Sake*), kidnapping and even fellatio (in *Ladybug, Ladybug*...). The attempted balance, whether the male protagonists' affection for their 'little girl lost' daughters or substitute daughters, or the wildly inventive humorous set-pieces – Carlyle selling lingerie in the whorehouse in *The Vanishing Point*; Colin Dobbs and the dead dachshund in the refrigerator in *Since Daisy Creek*; the mayor, his ulcer, and the balloon ride in *For Art's Sake*; to name only a few – are never sufficiently related to the main plot.

Who Has Seen the Wind contains a number of apparently self-contained incidents, but they are invariably integrated (generally through unifying imagery or symbolism) into the whole.[3] In other words, *Who Has Seen the Wind* achieves its artistic success, at no sacrifice of popular appeal, by virtue of its art. I cannot but consider it significant that, in the O'Rourke interview, Mitchell rails against what he calls 'the harness, craft' (150). The whole passage is revealing. He claims that the writers of his generation (he names Ernest Buckler, Margaret Laurence, Wallace Stegner, and Alice Munro) tended to be inhibited by an overemphasis on the craft of fiction: 'Like I would read in *Writer's Digest* an article ... on handling of viewpoint in the short story. And I would be paralysed for a whole year ... [W]e studied that craft harness but we hadn't captured our horse and the name of the horse is Life. So, at some point, I suddenly realized that technique and gimmicks and craft were not enough ... I had to first find the lumber out of which I would build my illusions, and then this found lumber would determine the structure that I would build' (150). This is an infuriating mixture of basic common sense passing as profound illumination (of course 'technique and gimmicks and craft are not enough'), the homely simplistic imagery of Jake Trumper ('the name of the horse is Life,' 'this found lumber'), and, I fear, the sentimental romanticism that is bedrock W.O. Mitchell. I do not believe that writers like Stegner and Munro solemnly consulted *Writer's Digest* as a guide to their art; nor do I believe that they ever turned their backs on craft. (The reason *How I Spent My Summer Holidays* never matches its obvious model, *Wolf Willow*, is that it lacks Stegner's exquisite artistic control.) The notion that, once he has found his horse, he can let lumber determine the structure of the stable to contain it will not bear a moment's serious consideration. F.M. Salter insisted on Mitchell's paying due attention to the craft as well as to the life – and the result was his one undisputed artistic success.

Mitchell is not, of course, to be judged wholly on off-the-cuff remarks made during an interview session. I quote them – and place emphasis upon them – because I believe that they help to explain oddities, anomalies, and incongruities to be found within his work. The cast of mind revealed here is, I suggest, the cast of mind whose lineaments can be traced in the novels and stories. It is endearing, sympathetic, warm, impassioned, and unquestionably sincere, but it shows little sign of being either sharply focused or intellectually rigorous. The author of *Who Has Seen the Wind* is clearly a writer to be reckoned with. I cannot, however, resist the conclusion, arrived at reluctantly and with regret, that he lacks the profound vision that characterizes a truly great artist.

NOTES

1 For a detailed examination of the literary geography of these stories, see Catherine McLay's 'Crocus, Saskatchewan: A Country of the Mind.'
2 Similarly, the 1964 novella, *The Black Bonspiel of Wullie MacCrimmon*, written, according to the author's note, in 1950 (55), though set in 'Kartoum, Alberta' (18), shares various characters and places – Drew's Pool Hall, Chez Sadie's, MacCrimmon's Shoe and Harness, Malleable Brown's blacksmith shop (5, 6, 21), and several others – with one or more of the Jake and the Kid stories, the books set in Shelby, and *Who Has Seen the Wind*. In its revised form as a novel – *The Black Bonspiel of Willie MacCrimmon* (1993) – the setting is Shelby.
3 I have discussed this in some detail in the Mitchell chapter of my *A Sense of Style*, especially 63–68.

Images of Transgression:
The Threat of Sexuality in
W.O. Mitchell's Fiction

DICK HARRISON

Explicit sex is not touted as a main attraction of W.O. Mitchell's fiction. By my count, coitus between major characters occurs as a narrative event three times in the course of his eight novels. Yet the body count is not a fair measure of the importance of sexuality in Mitchell's fiction; its exclusion can be as significant as its inclusion. Mitchell adopts unusual strategies that effectively write sex out of the central narratives of most of his major novels; however, in spite of, or perhaps because of, that exclusion, sexuality lingers in the margins as a threatening presence, and when it does break through its social and narrative constraints, it is usually in forms that appear distasteful rather than alluring, more openly exploitive and predatory than seductive. Sexuality is thus primarily a negative force in the action of the novels, but it also serves as a complex signifier of moral structures in Mitchell's fictional world, a marker of boundaries through signs of their transgression.

Mitchell's characters are created out of, and into, a milieu of prairie puritanism, where sexual repression and guilt are to be expected, and Mitchell's narrative conventions descend from a tradition in which sexual reference is muted if not suppressed. Henry Kreisel, in his 'The Prairie: A State of Mind,' traces the sexual repression portrayed in prairie fiction to the pioneers' need to 'curb their passions and contain them within a tight neo-Calvinist framework' (263). Rather than weaken the force of sexuality in the fiction, the curbing exacerbates its effects. As Kreisel explains, 'it is not surprising that the passions, long suppressed, should burst violently into the open and threaten the framework that was meant to contain them' (263). An inherited neo-Calvinist framework is a major determinant of Mitchell's portrayal of sexuality, but Kreisel's explanation of its effects applies better to such writers as Grove, Ostenso, and Ross. In Mitchell's fiction the passions rarely 'burst violently into the open'; repressed sexuality may threaten the framework meant to contain it, but its effects are more insidious and far-reaching, especially on the young. The passage from innocence to experience that forms the foundation narrative of Mitchell's fiction is threatened by what neo-Calvinism has done to sexuality, and Mitchell's adult characters suffer lingering effects. One way of understanding the significance Mitchell assigns to sexuality is to trace its effects on that narrative.[1]

Bracketing Sexuality

In the lives of Mitchell's early protagonists, puberty and the sexual urgency of youth are conspicuous absences. *Who Has Seen the Wind*, for example, traces Brian O'Connal's passage from sensuous innocence to an uncommonly mature spiritual and philosophical awakening for a boy of twelve, but his passage is arrested at a significant point. As Laurence Ricou says, Mitchell examines the distinct stages of Brian's growth so carefully that the reader is aware of the next stage: 'This next stage, of course, is adolescence, a period of sexual awakening' ('Notes' 15). Understanding the significance of Brian's loss of innocence depends on an awareness of the adult world he will inhabit, but narration of that world is accomplished mainly through another focal character, Mr Digby, who serves as an alternate protagonist. This narrative strategy solves a number of problems arising from a child protagonist. It also serves to bracket that stage of sexual awakening; Digby is safely beyond the anxieties of adolescence and apparently beyond avid sexual desire. A similar pattern can be seen in most of Mitchell's early fiction. In the *Jake and the Kid* tales, the Kid is again pre-pubescent, living in a home free from sexuality. His mother is alone, his missing father replaced by a hired man too old, by character type if not in years, to pose an adult threat of sexuality. In *The Kite*, there is no symmetrical pairing, but puberty is again omitted from the ages of male characters played off against each other in the action. There is the child, Keith; David Lang, a jaded, prematurely middle-aged journalist capable of a romantic but virtually asexual attraction to Keith's mother; and Daddy Sherry, who owes his longevity partly to shunning women and remaining faithful to the memory of his old friend 'Ramrod.' In *The Vanishing Point*, sexuality is immanent in the Native community, but the bracketing pattern persists in the protagonist's recollections. Carlyle Sinclair recalls his recent past on the reserve and his early childhood, but his flashbacks stop short of puberty even though he believes his present alienation has roots in the sexual repression and guilt instilled by his Aunt Pearl's antiseptic prudery. Mitchell's narrative bracketing of his protagonists' traumatic loss of sexual innocence becomes more apparent in retrospect with the publication of *How I Spent My Summer Holidays*, where that trauma is directly addressed. Again, the focalization is dual, with an older narrator, Hugh, recalling a childhood self, but here the brackets are removed, the recollections allowed to extend to the point of sexual awareness. If Mitchell's earlier narratives could be said to skirt the abyss of sexuality, Hugh stops to look into it, with horror and repugnance.

This elision of sexual awakening from his earlier narratives is the more remarkable given that Mitchell represents the child's loss of innocence as analogous to the biblical 'Fall.' In *Who Has Seen the Wind*, he establishes a paradigm for the condition of mortality faced by virtually all his protagonists. The child's 'Fall' is a loss of primal unity with nature, shattered by a dawning awareness of self. In an interview, Mitchell cites Erich Fromm's proposition that consciousness of self separates man from the living whole as a 'constant theme' in his work ('Developers' 29). Separated from the eternal, cyclical processes of nature, the conscious self is, like Adam, morally responsible, separate, unique, and therefore mortal and isolated. Brian becomes aware of his 'apartness' during his night on the prairie; after his father's funeral he identifies it as the condition of human mortality.

In *The Vanishing Point*, Sinclair applies biblical terms to this fall into self-awareness and responsibility, cursing Eve and the apple of 'early winter knowledge' (185), but Brian is turned out of his Eden without an Eve. His fall seems to be accomplished without the sexual implications usually attached to the Genesis story, especially in puritan traditions. His 'forbidden' knowledge appears to be asexual, but a revelation of sexual biology does play a part in his fall. Brian's prelapsarian state of unity is signalled by something he calls 'the feeling,' an intuition of cosmic harmony usually associated with nature. When he learns from his playmate, Art, that babies are not sent by God, that men and women copulate 'just like dogs an' gophers,' Brian has an extraordinary and violent reaction. He is 'ashamed and frightened,' then outraged at the suggestion that humans are like 'dogs on a boulevard' (200), then disillusioned with his cherished intuitions: 'The feeling had nothing to do with anything. It wasn't any good' (201). At the age of eleven, Brian's rational, acultured, moral self is already recoiling from the brute processes of nature. Even in this first novel, where sexuality is written out of the main narrative, it appears briefly as a disillusioning revelation and as a sign of the boy's passage and a marker of the borders of self.

The Mental Hole

When the narrator of *How I Spent My Summer Holidays* revisits his childhood, he focuses on the summer when he was twelve or thirteen with the express purpose of understanding his fall from innocence. There is a mystery at the heart of it, he says, which has eluded him for decades and which he now hopes yet fears he may decipher. In the older Hugh's mind that mystery centres on an association between sexuality and adult betrayal of the vulnerable young, as suggested by a recurrent dream in which he is solicited by a respectable matron of the town to sodomize a row of child prostitutes. Only at the end of his narrative can Hugh interpret his dream and accept what he has 'refused to know all these years' (223), that even his childhood hero betrayed the trust of the young.

Young Hughie does not physically experience a sexual initiation, but the narrative of his fall, unlike Brian's, is rife with sexual incident and imagery. He has a boy's prurient curiosity about budding female bodies, he knows what goes on at Sadie Ross-dance's cottages, and he accidentally discovers masturbation, with attendant guilt and shame. Like Brian's, his first impressions of sexuality are ugly and distasteful. When he happens to witness a nude swimming party of seven prostitutes, his curiosity immediately gives way to disappointment and disgust at the sight of female bodies: 'I felt sick. Then – quickly – disappointed. After all the years of wondering and wanting to see, there was nothing to see! Tits were quite unnecessary. They did not belong there. The whole female form was wrong!' (159). Hughie's reaction is as extraordinary as Brian's outrage at the sexual facts of life, and both boys suffer a violation of their sense of order as well as a puritanical shame. But Hughie is exposed to more than the idea of sexual biology; he encounters the physical and emotional aspects of sexuality, both in their most distasteful forms. He sees the gross physicality of the human body and desire that is debased, distorted, and destructive. All the sexuality of the town that the older Hugh recalls is tainted with guilt and with overtones of depravity: Mrs Kidd's aggressive lesbian advances to Hughie's mother; Bella Motherwell's prostitution, infidelity, and disease; the hint of pedophilia in King Motherwell's association with the boys.

Through King, sexuality is directly linked with biblical imagery of the Fall. An indelible tattoo gives Hughie's childhood idol the appearance of being caught in the coils of a serpent: 'Vein blue and faint rust-pink and green it came out of the black bush of his pubic hair; scaled and about half as thick as my wrist, it coiled around his belly button and then up under his left nipple and across his chest to loop around his right nipple' (26). King later associates this serpent with his faithless wife when, in a state of delirium tremens, he imagines the tattoo to be alive and cries out 'No! No!... Not – her – poison kiss!' (207). In Hugh's narrative,

Bella, described as 'Proserpine-lovely,' makes a convenient, one-dimensional Eve figure, tempting her man to his damnation and death. While Hughie himself is not tempted, the serpent in his childhood garden is decidedly sexual and specifically associated with the depravity of female sexuality.

The point Hugh identifies as the end of his innocence, the moment he 'stopped being a boy,' is directly a result of violence rather than sex. It is his discovery of Bella's mutilated and decaying corpse in the cave he and his friend have dug on the prairie. But, as the older Hugh must finally acknowledge, King has beaten his wife to death in a jealous rage provoked by her infidelity and prostitution and her lesbian liaison with Mrs Kidd. The personal (though not precisely the legal) consequence of her murder is that Hughie's hero later hangs himself in the mental hospital. Sexuality is thus associated with horror, nausea, guilt, shame, disease, degradation, depravity, violence, madness, and death, and with virtually nothing positive in Hugh's narrative.

The adult betrayal of the young that Hugh laments consists partly in exposing children to the consequences of adult sexuality and partly in inculcating in them a Calvinist code which makes the advent of sexuality traumatic. The classic product of this life-denying code is the anal erotic Austin Musgrave with his compulsive propriety and malicious gossip, but Hugh considers himself and all his friends victims. The caves of their unconscious psyches have been defiled. Some grown-ups, he concedes, may have been well intentioned, entering the caves of childhood only to make them safe for their vulnerable young. 'They did not know, nor did we, that they could be carriers, unintentionally leaving serpents behind, coiled in a dark corner, later to bite and poison and destroy' (222).

In trying to understand his fall from innocence, Hugh envisions it both as a tragic fall into mortality and as a reluctant and dangerous passage to adulthood, and sexuality is among the perils that beset the passage. Hugh divides the village of his boyhood into four distinct societies: 'The largest and most dominant was adult of course, but our child society was real and separate, and we tried to keep it for our own' (5). Their 'child world,' as he calls it, is in constant, covert rebellion against the authority of the adult world. The river, where the boys sport in innocent nakedness in the 'Mental hole,' marks the separation; beyond the river, Hughie and his friend dig their cave as a symbolic haven from adults in their upper world. Crossing the gulf that separates the worlds entails the pain of loss and the threat of adult mysteries, including an element of sexual threat suggested by the sinister associations of the bridge, where Hughie encounters female nakedness, King's serpent, and Bella's obscene dance with a bulrush phallus. The last two distinct societies of the village presumably await those who fail to navigate the passage: Sadie Rossdance's cottages and the mental hospital, the refuges of sexuality and madness.

The perils of the passage to adulthood are rooted as much in gender as in sexuality itself. Hughie's fear and loathing of female sexuality, for example, arises from puritan repression and guilt, but also from insecurity about gender identity or manhood. And the same insecurity underlies the boys' resentment of authority and attraction to a delusional world of heroism that Hughie projects on King Motherwell, the one adult admitted to the child world as both man and boy. King himself warns the boys about the illusory nature of heroism, but he is an ideal object for their projection of heroic fantasies. King is handsome, dashing, and violent, a hunter, war hero, and athletic champion, glamorously mobile and mysterious, proprietor of the forbidden pool hall, a rebel who scorns the hypocrisy of the adult world, and outlaw who defies authority. In his wistful reflections, Hugh identifies King with a lost heroic age destroyed or unmanned by a puritanism implemented by women. (He conveniently overlooks the patriarchal origin of puritanism.) King is cast as the transcendent hero of classical myth, like Heracles grappling with the serpent which represents earthbound destiny. Hugh sees himself and his playmates as representatives of an earlier, matriarchal culture, unable to pass into that heroic age: 'Hesiod could compare us to the pre-Aryan silver age heroes: "eaters of bread, utterly subject to our mothers, however long they lived"' (3). The ultimate threat is not so much female sex as female gender, threatening male freedom, order, and control.

Hugh's resentment of puritanism, then, is based paradoxically on an unregenerate faith in patriarchal values. It could also be argued that he shares that faith with a number of other Mitchell protagonists, but my primary interest here is not in a study of gender constructions in Mitchell's fictional world, rewarding as that would be. My more limited concern is with the way sexuality in that world signals such constructions. Increasingly in the later novels sexuality serves not only as a representation of anarchic natural forces and the site of unnatural repression and fear but also as a sign of sensitive gender boundaries.

Hugh's quotation from Hesiod suggests another way of conceiving the boys' passage to adulthood in which sexual imagery reflects gender anxieties. On a simplified Freudian or Lacanian model, the boys must progress from a world of being to a world of meaning, from a state of unity with the mother, through a traumatic passage involving sexual differentiation, to a symbolic world of the father and of society. In that intermediate Oedipal stage, boys feel threatened by parental disapproval and by adult authority in general, and rebellious toward the cultural values and prohibitions it embodies. Hughie and his playmates are literally in that Oedipal stage. His childhood hero also reflects Oedipal associations and anxieties. King may inspire classical comparisons, but he more nearly resembles the typical hero of the American western who seeks justice beyond the law and is generally interpreted as acting out the Oedipal fantasies of his reading or viewing audience. Like the archetypal frontiersman, King is even a pseudo-Indian, complete with his own medicine bag, and late in the novel Hughie finds King in an alcoholic delirium, clutching his bag (said to resemble a severed scrotum) and crying 'Can't take it from me' (210). In the symbolism of the novel, King is evidently mistaken. The puritan matron in Hugh's recurrent dream wears, like a trophy, a similar leather bag 'hanging down like a sporran before her' (2). The hero is unmanned, the castration fear realized, the passage unsuccessful.

It may be more than coincidence that *How I Spent My Summer Holidays* is the only Mitchell novel to treat the loss of sexual innocence and the only one with a tragic rather than a comedic resolution. In whatever terms – biblical, classical, or psychoanalytic – the passage to adulthood is conceived, Hughie, his playmates, and their hero cannot be seen to accomplish it successfully. The older Hugh ends his narrative with a lament for himself and his fellows: 'Poor Austin!' 'Poor Peter ...!' 'Poor King!' 'Poor me!' (222–23). He remains, at fifty, a bitter, self-pitying, and confused man, nursing his misogyny and his love for a childhood hero. His resentment of adult authority has advanced only to an uneasy suspicion of his own complicity in it, as his child-brothel dream implies. He faces the isolation Brian O'Connal discovered as the condition of human mortality but has found no compensating relief in community. *How I Spent My Summer Holidays* thus participates in two major movements in Mitchell's fiction. It concludes the earlier exploration of innocence and the Fall, and the imagery with which it surrounds sexual awakening suggests a reason for Mitchell's earlier narrative bracketing of that stage of adolescence. Through its older narrator, the novel also contributes to the search of mature protagonists for reconciliation with their mortality that occupies the earlier and later novels, and many of the same motifs recur: the problematic passage to adulthood, the need for community, the failure of community conceived as a betrayal of adult responsibility to the young, and the implication of sexuality in that betrayal.

Bridging the Gulf

In Mitchell's later novels, relief from the mortal isolation of the self depends on bridging the gulf between individual souls. In *Ladybug, Ladybug...*, Kenneth Lyon articulates this answer to mortality quite explicitly in his convocation address. The prairie, he says, 'teaches early that to be human means to be conscious of the self and of being separate from the living whole.' Further, 'it is impossible to rejoin the living whole to ease the human pain of loneliness' (137). 'In my young world, at a very early age,' Lyon says, 'I learned that I was mortal' (138). Thus the problem of human mortality concretely represented in earlier novels can simply be stated and the solution proposed: 'It is for this reason that humans build their bridges from lonely human self to lonely human self' (138). These bridges can be built individually only through love and collectively only through art and the humanities. The bridge metaphor Lyon elaborates actually emerges earlier, in *The Vanishing Point*, both tangibly in the swinging bridge that connects the Paradise Valley Reserve to the outer (White) world and intangibly in the equally precarious bridges between Carlyle Sinclair and his Native charges, between races and individuals. When trying to secure a bond with his protégée, Victoria, Carlyle recognizes how difficult and uncertain such bridges are: 'Out of my skin and into yours I cannot get – however hard I try ... What a weak bridge emotion was for people to walk across to each other' (216). Carlyle's bridges swing over gulfs and are as emotionally perilous as the bridge that later appears in *How I Spent My Summer Holidays*.

Sex plays an ambivalent role in this bridging. The Calvinist milieu Mitchell represents in his fiction determines that sex will be implicated in the fall into mortality and become a terror besetting a boy's passage to adulthood. By the same token, in fiction exposing the tragic effects of that milieu, one might expect mature sexuality to offer an answer to that mortality, as a mitigation of its finality, a relief from isolation, a means of breaching the 'envelope of self,' or even a symbolic liberation from the life-denying constrictions of puritanism. Yet *The Vanishing Point* is the only Mitchell novel in which physical sexuality contributes directly to a bridging between 'lonely human selves' or to a protagonist's reconciliation to his mortality. Even there, sexuality initially appears to represent all the obstacles to understanding between races and individuals. The drumming in the Stoney dance tent expresses the natural anarchic and visceral energies that resist the rational civilized order of which Carlyle is the agent, and it is directly equated with the drumming in the mating rituals of the ruff grouse. Yet it is at that visceral level that Carlyle eventually finds his bond of humanity with the Stoneys.

For Carlyle sex is less a threat in itself than a measure of the gulf that divides him from these people, an index of alienation, and a marker of the cultural boundaries between Red and White, natural and civilized. Sex and, in an analogous way, excrement, function as complex signs of such borders, internal and external, which Carlyle is committed to guarding and yet must ultimately cross. The border between the instinctual, amoral order of nature and the rational, moral order of civilization can be negotiated only in certain ways. The osprey shits blamelessly in the stream, but when Harold Lefthand dumps horse manure in the agency water supply he violates the borders of civil order. White society transgresses the borders of nature by sterilizing dung and selling it as a commodity just as it seeks to sterilize the natural vitality of the Native people by civilizing them. The spontaneous, unself-conscious lust of Marth Bear is merely comic in its excess, but the Catfaces' commercial use of sex in the city is a violation of nature. Conversely, Heally Richards's use of Gloria as his born-again whitened Christian Indian crosses cultural borders illegitimately. The sealing off of the border between the natural and spontaneous and the rational and moral within Sinclair is signalled by the same two strains of imagery. In memory, Carlyle links his Aunt Pearl's white stool and burning of string in the bathroom with her total rejection of him for enlarging his penis in the magic lantern. Carlyle also recalls Old Khaki's perspective exercises as a moment of being fragmented, 'vanished' from himself. His response to that violation was to defecate in the teacher's desk. Sexual and excremental imagery thus signals a variety of borders which are important lines of definition but can become life-denying confinements that fragment and isolate humanity. They cannot be carelessly violated, but they must somehow be negotiated if Carlyle is to be whole.

For Carlyle these internal and external borders are at first impenetrable, opaque. Confined to his White rational order, he can perceive the Native culture only as chaos, his own perspective only as necessity. He cannot see that he is projecting on young Victoria his White middle-class values and an illusion of his own lost innocence. Carlyle becomes aware of his borders through a rudimentary sexual image. While watching Fyfe control the fertilization of his orchids to produce a pure white strain, he recognizes sexual prohibition as a power to control and manipulate. When he later abandons Victoria because she has become inappropriately pregnant (like the orchid Fyfe rejects for having been randomly fertilized by a bee) he recognizes how thoroughly he has internalized the system of control he administers.

It is the primitive erotic rhythms of the dance tent that enable Carlyle to cross his borders, to reach the natural, spontaneous side of himself that had been 'vanished' by the Victorian perspectives of Old Khaki and Aunt Pearl. Under the influence of the drums, he can at last conceive of lifting 'bridges between himself and other men so that he could walk from his own heart and into other hearts' (385). The Prairie Chicken Dance, by liberating him from the 'trap of self,' enables him to encounter the actual Victoria rather than his sanitized, denatured image of her. Their love-making is, for Carlyle, the necessary bridge, the answer to human mortality. It is also rare in Mitchell's fiction in other respects. Love is given a sexual expression; and while their sexual intercourse is not narrated or explicitly reported, it is an incontestable event in the narrative. The physical and emotional manifestations of sexuality are both represented together, positively, and not humorously. At least for Carlyle, erotic excitement has engendered a surrender of the self in sexual union and mutual satisfaction. Through sexual love, the borders of self have been negotiated. This may seem a tedious and unnecessary cataloguing of the obvious, but to my knowledge, Carlyle and Victoria's implied love-making is the only occasion in Mitchell's fiction on which all of the above conditions prevail.

Carlyle's sexual union with Victoria, together with his resolve to marry her, signals a classic comedic resolution. The waters of Beulah Creek flow again as the natural order participates in the comedic renewal of a world corrupted by civilization. But there are shadows, if not serpents, in this restored garden. Carlyle is aware of the ructions he will cause by crossing these social and racial borders; as he says, 'there'll be hell and heartburn all the way to Ottawa!' (387). He does not reflect on another, more ancient, border he has crossed. Carlyle has been Victoria's teacher and mentor for nine years, since she was a child of ten, and has assumed a parental role in her upbringing. About three days before their love-making, Carlyle says to Victoria, 'I haven't a daughter of my own – but you are my daughter' (365). This is not an impulsive gesture. On the night of the Prairie Chicken Dance, he again considers her in the same terms: 'My child – my child! Oh God, you were my child' (382). After Carlyle discovers his erotic love for Victoria, he is presumed to regard his earlier belief as a self-centred failure to acknowledge Victoria's womanhood, but the reader is not allowed to forget entirely their earlier relationship. When Carlyle wakes with Victoria naked in his bed, he remarks the childlike quality of her face, with its 'freckles still spiced beneath her closed eyes' (387). Carlyle does not, of course, literally violate any incest taboo of either society. The 'hell and heartburn' he anticipates will not be on that account; in White society his marriage will probably be regarded as merely improper. Yet this most positive of sexual resolutions is nonetheless faintly shadowed by anxieties about incest and pedophilia. In Mitchell's subsequent novels such anxieties resurface and come to represent the ultimate betrayal of adult responsibility to the vulnerable young.

Borderline Cases

The protagonists of Mitchell's 'Livingstone' novels, *Since Daisy Creek, Ladybug, Ladybug*..., and *For Art's Sake*, are all older men coming reluctantly to terms with their own mortality. Like Carlyle and Hugh, they show signs of an unsuccessful or imperfect passage to adulthood; all are alienated from the living whole, caught in the 'envelope of self,' and in need of those bridges Kenneth Lyon proposes. Unlike Carlyle, they are not able to build their bridges through sexuality, with the possible and qualified exception of Colin Dobbs in *Since Daisy Creek*. But sex again serves as a complex sign of borders and the interchange along borders in these novels. Colin Dobbs, Kenneth Lyon, and Arthur Ireland are all, in a sense, borderline cases.

Physical sexuality in the Livingstone novels is written out of the central action not so much by narrative strategies as by plot structure. The protagonists are alone, widowed or divorced, their mates surviving only in memory or imagination. These older men are instead paired with young women with whom the redeeming act of bridging must begin, but sex can play no overt part in the love bridge, not only by virtue of their age differences but because the women are, literally or figuratively, daughters to the protagonists. Sex is denied by the incest taboo, and Mitchell's repeated use of this dramatic structure draws attention to the effects of that taboo. Most simply it could be seen to purify the love at the centre of the action, shielding it from carnal motives and the anarchic forces of sexuality and focusing its effects on the building of community – love as *caritas* rather than *eros*. At the same time, the very prohibition of sexuality ensures it a presence in the action; it becomes more emphatically a sign of borders which must not be crossed. Incest would be the ultimate transgression of the parental bond, that most sacred of the adult responsibilities to the vulnerable young which constitute the soul of community in these novels. The young women are obtrusively marked by their language as beyond innocence in the usual sense, but have all been traumatized in some way by male sexual aggression. They are vulnerable, and their vulnerability is sexually signalled. Elsewhere in these novels sex also serves as a more general marker of necessary borders between selves and sexual aggression as a sign of failure to negotiate those borders.

Colin Dobbs, in *Since Daisy Creek*, is the most obvious casualty of the perilous passage to adulthood. He feels his manhood threatened, especially by females, and he focuses his fear and hatred on a mauling he has taken from a – significantly female – grizzly on Daisy Creek. His mutilated body becomes a visible expression of his lacerated ego and a mark of his apartness from the rest of humanity, while his pain and disfigurement keep him as self-absorbed physically as he is emotionally. But it is apparent that his insecurities have earlier origins, in his wife's divorcing him and probably in his childhood, when he was raised fatherless by a mother given to knocking him down and telling him she 'would not piss in my ear if my brain was on fire' (150). Dobbs's fears are gender-related, and he has reacted to the threat with aggressive self-assertion; as he puts it, 'he had taken up something less dangerous than marriage: bear-hunting' (94). He has made a romantic attempt to become a Hemingwayesque boy-man, or that classic figure of Western literature, the individualist male who seeks to transcend his mortality through symbolic achievements, and who flees from woman as the reminder and agent of that mortality.

Dobbs shores up his threatened manhood by making sex objects of the female hospital staff, his nurse who could have stepped 'into a Playboy centrefold' and his physiotherapist, a 'medieval bitch' with whom he imagines 'intercourse would be an olympic event' (4). In gender terms, he might be seen as aggressively asserting a stereotyped male identity in violation of the female selves around him. For Dobbs the most notable event of the narrative before his daughter arrives is an erection, yet the significance of his erection is more phallic than genital. It is auto-erotic, raised by his solitary speculations about nurse Bews, primarily a confirmation of his potency, to be boasted about and alluded to in conversation. At the same time, Dobbs is shown to be apprehensive about real heterosexual activity. The only two specific intimate embraces he recalls are both loathsome. The first is from his sexually predatory colleague Liz Skeffington. This is the only graphically described sexual act in Mitchell's fiction, and while Dobbs's distaste is comically displaced into a sneezing fit, it is confirmed by his later warning to the woman to stay away from him or he would 'bust her jaw.' The second is by the sow grizzly he has shot, whose 'embrace' he compares to rape (5).

Like Carlyle Sinclair, Dobbs is asserting his fragile self near the borders of pedophilia and incest. The usually contentious inter-play between Dobbs and his daughter Annie is the dramatic heart of the novel and the means of Dobbs's redemption, but it is shaded with sexual nuances one would not expect in a father-daughter relationship. The unusual details of behaviour are trifling and innocent enough in themselves, but cumulatively suggestive. When his daughter reappears at his bedside after five years' absence, Dobbs quite naturally requests an exchange of kisses. Shortly after that, she kisses him again while helping him to sit up: 'This time he did not have to ask her to kiss him. She held him in her arms much longer' (9). Neither detail would attract any attention if Dobbs's first thought on seeing his daughter had not been, 'Oh, Annie, dear Annie, won't you marry me!' (6). That line, possibly from an old song, would be only slightly puzzling except that, as Annie is leaving, he neglects to introduce her to Velvet Bews, though he judges they are about the same age and would approve of each other. Dobbs recognizes this as an 'interesting omission,' and though he explores it no further, the omission could be 'interesting' only if Dobbs subconsciously regards the girls as in some sense rivals. Dobbs's erotic response to Velvet is known, and she soon reveals her sexual attraction to him, betting that he could even 'turn on' her straitlaced supervisor Miss Learmonth. These quizzical sexual suggestions generate a complexity of tensions and displacements beneath the surface of the father-daughter relationship. Annie replaces Velvet as Dobbs's nurse; Dobbs claims Velvet as a second daughter but she repeats that her interest in him is not daughterly; Dobbs tells Annie about the erection Velvet excited in him. At this, Annie objects, saying 'Tell it to her – not me, God Damn it!' (36), but usually she joins freely in the sexual reference and innuendo that spice their conversation, occasionally troubling her father with more details of her sexual experience than he cares to hear, including the sexual aggression of her stepfather, which she has rejected as incestuous. There is a sexual undertone, even undertow, to the interplay between father and daughter, which often gives their disputes as much the tone of lovers' quarrels as of family contention.

The faint tension created by implicit sexuality in the shadow of the incest taboo is potentially distracting but fruitful in several ways. It underscores Dobbs's preoccupation with manhood, and the resultant tension between egocentrism and responsibility generates the main action of the novel. It also emphasizes the importance of family as a delicate web of love and obligation, vulnerable to betrayal. It draws attention particularly to the place of sexuality in that web. Dobbs has sentimental flashbacks to the time of Annie's childhood, when father and daughter enjoyed an unguarded unity as he comforted her and made her his companion, almost his conspirator, in camping and flyfishing. At the time, their closeness may have contributed to his failure as husband and father; his wife complained that he came between her and her daughter, and identification with her father may have impeded Annie's development of gender identity. But Dobbs recalls that phase of his life with wistful yearning. Now, because of sexuality, a return to such idyllic childhood unity is impossible. Sexuality is the flaming sword at the gates of Eden, barring the return. Dobbs must forge a more difficult, delicate, and unselfish bond between them. Sexuality signals a border which must be negotiated, accommodating sexuality, gender, and parental responsibility.

Annie is brought back to Dobbs not only to nurse a wounded father to health but to animate his growth, in middle age, to an adulthood he has never quite achieved. She shows Dobbs to himself, literally, forcing him to sit for a portrait. Her presence helps him to acknowledge his self-absorption and consequent failure as a husband and father, and she exposes his attempt to 'load everything on that bear' as a 'romantic cop-out' (241) from his real problems. She also ridicules the 'white hunter icon' of the bear's hide over which he is suing the taxidermist, and with Annie's help, Dobbs recognizes that everyone else involved in the dispute over the hide has been sacrificing for friends and loved ones while he has been intent only on symbolically shoring up his ego. Finally, she directs him to his neglected writing as a form of self-expression that can rebuild the bridges he has been petulantly destroying. Annie plays an essentially maternal role to Dobbs, her last gift being a firm insistence on their separation and his independence. There are signs of her success, signs of his readiness to build bridges to other selves, and sexual signs are again one measure of his progress. The narration ends with Dobbs's thoughts of a woman he has met in the university's coeducational sauna. Their meeting contrasts with the opening hospital scenes in encouraging ways. Helen Sweeney is not a girl to be objectified as a centrefold, but a mature woman, a mother, and a professor of philosophy. Like Dobbs, she has been physically disfigured by life, and they meet frankly, on common ground, in 'naked candour,' and 'glorified by sweat' (147), as Dobbs puts it. But not all the signs are as promising. Dobbs witnesses Helen in a maternal role, responding patiently to an importunate child, and, like Dobbs's own mother, she has had a mastectomy. Unlike Dobbs's disfigurement, hers is specifically sexual, the loss of one breast, one physical sign of her femaleness. On the one hand, her loss may be seen to balance his sense of diminished manhood, but on the other it suggests that for Dobbs the borders of self to be negotiated are still threatened by sexuality. It is not clear whether Dobbs has outgrown his fear of female sexuality or his adolescent tendency to manifest that fear as aggression or regression. But then, there are no miracles in Mitchell's comedic resolutions, and Dobbs has clearly come a long way towards a mature reconciliation with his mortality.

In *Ladybug, Ladybug ...*, Mitchell again creates a father-daughter relationship, at least in spirit, between the protagonist and his live-in housekeeper Nadya, but in this case it serves more simply to preclude sexuality from their familial love. Kenneth Lyon is seventy-seven, and if age were not a sufficient bar to sexual interest, he is aware that Nadya is about the age his lost daughter Susan would be, and is performing a daughterly role. By extension, sexuality in the novel is excluded from the bridges between human selves that can, in Lyon's own terms, unite the 'mortal family' against 'the heart of darkness,' the unreclaimed savage within (140). As the nursery rhyme invoked in its title suggests, *Ladybug, Ladybug ...* is about family, not as a site of innocence and primitive unity, but as a paradigm for human community, complete with the delusions, failures, and betrayals that beset human relations.

While the central relationship between Lyon and Nadya is free from the sexual ambiguities found in *Since Daisy Creek*, sex is more unambiguously a threat to the mortal family. Sexual reference is confined almost exclusively to the character of Charles Slaughter, the sociopath who stalks Nadya and kidnaps her daughter Rosemary. As a result, sexuality is excluded in its benign and appealing forms and represented only by gross physicality, especially with images of penises, abusing and abused, and by desire that is distorted, perverted, and manipulated. The university's dubious experiments in calibrating penis expansion as a quantification of sexual arousal provide a telling image of society's corruption of sexuality. Slaughter himself is a victim turned victimizer. The mother he recalls as a pious and sadistic puritan is Mitchell's most complete embodiment of the terrible mother archetype that haunts his later fiction. She beats and dominates her child with an unmistakably sexual relish. The young Charles is also seduced and sodomized by the Reverend Elijah Matthews, and his own later psychotic violence takes similarly perverted sexual forms. He kidnaps Rosemary in revenge against Nadya, who earlier fended off his sexual assault by biting his penis. The root cause of the evil that threatens the young is clearly puritan repression and the perverted sexuality it generates.

Sexuality is again associated with violence, madness, degradation, and death, and it again marks the violation of borders, moral and social borders between civilized and savage behaviour and personal borders between selves. As in *The Vanishing Point*, society violates the borders of nature, and in Slaughter's rebellion a natural savagery emanating from what Lyon calls 'the heart of darkness' violates social and moral order. The terrible mother and false priest commit fatal violations of young Slaughter's self, and he in turn goes on to violate the selves of Nadya and Rosemary. It is made clear that Slaughter's attack is specifically on the child's *self*. He separates her from herself by forcing her to depersonalize herself as 'it,' an object to be despised. In Lyon's terms, Slaughter is a destroyer of bridges between selves who finally destroys himself, appropriately enough, by riding his motorcycle from an escarpment into the river beside a bridge.

Mrs Slaughter and the Reverend Matthews, by their sexual abuse of a child, are made grotesque representations of adult failure of responsibility to the young, a failure that characterizes the society and occupies the internal action of the novel. Lyon himself would like to attribute the loss of his daughter entirely to fate, but she strayed into the mountain wilderness while in his care, probably while he was resisting the advances of a 'blond poetess.' Sex is thus not unrelated to his lingering guilt, but it remains an external threat. Lyon's failure is rather self-absorption, a failure to anticipate dangers, as he realizes when his experience of loss is repeated with Rosemary. His negligence becomes an image of society's failure when he nods on a bench while Rosemary plays in a park overlooked by Slaughter's cave. Metaphorically, the old sleep while the vulnerable young stray toward the dark caves where monsters created by adult desire and repression are lurking. Bridges are necessary because self-absorption is in its own way as culpable as the self-assertion and violations of other selves that are represented here in images of sexuality.

Dammed Sexuality

Arthur Ireland, in *For Art's Sake*, is another aging protagonist whose love is isolated from sexuality by the fact that his wife is dead and his young artist protégée takes the place of the daughter he never had. Arthur Ireland, like Mitchell's other artist protagonist, Colin Dobbs, is in need of female nuturing and guidance because he has never quite grown up. He is arrested (literally) in an Oedipal rebellion against adult authority. His scheme of stealing art treasures from private collections so that they will later be bought from insurance companies by public galleries and hence returned to the people is grandly democratic, but it springs from the same emotional sources as the tricks he plays on the dean who has denied him tenure.

Art's passage to manhood seems to have been obstructed by the usual terrors of witches and sexuality. His 'loss of innocence' (65) he identifies with a trip to Paris for a summer art course at the Sorbonne at the age of seventeen, when he appeared to the world to be fourteen and to his mother ten years old. He takes passage on a Greek packet, where he is warned, 'Keep your eye peeled and your asshole covered at all times' (52). In England he is poisoned and robbed by an aged whore, and in Paris importuned, harrassed, and beaten by a particularly ugly, witchlike old prostitute whose 'cartoon ghost face' is 'luminous in the lamplight shadow' (63) as she waylays him. Art reacts to this outrage in the same childish way that the young Carlyle Sinclair protested old Khaki's violation of his selfhood, defecating in the bidet before checking out of his room in what he should have recognized as a brothel, sex and other bodily functions again marking the borders of self and civilized behaviour. The final shred of Art's innocence is said to be lost to a performance of the Folies, which combines perversions of religion and sexuality, 'the priest and his religious-rite copulation with the nun – dog fashion' (65). But Art does not pass decisively from innocence to experience. Instead, in Paris his mentor Louis Simard gives him 'back his innocence' by showing him paintings of a nude who is pregnant and thereby 'no longer naked' (66). Through art, sexuality can be disarmed, and the fallen can apparently be redeemed.

For relief from his loneliness Art depends on the male companions he has gathered on his acreage and on silent communion with the memory or the spirit of his wife Irene. From her he seeks guidance and, especially, approval, casting her in a quasi-maternal role. Until the last scenes of the novel, his recollections of his wife are almost entirely purified of sexual reference. Even their honeymoon lovemaking is comically disarmed by shifting beds and an intrusive child. Ireland's love for his protégée, Kate, is equally innocent of sexual desire, as they claim each other as father and daughter. The two are strangely complementary. Ireland claims for art an aesthetic value that transcends the encoded moral values of society. Like Robin Hood or the individualist Western hero, he defies authority to seek natural justice beyond the law. Kate is a police officer dedicated to preserving the law and the constituted authority of society against such anarchic forces. The source of Kate's dedication is curiously coincident with Ireland's loss of innocence. Before meeting Ireland, she has given up her painting to enforce the law because her sister, a gifted dancer, was 'raped and strangled to death in the Rue Madeleine alleyway' (127). Both are in a sense defenders of art, and for both sexuality has its dark, exotic, and violent associations, but Kate's dedication is specifically to institutions designed to constrain male self-assertion. Like Irene, she is a guide to Ireland in his progress from Oedipal arrest toward mature participation in community.

Ireland's self-assertion, like Colin Dobbs's, also leads to a betrayal of his responsibility to the young. By sheltering them in his home, he earns the trust of the fledgling actor Win and the aspiring poet Darryl. He violates that trust when he involves them in the art thefts that lead to their imprisonment and Darryl's subsequent suicide. Ireland's betrayal is not itself sexual, but Mitchell provides a demonic counterpart to it with the reappearance of the Reverend Elijah Matthews. Imprisoned on multiple charges of pederasty, Matthews convinces the impressionable Darryl of his innocence with the same tale he had told Slaughter in *Ladybug, Ladybug ...* Surprised by Matthews's sexual advances, Darryl is unable to live with his shame and sexual insecurities. Sexuality again becomes a sign of the vulnerable borders of the self and the ultimate sign of adult betrayal of the young.

When Ireland turns his acreage into a retreat for artists, he is building bridges of community, but his redemption depends first on an internal bridging or border crossing achieved through the help of his guides and the power of art. In *Since Daisy Creek* it is implied that Dobbs's way back to community will be through his literary art, but here Mitchell shows the stages of Ireland's transformation in a sequence which subsumes most of his earlier motifs of gardens, borders, and passages. In his cell Ireland experiences a vivid recall or sensory repetition of a visit to his beaver pond after his wife's death to 'wash sorrow away.' There he and Irene had christened their new home by swimming naked together, so in memory Ireland is approaching love, sexuality, and union with the living whole in nature when he gives himself to the 'cool and fluid intimacy of water on nakedness' (249). Self-forgetful, he is 'caught in the spring race that would spill with fury over the beaver dam' (249). Fluid intimacy having drawn him into orgasmic violence, Ireland is stunned and granted a momentary vision or hallucination of his wife: 'How white she was against the silver willow over there, pale and lithely naked with her arms up and her head tilted forward as she tied up her hair. He saw clearly the shallow bend of her back, the soft curve and thrust of her breasts – Gone! The eddy had sucked him down and into underwater darkness, then total blackout!' (249). Ireland is apparently pulled from the water by his dog, to wake in a state of natural serenity rendered the more Edenic by the immediate appearance of a serpent, which turns out to be a harmless bull snake. The original experience achieved for Ireland a spiritual union with his deceased wife in which they were able to 'talk with each other whenever he needed her' (250). The reader is invited to interpret the recollection not only by its foregrounding as a discrete embedded narrative but by Ireland's own curiosity about it: 'Could this dream image be some sort of creative promise? Could visual remembrance be translated into paint?' (250). For Art it can, and, like water bursting over a dam, the vision releases a flood of visual images in Ireland's imagination, images of nature and sexuality, with a hint of violence: 'not just dark sky and cloud but the long roll of surf and the snow-capped geometry of mountains. A bloody dumbbell kept coming back. So did a large and formal key hole followed by a vagina and then a penis' (250). The images break Ireland's five-year artistic block.

It would probably be too literal an interpretation of these images to say that sex is the key to Ireland's artistic regeneration, but obviously it is integral to the unity he expresses in his new paintings. The 'inscapes' that he paints are said to suggest breasts or clouds or snowdrifts with a red 'fireglow' at their centres. His art, in effect, mediates the threatening aspects of the sexual images triggered by his vision, transforming the raw images of genitalia and violence into a gendered and maternal landscape, with passion a safely banked fire at its heart. The vision itself contains potentially threatening images of violence associated with sexual desire, even an image of female nakedness by the water, but it is quite unlike those in *How I Spent My Summer Holidays*. This is the most sexually alluring image of his wife that Ireland retains, but he is addressing her sexuality at two, or perhaps three, removes from experience. It is a memory of a vision, and it is further distanced and disarmed by its style. The details of pose and of anatomy it presents are those of a conventional and chaste artistic composition (like Louis Simard's nudes that are no longer naked). Ireland recalls his wife with a painterly eye, and that may be the most important promise of the vision. To push its interpretation a little further, in reverie and through art, Ireland can symbolically cross the borders of self, braving the dammed and potentially destructive energies of sexual desire to achieve unity with another self and with the living whole. On the evidence of his 'inscapes' he might be accused of negotiating a regression to a childlike illusion of unity with the mother, but the details of the vision imply a more complex state. What he reaches is not an unfallen Eden – the snake is there, if harmless – and not the primal, unselfconscious unity of childhood, but an adult, civilized unity mediated by art. It implies that even the terrors of sexuality that guard the borders and points of passage can be mastered through reverie and art.

For a writer of comedy and humour, Mitchell presents a surprisingly dark and disturbing impression of sexuality. In part it owes its threatening and distasteful quality to the neo-Calvinist milieu Henry Kreisel identifies; Mitchell is representing faithfully a sexuality made ugly by repression. But the cumulative impression is reinforced by the aspects of sexuality Mitchell does not represent. It is surprising, for example, that a writer of such vividly sensuous prose does not celebrate the sensual beauty of human flesh. There is love in Mitchell's novels, but it rarely keeps company with sex. What is written out of the narrative even more consistently than the flesh is sexual desire in its benign physical and emotional manifestations: erotic excitement and longing leading to self-forgetfulness, sexual union, and mutual fulfilment. Satiric denigration of puritan repression implies an ideal of natural, untrammelled sexuality, but that ideal is not clearly realized except among 'uncivilized' characters. These exclusions are probably related to the symbolic function of sexuality as a threatening presence and a marker of borders in Mitchell's fictional world. As we see in *The Vanishing Point* and *For Art's Sake*, even benign sexuality retains its threatening aspect.

A sexuality that is threatening is particularly effective in marking the presence of borders – moral, social, personal, and psychic borders – by providing images of transgression and violation at several symbolic levels, from serpents and flaming swords to castration and rape. Pedophilia, for example, is a shockingly emphatic signifier of the border between child innocence and adult desire. By its distastefulness it signals not only the location of a limit but the need for borders, a need that is implicit in Mitchell's fiction from the time of *Who Has Seen the Wind*. Brian O'Connal discovers the borders between the 'self and the not-self,' to use Mr Hislop's phrase, between the conscious self and the living whole, in his night on the prairie when the wind threatens to deprive him of his 'very self.' While Brian's puritanical outrage at the biology of human reproduction is comic, his disgust at the picture of humans 'like dogs on a boulevard' marks a necessary border of his self.

At the same time, borders must be traversed if mortal isolation is to be relieved, as Mitchell illustrates with Carlyle Sinclair's sealed borders, but bridging is perilous. Leaving the 'envelope of self' entails vulnerability; entering another self risks violation, and most of Mitchell's sexual images of transgression signal these dangers. In the novels that do venture a negotiation of the borders of self, some benign sexual imagery usually attends the resolution; Dobbs finds his Helen in the sauna; even Lyon's return to the mortal family is sparked by his conjecture that Mark Twain is the love child of William Lyon Mackenzie – the product of a fortunate transgression. *The Vanishing Point* and *For Art's Sake* are the most complete negotiations. In *The Vanishing Point* love is the bridge and the mediation, but physical sexuality sits uneasily with the family motif; there is a lingering uncertainty about how legitimately the borders have been negotiated.

In *For Art's Sake*, Ireland explicitly breaks through an artist's block, but the imagery of his passage suggests that it coincides with several internal and external borders. Going over the dam, Ireland is breaking through to his own remembered desires as well as uniting with his soul mate – effectively a reconciliation of flesh and spirit. The garden imagery implies a negotiation of the border between the self and the living whole, the self and the 'other.' The sexuality marking these borders is still potentially threatening and violent but can be civilized by art. Sexual imagery, by signifying the necessity of these borders, confirms an important feature of the cosmology of Mitchell's fictional world.

In the polarity that regularly develops between culture and nature, it is sometimes carelessly assumed that Mitchell favours nature. What is apparent from the sexual imagery is that the reconciliation of the mortal self with the living whole is to be effected only through the mediating forms of culture, through what is broadly termed 'art.'

NOTE

1 In tracing those effects I will be touching on all of Mitchell's major novels except *Roses Are Difficult Here*. That novel sustains Mitchell's general pattern of sexuality as a potential threat to social order, community, and family, but possibly because of its time of writing and publication or its origins in a specific issue of community values, its place in the evolving narrative I trace in Mitchell's fiction is not clear. I have therefore decided to set it aside.

Garden with Serpents: Mitchell, Kurelek, and the Boy's-Eye View of Prairie Life

MURIEL WHITAKER

W.O. Mitchell's novels *Who Has Seen the Wind* and *How I Spent My Summer Holidays* present, in King Motherwell's image, a Garden of Eden with serpents crawling out of the buffalo-berry bushes. The Edenic myth of acquired knowledge and lost innocence is Mitchell's controlling archetype. In each novel the central consciousness belongs to a boy living in a small Canadian town surrounded by 'the least common denominator of nature, the skeleton requirements simply, of land and sky – Saskatchewan prairie' (3). The child's acute perception enables the author to recreate convincingly, through visual, aural, tactile, olfactory, and gustatory images, the physical landscape that has psychological implications.

Like W.O. Mitchell, the Ukrainian Canadian artist William Kurelek views the prairies as a flawed paradise where childhood experiences modify an initial impression of nature's awesome beauty and innocence. In *A Prairie Boy's Winter* (1973) and *A Prairie Boy's Summer* (1975), the text and illustrations are based on recollections of his Manitoba boyhood, a period of his life when persecuting humans vitiated the child's response to the prairie seasons, God's wonderful creation. Autobiography underlies the artistic works that Mitchell and Kurelek devise by applying the child's-eye view technique to a particular place – the Canadian prairies – during the period bounded by the two World Wars. The two visions are explicitly juxtaposed when Kurelek illustrates the 1976 and 1991 editions of Mitchell's first novel, *Who Has Seen the Wind*, thereby facilitating a comparison of the two perspectives.

To a degree, Kurelek's William – the twelve-year-old 'eye' of the 'Prairie Boy' books – and Mitchell's protagonists – Brian and Hugh – share a common repertoire of boyhood experiences: killing gophers, gathering at the swimming holes, watching the killdeer's diversionary tactics, marvelling at the brilliance of winter fields, witnessing the violence of summer storms, and participating in the triumphs and humiliations of school and schoolyard. What differentiates the boys and their creators is the opportunity to free their spirits into game-playing. While summer allows Brian and Hugh to act out the heroic roles which their imaginations have created and which Mitchell approved of as a form of education, William is constrained by the fact that 'summer always meant a lot of farm work' (8). Only one of the twenty paintings and commentaries that make up *A Prairie Boy's Summer* presents an activity that William thoroughly enjoyed – archery, a sport in which he excelled and in which he could imagine that he was 'conquering the awesomeness of the prairie expanses at last' (46). The remainder largely record the relentless toil required of a physically small and inept boy on an immigrant farm, where success was measured in monetary terms and children were valued as unpaid labourers. Aside from their prairie origins, what encouraged Kurelek to approach Mitchell when he was writer-in-residence at the University of Toronto was a conviction that the author of *Who Has Seen the Wind* was a sincere Christian. Though that novel's religious observances are Presbyterian rather than Catholic, the pantheism of Mitchell's natural world conformed to Kurelek's view of Nature as God.

When the protagonist of *Who Has Seen the Wind*, four-year-old Brian Sean MacMurray O'Connal (the names aptly convey the British origins of the dominant society), escapes from the backyard sandpile into sudden emptiness, the prairie materializes initially as sound: the hum of telephone wires, the clicking of crickets and grasshoppers, the meadow lark's song. Then he feels the warmth of a rock, the tickle of grass, the 'warm and living' wind.

The shadow of a hawk, the shimmering of a dragonfly's wings, the stripes of the flax flower, and the haloes of foxtails impinge upon his field of vision (10–11). The effects of light, which young Brian perceives as a pervasive aspect of the prairie, persist until the novel's final scene, sustaining paradisal associations.

The centrality of wind as a persistent aspect of prairie life is signalled by two epigraphs, one from Christina Rossetti's 'Who has seen the wind,' and the other from Psalm 103:15–16. Brian notices the 'fervent whirlwind' circling around the church as he goes looking for God;[1] the pervasive sighing through great emptiness when he first sees the Young Ben; the crying along the eaves-troughing as the baby sickens; the whispering through the prairie grasses that his father will never hear again. The bright wind-swept prairie comes to represent, in addition to tangible beauty, an expression of transcendental reality: 'Prairie's awful, thought Brian, and in his mind there loomed vaguely fearful images of a still and brooding spirit, a quiescent power unsmiling from ever-lasting to everlasting, to which the coming and passing of the prairie's creatures was but incidental' (125).

For twelve-year-old Hugh of *How I Spent My Summer Holidays*, the prairie world centres on 'the Little Souris River, a wandering prairie vein ... almost a miracle' (5), a place of amusement and freedom in all seasons. It is potent with the scents of mint, wolf willow, and potter's clay, which evoke a memory resonance when the narrator, forty years later, attempts to recreate the summer of 1924. Crocuses, violets, wild roses, buttercups, buffalo bean, bluebells, tiger lilies, and goldenrod are miniatures of beauty.[2] Adam-like Hugh catalogues the abundant and benign wildlife – a killdeer faking an injured wing, prairie chickens that can be speared and cooked over a willow fire, coyotes that emit untidy barks or long, lifting howls. This is the kind of knowledge a prairie boy would have, along with the ability to recognize that 'the shit incense of death ... could vary so in revulsion weight, depending on time and distance and creature size' (173). The prairie is a boy's paradise: 'There was nothing frightening at all left on our great grass sea' (53), says Hugh with unconscious irony. The novel's focal setting, the cave which Hugh and Peter

Deane-Cooper dig during their summer holidays, depends for its feasibility on the prairie's plenitude.

Juxtaposed to the romantic natural world, a place of adventure and freedom from adult prohibitions, is the puritanical, shabby small town, which physically and psychologically imitates the older settlements in Ontario (Morton 168–69). Churches, schools, banks, lawcourts, businesses, and well-furnished houses assure the frontier society that morality, justice, and social and economic order will be maintained. The O'Connals' superior social position is certified by their three-storey house, towering above the cottage to the left and adorned with Virginia creeper, spirea, and honeysuckle. Hugh's mother asserts her gentility by following Victorian manners and mores. 'Our girl never goes covered-wagon,' her husband confides to his son. 'Calling-cards and hall-marked sterling and Royal Crown Derby all the way' (111). What Margaret Atwood refers to as 'a cosmic rigidity [that] goes far beyond the strength necessary to build and sustain a pioneering community' (Atwood, 32–33) is a source of conflict in both novels. Yet the fact that the protagonists belong to respectable 'establishment' families provides a security that encourages confidence and independence.

Mitchell enriches the sparse associations of what the settlers regarded as a country without a mythology by furnishing story-telling adults. King Motherwell's tale of the magical buck and the Indian hunters, though rationalized, retains a heroic dimension. Hugh's father relates the Persephone myth to the prairie's seasonal cycle. Brian's Uncle Sean transfers to his south forty an Irish leprechaun. Most importantly, the boy's Scottish grandmother, who had come west to homestead during the Riel rebellion of 1885, is a purveyor of both family and prairie history. Gradually, the material landscape becomes for the perceptive boys a landscape of the mind.[3]

Although *Who Has Seen the Wind* and *How I Spent My Summer Holidays* share a similar setting – small Saskatchewan towns in the period between the two World Wars – and a similar narrative technique – the use of a boy as the central consciousness – they differ substantially in subject matter and attitude. Mitchell has two purposes in the earlier novel: to explore a boy's acquistion of knowledge about 'the realities of birth, hunger, satiety, eternity, death' (ix), and to reveal the cruelty, vindictiveness, and hypocrisy that motivate some of the town's most influential citizens. Because the actual vocabulary of a young child is limited, the author uses the technique of a central consciousness (the child's) expressed in third-person narration. This device allows a more sophisticated verbalization. And because the child's limited experience makes him an unsuitable vehicle for persistent social satire, two adult narrative voices are intermittently heard: those of the humane school principal, Digby, and of the primary teacher, Miss Thompson.

Mitchell's conception of Brian is obviously influenced by William Wordsworth's poem 'Ode: Intimations of Immortality from Recollections of Early Childhood.' Digby makes the connection specific when he ponders the 'maturity in spite of the formlessness of childish feature, wisdom without years' (292) reflected in the boy's face. Allowing for the generic difference, we may note that Lionel Trilling's explication of the ode's theme applies equally well to *Who Has Seen the Wind*:

> It is a poem about growing; some say it is a poem about growing old, but I believe it is about growing up. It is incidentally a poem about optics, and then, inevitably, about epistemology; it is concerned with ways of seeing and then with ways of knowing. Ultimately it is concerned with ways of acting, for as usual with Wordsworth, knowledge implies liberty and power. (Trilling 130)

Brian's transcendental yearnings, which he calls 'the feeling,' are associated with the prairie, the wind, horses, and God, with a dead pigeon, a tailless gopher lying on the prairie, a dewdrop brightening a spirea leaf, 'a star's cold light in its pure heart.' His wild *alter ego*, the Young Ben, fused with prairie images of wind, grass, and coyotes, is also part of the 'excitement, akin to the feeling that had moved him so often' (123). Ben's sharing, actively or as a spectator, in the succession of deaths and burials (pigeon, dog, gopher, father) that mark Brian's *rites de passage* reinforces his role as a bond between Brian, seeker of knowledge, and the prairie, transcendental source of reality. Trying to verbalize 'the feeling' in the context of a Berkeleian discussion between Digby and Milt Palmer, he describes it as 'want[ing] to know something, only you don't know what,' as feeling 'as if you are going to spill over'(285). It is Digby who legitimizes 'the feeling' as a source of knowledge, and it is Digby who confirms its loss as a sign that 'You've grown up' (290). Only a Wordsworthian recollection of experienced feelings remains.

In the education of the hero (a common romance motif), home, school, and church impart factual knowledge and acceptable values. But Brian also engages in a personal quest for what, lacking a sophisticated vocabulary, he baldly characterizes as 'right' or 'wrong... not right.' The Young Ben's swift and bloody punishment of Artie, torturer of gophers, fills him with 'a sense of the justness, the rightness, the completeness of what the Young Ben had done – what he himself would like to have done' (124). A freak of nature, the two-headed calf, appals and bewilders him as something that 'isn't right,' that he would never understand. When he attempts the correction of another defect of nature, the terrible cast in Annie's right eye, his ignorance of adult psychology renders his advice counter-productive; right intentions do not always bring desired results. Refusing to accept the establishment view of the Ben's crime and punishment, he feels that there is 'a wrongness in the Lord's punishment and with this he experienced a feeling of guilt at being upon the Ben's side rather than that of Mr. Powelly and the Lord' (252). The Lord, at least, is rehabilitated as an embodiment of justice when He rides the whirlwind to save Saint Sammy from Bent Candy's malice and greed.

The philosophical questioning brought on by his grandmother's death leads the boy to conclude, 'It was awful to be a human. It wasn't any good' (291). But a Wordsworthian natural world remains to console him with the exquisitely stamped tracks of a prairie chicken and the glinting ice crystals on a wild rose bush. As at the conclusion of the ode, the philosophic mind (even that of an eleven-year-old boy) uses knowledge of mortality to make experienced life significant.

Thirty-four years separate the publication date of *Who Has Seen the Wind* from that of *How I Spent My Summer Holidays*. The later book is concerned not so much with the acquistion of knowledge as with the loss of prelapsarian innocence. (The mundane title, an essay topic commonly assigned to school children in September, ironically denotes the perversion of carefree pursuits.) First-person narration promotes a more immediate but less philosophical account of a boy's experience. Biologically Hugh is a continuation of Brian, for he is twelve years old in the summer of 1924, when the main events occur. But he is a different breed of boy. While Brian is amenable, responsible, contemplative, generally obedient and anxious to please, Hugh is extroverted, prone to scatalogical language, obsessed with sexual organs, knowledgeable about local scandals (information gleaned by his eavesdropping friend, Musgrave), and skilled at manipulating his parents through lies and evasions, pretended illnesses, appeals to parental sympathy, and an ability to take advantage of parental moods.

Yet despite the brash, self-assured persona which the narrative voice creates, Hugh still belongs to the age of innocence. He revels in the romantic adventures of G.A. Henty, Mark Twain, and the *Chums* annuals, and participates in such childhood rituals as pursuing the Sunday school attendance prize, saying his evening prayers, and distributing May Day baskets. Lacking the protective cover that adults develop, he indulges in outbursts of raw emotion, shouting obscenities when King teases him, crying when his father laughs at his newly acquired glasses, yelling in terror after a nightmare. Wonder and joy are his response to prairie flowers and a skylark's song. Adults are a mystery; about the murkier aspects of adult life – secret drinking, masturbation, bootlegging, insanity, and lesbianism – his knowledge is incomplete, erroneous, or non-existent.

The most significant aspect of his innocence is his uncritical worship of King Motherwell, the decorated soldier, hockey star, pool hall operator, gambler, alcoholic, bootlegger, and murderer who is the hero of Hugh's story. The epigraph from Virgil's *Aenead* – 'arma virumque cano' – portends an epic theme. Based on Hugh's evidence, the reader may judge King admirable in his common sense advice to the boys, and pitiable for his haunting memories of the Western Front. But he is culpable in encouraging the boys' deviousness and in ruthlessly exploiting their innocence. Accepting him as being 'on our side against all the adults in their upper world' (107), the boys make him part of their game-playing without realizing how much he controls them.

The great adventure of the summer holidays begins when Hugh and his friend Peter Deane-Cooper dig a secret cave. Before they can enjoy it, King persuades them to harbour an escaped lunatic, Bill the Sheepherder. The boys become involved in a 'fabric of lies, pretence and dissemblance' that only ends when Hugh discovers outside the cave 'a leg with only part of the foot left and the flesh gnawed off from the ankle to the knee' (173). Inside are grislier remains, the head of King's wife Bella 'alive with maggots, black with clotted blood, bruised like an apple and keg-swollen' (174). With that discovery, says the narrator, 'I stopped being a boy' (173).

The adventure-producing prairie, with its pristine flowers and unthreatening fauna, is made sinister by human trespassers. Holy Rollers are baptized in the muddy river to emerge choking and coughing, with, as Hugh notes, their gowns sucked into crotch, belly button, and the crack of buttocks. Prostitutes from Sadie Rossdance's nearby cottages strip, swim, and indulge in obscene gesturing and repartee, as Hugh spies on them from a demonic hiding place of thorny rose and buffalo-berry bushes and hairy nettle leaves. Lunatics from 'the Mental' wander about. There is gratuitous violence unrelated to plot development and characterization, as when we are told that Blind Jesus 'got spattered against the cow-catcher of the northbound Soo Line passenger' (213) and that Buffalo Billy was paralysed from the waist down after being gored by a bull. Violence, combined with prurience, insanity, perversion, disease, and crime, effects a shift from romance, the conventional genre of the boys' adventure story, to a dark and cynical realism with no happy endings.

The child's-eye view technique has several advantages, aesthetic and psychological. Like Jane Austen's little bit of carved ivory, the child's world is a microcosm centred on home and spreading into a small town and its environs where everyone is known and categorized. Brian and Hugh inhabit the milieu of Mitchell's own prairie childhood in Weyburn, Saskatchewan. Scrupulously retrieved period details – a farm rack held together by haywire, drought-stricken crops, muddy swimming holes, school children memorizing uplifting poetry, Mission Band collections, outhouses, harness shops, Old Stag chewing tobacco – fix in time a particular locale that is simultaneously generic.

The child's sensitivity to emotional climates, his curiosity, his skill at eavesdropping, and his acute perceptions make him an admirable reporter, while his ignorance and inexperience limit his ability to interpret what he perceives. This disparity between the child's limited view and the reader's interpretation of evidence produces the irony that is Mitchell's most important effect. Seated in the Presbyterian church, Brian notes the China kids, isolated in the front row; the Ben's gently moving jaw; the Young Ben's wary eyes assessing the people who hem him in; Mr Powelly's stringy hair carefully combed over his balding pate, and his speciously benign, thin-lipped smile; Mrs Abercrombie's conspicuous position and upcast eyes. He naively thinks that the act of worshipping together can unify this assembly of persecutors and victims.

Hugh can encounter his beautiful mother's overturned tea wagon and tearful face; can enumerate and be disturbed by virile Mrs Inspector Kydd's visits to Bella, the illegitimate daughter of a hired girl; can observe Bella's acquisition of a new pink dress and hear her lying denials without suspecting the lesbian proclivities that the reader deduces.

How I Spent My Summer Holidays is so carefully structured that the narrator's epiphany is deferred thirty-eight years. On a time return to his boyhood home he finally realizes, not only the identity of Bella's murderer, but the part that he himself played in his hero's descent into murder, alcoholism, insanity, and suicide. The handcarved teal decoy, King's last gift, assumes ominous resonances.

The Wordsworthian liberty and moral awareness which knowledge bestowed on Mitchell's heroes were unacceptable attributes in the Kurelek home, where to sin was to allow the cows to stray into the cornfield or the machinery to break down. Education was valued only as a route to a prestigious and lucrative profession, such as medicine. The Kurelek parents' unsociability, along with their poverty and ethnicity, effectively isolated the future artist from the kind of mainstream Canadian life that Mitchell's novels depicted. Opportunities for play and reflection were adjuncts to work.

Like W.O. Mitchell, William Kurelek had a prairie boyhood. He was born in 1927 near Whitford, Alberta, where his immigrant father had a quarter section; in 1934 the family moved to a dairy farm at Stonewall, twenty miles north of Winnipeg, remaining there until 1946. This is the setting particularly associated with the artist's childhood memories. Kurelek's practice of writing explanatory notes for books and exhibition catalogues provides insight into his youthful experiences and attitudes. Like Mitchell, he was awed and fascinated by the prairie's immensity of land and sky: 'From the scenic viewpoint, by far the most magnificent feature of the prairies is the panorama of the sky, awesomely grand and varied ... Even the wind is visible, as in W.O. Mitchell's wonderfully evocative book, *Who Has Seen the Wind*. The land is so flat it is like being on an ocean' (*Kurelek's Canada* 88, 91). His painting 'By the Breath of the Spirit II' (1975) illustrates the wind's transcendental symbolism.

He also found nature beautiful and heartless, but his vision accommodated Wordsworthian pantheism. A note 'About Nature' appended to *Kurelek's Vision of Canada* reads, 'Nature gives not a drop of comfort ... living beings are trapped by her pitiless laws' (Murray/Kurelek 71). The dedication of a *Prairie Boy's Summer* (in words composed by W.O. Mitchell) reveals a different attitude:

With love for my sister Nancy
Who more than anyone else shared with me the surprise and won-
    der of prairie seasons as a child
Who has added to that surprise and wonder a sense of awe and
    love for the creator of those wonders, many call it the Living
    Whole –
Ultimate Cause – Nature. We two call it: God.

Kurelek differed from Mitchell in being a farm boy rather than a town boy and in being a member of an ethnic minority (Ukrainian) rather than of an Ontario-British establishment. As described in his autobiography *Someone With Me*, his childhood was a nightmare of fear and humiliation both at home, where he was frequently tongue-lashed by his short-tempered father, and at school, where he was bullied and ridiculed. The bitter, desperate parent expected 'immediate perfection' from the young sons, who had to become farm labourers when potential hired men went off to war. William was blamed for broken binders, frozen waterlines, leaked oil, and runaway sweeps and wagons. Kurelek describes the rancour of the father-son relationship at the conclusion of a chapter entitled 'Hard Times': 'But it was obvious to me that, except for my good standing at school, I was in no way fulfilling his concept of what a son should be. No matter what the circumstances, what I said disappointed him. "Stupid" was the most common adjective I was branded with. "Deaf," "dumb," "blind" were close second-favourites, heaped on my head as it hung in shame' (*Someone With Me* 77). 'Depersonalization,' a defence mechanism that suppressed feeling, led to chronic depression, eye trouble, and a period in English mental hospitals. Conversion to Catholicism in 1957 provided comfort, stability, a philosophical basis for appreciating beauty, and a view of his painting as 'a vocation, a calling by God to serve Him in a specific way' (*Someone With Me* 173).

Kurelek's first concerted evocations of his prairie boyhood were two picture books published by Tundra Books of Montreal, *A Prairie Boy's Winter* (1973) and *A Prairie Boy's Summer* (1975). When the original paintings were exhibited in 1977, a critic noted that the images symbolized 'the boyhoods of thousands of others in hundreds of different towns' (Newton). The book illustrations were praised as 'romantic,' 'idyllic,' and 'nostalgic' impressions of happy and innocent youth; however, a closer examination of the paintings and their accompanying text reveals darker elements. Repeatedly Kurelek refers to his ineptitude, victimization, and physical discomfort. For example, during the winter season William snags his jacket on a barbed wire fence as he attempts to join a game of Fox and Geese (4); he dislikes hockey or other rough sports 'because he wasn't strong, athletic or quick' (5); he dreads 'Hockey Hassles' that erupt over his goalkeeping, a role to which his poor skating confines him (6); and he has early experience of wettings during the spring run-off, when older schoolboys bullied the younger children (19). The summer season brings its own tribulations, as he dislikes the school field-day (1, 4), softball (2), harrowing (8), hay raking and stacking (9), milking (12), plowing (15), cutting grain with an old tractor (16), and stooking during a wet spell (17).

Though the children's bright clothing,[4] the intensely blue skies, red barns, and green fields are visually charming, the negative memories which the accompanying text retrieves affect the picture content by suggesting threatening situations and ominous moods. For example, the usually enjoyable activity at the neighbourhood swimming hole is marred by William's fear of catfish and crayfish and practical jokes; and the fun of skating on the ditch is spoilt when he alone gets caught in the reeds. Examining Kurelek's picture books for children, Jetske Sybesma-Ironside discusses the parallels between the autobiographical accounts of painful experiences in *Someone With Me* and the pictured recollections. The boy's dereliction in failing to close the chicken coop has suggested 'Chasing a chicken in the snow' (11); 'Watering cows in winter' (10) derives from the occasion when the boy allowed the waterline to freeze, engendering 'the uncanny feeling that I was actually sabotaging farm operations' (*Someone With Me* 73). After discussing additional examples, Sybesma concludes that the picture books reveal 'a tragic child whose internal landscape of the mind was torn because of the impact of his terrifying father' (Sybesma-Ironside 16).

Stylistically, the illustrations are realistic and descriptive, the kind of pastoral prairie scenes that the artist called 'pot-boilers' in contrast to his moralizing religious works. The human figures (mostly boys) are characterized by gestures rather than facial expressions.[5] An emphasis on contour focuses the viewer's attention on physical action, as when the boy struggles to move a huge snowball or forcefully jabs a pitchfork into the haystack's frozen surface. The painting of setting is strongly linear. Barbed wire fences, dark strips of ploughed land, rows of cabbages, herds of cows parallel a high, distant horizon; the lack of natural closure – animals, cars, buildings, and farm machinery are frequently cut off by the page's white edge – increases the sense of space. Contrasting with the immensity of land and sky are a tiny frog leaping away from the hay rake, a sling shot half hidden in the grass beside an outstretched boy, the first snowflakes falling into a child's open palm, and the tiny humans working distant fields.

When Mitchell was writer-in-residence at the University of Toronto, Kurelek, introducing himself only as 'a painter,' sought help in revising his autobiography. The most important result of the friendship that grew out of that encounter was the 1976 edition of *Who Has Seen the Wind*, with eight paintings and thirty-two black and white headpieces executed by Kurelek. Onto a masonite base, he applied a mixture of media, 'something I developed myself ... predominantly oil, but there is also lacquer, graphite, coloured pencil and pen-and-ink on a gesso base which I scratch through in places where I need a fine white line' (*Kurelek's Vision of Canada* 72). Poster paints were also liberally used in the Mitchell series.

Kurelek divided his paintings into two categories: the nostalgic pastoral scenes drawn from his farm experiences and the didactic works with socio-religious themes. Although he sometimes chose overtly Christian subjects such as the Crucifixion and the Nativity, he also invested apparently secular scenes with a 'hidden religious message.' Explicating the representation of a country schoolyard in a painting entitled 'In Search of the True God #5' (1964), he writes, 'if I meditate sufficiently on it country images always suggest themselves as illustrations for Biblical parables' (*William Kurelek: A Retrospective* no. 34). He also remarked that 'growing up with farm animals I began to see animal imagery in human behaviour and eventually this furnished the basis for much of the symbolism in my message paintings' (*Someone With Me* 68). The painting for chapter 6 of *Who Has Seen the Wind* is a stunning pastoral landscape assembled from disparate textual details. Across a flat table-top of land a man in blue overalls and red shirt, 'leaning slightly backward against the reins looped round his waist' walks with his team towards the 'lone farmhouse' (to which the artist has added a red barn, a windmill, some outhouses and grain bins). The stippling technique which Kurelek learned as a picture framer animates the dark, newly ploughed field with specks of orange. On the horizon are massed the purple thunderclouds which had brought rain too late to help the crops. Between the areas of darkness lies a bright strip as stubble, stooks, and fence posts are gilded by the setting sun. In the highest visible corner of the 'stark blue' sky a lonely goshawk hangs: 'It drifted low in lazing circles, slipping its dark shadow over stubble, summer fallow, baking wheat. A pause – one swoop – galvanic death to a tan burgher no more to sit amid his city's grained heaps and squeak a question to the wind' (73).[6] As this quotation illustrates, reading the text can affect a viewer's response to an apparently innocent scene. A more powerful example of revision effected by context is the third painting, showing four jolly boys and their frisky dogs walking down a country road between green fields. The spacial treatment is conical, with the straight lines of road, verge, fenceposts, and telephone lines leading the eye to the distant town, where the row of red grain elevators confirms the nature of the crops and the presence of the railway. The youngest child carries red lard pails and the two middle ones also have a washtub. They would seem to be engaged in some insouciant summer adventure; in fact, their object is to drown out gophers. During the events that follow, Brian observes torture, death, and retribution with emotions that range from disgust and fear to fierce exultation.

Kurelek was fascinated by night-time and sometimes stayed outside all night to record its manifestations with camera and paint. Darkness could be recorded literally, as in 'Wiener Roast on My Father's Farm' (1974), but it could also evoke the sense of impending doom which permeated his vision of contemporary society. His use of light and darkness in the *Who Has Seen the Wind* series is a clue to the hidden messages which he insisted were present, though he acknowledged that he could not force the viewer to accept them. In the intimate semi-darkness of the Hoffmans' hayloft, Forbsie and Brian on their stomachs gaze into the nest of baby pigeons, pondering the origins of life. Through the dusty window streams a solid bar of light, symbol of life and the Creator, illuminating the young boys and the newly hatched birds (which iconographically represent the soul). Contrasting with this scene is the almost complete darkness of Mr Hoffman's rabbit shed; only a raking light from a crescent, cloud-shrouded moon allows us to pick out Mr Hoffman in his train conductor's uniform, Mr O'Connal, and Joe Pivott as they go about their murderous work of destroying the burgeoning animal population. Joe's setters sit, eagerly pointing, and ready to attack any that try to escape. It is not difficult to connect the helpless, doomed rabbits with human victims of violence.

In the sixth painting, light and darkness are used to convey a religious message. Brian, having run away from the farm, lies in a foetal position beneath a huge dark straw stack, which occupies nine-tenths of the picture space. The artist has created a feeling of rough-textured straw by scraping into the paint surface and accentuating the marks with coloured pencil. The stack seems to represent Brian's loneliness, shame, fear, 'the feeling of nakedness and vulnerability that terrified him,' all the sorrows that weigh down his spirit and that are about to be multiplied by his father's death. In the upper right-hand corner (a position that iconographically in medieval illuminations often represented the place of God) there flashes an apocalyptic sunrise, symbol of salvation. The metaphor of wind as spiritual power appears in the seventh painting. Streaking clouds, bending grass and trees, Brian's flying coat-tail, and Bent Candy's disintegrating barn convey its strength. Like an Old Testament prophet, elongated in the manner of Byzantine icons, Saint Sammy raises his forefinger heavenward.

For the final painting Kurelek chooses, not the daytime prairie where Brian, thinking of the dead, walks on the frozen crust, but the darkness of a winter night. Under a full moon, which brightens the windswept snow and tall weeds, a lone coyote gives voice to a howl, 'his throat line long to the dog nose pointing out the moon.' The scene seems to represent the plight of humanity. Isolated and bereft in 'the Dark Night toward which present materialism is tending' (*William Kurelek: A Retrospective* 2), the only recourse is divine Providence.

Kurelek's black and white headpieces are vignettes closely related to each chapter's content. As well as genre scenes, there is some portraiture and a characteristic use of symbolism. In the illustrated Macmillan edition (1976), the large drawings occupying more than half a page are unframed, though they are generally devised to fit an oval. In some cases, such as the scene where Brian, supported by the Young Ben, walks homeward through wind and snow (chapter 10), or the summer scene of boys on a country road (chapter 21), the illustration expands into the page's border, increasing the sense of immensity. In the McClelland and Stewart edition (1991), the illustrations are reduced in size and enclosed in rectangular frames which distance the viewer, and produce the effect of pictures hanging on a wall. The headpiece for chapter 1 is a portrait of Brian. With his round head, high cheekbones, dark hair and eyes, straight, wide-nostrilled nose, protruding ears, and serious mouth, he seems a portrait of the artist, more Ukrainian than Celtic. The drawings' most remarkable aspect is the skill with which Kurelek reproduces, quite literally, the child's-eye view. Many objects are seen only at or near floor-level; adults are represented by the lower part of the body. Mrs MacMurray is a long skirt and a leg brace, Miss MacDonald a midriff at which Brian aims his water pistol. When Brian crouches by the two-headed calf, a phalanx of trouser legs and boots surrounds him. When Mr Digby and Miss Thompson look down the main street, their figures are elongated as if seen from below; the vanishing point conforms to the boy's, not the adult's, perspective. Significant gestures convey emotions. A woman's hand laid on a man's beside a teapot and bowl of sugar cubes conveys the love, tenderness, unity, and domestic harmony of Maggie and Gerald O'Connal. The grandmother's leg brace lies unneeded on the patchwork quilt of her brass bed after her ascent to a Presbyterian heaven.

Though both Mitchell and Kurelek confronted the problem of evil, they differed in their conceptions and evocations. Mitchell associated evil with the kind of damaging individuals found in any community – the envious, vindictive, hypocritical, malicious, and selfish people whose actions reflected their flawed natures. In *Who Has Seen the Wind*, he manipulated the plot to effect happy endings – the unions of Miss Thompson and Digby, of Annie and Abe; the routing of Mrs Abercrombie, and the Young Ben's escape from reform school. The romantic solution was not repeated in *How I Spent My Summer Holidays*, where the characters' postludes were less euphoric. Kurelek's concerns were such global evils as war, nuclear fall-out, torture, abortion, and materialism. To the question, 'If God is Good, then how come there is so much pain and evil in the world He has created?' he replied, 'if He does exist, then those who suffer innocently or those who suffer with hope in Him will at least find restitution and an end to the pain after death' (*Someone With Me* 154). His practice, following the example of the English painter, Stanley Spencer, was to impose on conventional local scenes moral and spiritual symbols that, if recognized, expanded their meaning, offering warnings and spiritual consolations. Finally, in comparing the perspectives of the two prairie artists, it is apparent that Mitchell's perceptions of the boy-on-the-prairies theme emphasized play and contemplation; Kurelek's emphasized work and oppression.

NOTES

1 In the Greek text of John 3:8, 'the wind bloweth where it listeth ... so is every-one that is born of the Spirit,' the same word *pneuma* represents both 'wind' and 'spirit.' Cf. also Job 38:1, where God speaks to Job out of the whirlwind.
2 The abundance of wildflowers led early settlers to describe the prairies as the Garden of the West. See Nellie McClung's *Clearing in the West: My Own Story* (Toronto: Thomas Allen, 1925) and Mary Hiemstra's *Gully Farm* (Toronto: McClelland and Stewart, 1955).
3 See W.L. Morton's seminal essay, 'Seeing an Unliterary Landscape,' *Mosaic* 3 (Spring 1970): 1–10.
4 The artist told his publisher May Cutler that *A Prairie Boy's Winter* was not honest because 'I gave all the children bright clothes, but we had navy blue, brown or dark grey.' Patricia Morley, *Kurelek, A Biography* (Toronto: Macmillan, 1986), 250.

5 Kurelek was largely self-taught, his chief source of instruction being Kimon Nicolaides's *The Natural Way to Draw* (Boston: Houghton Mifflin, 1969). Nicolaides emphasized contour and gesture.

6 Paginated textual references related to illustration refer to the McClelland and Stewart edition of 1991.

W.O. Mitchell and the Pursuit
of the Homosocial Ideal

TERRY GOLDIE

In spite of the many other candidates, W.O. Mitchell remains the quintessential prairie writer. His 1947 novel *Who Has Seen the Wind* begins with his oft-quoted definition of this broad band of flatness which lies at the heart of North America: 'Here was the least common denominator of nature, the skeleton requirements simply, of land and sky – Saskatchewan prairie' (3). And in the heart of this heart is a boy, Brian, searching for the 'ultimate meaning of the cycle of life' (1).

But emphatically a boy rather than a child. For the novel is a highly gendered portrait of Brian's dedicated pursuit of male homosocial bonding at the fringe of society, usually in direct opposition to attempts, often female, to produce other social integration. This rebellion can be glimpsed throughout Mitchell's work, from the kid's apprenticeship to the hired hand in the *Jake and the Kid* stories to the various White men who apprentice to Archie Nicotine in *The Vanishing Point* and *Since Daisy Creek*. The pattern culminates in what is to date Mitchell's last major new work, published in 1992. *For Art's Sake* describes an old man, Art, as he attempts to follow his muse in spite of the obstacles presented by greed, the law, and university bureaucracy that impede him.

I do not mean to suggest that the pursuit of the homosocial is the primary statement of either text. I presume most readers would maintain that *Who Has Seen the Wind* is first about the human need to come to terms with the land, which provides the source of both birth and death. A representative view is provided by Laurence Ricou's look at prairie man in *Vertical Man/Horizontal World*: 'His visual focus on sky and horizon is a metaphor for man's emotional and intellectual focus on the nature of the infinite, upon that which is normally beyond human comprehension' (95). Similarly, the punning title of *For Art's Sake* asks whether creativity can survive in the face of the decadence of the modern art market. Still, each novel suggests that such answers as exist will arise through intense male relationships.

In *Between Men*, Eve Kosofsky Sedgwick discusses many elements of what she calls 'homosocial desire,' including 'male friendship, mentorship, entitlement, rivalry, and hetero- and homosexuality' (1). The first four of these elements are important to various degrees in *Who Has Seen the Wind*. Male friendship provides the Platonic dialogues which shape most of the philosophical discussions in the novel. Discovery through childhood experience is always moulded by the complications in the relationships among Brian, Forbsie, and Artie. When Brian posits a heaven which exists in the phenomenal world and might be reached by tying feathers to their arms, Artie says, 'It's dumb to think that.' Brian turns to Forbsie: 'Don't listen to Artie – to what he says. He doesn't know' (28). The same pattern emerges in adult connections as the principal, Mr Digby, explores questions of existence first with the minister and then with Milt Palmer, the shoemaker: 'He could exercise a natural talent for dialectic which had been neglected much since his old friend Hislop had left the town' (132). As in the less sophisticated exchange of the boys, dialogue is both a statement of the bonds between males and an analysis of the meaning of life, a Saskatchewan Symposium.

Mentors are the stations of Brian's youthful picaresque experience around the town and out to the prairie. His first stop is his Uncle Sean, who spins a tale of a leprechaun, but he then moves on to Reverend Hislop. Throughout the novel he makes similar demands on his father, on his uncle's hired man, Ab, and on the reclusive religious fanatic, Saint Sammy. He is also an eavesdropper for some of the conversations between Digby and Palmer.

Like the boyish competition that is in evidence throughout the adventures of the three boys, there are various struggles between men. These range from the subtle fraternal rivalry between Sean and Gerald to the overt, literally earth-shaking, war between Sammy and Bent Candy, a local farmer who wants Sammy's sacred Clydesdales. It has often been noted that the romantic triangle of one woman and two men presents less a question of who the woman chooses than of which man wins the prize. This rivalry of heterosexual exchange arises when Dr Svarich and Digby both seek a romance with the new teacher, Miss Thompson.

The element of entitlement, which involves a passing down from father to son, is first an issue of material property, but it also appears in the inheritance of character and in the connections between mentors and their metaphorical sons. All of these factors come into play when Brian's father dies. Although Brian is very young it seems necessary to him that he find a clear role for the future. His decision to become a 'dirt doctor' is one that he feels will make him an appropriate progeny for both his educated father and his childless farmer uncle.

The absent heterosexuality suggested by the role of the bachelor is an undercurrent of the novel. While sexuality and reproduction are significant in Brian's studies of nature, they seem rather oblique among humans. Normative heterosexual relations presumably take place between Brian's parents, but outside of that they appear only between minor characters. The central mentors for Brian tend to be bachelors, most obviously Sean and Saint Sammy. They exist outside of and in opposition to female society, as shown by Sean's confrontations with anything that seems feminine, except for his land: 'farm her with yer hearts an' brains' (18), and Saint Sammy's diatribe against 'the harlot an' the fornicator' (192) and 'the bare-ass adulteresses' (192). One initial bachelor, Ab, seems the exception in his marriage and production of children, but again he conforms to the social order in a rather diagonal fashion, with a woman chosen apparently because she reminds him of the runt pig and the snuffy cow.

The role of heterosexuality is reflected by the position of women. Two of the primary villains are female, the teacher Miss

MacDonald and the schoolboard harridan Mrs Abercrombie. The grandmother at first appears as a similar agent of social restriction but changes during the course of the novel through her developing senility. Brian's mother and the new teacher Miss Thompson are, on the other hand, very positive figures, but they are so less because of what they do than of what they allow. They are two females who seem willing to at least modify their socializations and allow the boys the freedom of discovery through contact with nature and with men.

The essential male bonding in the novel is between Brian and the Huck Finn–like character, the Young Ben. The child of the town ne'er-do-well, the Young Ben's primary significance seems to be his identification with nature, as revealed in Brian's first encounter with him:

> Brian was not startled; he simply accepted the boy's presence out here as he had accepted that of the gopher and the hawk and the dragonfly.
>   'This is your prairie,' Brian said. (11)

Eventually Brian realizes that, like other elements of nature, the Young Ben can produce that overwhelming sense of the mystery of the cosmos which Brian comes to call 'the feeling': 'He looks like a coyote, thought Brian, like a watching coyote. He realized with a start that an excitement, akin to the feeling that had moved him so often, was beginning to tremble within him. His knees felt weak with it; the Young Ben could cause it too' (123).

Critics have offered a variety of interpretations of the Young Ben's position in the novel, but they all are shaped by the associations noted by Ricou: 'The combination of these characteristics: reticence, solitude, exemption from restrictions, and love of life in all its forms links the Young Ben to the simple, primary elements of his familiar landscape' (*Vertical Man* 102). Mr Digby and Miss Thompson accept the Young Ben's asocial behaviour as essential to his being and acknowledge that he doesn't belong in school. Mrs Abercrombie believes he is a dangerous non-conformist who should be in a reformatory. The two factions represent the divisive pro-prairie and anti-prairie attitudes with which Brian must deal.

Although all critics comment on the Young Ben's symbolic value, they pay little attention to the nature of Brian's response. In school, Brian was 'aware of a strange attraction to the Young Ben,' which left him 'fascinated and confused' (86). 'There grew a strengthening bond between them, an extrasensory brothership' (86). As the novel continues this bond is referred to as 'magic' (124) and instinctive: 'Brian stopped and stared across at the Young Ben; he never saw the other boy without excitement stirring within him; as ever it was a wordless attraction strengthening with each additional and fleeting glimpse he got of the Young Ben. He felt an impulse now to cross the street and walk along with the Young Ben, felt instinctively that somehow it would help him' (201). Brian's father's death overturns his world but 'One thing had not changed – the Young Ben's attraction for him' (245). Still, after the Young Ben quits school, the text does not refer to him.

Ricou's later study, *Everyday Magic: Child Languages in Canadian Literature*, notes the importance of Brian's age:

> As Mitchell tells us at the beginning, his novel is most assuredly a story about a boy. He can best stop, therefore, where Brian is no longer quite a child but is still a long way from being a man, where he can think of becoming a 'dirt doctor' close to the soil and to the cerebral world of science, where the wholeness of the child's vision is still intact, where birth and death, love and hunger, can still be combined in a vision of unity and integrity, where awesome mystery is a feeling sufficient unto itself. (59)

This 'stop' also might explain the limited sexuality. Perhaps the novel is stating that at Brian's age sexuality is a biological truth visible in animals more than humans. Brian shows no awareness of his own sexual interests. The only element of his perception which might be termed erotic is his response to the Young Ben.

To some, this reading might seem an unnecessary sexualization of this attraction. There are a few markers of the stereotypical homosexual youth in Brian – his introspection, his closeness to his mother, and his glimpses of 'difference' in himself – but to make of these a gay *Bildungsroman* would be an extreme over-reading. Still, a comment by Sara Suleri on Kipling's *Kim* is appropriate: 'While it would be unnecessarily reductive to read the desire that obtains between the lama and Kim as a figure for the submerged homoeroticism that attends on colonial encounter, it would be equally injudicious to ignore the passion that describes their connection' (120–21). The same is true of Brian's feelings for the Young Ben.

As Sedgwick observes, 'To draw the "homosocial" back into the orbit of "desire," of the potentially erotic, then, is to hypothesize the potential unbrokenness of a continuum between homosocial and homosexual – a continuum whose visibility, for men, in our society, is radically disrupted' (1–2). Perhaps I am similarly disrupted if I suggest that it is much more useful, at least in the case of this novel, to stop the continuum at the homoerotic. Arguably, this might be because it is the novel of a boy, sexual orientation unknown, rather than of a man. But both the intensity and the asexuality of the response to the Young Ben offer a passionate charge that transfers to other homosocial relations which have no apparent erotic component. Most critics link the Young Ben and Saint Sammy, but Tallman goes beyond the others: 'And what is old Sammy in his age and insanity but young Ben later on and farther out on the road leading away from contact with other human beings' (235). Tallman's transformed Young Ben would not be accepted by most readers, but it is difficult to see what the homoerotic glow of the Young Ben could become in adulthood if homosexuality is not a possibility. A sexually repressed religious fanatic might fit.

Thus, the homoerotic in *Who Has Seen the Wind* remains at the level of a hint of potential while the homosocial is a beginning apprenticeship, as Brian seeks through peers and mentors a way to achieve the 'natural life' in spite of the repressive powers around him. In *For Art's Sake*, Art Ireland, the main character, is at the end of the journey. Art's guiding lights have been painting and his wife Irene. Now a widower he tries to fulfil his promise to her by giving up teaching to devote himself to creation. Part of the process has been to start what he calls an 'art colony' in an abandoned church. His first colleague, Charlie, moved in when 'both of them had lost their life companions' (21). Then came Winston, an actor, and Darryl, a poet.

The group decides to steal art collections and return them to public ownership. At one level it becomes a comic buddy yarn, the 'unlikely crooks' story so popular in films. At another level, it touches on the metaphysics of the meaning of art, for both creator and observer. As Art goes from artist-teacher to artist-thief to artist-convict, he, like Brian, ruminates.

One element of the homosocial which is again important here is the mentor. Art himself is a mentor for the other colonists and has played that role for a variety of students. At various stages of his own life, beginning with his first trip at sea, he encounters a series of male teachers. The primary such figure is his first art teacher Louis Simard, who seems to have brought out the Brian in the adult Art: 'Bless you, Louis, wherever you may be. You gave me back my innocence. I have never stopped trying to discharge my debt to you!' (67)

Unlike the repressive female figures in *Who Has Seen the Wind*, the villain in *For Art's Sake* is male, the ambitious dean of the university. His main competition is another male, a rapacious farmer named Ottowell who is much like Bent Candy. The only evil female is a minor character, Mrs Sage, a landlady who steals from Art when he is on a youthful trip to Europe. There is a female similar to Miss Thompson, Kate, the detective assigned to Art's case. Unlike Miss Thompson, however, she is not defined as a romantic target. Instead, she has a number of masculine attributes, as suggested by the style of her comeback to a colleague who dislikes working with a woman: 'What you have beside you here, Laverty, is a partner still in training who, although she does squat to piss, does not intend to take any more shit from you for the next three months!' (129) While said by Art to resemble Irene, she is less the object of Art's desire than a typical ambivalent opponent, one of the boys yet, because of the legal system, on the opposite side.

When Art is in prison, he encounters another virtuous companion, the warden. He shows his gratitude with a painting of the warden's 'dear departed' on their honeymoon. Thus, he is the third major widower in the novel: in other words, a man clearly defined as heterosexual but with no apparent heterosexual activity. The constant references to the deification of the various departeds would seem to make such activity impossible. Katie laments, not a dead spouse, but a dead sister, to whom she was similarly devoted. This relationship does not seem erotic but the specifics of the death are sexual in that the sister was raped and murdered. This violence is the stated reason for Kate's having become a policewoman. It is perhaps the unstated explanation for her own lack of participation in the heterosexuality of society as well.

The asexuality of most of the other characters is simply an absence: no partners are depicted or mentioned. Most of the actual references to heterosexuality are to prostitutes, such as the suggestion made by Laverty that Kate was a hooker, or the depiction of the whore who attacks Art on the street, or the reference to the sexual habits of Mrs Sage. This lack of positive heterosexuality extends to the lack of progeny. Art thinks of Kate as the daughter he never had: 'Hadn't been for the three miscarriages and the final hysterectomy she could have been the daughter that might have been' (141). Art's own father died when he was an infant. Throughout, the novel rejects biological parenting for the symbolic fathering of mentoring, as in the admonition by the policeman who saves the young Art from Mrs Sage: 'Look son, I'm a father. And if you were mine I wouldn't let you out of me sight for the next five years. Not till you could smell danger off a bitch like her' (60).

Unlike *Who Has Seen the Wind, For Art's Sake* makes overt reference to homosexuality, but only in homophobic representations, such as the jokes when Art is on shipboard: 'She's a Greek packet, sonsy boy. Keep your eye peeled and your arsehole covered at all times' (52); or, when they first enter prison, the guard's confrontation of Elijah, the evangelist child abuser: 'From now on you keep your fucking Good Shepherd's crook in your pants' (210). He represents, perhaps, the sexual expression denied Saint Sammy. His demonic character is revealed when he befriends Darryl only to attempt to seduce him, which apparently leads to Darryl's suicide.

For Art's Sake offers the institutionalized homosociality of the ship and the prison as dangerous places of homosexual lust, in spite of moments of camaraderie. The created and creative asexual homosociality of the art colony is a haven, but a temporary one, as the colony's attempt to change the outside world leads to its removal and destruction. It is interesting that in this realm of adults, as in the realm of children in *Who Has Seen the Wind*, while sexuality, whether hetero- or homo-, is to be avoided, it aids in the destruction of only two people: Darryl and Kate's sister. For the rest, in both novels, it is the general social rules of the community that interfere with the homosocial potential of those good-hearted males who would choose to bond with like souls. As Charlie says to Art of Darryl and Win: 'For those boys you call all the shots because they respect and love you ... Almost as much as I did. Once' (82). But all must separate as a result of the theft and incarceration, just as Brian will leave the Young Ben and Saint Sammy as he pursues his education.

I am not suggesting that homosexuality is the answer to the puzzle of either of these novels. While discussing Sedgwick's *Epistemology of the Closet* in 'Queer, Query? Identity, Opacity, and the Elaboration of Desire,' Christopher Lane confronts the view of homosexuality as the skeleton which must be revealed:

> To these critics, opacity therefore signifies an implicit refusal – and performs a *preterition* of unbreachable silence – as though the difficulty of meaning were not itself a phenomenon that modernism would repeatedly address, or that sexuality – and especially homosexuality – were the privileged site of unknowing on which all other difficulty can ultimately be appended, and all coherence seen to flounder. (4)

Homosexuality is not the key to these novels. However, bearing in mind Suleri's warning not to ignore 'the passion that describes their connection,' we can acknowledge the *eros* of the Young Ben, the careful absence of sex, and the idealized homosociality as significant factors.

Some years ago, the feminist critic Annette Kolodny asked for a 'turn of the lens': 'In asking different questions of, or in bringing different analytical methodologies to, any text, different literary critics necessarily report different gleanings or discover different meanings, meanings which reflect not so much the *text qua text* but *the text as shaped by* the particular questions or analyses applied to it, (329). Yet these shaping questions suggest ways in which novels reflect society, here through the assertion of homosociality, the homoerotic undercurrent of that homosociality, the homophobic response to active homosexuality, and the implication that the bonds of heterosexuality, and the institutions associated with such cultural norms, are an interference with the potential adventurous liberation of freely chosen homosociality. It might seem another example of the reduction which Suleri, Sedgwick, and Lane all claim to fear, but perhaps both texts, and their contexts, simply show a few of the possible results of a social order in which, to use a paraphrase through which a famous non-male, non-heterosexual commented ironically on textuality and reality: 'a boy is a boy is a boy.'

Return to the Scene of
Revelation and Loss:
Mitchell's *Who* and *How*

R. ALEXANDER KIZUK

Of W.O. Mitchell's works, the novels *Who Has Seen the Wind* and
How I Spent My Summer Holidays examine most carefully the
imaginary or semiotic play that underlies the author's depiction
of a boy's first encounters with the world, the flesh, and the prairie. Nearly all of Mitchell's work devolves from the 'world of crocus,' in W.J. Keith's phrase, but these two narratives, and the *Jake
and the Kid* radio plays, especially concern boyhood, and a boy's
perception of a predominantly male environment. In both works,
the mother and woman are, as narrative figures, subordinate to
figures of male heroes, fathers, and mentors. In the later novel,
indeed, woman is prefigured as the site of violence, defilement,
and expulsion. This undercurrent of ferocity is a primary theme
in my reading of Mitchell's return to the *rites des passages* of Canadian prairie boyhood in *How I Spent My Summer Holidays*. My
object, however, the ground tone, the lay of the land, is necessarily the 'horror' about which twelve-year-old Hugh says, at the
novel's close: 'Finally I may have sorted it out' (224). This statement inevitably recalls Brian O'Connal's words to his teacher,
Digby, in the closing pages of *Who Has Seen the Wind*: 'I've been
trying to – to figure out for a long time, and it won't! Everything
has to figure out, doesn't it?' (286).

How I Spent My Summer Holidays, published thirty-four years
after the author's debut as a novelist, seems to be Mitchell's bid
to 'sort out' the darker side of the narrative possibilities first
enunciated in the fictional psyche of Brian O'Connal, the child-

protagonist of his extraordinarily successful 1947 novel. In a sense, the first novel asks *who* it is who steps into the scene of loss and revelation that is the psycholinguistic ground of both novels. The second novel returns to this scene to investigate *how* that process works. In another sense, *How I Spent My Summer Holidays* is a continuation, almost a sequel, to *Who Has Seen the Wind*. In *How*, Mitchell captures twelve-year-old Hugh in the midst of puberty, whereas Brian, at the same age at the end of *Who*, has not yet embarked on that adventure. Both boys are the sons of loving parents who are morally superior, in the main, to many of the minor characters of the small Canadian prairie town, modelled on Mitchell's own home town of Weyburn, Saskatchewan, in which the stories are set. A few of the minor characters appear in both books. (These novels, with *Roses Are Difficult Here*, are the most cutting of Mitchell's satires of Canadian prairie life.) Both boys are, as well, profoundly affected by a mentor, an older male who is not a father-figure: Brian's teacher, Digby, and Hugh's boyhood hero, King Motherwell.

The growth and development of both boys – as males – are deeply scarred by encounters with death, an 'inevitable vision' given to the boys 'too young' (*How* 173):

> for the first discovery of mortality is given early to a prairie child. We were by the age of twelve quite used to that smell – or rather smells; they could vary so in revulsion, weight, depending on time and distance and creature size: gopher, cat, dog, jack-rabbit, badger, skunk, coyote, horse or cow, near or far, putrid rot smell of new, to slightly soured smell of old, death, long after crows and magpies, beetles and maggots, and other prairie undertakers were through their work. By ten we could tell what had been at a larger cadaver, whether crow or magpie, bobcat or coyote, for the coyote always began to eat out at the anus, the bobcat at the soft belly, magpies almost anywhere. The Liar said they always went for the eyes first. (*How* 173)

It is not this raw and impersonal mortality, however, that does the wounding. The permanent scarring is caused by excessive guilt

trauma constructed within an economy of desire that is psychologically appropriate for a twelve-year-old boy. In the fictional
psyches of these two boy-protagonists, the removal (by death) of
the beloved object is suffered as a punishing loss. The child
mourns this loss within himself in such a manner that he believes,
while withdrawing from human community, that his encounter
with death is all too personal.

For Brian and Hugh, death is not simply a fact, not even a Dar-
winian fact. It is rather an *act* – one perceived in terms of punishment and cruelty, to be sure, but also of defilement and deception.
This appears to be the import of the carrion-eating imagery
and the gratuitous quotation of the minor boyhood character The
Liar in the passage cited above. After the discovery of Bella's
corpse, in *How I Spent My Summer Holidays*, Hugh struggles to
cope, and wishes that he had inherited 'that blessed ability at self-
deception' that characterizes his mother, who quickly convinces
herself that 'the whole thing didn't happen at all' (183). As Dick
Harrison put it, adults 'sleep while the vulnerable young stray
toward the dark caves where monsters created by adult desire
and repression are lurking' ('W.O.' 192). Gradually, however, the
nightmares do stop: Hugh does cope; there are compensations.
But Mitchell makes it clear that one thing will remain the same
after Hugh becomes a man:

> I could no longer trick my fear by telling myself that wicked people
> robbed and wounded and killed only adults and never children.
>   I now realize they often do and that Saint Simeon just had to piss
> off his pillar and out into the dark. (184)

The man the boy will become will never be able to trust society
beyond its capacity to deceive itself with high ideals and beliefs in
human goodness. Hugh's first step in this direction is perhaps to
caricature his teacher Mr Mackey for his idealism when school
starts up in September, after the murder, while at the same time
experiencing a sense of vertigo upon contemplating the composition topic Mr Mackey puts up on the blackboard, 'HOW I SPENT
MY SUMMER HOLIDAYS' (180). It is for a reckoning of this ver-

tigo, 'a dark abyss opening between childhood and maturity,' as Harrison says, 'surrounded with imagery of caves, anuses, castrating women, violence, guilt, perversion, and madness ' (197), that the novel's adult narrator is searching, many years later, on the town's fiftieth anniversary.

In these novels, a too-intimate Death takes away the father, for Brian, and it takes away the hero/mentor, for Hugh. This act – a robbery and a wounding – is also an act of deprivation, of denial and a withholding, the effect of which is excoriating for the developing male ego. In the scene in which Brian and the Young Ben bury Brian's dog, the first novel captures succinctly this sense of a *hollowing-out in a boy's psyche*, following an encounter with death. 'Kiyoots can't git him now,' says the Young Ben. 'Somewhere within Brian something was gone; ever since the accident it had been leaving him as the sand of an hourglass threads away grain by tiny grain. Now there was an emptiness that wasn't to be believed' (177). Following upon the father's death shortly thereafter, this grief deepens into psychic damage that can never heal, precisely because it cannot be believed. Nothing can ever replace this lack:

> *Fathers died and sons were born*; the prairie was forever, with its wind whispering through the long, dead grasses, through the long and endless silence. Winter came and spring and fall, then summer and winter again; the sun rose and set again, and everything that was once – was again – forever and forever. But for man, the prairie whispered – never – never. For Brian's father – never. (*Who* 239; my emphasis)

In the later novel, twenty-five-year-old Hugh returns to his home town from college to bury his father (it is not until he is fifty, returning to the town on their shared anniversary, that he finally thinks he has 'it sorted out'). When Hugh views his father in his casket, he cannot believe what he sees: the words 'This was not my father' are repeated in the text as a mournful refrain (215). His father, for Hugh, was not the man he had been, but more a principle of inner surety: 'I did not have to defend my interior from my father' (215). Many years later, Hugh realizes that the town had 'stained me during my litmus years, fixing my inner and outer perspective, dictating the terms of the fragile identity contract I would have with myself for the rest of my life' (10). Thus the cleansing of this 'stain' of loss is withheld, and neither Brian nor Hugh can accept the presence of this unprotected interiority, this lack and its stain, and remain secure within sound ego boundaries. Even at twenty-five, Hugh defends himself inadequately against his mother, who 'still tended to come on too strong, right through neutral territory' (215).

Mitchell has inscribed this clinging-to-the-absence-of-the-father – this hollow that can neither be believed nor beloved – this stain that will never wash out – quite differently in the two novels, but the figure is dominant in both nonetheless. The narratives of Brian's loss of his father and Hugh's loss of esteem for his mentor (superimposed upon the scene of his father's death [214–21]), are conceivably variants of the story of Mitchell's own fatherless childhood. Mitchell's widowed mother took him to Florida at the age of twelve due to his ill health. This personal experience of fatherlessness stands behind both novels like a fathomless backdrop. And in the foreground stands the figure of an *empty* boy: a hollow the wind blows through, a hollow in the prairie, hollow summers and unhallowed ground – hollow recompense; short solace.

Let us consider what consolations there are for these two boy-protagonists, before returning to the significance of the strange trope of the unfathered child ('Fathers die and sons are born') as a hollow, void, or cavity that cannot be filled.

In *Who Has Seen the Wind*, it is certainly not God Who tenders any surety to man. On the contrary, it is God, in the carefully elaborated controlling metaphor of the prairie wind, Who withholds both the most cherished life and the most yearned for explanations for human grief. The God of this book is both personal and cruel: for a breath of air, He reaches into the grandmother's window in the O'Connal home to take her life and along with it the hockey stockings for which the boy has hungered (283). The hockey stockings, which symbolize for Brian his right to enter the world of men, are thus withheld. For all her womanly love, the grandmother cannot initiate him; she cannot replace the father's role in this. Similarly, in *How I Spent My Summer Holidays*, woman and the mother are inadequate for the purposes of preparing Hugh for the life of an adult heterosexual male.

Hugh is self-conscious about his physical smallness – 'I was *all* small, particularly where it mattered most to me' (11). Hugh experiences penis envy of other boys and feelings of guilt, shame, and 'uncleanliness' following 'exercise' intended to bulk up that important member (13). Uncleanliness becomes a recurring motif in the novel. His eyeglasses, his family's relative wealth and culture, his sensitivity, his somewhat frail health and his mother's care, 'deer-alert to coughs and sniffles' (52), all emburden him in his quest to become manly, as gender identity was conceived in his time and place. His first erection from heterosexual desire occurs as he accidentally watches the town's prostitutes undress and go swimming in his out-of-the-way swimming hole, 'phallic with cat-tails' (10), under the CPR trestles. 'Until then,' Hugh narrates, 'the worst thing I could think of happening to a person was to find himself in the center of an open field with Vonnegut's Holstein bull, magnificent candy-pink knackers swinging ... as he bore down on you in full charge. This was worse' (158). Hugh is shocked and aroused by the revelation of the naked female body – 'The whole female form was wrong!' (159) – yet that moment of witness will always mark the quality of sex for him in later life: 'The perfume of wolf willow was all around me. Perfume sweet, yet musk wild! Many years later I would pin that lovely smell to a woman's sexual scent' (159, cf. 10). Hugh is especially smitten by the beauty of his hero's wife, the 'Proserpine-lovely' (119) Bella. But this poetry is undercut by the bawdy of the scene that follows.

The whores' madame is the last to undress. Before her swim, she backs into the bushes and nettles where Hugh is hiding, hunkers down and urinates:

> ... but she didn't stand up right away, not until she let go a fart. When she stood up she stepped out of her bloomers. The backs of her thighs and her buttocks were traced with blue veins, the flesh lumpy like badly made porridge.

> As she walked away from my hiding place, her great Roquefort buttocks alternating and asking for harness, I thought of the fire-wagon team and the two blacks Mr. Candy hitched to the honey wagon. I wondered if after she had finished her leak Miss Ross-dance had opened and closed and opened and closed again like a camera shutter, the way mares did. Likely not.
>
> I had lost my hard on. (161)

The scene (implied sweetness becoming repugnant) changes from bawdy to sordid, moreover, as Bella, the wife of the man who is initiating Hugh into adulthood, transforms herself with a cat-tail into an image of a phallic woman, then calls out to one of the other whores, 'Suck this one, Loretta!' (164).

Later, the narrative goes beyond sordidness to *noir*, when Hugh discovers Bella dead in his cave, her skull crushed and her 'Pros-erpine-lovely' (119) body eaten by animals. Hugh's 'horror' (171) of this 'terrible revelation' of 'the ultimate corruption of human death' (174) causes the boy to become withdrawn. In the days that follow, he becomes obsessed with disease and corruption, at one point fixating on lepers 'tinkling a little bell and crying, "Unclean! Unclean!"' (172). Hugh's mother, in an effort to revive his spirits, gives him his first set of long pants for his thirteenth birthday, 'in 1924, when no male wore long pants before the age of eighteen,' knowing that becoming a man is very much on the boy's mind: 'I pulled them on over my pajama bottoms and looked down at my no-legs. A balloon was inflating inside me and I had grown one foot. I was taller; I was maler as I stared down the long and unbroken creases "with a wild surmise ... silent upon a peak in Darien"' (204). More than anything, Hugh desires his hero and mentor to see him in his long pants. King Motherwell is one of the town's ruffians, a bootlegger and a war hero. He is idolized by the young boys of the town, and, when he goes swimming with them in the summer, the boys marvel at his tattoo: 'Vein blue and faint rust-pink and green it came out of the black bush of his pubic hair,' coiled over the torso, 'forked tongue' at the throat (26). (This carnavalesque tattoo suggests a priapic aspect to Motherwell's character; the scene in which Motherwell and Hugh swim naked alone is not without romantic/sexual colouring, which Mitchell underscores by evoking the cinema stars Colleen Moore and Rudolf Valentino.) Hugh races to Motherwell's pool hall, proudly wearing the symbol of his new manhood given to him by his mother. What he finds, however, is his mentor and hero out of his mind with drink. In delirium tremens, Motherwell 'threw himself round, clutching and scratching at his crotch, at his stomach – his chest. Then I saw why. His serpent had come alive.' 'Don't let her! Don't!' screams Motherwell. 'Not – her – poison kiss!' The hero out of control, repulsive, cowardly, the phallic tattoo become a figure of *feminine* terror and death, the boy says plainly, 'Having my first pair of long pants was no longer very important to me' (207).

The way to manhood is initiated by the mother in *How I Spent My Summer Holidays*, and that way becomes a phallic horror for Hugh. *Who Has Seen the Wind* may be said to have prefigured this symbolic construction of yearnings and terrors, however, even in its opening scene of the four-year-old Brian playing in the sand. Here, the unflatteringly detailed description of the grand-mother's body recalls that of Sadie Rossdance, including the flat-ulence. Where Hugh associates woman and the scent of wolf willow in his mind, Brian associates his grandmother with stern-ness and the scent of apples. Both Sadie and the grandmother are domineering women, quite capable of laying down the law: 'He hated his grandmother. She made him go out to a sand pile where there was nobody.' Brian makes a mound of sand and punishes it murderously with 'an old shovel'; he 'wished it were his grand-mother ... He was hitting his grandmother so awful ... He began again to punish the sand pile' (5–6). Another boy joins him, call-ing himself 'Benny Banana.' The boys then go to visit the house 'where God stays,' so that Brian can 'get Him after my gramma.' On the way Brian adapts the 'Step on a crack' nonsense rhyme to 'break your gramma's back' (7–9). Earlier he had thought to get the town policeman to use his knife to 'chop her into little pieces and cut her head off' (5).

The ferocity of four-year-old Brian's fantasies, like the violent horror of Hugh's discovery of Bella's mutilated corpse, is certainly remarkable. Julia Kristeva's *Powers of Horror* argues that the 'abject' acts as an intermediary stage in the formation of the subject and his or her separation from the maternal object. In this context, it is worth noting that the narrator tells us, in the opening of *How*, that 'Hesiod could compare us [the boys of the town] to the pre-Aryan silver age heroes: "... eaters of bread, utterly subject to our mothers, however long they lived"' (3). In Kristeva's analysis, all the world belongs to the mother at the pre-symbolic level – and this includes any unpleasant messiness. Gradually, the subject may encounter 'a violent, clumsy breaking away, with the constant risk of falling back under the sway of a power as securing as it is stifling' (13). Defilement functions in this construction to help define the boundaries between the body of the subject and the oceanic mother. Lacan, the psychoanalyst, tells us that 'castration turns phantasy into that supple, yet inextensible chain [of signifiers] by which the arrest of the object-investment, which can hardly go beyond certain natural limits, takes on the transcendental function of ensuring the *jouissance* of the Other, which passes this chain on to me in the Law' (324). Kristeva, the feminist, says that the *abject* as *defilement* draws the line in the 'two-sided sacred' (57) that separates, primordially, the semiotic authority of the Mother and the symbolic law of the Father. 'This authority shapes the body into a *territory* having areas, orifices, points and lines, surfaces and hollows, where the archaic power of mastery and neglect, of the differentiation of proper-clean and improper-dirty, possible and impossible, is impressed and exerted' (72).

The Kristevian analysis seems to be more efficient in the case of Mitchell's two novels. It seems clear that both boy-protagonists are very much concerned with marking out such a Kristevian *territory*, within which they may become proper men. The pervasive excremental imagery of *How* can be immediately comprehended in this figure, and the same can be said of the recurring motif of cleanliness. But *Who* is not without its dark side either. One character, at least (as Keith notes, 145), believes she has seen 'the heart of darkness' in the town's pettiness (279). But the same character says, 'Isn't it about time for a little sweetness and light around here?' (280). This small compensation of sweetness and light has been captured in another literary allusion, earlier in the text, one which functions to structure 'the feeling' that Brian carries with him to the end of the novel. In the famous scene in which Brian finally learns to grieve for his father, he walks 'on with the tall prairie grass hissing against his legs, out into the prairie's stillness and loneliness ... ringing him and separating him from the town' (238) – the town, that is, 'where his mother was' (240). The boy stands, 'with the prairie stretching from him,' as if it were a continuous part of him. Suddenly, he realizes his responsibility to his widowed mother, the tears flow, and a meadow lark 'splintered the stillness,' again and again, charging him with 'a sudden breathlessness' and 'fierce excitement' (240). The model for this epiphany is Keats's nightingale, and Mitchell returns to this ode ironically for certain structuring motifs in the later novel. The 'Ode to a Nightingale' may have seemed appropriate for this moment in the earlier novel, however, insofar as Keats is 'the most reverent and affectionate of nature-sons, finding in the moist [female liquidity] not annihilated consciousness but enhanced imagination, a new paradise garden,' according to Camille Paglia, at least, commenting on Lionel Trilling's idea of Keats's '"manliness," or "mature masculinity"' (383). Yet surely the predominant intertextual echoes in *Who* will be heard in the lines: 'Still wouldst thou sing, and I have ears in vain – To thy high requiem become a sod' (59–60).

At the close of the 1947 novel, Brian's boyhood ambition is to become a 'dirt doctor,' after his uncle Sean tells him that 'the prairie's sick.' The mother and the uncle decide to send the boy away, first to the uncle's spread, then to university, so that he may return one day (a proper man) to heal the drought-stricken land (288–89). In one sense, Hugh, in the later novel, is the 'dirt doctor' invoked here; more importantly, however, this desire to return in order to heal the prairie is bound to the wish of the boy to heal himself as an extension of the land, a sod. Mitchell's prairie boy is a savage, a native of the land. Hence, in the later novel, the town – human society as represented by the town – is the site of defilement and horror that is exactly the same age as the boy.

In either case, the body is continuous with the prairie, though connected to (disconnecting from) the town through abjection and defilement. Through the colourful character of Saint Sammy, Mitchell explicitly invokes the Edenic motif in *Who Has Seen the Wind*, with particular emphasis on the Adamic concept of earth:

> 'An' He got to thinkin', there ain't nobody fer to till this here soil, to one-way her, to drill her, ner to stook the crops ... so He took Him some topsoil – made her into the shape of a man – breathed down into the nose with the breatha life.
> 'That was Adam, He was a man.' (193)

Mr Digby tries to teach Brian Christian phenomenology near the novel's close. This is the scene in which Brian tries to articulate 'the feeling' that he has been carrying with him at least since his father's death, which contains the ferocity kindled in him by the meadow lark. Brian's 'feeling' has now evolved into something of an epistemological imminence of frustrated revelation: 'like – well – you wanted to know something, only you don't know what,' and 'It's like you are going to spill over' (285). Digby confronts this 'feeling' with a free-association test. Brian's responses reflect his preoccupation with playing hockey soon, and an amusing reference to a common defilement in rural communities: 'Brian thought: skates – ice – snow – road apple' (286). In the later novel, Mitchell uses road apples, horse's droppings, to signal the loss of any unironized sweetness and light and the beginning of a dark revelation – Saint Simeon pissing into the darkness of human community.

For all its lachrymose sweetness, *Who Has Seen the Wind* offers no succour to its psychologically scarred, fatherless protagonist. In the end, Brian is haunted by his desire to know 'the thing that cannot hide from him forever,' though he surmises the Young Ben and Mr Digby are 'part of it' (292). Alone in his grandmother's room, he is unable to accept the fact of her death. Indeed, he feels as if at any moment she 'would return to find him uninvited in her room.' He is '*suddenly* aware of an emotion long familiar to him ... his grandmother was not dead ... *They* had died. For hun-

dreds of years they had been dead. His own father had died and
his father, and his father, and his father before him' (291; Mitchell's emphasis). Fathers die and sons are born. On the grandmother's bed lies her leg brace, 'left behind ... as though she
would return to put it on at any minute. The feeling of guilt deep-
ened' (291). This object does not belong in the grandmother's bed;
nor does Brian belong in her room. Things are out of joint. To be
sure, out in the 'rapt and endless silence' of the prairie, Brian
hears a 'sound distinct and separate in the night: a shout, a
woman's laugh. Clear – truant sounds' (293). And even if she is
only a 'splinter' made by the meadow lark's song, *she* does not
properly belong *out there*, on the silent and lonely plains of the
Adamic body. Yet there she is.

These motifs, allusions, and symbolizations are all repeated in
How I Spent My Summer Holidays. They are, however, shockingly
internalized in what amounts to a mentally ill, psycho-narrative
of the prairie male suffering a mid-life crisis. As Harrison says,
the story of the cave nurtures 'the sick, subterranean soul of man
(or child)' (184), and the narrator 'is literate, sensitive, even
poetic, ... [but] clearly a bitter, maladjusted old man' (186). Much
more consciously structured, it poses a new set of pagan allusions
which counterpoint the (Judaeo-Christian) literary and cultural
forms present in *Who*. In a manner not unlike Kroetsch's in *The
Studhorse Man* (1969) and *What the Crow Said* (1978), Mitchell
allows the mythologies he invokes to allude and elide playfully.
Mitchell's allusions to the 'Ode to a Nightingale' are playful, too,
at first, then profoundly ironic: Hugh returns to view his dead
father in Orrin Nightingale's Funeral Home (214).

The 1981 novel is explicit about the 'Psychology. Abnormal.'
(218), which shapes the protagonist's 'fallen' psyche. Hence the
depiction of the sick, 'dirty,' pederastic dream in the opening
pages (1–2). The narrative invokes the Edenic motif when Hugh
first sees Motherwell's serpentine tattoo and the mentor laugh-
ingly quips, 'Another serpent crawling out of the buffalo-berry
bush in the Garden of Eden' (26). Motherwell then instructs Hugh
in the proper interpretation of the Ten Commandments. Hugh's
mentor teaches him to despise the Law: 'There has been too much

thou-shalt-notting going on all through the centuries of man and all of this thou-shalt-notting has got to stop. Kingsley Spurgeon Motherwell's commandment is: "Thou shalt not – shalt not." *I* shalt not – that's all right – but no more of this "Thou shalt not. Thou shalt not *thou* shalt not."' (*How* 27). When Hugh later enters Mr Nightingale's funeral home to view his dead father, he remembers that the room 'smelled not so much of lilies and carnations as it did of apples' (214). Once Hugh has more or less managed to repress his horror at the murder of Bella, and again feels the quickening within him of heterosexual desire, the deceiving serpent returns, and in the guise (or wig) of woman. Hugh is delighted by the sight of girls playing in his street, but the 'skipping-rope was lisping as Daisy darted in and out like a garter-snake's tongue,' and in Hugh's memory (in the mind of the adult narrator), their song is 'unclean':

> *Charlie Chaplin*
> *Went to France.*
> *Teach the ladies*
> *How to dance.*
> *When he got there*
> *Sat on a pin.*
> *How many inches*
> *Did it go in?* (194)

In the Judaeo-Christian context, these fantasies are the consequences of a boyhood fall from grace. As Hugh is taught in school, 'consequences were something to be *suffered*; our lives had been mined with them so that all pleasures must be followed by an explosion of unpleasant consequences' (7).

This context is alien to the savage and pagan prairie boy of such texts as *Wolf Willow*, *The Studhorse Man*, and Mitchell's books. 'The superlative sun that shone down on us was Greek' (3), the narrator says at the start of *How*. Hugh's hockey team, coached by Motherwell, is called the *Trojans* (21), and his mother's name is Helen (116). Hugh calls Bella 'Proserpine-lovely,' explaining that, 'I got that out of my *Golden Book of Legends*' (119). At the highest point of psychological crisis in the narrative, the boy's father describes winter's coming on as 'Persephone's getting ready to go downstairs,' and briefly explains the Eleusinian myth: Demeter's 'Sorrowing for her daughter, so she's ready to wander again' (192). Another source of 'pagan' or 'savage' references is North American Indian legend. Towards the end, it is revealed that Motherwell is Native, but, more importantly, that he has achieved the status of a shaman in Hugh's recollections (200, 210–11). Indeed, Motherwell represents a juncture between Judaeo-Christian and pagan mythology. At one point, he shouts at a Baptist employee: 'I got the Wendigo in me now! That's Cree, Leon. Look up Satan in your Bible there' (200). Mitchell brackets his satire of idealism, denominational self-righteousness, and, in particular, the concept of Christian salvation, between these Edenic and pagan antipodes. Moreover, as in Kroetsch's novels, there is communication between them, which results in carnavalesque icons. Saint Sammy is one such figure in *Who Has Seen the Wind*, rather more developed as a character than the iconic figures of the later novel, 'Horny Harold, Buffalo Billy, Blind Jesus, Isaac the Bird' (55), and Bill the Sheepherder, all of whom are inmates at the mental asylum that either employs or lodges many of the town's people. One such inmate is Mrs Eddie Crozier, the mother of Motherwell's best adult friend; she is said to have lost her mind due to her son's having 'lusted after strange flesh' (56). After the murder of Bella, King Motherwell (Satan and shaman) joins the other icons in 'the Mental' (213).

There are three overlapping time lines in *How I Spent My Summer Holidays*: Hugh at fifty, the time of the writing; Hugh at twenty-five, returning to his home town to bury his father; and Hugh at twelve, the time of formative experience. Recurring 'brothel-ugly' dreams of temptations to pederasty in middle age drive him back to the town. In these dreams, 'child anuses,' 'caves,' and 'my own mother' are chillingly and cruelly associated (2). 'I was on a time return' (7), as he says, to investigate 'it' (1; but see also 3). When the elder Hugh recounts the story of the Soo Line engineer who ran over Blind Jesus because he thought 'He wasn't real' (213), and the story of Buffalo Billy's paralysis, gored by the same bull he had feared as a child, he establishes an iconic context for his own sense of fatherlessness and its consequences. These stories are narrated almost in the same breath as his account of the funeral, in which he laments that the body in the casket 'was not my father' (214–15). At twelve, consequences were something to be *suffered*; at twenty-five, the consequences were guiltless, ironic, iconic; at fifty, however, the consequences amount to the novel itself: what Kristeva would call *felix culpa*, the transformation of evil and horror into a 'speaking sin.' This type of narrative nurtures 'a wholly different speaking subject,' one which Christianity may only encounter in art and literature (113). This subject, guilt-ridden and morbid as it is (like Celine's writing, which Kristeva studies as exemplary of *felix culpa*), constitutes a narrative that *controls* the symbolizations of abjection, as opposed to the younger Hugh's fantasies, which had been controlled *by* them.

Thus, the story, the composition – 'How I Spent My Summer Holidays' – is a form of compensation and consolation for the middle-aged Hugh. But his analysis is not sustaining. Both Keith (146) and Harrison (197–98) note the novel's apparent inconclusiveness and loss of tonal balance. This, however, may be inevitable, not to say deliberate. I have argued elsewhere that certain types of contemporary fiction present the 'myth of the child' as though it were an early myth of postmodern times. Other novels of this sort, such as Davies's *What's Bred in the Bone* or Atwood's *The Handmaid's Tale*, seem to return to a pre-Oedipal stage or matrix of symbolization, in the construction of fictional psyches, which 'put to rest or at least critique much of the discourse in our culture concerning the Father's No and the Mother's Yes' (Kizuk 8). Hugh's mother, an 'eminent Victorian' and his 'major adversary' (*How* 111), 'knew how to make a person feel ashamed of himself' (77), and too often interfered in the relationship between the boy and the father (176–77). Though he cites his 'father and mother' as having 'marked me most in boyhood' (18), Hugh turns from his father to Motherwell for his initiation into manhood: 'That summer I drew further from my father and much closer to King Motherwell ... My father never swam with us in the river. He could not swim' (38–39).

Guy Corneau's research into male psychology suggests that the 'signature of a missing father is the fragile masculine identity of his sons' (38); 'sons who had inadequate relationships with their fathers have actually been left with psychological holes that quickly fill with dangerous fantasies' (40). 'The major result of this is that *the son will not develop positively in relation to his father's body, but rather will develop negatively against his mother's body and against the female body in general*' (23; Corneau's emphasis). In the fictional psyche of Mitchell's boy-protagonist, Hugh in maturity discovers that the defilement and horror he has associated with woman are expelled by the most violent means possible. In the end, Hugh can forgive himself for his own sullied analysis and forgive his friend Musgrave for telling him (on the occasion of his father's death) 'what I have refused to know all these years' (223): that Motherwell 'must have beaten the lovely whore to death in a drunken rage of frustration' (224). 'Finally I may have it sorted out,' he says, but it is only a wish that the ghost of King Motherwell will have 'haunted me for love!' (224; see also 34).

In the final pages, any doubt that this form of boyhood love can have been anything other than pure – before 'the sick void within me' (220) took hold – is conclusively exorcised through the character of Austin Musgrave. The opposition in the novel's imagery of defilement and cleanliness clearly opposes Musgrave and Motherwell in terms of profanity and cleanliness (23–25; cf. 186– 91 and 222). Motherwell never swears and is 'just about the cleanest person in our district' (25). Musgrave, whose 'totem' is the coyote (41), 'was the worst; he could talk dirty without using any words – just ones out of the Bible' (23). In the end, and in a manner that is reminiscent of novels like *The Studhorse Man* and Nabokov's *Pale Fire*, Hugh confounds analysis by ridiculing Musgrave (who became a psychoanalyst): 'I can just imagine an analysis session with Austin in Seattle or Portland or San Francisco after his receptionist, Miss Cromwell, has said, "Dr Musgrave will penetrate you now"' (221). Here, the implied reader is prefigured as unclean and improper, and as a carrier, 'unintentionally leaving serpents behind, coiled in a dark corner, later to bite and poison and destroy' (222). In its very inconclusiveness, the novel challenges the reader's interpretive strategies.

The dark corner into which we peer is also the underworld of boyhood adolescence, 'the site of the cave Peter and I had dug in the summer of 1924' (16). No one can look into this darkness without leaving 'adult footprints in our child caves' (222). When the adult Hugh follows his child self through the narrative of that summer, and thus, finally, returns, alone, after the murder, to his cave, he writes down the words 'Forlorn – forlorn – forlorn!' (193) to toll him back to his sole self. But this cave is also the site of every revelation and every loss that he will ever know. 'They'd filled it in! ... In time the earth would settle and the prairie would heal over its own scar' (194). In this novel, the corpse of the defiled and mutilated woman is well buried. But fancy cannot cheat so well as she is famed to do, deceiving elf. The shock to Hugh's psyche at the difference that exists *within* sexual difference has created a rift between 'absolute self-love, or primary narcissism' and the self-esteem that is 'restored through admiration of the parent of the same sex, but only providing that the parent reciprocates with a similar admiration' (Corneau 69). It is the role of older males to step in here, in the place of the absent or inadequate father, to recognize where the boy's aptitudes may lie and give direction. Both novels contain recognition scenes of this sort (*Who* 290; *How* 106). However, when mentoring also fails, as it does for Hugh, there can be only emptiness ... a hollow, a windy cave, Blake's 'grave of the soul,' flickering from the flames and shadows of an uncathected desire, in the place of this proper form of personal recognition among males.

'What's Ahead for Billy?':
The Stoneys, 'The Alien,' and
The Vanishing Point

O.S. MITCHELL

The Vanishing Point (1973) had the longest gestation period of any of W.O. Mitchell's novels. It is deeply rooted in, yet very different from, 'The Alien,' an earlier failed novel whose genesis was sparked by Mitchell's involvement with a small Native community in the southern Alberta foothills. He began writing 'The Alien' in 1946 and finally, after it had grown into an unmanageable 900-page manuscript, abandoned it in 1954. This novel's failure was a major disappointment for Mitchell. It had been seven years since the publication of his first novel, *Who Has Seen the Wind* (1947), and he believed at the time that 'The Alien' was his 'major bid as a novelist' (Mitchell to Cloud, 22 July 1952). Although on several occasions over the next fourteen years he tried to revise 'The Alien,' he failed each time, and it was not until the fall of 1967 that he found a strategy which freed him to begin the rewrite which grew into *The Vanishing Point*. An examination of the growth of 'The Alien' and its transformation into *The Vanishing Point* will reveal some of the essential characteristics of Mitchell's creative process, of his aesthetics, and of his sensibility.

The Stoneys

Mitchell's creative imagination has always been attracted to individuals and groups who are controlled by a dominant culture or class: the socially outcast (the Bens in *Who Has Seen the Wind*, the Napoleons in *Roses Are Difficult Here*); the mentally 'different'

(Saint Sammy in *Who Has Seen the Wind*, the three mad women in *Back to Beulah*, Bill the Sheepherder in *How I Spent My Summer Holidays*, Howard Arnold in *For Those in Peril on the Sea*); the vulnerable young (Brian in *Who Has Seen the Wind*, Hugh in *How I Spent My Summer Holidays*); and racial or cultural minorities (the Wongs in *Who Has Seen the Wind*, the Hutterites in *The Devil's Instrument*).[1] One of the central elements in 'The Alien' and *The Vanishing Point* was Mitchell's experience and friendship with another marginalized group: the Bearspaw sub-band of Stoney Indians from the Morley reserve fifty miles west of Calgary.

Mitchell first met the Stoneys in the fall of 1943, when he became involved in their cause to obtain more land. The Stoneys had been lobbying the government for about five years for additional land suitable for agricultural purposes. The 90,000 acres of land at the Morley reserve granted them in 1876 by Treaty Number Seven were no longer able to sustain their hunting culture. They had become hunted, trapped, and timbered out, and were unsuitable for grazing and agricultural purposes. As a result, the Bearspaw sub-band, about 175 people, had left Morley and were scattered through the foothills to the south. They barely managed to survive by doing seasonal work, such as haying and fencing, for farmers and ranchers. They camped in canvas tents wherever they could get permission, and for a number of generations had been living a 'nomadic life in the foothills west of High River' (*High River Times* 14 October 1948: 1). On an afternoon in mid-October 1943, Mitchell attended a council meeting held on the Macleay ranch at which the Stoneys discussed their case and signed a formal petition to the federal government requesting that land be purchased for them in the foothill country of their traditional territory. Mitchell was impressed by the various Stoney speakers. Some of their images and phrases, such as John Dixon's, 'Now I am in a sack, can't get out. Happy days are lost' (*High River Times* 21 October 1943: 5), would later find their way into his fiction.[2]

In the dance tent later that night, Mitchell apparently enjoyed himself very much. A few weeks later, Hughena McCorquodale wrote Mitchell and jokingly suggested that Mitchell's enthusiastic participation in the festivities may have been viewed by Mr Macleay as diverting attention away from the main cause (the petition to Ottawa): 'We still carry the picture of you sitting in the Indian teepee at 1:30 a.m., or bowing and capering with little Rain-in-the-Face. That was quite a night and I'm afraid Mr. Macleay will think I haven't done his cause justice. He is a man of one idea, and he does concentrate' (3 November 1943). Mitchell was moved by the dances, particularly the Prairie Chicken Dance, and his interest in the Stoneys obviously went beyond their immediate land claims. During this first brief encounter he began some lasting friendships as well as a long-standing fascination with the Stoney culture and the impact of White culture on it.

When he returned to New Dayton, where he was principal of the high school, he wrote a partially fictionalized article, 'What's Ahead for Billy?' which dramatized the proceedings of the October council meeting from the point of view of a fictional character. A young Stoney called Billy peeks through the window of the cabin in which the meeting is being held and listens to the speeches of his elders. Finally, 'the old, blind chief' is helped to his feet:

'We been here first our color people. At Treaty Number Seven we were promised help if we need it – as long as water flowing in the Bow River. We need help. Water still flowing in Bow River. I very anxious to hear answer from Ottawa. That's all.'

And that was all that Billy heard, for at that moment his deaf-and-dumb mother had pulled on his shirt, had taken him back to the camp with her in the buckboard. That afternoon he had watched the squaws set up the dancing tent, and that night he had watched the dancing, had himself danced the Prairie Chicken dance after all the men had signed the piece of paper.

And, though Billy did not know it, the piece of paper that was to go to Ottawa concerned him; it asked for new land for all the Stoneys, but it concerned Billy, all the Billies of the Stoney people, and those who were Billies ten and fifteen years ago – it concerned these most.

One wonders what is ahead for Billy, and for the 715 Stoney people, who live from day to day on the edge of starvation, acquainted with all it stands for, and, in spite of that, a loyal and peaceful group of people. (85)

Mitchell's choice of the name 'Billy' for his representative Indian child in this scene suggests one of the central paradoxical themes he will later explore in 'The Alien' and *The Vanishing Point*. Giving the Native child his own childhood name suggests Mitchell's desire to fully understand and identify *with* the Stoneys. But at the same time the scene implicitly reveals his sense of being alien, of being on the outside of this situation. Both protagonists in 'The Alien' and *The Vanishing Point* will grapple with the twinned but conflicting tensions of alienation and bridging, of the seeming impossibility of communication between individual consciousnesses and cultures and the desire for alien consciousnesses to connect.

The fictionalized Billy character and scenes implicitly highlight some of the central concerns of the Stoneys at the October meeting and Mitchell's sense of their dilemma. The younger generations of Stoneys are perilously caught between the old ways of their Stoney hunting culture and the new ways of the so-called 'civilized' White culture. The strategies for untying the 'sack' in which they are caught include education for their children and opportunities to achieve an adequate standard of living. The younger generations must learn to speak and hear the language of this foreign White culture in order for their own culture to survive within it – they cannot simply ignore it and retreat to their traditional ways of surviving, which are no longer tenable.

Mitchell wanted to do whatever he could to bring public pressure to bear on the government to help the Stoneys and hoped that *Maclean's* would publish 'What's Ahead for Billy?' thus giving their cause a large audience. But *Maclean's* rejected the article because they felt that the mixture of fictionalized story and factual article did not work. They were, however, impressed by Mitchell's feeling for the Stoneys and asked him for a 'pure' story using Native atmosphere and characters. Mitchell sent 'What's Ahead for Billy?' to *Canadian Forum*, which published a much shortened version of it in July 1944. Much of the fictional material was removed from this version, including a detailed description of Billy taking part in the Prairie Chicken Dance, a scene which Mitchell would re-work and expand at least four times over a thirty-year period in the manuscript stories 'Billy Was a Stoney' (1944) and 'Catharsis' (1947), in 'The Alien,' and, finally, in *The Vanishing Point*.

Mitchell's next encounter with the Stoneys was seven months later on the Easter weekend of 1944. He and his wife Merna were invited to the Macleay ranch to lend their support to the Stoneys, who were having another council meeting to renew their pleas for more land. Again at this meeting a number of Stoneys spoke eloquently of their plight. Isaiah Rider, a great grandson of Chief Bearspaw, who signed the original treaty of 1876, said, 'In future if we could get land like this round about us now, we don't even want to go to heaven, just stay right here and be happy' (*High River Times* 13 April 1944: 1). One of the other speakers was Peter Dixon, who spoke of his hopes and fears for the future of his young baby and other Stoney children. The Whites present were also invited to speak through an interpreter and, following Senator Riley and A.Y. McCorquodale, Mitchell said a few words:

> Yesterday, my wife and I went to your church meeting. It was a good service. I noticed Peter Dickson's baby at the end of the tent. Peter's baby is eight months old and has four teeth. My son is nine months old and has four teeth. Both babies are Canadians, Peter's just as much as mine. I'll do everything I can to see that my baby eats, and I'll do everything I can to see that Peter's baby gets his chance too for the right food. (*High River Times* 13 April 1944: 4).

Mitchell vividly remembers this occasion and recalls how emotionally caught up he had become in the meeting. He felt that he had really 'bridged' with the Stoneys. He certainly made true friends with the Dixons that afternoon.[3]

Five months later, F.M. Salter[4] submitted the story 'Billy was a Stoney' to Dudley Cloud, managing editor of *Atlantic Monthly*. In his covering letter Salter gives a description of Mitchell's background and comments on his interest in the Stoneys: 'He is a lad of enthusiasms – and "Billy was a Stoney" is one of the new ones. He has been very much interested in the Stoney Indians – and the terms in which he condemns governmental treatment of the Indians would curl your hair. You may take this Billy story as authentic stuff; he knows what he is talking about' (29 August 1944). 'Billy Was a Stoney' begins with Billy getting a ride in a democrat to a nearby ranch with Mrs Rider. She is grieving over the death of her young son and is going to the ranch to have a 'burying box' made for him. Billy watches as the ranch hands build the coffin and then paint it with green Kalsomine. He is given the small amount of remaining Kalsomine, which he uses to paint himself 'green from the blue-black bowl of his head to the soft, buck-skin soles of his mocassins' (5) for the dance that evening. The last four pages of the partial manuscript describe Billy's first awkward rounds in the Prairie Chicken Dance. *Atlantic Monthly* rejected 'Billy Was a Stoney' because they felt that although it was a talented performance, it depended too much on atmosphere and needed more action.

The Stoneys' many petitions for more land finally bore fruit in the fall of 1948. The Department of Indian Affairs purchased the Eden Valley ranch, forty miles west of High River, for the Bearspaw band. The property had ranch buildings (which became a school, hospital, community hall, and teacher's residence) and a swing bridge over the Highwood River giving access to the small acreage on the north side of the river, which was bounded by the main road into the Eden Valley from High River and Longview. The Eden Valley reserve started operating as a sub-reserve in the summer of 1949 under the direction of Reverend Roy Taylor, who was a teacher and missionary, and Mrs Taylor, a registered nurse, who looked after the hospital. Hughena McCorquodale reported that when 'the wanderers are gathered in for the winter,' the reserve population would be about 140 people and concluded her last article on the Stoneys' land claims as follows: 'First impressions incline Mr. Taylor to believe that the Eden Valley experiment may develop very beneficially for these Stoneys of the foothills, who have been voluntary exiles from the nonproductive Morley reservation, but have suffered the handicap of lack of school, lack of hospital care, or constructive attention. They now have a home' (*High River Times* 8 September 1949). This small Native community of twenty-three families would continue over the next twenty-five years to deeply touch Mitchell's creative and personal life.

'The Alien'

As Mitchell worked on the final editorial touches to *Who Has Seen the Wind* in 1946, he had already started to work on his next novel, which grew out of his interest in the Stoneys and his experience of living in High River for two years. By January 1947 he had blocked out the narrative in chapters and had completed 50,000 words of rough material. His central character, Hugh (later named Carlyle), was a half-breed, and from the beginning he was conceived of as an idealistic but moody and embittered anti-hero who, unable to come to terms with his mixed blood, successively alienates himself from family, friends, and lovers in both White and Red cultures. In early rough notes for the novel, Mitchell wrote, 'The mixed blood motif must come up again and again and again'[5] and, 'This is a story of aliens [except for a few secondary characters, one of whom is Carlyle's wife]... These people have no experience of contingent persons. Some are beaten from within themselves – others by forces economic or social outside themselves' (MsC 19.12.5.f47). At this early stage Mitchell considered a positive ending for the novel, with Hugh, after his encounter with the lookout man, 'plunging blindly down the hog-back' of Mount Lookout 'to return to the more normal existence.' But three lines later he decided on a tragic end for his protagonist: 'And that's where it should end – with the failure of a man – with the shambles of other lives around – with his wife and what she thinks – and with his death –' (MsC 19.12.5.f55).

In July of 1947 Mitchell met with Stanley Salmen, the director of Atlantic Monthly Press, and outlined the narrative of 'The Alien' for him. Salmen disliked the negative hero and ending, for commercial reasons, and suggested that the main character undergo a regenerative change. Mitchell rankled at this suggestion. A year later in a letter to F.M. Salter he describes his meeting with Salmen:

> I made the mistake last summer in Victoria of telling Salmen the outline of the narrative, and he told me that he was very sorry to hear that the central character died in the end since 'negative endings' were poor business as far as novels were concerned. He wondered if it would not be possible for the central character to turn a corner and become regenerated. It is impossible for the central character to turn a corner, as a matter of fact I'm having a hard time to keep him from jumping off Look Out Peak in a most dramatic climax in which he not only dies but kills himself as well. That last sentence looks pretty confused to me, but I'll let it go. (21 September 1948)

In July 1948 Mitchell had moved his family to Toronto to begin a three-year stint as fiction editor of *Maclean's*, which considerably slowed down work on 'The Alien.' He worked at it on weekends, evenings, and during his summer holidays. On his three-week holiday at Bon Echo in the summer of 1949 he wrote the final sequence of 'The Alien' and, as he had written to Salter a year earlier, his tragic hero does commit suicide. Carlyle has given up on himself, his family, and the Stoneys, and listlessly rides towards Mount Lookout. As he climbs up to the look-out tower perched on top of the hog-back, the atmosphere is 'charged and crackling with the electricity' of an approaching storm. His knocks at the door are finally answered by the half-crazed look-out man. Interspersed in his babbling monologue are Caryle's impressions of him and his recognition that the look-out man is his mirror image:

> Carlyle could scarcely hear the voice droning on and on through an atmosphere filled with the terribly unfamiliar freshness of split oxygen. Through the flickering saffron light he stared at this gutless colorless man who seemed so deliberately divested of body flesh and grossness, freed here thousands of feet above the earth of

bogs and muskegs of obscurities and pettinesses and practicalities. By what process had he arrived here? Through carelessly lost faith in other men – discovery of insignificance in their lives – in his own? And what had followed then – the spent melancholy – the loosening tautness of mind, then the blinding flash of understanding contempt?

...

Though there might in time be surcease from the storm outside, there could never be escape from the torment within. Never could he retrace a step in his life to that funeral point when compassion had died its quick death. As though he had tapped some vibrant source of insight, he knew in the drained emptiness of his soul, that now he looked upon himself – as surely as in a mirror – here he was – this sterile, virgin and demented man – this Aristotle's God thinking its idiot self upon the mountain top. (MsC 19.14.3.f112, 114)

The final scene of the novel describes dawn breaking, details of bird sounds, and the movement of a porcupine as it climbs a spruce tree a few hundred feet below Carlyle's body. The scene is caught in the reflection of the lake at the base of Mount Lookout:

Reluctantly, lingeringly the last of the mist breathed from the face of the lake which reflected the sheer mountain side perfectly: the rust and tan and grey of the shale, the dark and sabering trees, the spruce and its porcupine. The reflection gave the illusion of incredible depth; half-way down it held the pine and the broken body at its base – steadily – like a fly in amber. (MsC 19.14.3.f21)

Mitchell says that the Bon Echo version of the ending of 'The Alien' remained virtually intact right through to the final 900-page manuscript completed in 1953. It is difficult to ascertain exactly what sections of the final three-part manuscript Mitchell had completed by the summer of 1949, but probably at most he had finished in draft about 400 pages. Most of part 3, leading up to Carlyle's suicide, had not yet been written.

In the final manuscript, part 1 (which was completed by May

1950) deals with Carlyle's university years, in which he meets and courts Grace. He is subject to irrational outbursts of anger and bitterness, ostensibly caused by his divided feelings over his mixed blood. He is ashamed that his mother was Native and conceals his background from those around him; at the same time he is outraged by racist remarks and attitudes and feels guilty for hiding his mixed blood. In part 2, Carlyle and Grace have moved to Shelby, a foothills town modelled on High River, where Carlyle is the school principal. During his time in Shelby, Carlyle withdraws more and more into a self-obsessed moodiness. He finds himself strangely attracted to the mountains forty miles away, particularly Mount Lookout. Part 2 of Carlyle's downward spiral into alienation climaxes when the townspeople discover that his mother was Native. After a bar-room brawl with Rory Napoleon, a half-breed who operates the town's honey-wagon, Carlyle resigns his principalship in Shelby, even though the town wishes him to stay on. During Mayor Oliver's speech at a town celebration in his honour, Carlyle thinks of how, three days before, he had walked to the river at the edge of town and 'lifted his eyes to Lookout still pure with snow against a brilliant and unstained April sky':

> There had been a slow release of tension as he stared to the clean edge of the mountain – aloof – aloof – cool and aloof – magnificently immovable and undeniable...
>
> Ageless rock and utter radiance slaking the parched sight. Glacial impersonality that could touch and freeze to unimportance his despair. He had been unfair; they deserved only his pity, for they were beyond all hope of redemption with no smooth conveyance from dull lives and the crackle of thorns. (156, personal manuscript)

Following Oliver's speech, Carlyle announces he is leaving Shelby to teach his people at the Paradise Valley reserve. In part 3, Carlyle, Grace, and their young son Hugh move to the Paradise Valley reserve, where he at first teaches and then also becomes the agent for the reserve.

Soon after writing the ending at Bon Echo, Mitchell ran into difficulties in continuing work on the Paradise Valley reserve material for part 3. He felt that he did not have enough first-hand experience with the Stoneys to convincingly portray Carlyle's reserve experience and his frustration with the Stoney's failures to meet his expectations. When he returned to Toronto from Bon Echo, he wrote to Dudley Cloud that he had hit a snag with 'The Alien': '– there is still one big hole that can be filled only after I have spent my two weeks holiday on an Indian Reservation' (23 July 1949). Whatever time Mitchell salvaged for 'The Alien' from his *Maclean's* work (and his CBC radio *Jake and the Kid* series) over the next two years was probably devoted to parts 1 and 2 of the manuscript. In the spring of 1951, Merna Mitchell decided that they had had enough of Toronto. She insisted that they move back to High River and that Mitchell go back to freelance writing so he could devote more time to his stalled novel. In a 1965 interview, Mitchell comments on how crucial the move back to High River was for his creative writing: 'The years in Toronto were sterile – I had to be near my subject – I can't fake it – I have to hear the right voices and the voices of Toronto were wrong' (Danylchuk).

In the fall of 1951 Mitchell moved a trailer out to the Eden Valley so he could be close to the Stoneys as he worked on 'The Alien.' In February and May of 1952 he taught at the reserve school for about four weeks for Reverend Taylor. The following fall, when Reverend Taylor and his wife took up positions at another reserve, Mitchell volunteered his services as the Eden Valley reserve teacher. He refused to accept a salary from Indian Affairs because he did not want his position as an observer and writer to be compromised. He wished 'to be honest and open' about what he experienced on the reserve and he knew that 'what came out in the novel may be an embarrassment to Indian Affairs' (interview, 27 December 1986). So, for the 1952–53 school year Mitchell lived on the reserve during the week and spent his weekends with his family in High River while he worked on completing 'The Alien.'

During his first year working with the Stoneys, Mitchell filled in most of the 'big hole' in part 3 which had stalled him two years before. Carlyle at first seems to have found his vocation and to relax into a more fulfilled life with his family and his teaching. Educating the Stoneys so that they can participate more fully and effectively in the advantages of White culture becomes an obsession for Caryle, and by throwing himself completely into this mission he appears to be less self-obsessed. He also becomes the agent for the reserve and initiates changes and improvements in the way the reserve's agricultural resources are handled. He pins his idealistic hopes on a young Stoney girl, Victoria Rider, who becomes the first Stoney to complete high school and enter the nursing program in the city hospital.

But Caryle inevitably submits to despairing moodiness. He broods about the impossibility of communicating with others, even with his own son Hugh:

> It was probably what every father sensed in his son, simply disparity in age creating two worlds which could not merge. They were on different planets! Was it any wonder he was visited with the same feeling of hopelessness he had with the Indian children – the hopelessness of ever knowing what went on in his own son's mind and heart! All communication between all humans was hopeless, wasn't it! Out of my skin and into yours I cannot get – ever – how hard I try – however much I want it! Just hope and desperately wish it were possible – fool myself – delude myself. It was like love – possessing a woman. There was the same defeat of imagined perfection dying instant death in physical realization. What a weak bridge emotion was for people to walk across to one another! Arching emotions lifting in their center the better to hold the heavy weight of communication which was just illusion after all, for once the passage was made the door was closed. He looked at blank wood! He called and no one answered. (241, personal manuscript)

Carlyle goes on to think that a father *should* be able to 'walk into his son's country of alien customs and accents, into the country of others' (242) and of how others, such as Grace and Dr Sanders, seem to be able to do so. The theme of communication surfaces earlier in part 3, when Carlyle angrily pulls Hugh away from the Prairie Chicken Dance at recess. Hugh, fascinated, had been watching the Stoney children dance and had been invited to join in. Carlyle demands to know how he was asked:

> 'How did they ask you? Which one?'
> 'Howard.'
> 'Howard can't speak English. Howard's – how could he – how could he ask you!'
> 'Not speaking.'
> 'Then how?'
> A faint frown wrinkled the boy's forehead, and it was his turn to helplessly find an explanation for his father. 'Like – I just – the way we do.'
> 'Do what?'
> 'With his eyes. Like that.'

There are some nice ironies here as Hugh struggles to communicate to his father how, through body language, he 'bridged' with children from an alien culture and participated in the circle of their dance, a dance which Carlyle sees as an impediment to his educational agenda for the Stoneys. Carlyle dismisses the drum and dance as primitive and escapist. He orders Hugh never to take part in the dance again saying, 'It's all right for them. It's not for you.' (154, personal manuscript), and arranges for baseball to replace the Prairie Chicken Dance at recess. In the last sequence of part 3, Carlyle's sense of the futility of connecting with others is echoed in the look-out man's narcissistic monologue, 'private words unintended for a listening ear' (MsC 19.14.3.f111):

> '– a sort of epistemological masturbation. The seeds don't come to anything – words can't be any good, of course. Take a word from one mind and plant it in another and it takes on unintended life – a strange fruit – strange blossoms – perhaps it doesn't germinate at all. They never can provoke an exact twin effect. Oh – a loaf of bread is a loaf of bread – a bed is a bed ...'

For a second Carlyle had a mental picture of him standing high on his mountain top, elbow crooked, upon the narrow edge, back arched in the supreme and perfect act of contempt over the world below. The picture as quickly dissolved, for it implied a function which had long since become vestigial in this aseptic man!

'– sleep in it – procreate in it – would you like – would you have some more similes – metaphors. They are worthless. They are pretty but useless. No use. Why should they have. They are not the thing – the thing is more like itself than anything else, isn't it? Do I bother you?' (MsC 19.14.3.f113)

Carlyle loses faith in his mission and capitulates completely to despair when Victoria becomes pregnant and Howard Powderface dies from tuberculosis. Victoria is 'grabbed hold of' (raped) by Johnny Education at one of the dances and she drops out of the nursing school. Howard dies unnecessarily because his father ignores Carlyle's repeated advice to get him proper medical attention. Carlyle sees Victoria as having failed him and abandons her (she lives at the edge of the reserve by herself and eventually gives birth to a stillborn child). He withdraws even more from his wife and children, and 'sells out' the reserve band when he persuades them to sign a power deal with a hydro company which will give the band members small monthly cash payments over a number of years (rather than advising them to continue to insist on a land trade which will give them more agriculturally suitable land so they can expand their herd). When Grace discovers he has advised the band to sign the power deal, she accuses him of using his mixed blood as 'a whipping boy – repository for blame' and tells him, 'You've just never grown up to contain the world, that's all! Or the other people in it. Me – your own children – you stop at the outer edges of yourself!' (306, personal manuscript; see also MsC 19.12.5.f57).

Grace leaves Carlyle, telling him she will come back when he has straightened himself out, and Carlyle begins the last stage of his regressive journey. He is attracted by the sound of the drum and outside the dance tent he confiscates some home brew from Matthew Bear, the band's star dancer, and begins to drink it himself. Then follows an eleven-page description of social dances (the Owl Dance and the Rabbit Dance) and three episodes of Matthew Bear doing the ceremonial Prairie Chicken Dance interspersed with Carlyle's thoughts about Victoria, whom he now sees for the first time in months (MsC. 19.14.3.f70–f81). Carlyle is 'stirred and dazed by the fierce assault of drum and liquor,' and as he watches a 'length of phallically carved bone' ritualistically passed around to invite partners into the dance he is filled with anger and jealousy. Victoria offers Carlyle the 'obscene bone' and, after doing the Rabbit and Owl dances with her, he takes her outside the dance tent and makes love to her in the shadows of the pines. The following morning Carlyle and Victoria leave the reserve and ride to the valley just below Mount Lookout, where they camp for two weeks. He grows more and more disgusted with Victoria, with her silence, her cultural habits (such as not eating until he has), and her features. Repulsed by her smell, he angrily orders her to bathe: 'Thereafter she went to the pool to bathe daily, and he knew that she did it simply because he wanted her to. The act had no meaning or value to her beyond his expressed desire that she should do it' (MsC 19.14.3.f100). Carlyle sends Victoria back to the reserve to get supplies, but assumes she will not come back. After telling her that he will meet her at the pass, he begins his ride to Mount Lookout, where he encounters the look-out man and plunges to his death down the mountain side in the storm.

Carlyle is a figure cut in part from the cloth of such Romantic tragic heroes as the Poet in Shelley's *Alastor* and the Byronic hero. Like Shelley's Poet figure, Carlyle is dissatisfied with the mundane and petty world of the many. Both the Poet's and Carlyle's idealism sours into a narcissistic and self-obsessed quest for the ideal which alienates them from humanity, and both are 'blasted by ... disappointment' and descend 'to an untimely grave' ('Preface' to *Alastor* 69) on the side of a mountain. Mount Lookout's cool aloofness, like Shelley's 'still,' 'serene,' and 'remote' Mount Blanc ('Mount Blanc' 91–92), symbolizes the Ideal, the Eternal, the One. In the early rough notes for 'The Alien,' Mitchell outlines his tragic protagonist and his mirror image, 'The Man at the Mountain Top,' along Shelleyean lines:

A hunger for the eternal – a dissatisfaction with the transient nature of the tactual the audible the visual.

Shelley: The One remains, the many change and pass;
       Heaven's light forever shines, Earth's shadows fly;
       Life, like a dome of many-coloured glass,
       Stains the white radiance of Eternity.   (MsC.19.12.5.f61)

This virgin pure ——— man – this gutless, colorless wraith of a man who had left the multitude to commune with himself ten thousand feet above the earth – freed of the bogs and muskegs of obscurities and pettinesses and practicalities – the ivory ivory tower.   (MsC. 19.12.5.f62)

And Carlyle in the end takes the advice Shelley offers in the remaining lines of this verse from 'Adonais.' Death will 'trample' the 'many-coloured glass' of life to fragments, so, 'Die, / If thou wouldst be with that which thou dost seek!' (405, lines 464–65).

Mitchell had a similar problem to Shelley's in *Alastor*. Shelley wishes to celebrate the Poet's Platonic idealism and intends him to be a tragic hero for whom the reader will find sympathy. But the Poet is not a sympathetic figure, being neither sympathetic to others nor evoking the reader's sympathy. Mitchell had been bothered by this lack in his hero about mid-point in the growth of the novel. Dudley Cloud wrote to Mitchell in December of 1950, saying that he liked part 1 but felt it was 'restricted.' Mitchell responded that part 1 was deliberately restrained and that parts 2 and 3 would have more 'fire and color' and adds, 'My main concern has been whether the reader would find sympathy in himself for Carlyle, and I'm awfully pleased you like him, for the book is a tragedy and you can't purge worth a damn if the central human is a heel' (28 December 1950).

However, it would be a lack of sympathy in and for Carlyle that caused Mitchell's two publishers, and finally Mitchell himself, to reject 'The Alien.' When he submitted part 1 to Macmillan in May 1951 and to Little, Brown about four months later, the readers' reports were very optimistic. A year later Mitchell wrote Dudley Cloud that he was almost finished part 3 and he was very enthusiastic and confident about the novel:

> I think it is excellent and may be my major bid as a novelist. Nothing like it has ever been done and the last two parts show the importance of the first part with its university setting which is at the opposite pole to the wild mountain setting of the agency period in this man's life. It is tragic as hell but has the light and varied surface of life, I think – form and theme and symbolism go right through the people and the incidents with what I hope is the right restraint...
>
> The last section in which Carlyle is an agency teacher and supervisor is not the Maugham in the English colony or Bates in Burma or Green among the British African exiles sort of thing. My natives are real; I have known them for ten years now, have been living on the reserve and teaching them for the past winter, have stopped short only of climbing under the cow hide with Mary Roll-In-The-Mud. The INDIAN QUESTION or WHAT SHALL I DO ABOUT MY MISCEGENATION does not form the core of the book at all any more than Melville concerned himself with the current evils of the whaling industry primarily.
>
> This thing is as good as Moby Dick and I appreciate your patience throughout my rude silences. (22 July 1952)

But three months after his ebullient letter to Cloud, Mitchell, although still certain of the novel's authentic treatment of the Stoneys, was having second thoughts about how good it was. He sent part 3 to his Canadian publisher John Gray of Macmillan and, judging from his covering letter, he had clearly begun to lose his confidence in it:

> Honestly, John, I cannot tell whether the thing is competent, bad, or good; I've been too long with it. I know it's authentic, for I spent most of the winter and fall living with the Stoneys; like Carlyle I taught them; his disillusionment in the hopelessness of work with them is very nearly autobiographical. I am now a regular drummer

for the Owl and Rabbit dances. I am seriously thinking of getting out a tape recorder then arranging to have little plastic discs cut to be inserted in the book jacket. One side would be the chicken dance to be read before the chapter in which Carlyle leaves with Victoria for the bush; the other side would have the Owl dance and the Rabbit dance. (23 October 1952)

Over the next five months Mitchell worked at rewriting parts 2 and 3 and writing a bridging framework through which the three parts of the novel are told. In this rewriting he tries to address Macmillan's concerns about Carlyle's lack of warmth. In March 1953 Mitchell wrote Cloud that he would shortly be sending him the completed manuscript but listed six problem areas which still concerned him and on which he would continue to work. Following these, he listed some of the things he had tried to accomplish in the novel, which included avoiding 'a tract on THE INDIAN QUESTION' but giving a 'true picture of the Western Canadian community's attitude towards mixed blood – a true picture of reserve conditions in Canada – of Indians in Canada.' He also described the rationale behind the novel's three settings and his protagonist's destination:

> Move from a highly civilized setting of University to the half-way point of the town in the foothills where the Indian motif is struck a little louder and a little more often – to the Reserve itself where the primitive takes over ..... to the mountain top, the logical end of Carlyle's selfishness ..... death where he is inaccessible to man and which is the inevitable conclusion, since it is the peace he has yearned for all his life. (2 March 1953)

The following day Mitchell wrote John Gray rejoicing that part 2 was being typed and that, although things still needed to be done, 'the main thing is that it is done and I like it after seven years' (3 March 1953).

Little, Brown's response to the completed manuscript, however, was negative. One of the reports dismissed it out of hand saying that it was 'beyond editorial therapy' (15 April 1953) and

Cloud wrote Mitchell on 27 April saying that Little, Brown and Atlantic could not afford to publish 'The Alien.' The main problems with the novel in their view were the slow downward trend of the story and Carlyle's character. Cloud's letter was a rather perfunctory one which offered no suggestions or hope for the novel and did not invite Mitchell to resubmit it after another rewrite. Macmillan expressed their concerns that the motivations behind Carlyle's and Grace's actions were unclear and unconvincing and that the Brontë-esque storm scene ending was melodramatic, but they liked it very much and wished to publish part or all of it. Mitchell was devastated by Little, Brown's rejection, but he did realize that the novel needed a major rewrite. Three weeks after Cloud's rejection letter, Mitchell wrote to John Gray describing his plans for a rewrite:

1. Take it out of the Grace–Senator–Powderface framework and recast it in one focussing on Carlyle himself. It will open with him riding alone into the mountains, troubled and disturbed after the signing of the power company agreement – coming back to Carlyle each time between the three parts until the inward course of the novel has caught up with him. The climax will then be contained in the Prairie Chicken Dance so that it will end in a blaze of fire-works and not in a gradual and tragic descent ending in his death where no man can reach him. He will not go into the wilderness with Victoria symbolizing his mother's people; he will not turn his back on her and go up onto the mountain to be confronted by himself in the form of the Lookout man. At the Prairie Chicken Dance he will understand the hopelessness of the Indians' lot, that their suffering in the song of the drum is much greater than his own selfish disappointment. He will understand their ability for the first time to achieve the strength to go on through the primitive anaesthesia of the drum and dance, will know then that he must throw himself again into his Indian work with a comparable fierceness, however hopeless the outlook. The book will end with a deliberate tearing up of the power company agreement which symbolizes all compromise.

2. Create Carlyle again... He will be gentler, more responsive...

and there will be no further blind and lashing angers which have their genesis in his miscegenation ... Altogether I shall warm Carlyle; he shall not do things I would not do myself. (23 May 1953)

Shortly after this letter 'The Alien' won the first *Maclean's* new novel award, and for the next three months Mitchell turned his attention to condensing part 3 into nine instalments for *Maclean's*. In this version of part 3, Mitchell incorporated some of the changes he had outlined to Gray in his letter of 23 May. During the climactic tent dance scene Carlyle has a moment of self-realization. Victoria's invitation to join the Rabbit Dance and Matthew Bear's performance of the Prairie Chicken Dance have a profound effect on him and, rather than moving him towards hopelessness and defeat, stir him to re-engagement:

And now, with the silent drum still numb in his blood, Carlyle sat shaken and moved as he had never been moved in his life before. By what process had he arrived in this tent flickering with lamp and firelight, surrounded by his mother's people finding the periodic and primitive anaesthesia that made their life bearable for them! How had he come through the bogs and muskegs of obscurities and pettinesses and practicalities – to an untenable territory of selfishness. Through a carelessly lost faith in other men – discovery of insignificance in their lives – in his own? How had he been able to blind himself to the vivid need of these people? ... That was it! Contempt for the ordinary, petty, distracting, turbulent and tyrannical and tawdry, the petty and pointless absurdities of human existence! He had truly found for himself with one rip of the veil the cheap value of a man clearly worthless in the wilting light of his contempt ... He was truly one of them and of the human race and he had failed them ... He must turn back to them, their hopelessness undiminished, for the turning back and being of them was the cardinal thing ... There would be other Victorias who would try with his help; they would go further or not so far, might even succeed, but at least there would be direction and that was the important thing. That was the important thing – that and being part of them and of all others. (*Maclean's* 15 January 1954: 33)

Carlyle decides to tear up the signed power agreement and to phone Grace. The final paragraph of the *Maclean's* version of 'The Alien' describes Carlyle leaving the tent as the Prairie Chicken Dance comes to an end: 'Just as he stepped out into the night, the drum was stilled with one lambasting sound. As though he had been held up by its solid beat, Matthew in a catalepsy of muscular tension, fell flat to earth – spread-eagled in utter exhaustion. Wonderful as birth, terrible as death, harsh as rape, unimportant as failure, the faultless Prairie Chicken dance was over and done' (33).

But Mitchell did not substantially revise the full manuscript of 'The Alien' as laid out in his letter of 23 May to Gray. He must have felt that the positive *Maclean's* ending, which *tells* rather than dramatizes Carlyle's self-discovery and desire to re-engage, did not grow organically out of the rest of the novel. It was a spliced-on *deus ex machina* ending which was out of sync with the novel's essentially tragic vision and protagonist (this ending is, however, very close in spirit to that of *The Vanishing Point*). John Gray offered, reluctantly, to publish the novel as it stood without an American publication, but only 'to get it out of your system and your way since it has been there too long' (5 February 1954). By the fall of 1954, however, Mitchell abandoned 'The Alien.' He realized that there was something deeply wrong with it which cosmetic changes, including splicing on a positive ending, could not rectify, and he had been with it too long to undertake the kind of major overhaul that it needed.

The Vanishing Point

Over the next fourteen years Mitchell on occasion pulled out the 'The Alien' and read it through with a view to starting a major rewrite. But each time he was overwhelmed by it and his efforts ended in defeat. In retrospect he realized, '[I had] put a finish on it that was good enough that it tyrannized me and I couldn't take liberties with it,' and, 'the other thing that was bothering me, that I was not fully conscious of, was this is completely out of harmony with what I sincerely in my gut believe about the nature of man' (interview, 26 December 1985): 'I like people – I hope for people and I say "yes" rather than "no" to man, because the human one is the only crap game in town – there isn't any other' (interviews, December 1981–January 1982). Mitchell's sense that 'The Alien' was 'finished' too soon may seem questionable given the seven years that he worked on the manuscript. But the key point here is that his anti-hero was conceived and the novel's concluding scenes were conceived and written quite early on. Its tragic vision grew out of a superficially cerebral and sentimental romantic pessimism which was conceived largely in the abstract. As a result, the kind of accidental and spontaneous creativity, which Mitchell's 'free-fall' method of writing is designed to tap, was stifled.[6] He still did a great deal of free-fall writing for this novel, particularly in the early stages, but almost from the beginning, in terms of his protagonist's character and destination, Mitchell had strait-jacketed himself. Carlyle, as a character, *never* ran away with Mitchell, was not allowed to take on a life that spontaneously grew and surprised Mitchell as he created him. As a result he comes across as a very mechanical and 'textureless' character whose tragic *angst* fails to effectively engage the reader's sympathy or interest. Most of what Carlyle does and says was done before it was done, had been blueprinted out 'cerebrally, intellectually' (interviews, December 1981–January 1982). It took Mitchell fourteen years to find the distance he needed to completely scrap this blueprint and let a more complexly motivated Carlyle grow organically within a vision more in harmony with Mitchell's sensibility.

Beginning in the fall of 1967, a number of things conspired to set the stage for the writing of *The Vanishing Point* over the next five years. First, Mitchell read a thesis on John Steinbeck which reaffirmed and helped clarify some thematic and formal issues for him.[7] He could now see clearly in light of Steinbeck's vision in *The Grapes of Wrath* how the nihilistic hero of 'The Alien' and its defeatist vision had gone wrong for him. Second, he accepted a writer-in-residence position at the University of Calgary beginning in the fall of 1968. The Mitchells moved to Calgary, and life in the city over the next five years offered Mitchell the same kind of experiential raw material for *The Vanishing Point*'s city milieu that his first-hand experience at Eden Valley had offered the Native milieu of 'The Alien.' This led to a new geographical and cultural 'axis' for *The Vanishing Point*: Carlyle's journeys *between* the 'civilized' city and Paradise Valley (rather than the regressive linear movement of 'The Alien' from the civilized university to a small foothills town to Paradise Valley and finally Mount Lookout). But probably most important was Mitchell's decision to start writing from scratch without looking at 'The Alien.' He knew he would use much of the material from part 3 of the manuscript, but he did not look at it until *The Vanishing Point* was in the final stages of completion some three years later. This enabled Mitchell to take the kind of large liberties necessary to do an effective rewrite. The result of Mitchell's final attack on 'The Alien' was a radically different novel with a more complex and engaging Carlyle, new secondary characters who play key roles in Carlyle's quest for self-discovery and meaning, new 'proliferating' images and symbols, a tighter organic structure, and a more comic (rather than tragic) vision which is open-ended and richer in its scope and depth. This is not to say that there is not a dark side to Mitchell's vision, but it is essentially existentialist – it faces squarely human limitations but refuses to give up, or, to paraphrase Daddy Sherry in *The Kite*, never settles for less.

One of the first liberties Mitchell took with his protagonist was to make him pure White. The original causes of Carlyle's 'fall' now lie in his childhood and cultural imprintings, and the motivation behind his character has nothing to do with miscegenation. In 'The Alien' Dr Sanders calls Carlyle an 'a-social, inhibited, Indian bastard!' (205, personal manuscript) which in *The Vanishing Point* becomes 'a hard man' and 'a puritan bastard' (156). *The Vanishing Point* opens with Carlyle awakening to the sound of drumming ruffled grouse on an early spring morning. He has been teaching on the reserve for almost nine years. In part he has been hibernating from the terrible emotional and psychological experience of losing his child and his wife (following the stillbirth his wife went into severe depression and died in a mental institute). Carlyle has also been damaged by a puritan and mate-

rialistic culture which programs its young to distrust the spontaneous and irrational whims of the emotions and imagination. So
Carlyle has been living on a reserve in a number of senses. He has
been holding himself 'in reserve' and has avoided forming any
deep or solid emotional attachments. He blinds himself to his real
feelings for Victoria, whom he has taught since she was a child.
He believes he has maintained a parent-to-child and teacher-to-
student relationship with her, when in fact it has been developing
into something else (just as the paternalistic attitude of the Whites
towards the Natives should have developed into something else).
But the next few weeks in Carlyle's life prove to be the culmina-
tion of a spiritual and emotional rebirth from nine years of hiber-
nation, from nine years of living his 'life... carefully [in] low key'
(4). With the exhilarating awareness that 'the alienating stun of
winter' has been reprieved by spring, 'young Grizzly Sinclair'
embarks on a crucial stage in his life which ends in self-discovery
and the salvaging of what is left of the wreck of his life. When Victoria disappears in the city and Carlyle searches for his 'little girl
lost,' he retreats into fantasies and memory trips through which
he begins to confront the emotional and psychological rape of
his puritan childhood (Aunt Pearl and Old Kacky), the rape of
'White civilization' (the city, little Willis's toy room) which alienates and threatens to 'vanish' all humans, and finally his own
unknowing complicity in perpetuating this rape on Victoria, the
Stoneys, and himself.

Not only does Carlyle run away with Mitchell and grow into a
much more complex character, but a number of other new major
characters introduce themselves into the novel. Heally Richards
becomes Carlyle's alter ego/mirror image, much along the lines
of the look-out man in 'The Alien.' Carlyle sees in Richards the
same kind of well-intentioned but blind and ultimately self-
serving egotism to which he has unknowingly succumbed (354,
366). But it is Archie Nicotine in particular who helps Mitchell
open up the restrictive closures of the original 'The Alien' and
breathe more life and action into it. Carlyle now has two good
angels, the White Dr Sanders (the Stoneys' 'disease brother,' 129)
and the Red Archie Nicotine. Just as Carlyle as a child had played
trickster to Aunt Pearl's well-ordered puritan world, Archie

continually needles, challenges, and upsets Carlyle's (and other Whites') puritan/'civilized' attitudes, presuppositions and projects. Carlyle dismissively stereotypes ('vanishes') Archie – he *knows* that Archie will never get out of the 'sack,' assumes that he will always have to bail him out of jail for being drunk and disorderly and that he will never get his truck going again. But when Carlyle gives up completely in despair and abandons Victoria on the city street when she tells him that she is pregnant, it is Archie Nicotine who refuses to quit and who by example helps bail Carlyle out of his despairing defeatism. Archie makes sure that Victoria will not be 'vanished' to the city streets as a prostitute by bringing her back to Paradise Valley, and it is Archie who urges (and taunts) Carlyle to go to the dance because Victoria is going to be there: 'There's some wicked ones around here too ... It comes free in Paradise, you know' (379).[8]

The title Mitchell originally chose, 'The Alien,' focused on the essential characteristic of his anti-hero – his isolation from human community. About two years into this final rewrite, Mitchell found a new central symbol and title for the novel, the vanishing point (its parallel in 'The Alien' is Mount Lookout):

> ... I do recall a morning when suddenly I was pulled back. I don't know why. It could be torque subconsciously exerted upon me by what was growing structurally about the novel I was committed to. But suddenly, for no goddamn reason, I remembered an art class back when I was eleven ... It had no relation in any way to what so far had grown in the novel at all. And then I remember pulling over a piece of paper. It was a doodling thing. I put the line in and just for the hell of it thought, 'I wonder if I can remember?' And I finally did the thing that Carlyle did in the art class ... suddenly I realized that the whole concept of the vanishing point is a convention of man, and that in the flow of man through the centuries there seem to have been times of hoplessness and despair, like the Dark Ages. But somebody at that point opened the converging lines that much. So man moved on – a new perspective – the Renaissance ... What I had found now made me change and this opened up the whole goddamn thing again. And it's this sort of thing happening through the growth of a novel so that it becomes what you can't

even dream it will become – and this really is the nature of the creative process. (Cowan 18)

In 'The Alien' Mitchell conceived of Mount Lookout as a regressive retreat to a dead end which 'vanished' the protagonist from humanity, from life. He did not allow this central symbol to 'proliferate' and suggest any potential positive implications. For example, the 'inward' looking look-out keeper who retreats up the mountain from humanity is also ostensibly 'looking out' for humanity, is on the mountain to warn the human community of potentially destructive forest fires. Typographically Mount Lookout might be represented as ∧, whereas the vanishing point would be ><. The vanishing point implicitly carries within itself the possibility of opening out, of connecting, of non-closure, of freedom from various kinds of tyranny. As Mate, Carlyle's school chum, points out, the 'vanishing point' as a concept is in fact an illusion (325). The vanishing point is a double-edged symbol which has obvious negative meanings, but these negative meanings are counterbalanced by the implicit paradox within the phrase. The vanishing point is an illusion growing out of an egocentric desire for simplistic and idealistic absolutes which, if obsessively and selfishly quested for (Shelley's Poet's quest for a female prototype of his self-conceived ideal, Carlyle's quest for a perfect 'Victoria,' White civilization's quest for a 'clean,' technological, ordered world) will lead to ennervating despair and alienation from humanity, to 'vanishment' of the self and others. The central image of the vanishing point is also supported by a wide array of other images and symbols which 'proliferate' and interconnect and are instrumental in Mitchell's exploration of the twinned themes of alienation and bridging and in his ironic and complex contrasting of the White and Native cultures. Some of these are salvaged from 'The Alien' and expanded upon (for example, the suspension bridge between the reserve and the road into the city is given more symbolic weight), and many new ones are woven into the fabric of the novel: mirrors, reversals, magic, excrement, food, Red and White, cleanliness, skin and bones, sexuality, disease, being lost and being found, Native oral narratives, fairy tales, technological 'toys,' the city's Devonian Tower,

Paradise Valley's Storm and Misty, Fyffe's greenhouse orchids, and Luton's garden ornaments.

As well as these new additions, Mitchell reworks the climactic Prairie Chicken Dance scene, counterpointing it against the revival tent 'Rally For Jesus' scene in which Heally Richards gives his rousing version of Ezekiel and the valley of dry bones and attempts to heal Old Esau, Victoria's grandfather, who is dying from tuberculosis, the 'Bony-Spectre' (10). Richards is the consummate evangelist crowd master who manipulates and reduces members of his congregation to twitching fallen bodies uttering gibberish. His 'dance' ceremony leads to anaesthetization of consciousness, alienation, and death. As Richards lays his hands on Old Esau, reduced to skin and bones by the 'Bony-Spectre,' the old man rises up momentarily from the stretcher and then dies. And just as Archie Nicotine is directly responsible for Richards's sudden fall from 'glory' (he challenged Richards to take a run at healing Old Esau), it is Archie who is partially responsible for a parallel but successful raising of the dead by bringing Victoria back to Paradise Valley and encouraging Carlyle to go to the dance. Now the drum and dance lead to connection rather than escapist anaesthetizing of consciousness. The phallic bone offered by Victoria is not seen by this Carlyle as 'obscene,' and Victoria is successful in raising Carlyle/Lazarus from the dead. She releases Carlyle from the 'Bony-Spectre' of his White puritan imprinting and from his fear of emotional and psychological pain, and prompts him to join the dance of the living whole. He had thought he was the white knight in shining armour who could help kiss awake Victoria and the Stoneys from their 'primitive' reserve/ sleep, when in fact this mission was a camouflage for his own problems. It is the Stoneys who save him when they help him realize that he and his White culture are in just as much of a 'mess' as the Stoneys. The city, too, is a reserve/slough that leads to alienation, to the psychological and emotional 'botulism' of its lonely inhabitants. Carlyle learns that the only game in town is the human one of indviduals *together* getting out of their alienated 'skins' and touching, bridging with one another.

The climax to Carlyle's search for himself, then, takes place in the dance tent on the Paradise Valley reserve. He had seen himself as a father figure searching for his little girl lost in the city, but in fact he has come to realize that he is a little boy lost (thus his memory trips to his childhood to help re-find himself). And it is Victoria, no longer a little girl lost but a woman who loves him, who helps him find himself by offering him the ritual bone as an invitation to join the dance – the dance from which he had angrily pulled her away when she was a child (208). Now the cathartic release of the drum and dance *do* assuage both White and Red grief and despair,[9] and initiate a true bridging between Carlyle and Victoria, a bridging where each player mirrors the other in a reciprocal way that transcends the alienating power relationships Carlyle has unsuspectingly been party to. In the context of *The Vanishing Point*'s vision, Victoria's name takes on new ironic resonances. On the one hand, it brings to mind all that we associate with her name-sake, Queen Victoria – puritan repression of the emotions and sexuality, civilized proprieties, nineteenth-century British imperialistic control of other cultures. But it also suggests 'victory' rather than failure, a victory not only for herself, because she was a failure only in the distorting 'Methodist glass' (384) held up by the Stoney's white 'guardians,' but for Carlyle as well. As he watches Ezra's grandson making miniature canal systems in the newly released flow of Beulah Creek, Carlyle pledges a new reciprocal approach to his Stoney children:

> Dear little bare-bum shaman, I am here – I'm standing here. Oh, let me show you to you – I want to mirror you so you may be more nearly true! Please perform your marvels for me – surprise me. Astonish me with your accidents. Trust me now. I promise you I won't destroy you with distorted image. I will not turn you into a backward person. At least I will try not to. Let's you and I conjure together. You watch me and I'll watch you and I will show you how to show me how to show you how to do our marvelous human tricks together! (389)

In *The Vanishing Point*, Mitchell succeeded in following through with the kind of major changes he had outlined to John Gray in his letter of 23 May 1953. He had known earlier that 'you can't purge worth a damn if the central human is a heel,' but he had been unable to re-create Carlyle, to 'warm Carlyle' and not make him 'do things I would not do myself.' The new Carlyle is much more autobiographical than the original Carlyle. In a way, Mitchell's twenty-five years of being 'lost' with 'The Alien' and finally being 'found' parallels Carlyle's being lost and finally found in *The Vanishing Point*. His living with the Stoneys in 1951–53 at first seemed to confirm the tragic vision and hero he had blueprinted in 1947, and he says that the despair and frustration Carlyle felt in his work with the Stoneys was very much his own. But one wonders how much of that despair, which went constitutionally against Mitchell's essentially positive and existentialist sensibility, was read into his Eden Valley experience because of the tragic vision and hero he had committed himself to in the beginning stages of 'The Alien.' Perhaps because of this there was little space for effective existentialist characters in 'The Alien' – there were certainly no such Stoney characters. In any event, Mitchell unties the tyrannical 'sack' of various closures of 'The Alien' (character, structure, theme) by starting with a blank page. Like Carlyle in Old Kacky's art class on the vanishing point, Mitchell was originally fascinated by the neat and rigid closure of the lines of road, fence posts, and telephone posts funnelling towards the vanishing point of Mount Lookout in the original blueprint of 'The Alien.' And also like Carlyle, who finally is not satisfied with his picture because it is 'empty' and needs a gopher or a tree (319), Mitchell opens up and enriches the original lines on the pages of 'The Alien' with many new spontaneous 'finds.' One of the most important of these was his Stoney character, Archie Nicotine. 'The Alien' began with Mitchell's fascination with and concern for the Eden Valley Stoneys and, thirty years later, *The Vanishing Point* ends in a scene in which Archie Nicotine gets his truck going again. It is perhaps not too much of an exaggeration to say that when Mitchell 'found' Archie and let him grow into the new novel, he finally managed to install the re-built rings and carburator for a stalled engine/manuscript that had been hanging from a tree for fourteen years (Archie's engine had hung from a tree for only two years!). So, rather than Carlyle's crumpled body at the foot of Mount Lookout, it is Archie Nicotine who is given the last scene in the novel. Carlyle has the last word in the novel, and significantly it is Archie's word, 'Hey-up!'

NOTES

1 He also wrote two radio plays, 'No Man Is' (*CBC Summer Fallow*, 29 May 1961) and 'Lady Bug, Lady Bug' (*CBC Summer Fallow*, 6 April 1964), which explore bigotry against the Hutterites in Alberta. See also the following articles: 'The Tragic Trek of the Mennonites,' *Maclean's*, 1 March 1951 (the story of John Wiebe); 'The People Who Don't Want Equality,' *Maclean's*, 3 July 1965; and 'The Riddle of Louis Riel,' *Maclean's*, 1 February 1952 and 15 February 1952. As a result of the research he did on the two-part Riel article he planned to do a novel on Gabriel Dumont and the Metis after 'The Alien' was completed.

2 Rod Macleay was the main organizer behind the petition. A.Y. McCorquodale, a High River lawyer, acted as a legal adviser and handled the formalities of the Stoneys' petition to Ottawa, and his wife Hughena, an editor of the *High River Times*, wrote a series of front-page articles covering and promoting the Stoneys' land claims from 12 August 1943 through to 8 September 1949. Senator Dan Riley, a prominent southern Alberta rancher and politician (he was elected High River's first mayor and was appointed to the Canadian Senate in 1925), also lent his support. Hughena McCorquodale's front page feature article, 'The Stoney Indians Petition Federal Government for Land Suited to New Skill,' gives an account of this meeting summarizing the interpreters' versions of the many speakers and the Stoneys' desire to obtain new land peacefully and without disturbing the established farmers and ranchers whom they viewed as their friends. See Mitchell's article 'What's Ahead for Billy?' for a more detailed account of the speeches at this meeting.

3 As a child and teenager, I recall some of the visits the Dixons paid to our High River home. On two of these occasions, when I was about nine and when I was fifteen, Mrs Dixon gave me smoked and beaded buckskin jackets which she had made. Their first son had died from pneumonia when he was about three years old and they had 'adopted' me because of my father's little speech and his continuing interest in them and the Eden Valley Reserve community.

4 F.M. Salter was a professor of English at the University of Alberta who played an important role in Mitchell's development as a creative writer. He worked closely with Mitchell from the summer of 1940 through the publication of *Who Has Seen the Wind* in 1947, both as an editor and an 'agent sans – ten percent.'

5 MsC 19.12.4.f4, University of Calgary Special Collections. Further references

to the early notes and various manuscripts for 'The Alien' held by the University of Calgary's Special Collections will be indicated with the call number in parentheses.

6 Mitchell uses the term free-fall to describe rough spontaneous writing with no thematic, character, or structural destination or closure in mind, and which leaves a work in process open to change and spontaneous accident, to what Mitchell calls 'finds.' For a detailed description of free-fall writing and its aims, see chapter 7 of *Since Daisy Creek* (98–104), where Mitchell ascribes to Colin Dobbs, a creative writing teacher, his own free-fall method of writing.

7 O.S. Mitchell, 'Prophecy in the Novels of John Steinbeck,' thesis, U of Alberta. In December 1967, Mitchell wrote, 'It [the M.A. thesis] had quite an impact on me and believe it or not pulled my understanding to a better view of novel structure – as achieved through symbolism particularly. Result – for the last two months I have been working on THE ALIEN ... Particularly Orme's reference to Steinbeck's GRAPES OF WRATH thesis: man goes forward four steps and slips back three – his faith in the flow of the life force – is precisely what I needed my attention called to. I knew that the inevitable tragedy of Victoria's failure wasn't right for me as a person and as a writer, but I was held helpless by it until I realized that her failure was not failure, for getting as far as she did was a triumph of sorts and that her bastard child will possibly go further – and then fail – and that each generation carries the movement on.' He ends this letter with, 'All our love and up the proliferating symbol!' (personal letter 10 December 1967). See also Mitchell's letters of 14 December 1967 and 7 June 1968 to John Gray (Macmillan Archive, McMaster University, Hamilton, Ontario).

8 Mitchell drew on a number of life models for Archie, including a Stoney, a Blood, a Hungarian, and his son Hugh. Archie Nicotine reappears in *Since Daisy Creek*, where he is literally as well as figuratively a guide for Colin Dobbs (who obsessively hunts for a grizzly bear), and saves his life. In this novel Archie and his cultural values are instrumental in helping Dobbs come to terms with his 'White' culture's anal erotic bent on 'winning' trophies and power, and it may be partly through Archie's influence that Colin Dobbs is able to overcome his writer's block of some ten years.

9 In 1947 Mitchell sent Dudley Cloud a short story, 'Catharsis,' about a Stoney father whose young boy dies. The father finds cathartic release from his grief and anguish by participating in the Prairie Chicken Dance. Interestingly, in the covering letter to Cloud, Mitchell indicates that at this time he saw the release offered by the Prairie Chicken Dance as 'Indian only': 'Here's the story. The grief is white and red – the assuaging, Indian only. It's a violent one, but by God it's true!' (7 April 1947).

'Breaking Free in a Fresh Place': The Significance of Childhood in *The Vanishing Point*

THERESIA M. QUIGLEY

The name of W.O. Mitchell is automatically associated in the minds of many Canadians with his first novel, the highly acclaimed *Who Has Seen the Wind*. Here we have the remarkable and rare feat of fiction intended for an adult audience presented from the point of view of a young child in such a manner as to completely captivate the reader with its ring of truth and authenticity. Unfortunately, however, due no doubt at least partially to the phenomenal success of his first novel, Mitchell's subsequent works have suffered from constant comparison and, to some extent, from critical neglect. It would seem that while readers enjoy a multi-faceted Mitchell, critics and reviewers, in a vain search for a reincarnation of Brian O'Connal, have determined to look no further into Mitchell's work.

As a result, the author's evolving view of childhood, as not necessarily happy but rather as an important formative period in the life of an individual, has largely gone unnoticed. Indeed, when *How I Spent My Summer Holidays* appeared in 1981, much was made of its portrayal of the shadow side of childhood, so different from the notion of the protected, nurtured state of innocence which had become associated with the author's fictional world. However, this more sombre depiction of childhood should not have come as a surprise to readers of Mitchell, since it was amply foreshadowed in his previous novel *The Vanishing Point*. This novel not only introduces the setting and some of the characters of the later work, but it also gives every indication that the author's view of childhood as a privileged state has undergone a change.

It is true that the principal focus of *The Vanishing Point* is the adult protagonist Carlyle Sinclair, a teacher and government agent on the Stoney Indian reserve of Paradise Valley in the foothills of Alberta; however, throughout the novel the author offers many pertinent glimpses into Carlyle's prairie childhood. He shows it, not as a preferred condition, but rather as an orphaned state, with the child, at the age of six, having passed from his brief, original state of grace, as Carol Pearson would describe it,[1] to the reality of 'living in a fallen world' (Pearson 4). Moreover, the author clearly indicates that this orphaned state influences the later behaviour of the adult character, suggesting that the childhood years are the formative years which the individual may leave behind but which somehow refuse to vanish.

As John Moss rightly suggests, 'the vanishing point provides the controlling metaphor of the novel' (264). But while Moss relates this metaphor primarily to the question of 'parallel races of people,' the Native and the White races, and to 'unlikely lovers,' Carlyle and Victoria, it may well be extended to encompass many other aspects of the novel. The importance of the vanishing point is precisely that it is an illusion. As Mate, Carlyle's childhood friend, states: 'It doesn't come to a point – it only comes almost to a vanishing point...' (325). However, a successful illusion must, of course, create the impression of reality, and it is here that many of the problems which the novel addresses arise. The first and most important problem relates to childhood itself which, having drifted into the nebulous past after the individual has reached a certain stage of adulthood, appears to have vanished to a point of insignificance, only to surface again and often adversely affect the adult who denies its significance. The second problem relates to power which the adult exercises over children or over other adults under care in an attempt to change them to a preconceived notion of being, which would vanquish the inner self and replace it with the empowered person's own self-projection.

Mitchell's descriptions of Carlyle's childhood have been

praised as 'marvellous digressions' (Moss 264) which bear witness to the author's comic genius, but not much has been said about the relevance of these chapters in explaining Carlyle, the adult. Nevertheless, upon closer examination, there can be little doubt that Mitchell had more in mind than humour when he created Carlyle, the child. Indeed, many of the childhood passages are far from humorous. It is much more likely that the author's intent can be explained by what Colin Dobbs, the protagonist of the later *Since Daisy Creek*, tells his students of creative writing: 'Most of what turns out to be useful seems to come after a time lag. Often out of childhood. The early years of your life – the first ten – are the litmus years, the ones that seem to stain us most vividly' (100). One suspects that Colin Dobbs speaks for Mitchell in this passage, particularly since the protagonist in *Ladybug, Ladybug ...*, Kenneth Lyon, makes a similar comment (13).

The plot of *The Vanishing Point* centres on Carlyle Sinclair's search for Victoria Rider, a nineteen-year-old Native girl who has disappeared from the hospital nursing school where she was studying. This search takes the protagonist from the wilderness passes of 'Storm and Misty' to the slum districts of the city, from bus depots to beer parlours to revival meetings, and finally, back to the reservation, in a journey of alternating hope and despair, love and anger.

Victoria is a 'special' Native girl: quiet, thoughtful, industrious, dedicated. She was the first child Carlyle met when he began teaching on the Paradise Valley reserve. He singled her out then as 'different,' surely not wholly 'Indian,' and definitely very smart. Throughout nine years of careful nurturing, he created a Victoria in his own image, a reflection of his achievement in Paradise Valley, a girl who, when she entered nursing school, dressed in a 'navy suit with lace at her throat – high heels' (238), looked thoroughly 'civilized' except for her eyes: 'Just the eyes now! not much – just a trace of smoke in the eyes' (238).

The Victoria that Carlyle is searching so desperately for is a product of his projection, a painstakingly pruned flower, cherished, trained, cultivated. Her disappearance 'shatter[s] something inside him' (323) and threatens his very existence, since, as his reflection, her loss indicates a loss of self. What Carlyle does not realize is that, like his friend Ian Fyfe, who grows orchids, nurturing, protecting, labelling them over many years to obtain a specific colour, a particular size, without ever considering 'what the orchid wants' (85), so Carlyle also, in his zeal to 'perfect' Victoria, has forgotten to ask her what *she* wants, what would make *her* happy, what would meet *her* needs. And thus, while he has transformed the outer shell and created a seemingly flawless product, the idea (ideal) he can love without shame, he has not changed her eyes, the smoky mirrors of her soul, her heritage, her very being. Victoria's 'Indianness,' to which he unconsciously objects, lies hidden beneath the white lace collar; it has not vanished. As a result, the search for 'his' Victoria is futile: he will not find what he is looking for because it is a mirage.

To be successful, Carlyle's journey must therefore be more than a mere search for a missing person; it must become a quest for who Victoria truly is, which can only be accomplished if Carlyle succeeds in finding himself first. For it is only in understanding how he perceives the world that he can begin to understand Victoria. This fundamental quest for an understanding of self turns Carlyle's search inward to his childhood.

The novel is divided into two principal sections. The first section begins with the adult protagonist Carlyle Sinclair preparing to go to the city to meet Victoria, and ends with his fruitless search for the girl in the mountains surrounding the reservation. Important characters like Archie Nicotine, Victoria's eventual rescuer; Esau Rider, Victoria's dying grandfather; and Ian Fyfe, the Indian Regional Affairs director, are introduced. The straightforward third-person narrative is interrupted by occasional memory flashbacks to incidents and individuals in Carlyle's childhood.

The second section of the novel begins in the past, with Carlyle remembering his first days in Paradise Valley. Carlyle has lost his wife and unborn daughter and has come to the reserve in the hope of escaping painful memories. His work on the reserve, his promotion to Indian agent, and his growing authority and influence are described. While these are ostensibly the protagonist's memories, the narrative flows in chronological order for some eleven chapters until the present is reached and Carlyle's search for Victoria is taken up again, this time in the city. At this point, various subplots which began in the first section are also reintroduced and the narrative becomes choppy as the story of Carlyle's search is interrupted with accounts of Archie Nicotine's release from jail, his subsequent involvements with Heally Richards, the faith healer; with Norman and Gloria Catface, the Native vagrants; and eventually, with the pregnant and confused Victoria. As Carlyle's search for Victoria becomes more and more hopeless, his childhood memories become more pronounced and eventually take over the narrative for two and a half chapters, again, in relatively chronological order. When the account returns to the present, the relevance of the Archie Nicotine and Heally Richards subplots to Carlyle's search becomes apparent. The final chapters of the novel bring about Carlyle's moment of epiphany and suggest a new beginning.

The novel begins with the promise of spring. Carlyle wakes to the drumming of the ruffed grouse and, when he steps outdoors, feels the warm winds of the chinook caressing his cheek, awakening in him all the emotions 'of young love' (4). Today is 'Victoria day' (4), the day he goes into the city to have lunch with his protégée Victoria. She is his symbol of success, reinforcing his illusion of victory over that which is different. His excitement at the prospect of seeing her also contradicts his assurances that 'there [is] no loved one at all' (4) in his life. Carlyle's emotionally charged behaviour with respect to anything relating to Victoria and his insistence that his concern for her is simply that of a father-figure or a friend create an atmosphere of disingenuousness from the beginning and serve as a forewarning that Carlyle's expectations are as misguided and over-inflated as the often-remembered balloon of his childhood, which 'died without warning in mid air' to drop 'to the floor' (5). Unable to admit the reality of his feeling for Victoria, naively insisting that it is somehow special, outside the realm of normal adult relationships, Carlyle's self-awareness is demonstrably flawed.

As the first section ends, Carlyle identifies with the 'Good Shepherd' in his painful and useless journey through the wilderness of 'Storm and Misty': 'He had not found her in Storm and Misty; he must find her in the city before she perished there ... *Jesus, dear Jesus, I'll find you, little lost lamb, Victoria!'* (115). Like the 'Good Shepherd,' Carlyle is prepared to leave all his other responsibilities to go in search of the 'one that is lost.' However, Carlyle's constant references to Victoria as his 'little lost lamb' result from a lack of understanding of Victoria and, more importantly, they underline his somewhat grandiose view of himself. Throughout much of his search, he tends to see Victoria as the personification of innocence, a child/woman unable to cope without his help, who has strayed and whom he must bring back at all costs. He is willing to endure hardship and privation to accomplish this goal, convincing himself that Victoria has simply made a mistake through fear, uncertainty, and low self-esteem, and that it is up to him to set her 'upon the right path' again.

Carlyle's trek through the mountains and the suffering this entails may be viewed as the beginning of his symbolic journey along what Robert Bly aptly calls the 'Road of Ashes'(79–86). His search, appropriately enough, takes him through burnt-over land, 'through a jack-strawed maze of grey trunks tilting, tangled, lying flat, spotted with the charred obscenities of spruce stumps, even their burn-bared roots checked and gleaming carbon. Appalling – ... through sable wasteland where no order of growth remained' (107). This passage through a place of decay and ashes and the eventual, unexpected, emergence from there to what Carlyle sees as a place of 'vision and solution ... where Beulah [begins]' (108) foreshadows his journey through a kind of spiritual death towards ultimate renewal: 'Here he could purify and prepare, and be absolved from self' (108). The protagonist is scarcely yet aware that his happiness is related to a process of breaking out of the self, 'to fly free of self' (108). As the name for the often mentioned river that runs through Paradise Valley, 'Beulah' (Isa 62:4, land of heavenly bliss) is significant in that the river appeared to have vanished underground during much of Carlyle's frantic search for Victoria, only to reappear again with renewed force, coinciding with the protagonist's own rebirth at the end of the novel. Mitchell's use of the word 'Beulah' for his fictional river, whose beginning is associated with a place of vision is derived from the Blakean view of Beulah, the world of vision and wonder, which, according to Northrop Frye, permits 'imaginative awakening,' promoting 'love and wonder' (*Fearful Symmetry* 49).[2]

Hence, this freeing, 'breaking out,' of the river during the spring run-off corresponds with Carlyle's own freeing of self and his acceptance of physical rather than Platonic love. It is the start of Carlyle's painful process of self-confrontation, although he does not yet know it. It is the start of his descent, his *katabasis*, which Bly explains as 'the Drop' (70), often caused in the lives of relatively successful and apparently happy individuals by a sudden misfortune: a loss of position, an illness, or 'the breaking of a long-standing friendship' (71). This drop into darkness may happen to persons whose 'way of dealing with the world was damaged' by a previous, often a childhood wound (72). The original wound becomes the opening through which *katabasis* occurs, eventually permitting the individual to face the shadows of his past and to live through the pain which still haunts his present and makes authentic living impossible. By allowing the descent into darkness to take place in his life, the individual, according to Bly, 'can use [the pain]... as an invitation to go through the door, accept *katabasis*, immerse himself in the wound, and exit from his old life through it' (74).

It is significant that this section of the novel ends as winter has returned unexpectedly. Carlyle's euphoria of a few short days ago has been replaced by dark dreams, depression, and a sense of confusion. The teasing winds of the chinook had created only the impression of spring – a false spring:

> It really meant to snow. He didn't bother with lunch – lay out on the couch and, with no sense of time passage whatever, stared up to the long windows above. The flakes falling, eluded; at glass touch they melted and ran. A flight of blackbirds scarved the length of the windows – disappeared – returned out of white nothing – only to vanish again. Individual flakes had become indistinguishable, just loosed from above without identity, myriads bewildering with vertigo. (114)

Rebirth, signalling a new beginning, clearly cannot yet take place.

During Carlyle's subsequent journey in search of Victoria through the 'wilderness' of the city streets, his suffering becomes more acute as his despair of ever finding the lost girl grows. It is important to note that when he is most deeply distraught (after a violent physical attack by a group of young Natives who chase him away from the city's Indian Friendship Centre as an unwelcome intruder, an outsider who does not belong), when he is hurt and in pain and in a state of total desperation, the memories of his childhood finally break through and demand his full attention. It would seem that Carlyle has now reached the point of his journey through darkness when he must stop to examine his past: his Aunt Pearl, his teacher 'Old Kacky,' and his father. At this stage, he recognizes his return to his childhood past as a search for pieces of a puzzle that are somehow missing in his makeup and that he must find to complete the picture of himself.

Carlyle is at this point in what Carol Pearson identifies as the Wanderer archetypal mode. She suggests that this is the stage which adult male individuals often enter after a period of achievement known as the Warrior mode. This earlier period signals power and a certain prestige in which individuals attempt 'to change the world in [their] own image' (4). In Carlyle's case, his Warrior period could be seen as his nine years on the reserve, during which he exercised a certain power and succeeded in marginally modernizing and thus changing the lives of the people under his guardianship to fit more closely the White Man's concept of civilized man.

Pearson warns that the Warrior mode is an often 'lonely and ultimately tragic period ... [during which] many men have discovered that, however satisfying it is in the short run, the urge to be better than, to dominate and control, brings only emptiness and despair' (2). The Wanderer mode is often borne out of the 'need to grow beyond the Warrior modality,' which acts like a prison from which the individual must escape (3). As its name implies, the Wanderer modality involves a journey of self-discovery – similar to Bly's passage through the 'Road of Ashes' –

which, while often extremely painful, will eventually lead to greater freedom through self-knowledge, as well as to yet another archetypal mode: that of the Martyr with its ability to 'give, to commit, and to sacrifice for others' (4).[3]

In Carlyle's case, the suffering which his futile search for Victoria engenders leads to the need to re-examine himself and hence to a return to his childhood. While it is true that the physical search through the city involves movement akin to wandering, the more significant aspect of Carlyle's 'wandering' is largely a mental and emotional exercise through what Heather Robertson rightly refers to as his 'personal inferno' (31), involving some of the more painful years of his early life. This journey eventually produces a sense of greater self-awareness, an openness to others' needs, and a readiness for permanent commitment.

The first person from his past with whom Carlyle must come to terms is his Aunt Pearl. It is immediately apparent from his hostile reaction that her memory is a most unwelcome one. 'Why should he remember Aunt Pearl and Willis's balloon! To hell with you, Aunt Pearl!... To hell to hell to hell with you!' (5) he thinks when she pops into his mind just as he is happily anticipating having lunch with Victoria. Thoughts of Aunt Pearl portend disappointment and loss: she is the person most closely associated with Carlyle's first fall from childhood grace when, upon his mother's death, he was immediately orphaned by his father, who could not cope with his own grief, let alone with a small child's needs.

At Aunt Pearl's, the six-year-old Carlyle has toys to play with and plenty of time on his hands, but no love. The big house is like a sterile tomb smelling of charred string burnt by his aunt to kill odours of any kind. The lonely attic playroom becomes a prison which Carlyle learns to hate, inventing reasons which will keep him occupied elsewhere. He routinely invades his aunt's pristine bedroom, where he moves the neatly placed items on her bird's-eye maple dresser to see if his aunt will notice and thereby become more aware of him. His actions become increasingly motivated by a need to assert his presence, to break through the vacuum of cleanliness, order, and neatness, in search of warmth and comfort. Thus, when he blows up the balloons, he does it not because he wants to play with them but because 'he had the feeling she wouldn't have liked it for him to blow them up and spoil their tight, smooth newness – like the wrinkled, blue one' (310). His final experiment with the magic lantern is motivated by that same need and is ultimately successful in securing his freedom and the right to return home to his father where he belongs.

His aunt, then, is the puritanical element in his life. Her obsession with neatness and order, her gentle but unyielding stubbornness, have left a mark on Carlyle which influences his later behaviour towards anything or anyone not 'quite civilized,' and leads him to try 'to keep the lid on a sensual, pagan culture he has been taught to abhor' (Robertson 31). One suspects that it is Aunt Pearl's influence that pushes Carlyle to find in Victoria that which is not altogether 'Indian': 'She can't be all Stoney, Peter... I mean – Indian' (146). This would explain his angry reaction when Victoria joins her friends in the 'Chicken Dance train, her head forward, face turned upwards, her right hand holding a twig to her rump for prairie-chicken tail-feathers' (207). When he grabs her roughly to pull her away from the other children, he cannot explain what motivates him:

> 'What's wrong with it, Mr. Sinclair?'
> What could he say to her! 'It's – I just don't want you to, Victoria.'
> 'Is there anything wrong with it, Mr. Sinclair?' she persisted.
> 'I don't want you to, and that's enough!' (208)

Aunt Pearl's obsession with smell may also be responsible for Carlyle's 'WASP respect for cleanliness' (Robertson 31) and underlies his action to 'purify' the air in the school room by keeping a mixture of disinfectant and water boiling on the school stove, ostensibly to kill germs.

The puritanical influence in Carlyle's childhood is further strengthened through contact with Mr Macky, his teacher in grade six. Old Kacky, as the children call him, is a man of straight and meticulous lines. Precision is his credo, except when it comes to the parts of the human anatomy which concern reproduction.

The drawing of the urinary system is 'terminally incomplete' and 'sex surfaced only in grammar, with the personal pronoun possessing the gerund and the chaste union of subject and predicate by non-thrusting copulative verb' (315).

Art class becomes an exercise in rigid accuracy: trees are not living organisms, they are skeletons with various names and have to be 'covered with short hair-strokes' or shaded 'in puffy clouds of leaves' (317). When Carlyle tries to 'beautify' his own drawing of the vanishing point by adding a few trees and bushes to the otherwise 'empty' landscape of straight lines (319), his brief attempt at individuality and imagination is brutally crushed by his teacher. A drawing of precision may not be spoiled by trees, gophers, and birds. What is in reality a statement of identity and an indication of creativity on the part of the young Carlyle is seen by his teacher as a deliberate act of insubordination, even vandalism, that merits a severe beating.

It is interesting to note that Carlyle realizes that his teacher's reaction is an attempt to diminish him; after the strapping, he is left in the teacher's office, isolated from the rest of the class, feeling threatened: 'Old Kacky had vanished him from them to vanishment. And then the really crazy thought happened. He was being vanished from himself ... stepping outside and apart and walking away farther and farther from himself, getting smaller and smaller and smaller ... dwindling right down to a point. That was crazy and enough to scare the shit out of a person!' (322). Through the striking repetition of the root word 'vanish' in various grammatical forms, Mitchell emphasizes the negative effect the ruthless abuse of power by adult care-givers can have on a budding child consciousness. Carlyle not only dreads exclusion from his peer group, but more importantly, he feels his very being, his personhood, under attack and fears annihilation. While he does not immediately regret his act of 'deliberate disobedience' (321), despite the painful punishment it engenders, his teacher's reaction nevertheless marks him. He learns that to succeed, one must follow rules, obey laws, and adhere to a 'proper' code of conduct designed to suppress individual impulses. To do otherwise implies personal suffering, shame, and guilt. Thus, as an adult, he can accept the other Native children on their own terms because they do not matter to him personally, but Victoria, being his favourite and, unconsciously, the sum total of his own projected accomplishments, must be made to conform to a 'proper' standard. Instead of learning from the pain of his own experience, he perpetuates the tyranny, albeit in a gentler form. He expects Victoria to vanish into his vision of her and forgets his friend Mate's warning that, while the vanishing point which they were taught to draw with meticulous precision by Old Kacky might indeed look real enough, it is, in fact, only an illusion.

As Carlyle's search for Victoria becomes more desperate, he begins to realize that finding her has become crucial to his own survival and is in some strange way linked to the search of his past: indeed had never lost her – or Old Kacky. How about his father?' (324) He realizes that he has difficulty remembering his father's face: he cannot associate it with any concrete sign of love or emotion of any kind: 'No ears that called attention to themselves – no eyes that committed in any way; forehead, chin, nose making no statement of their own. Plato's pattern of a face' (324). He can remember the housekeeper Olga, her warmth, her tenderness; he can remember Mate, his best friend. But his father's memory produces only a sense of void: 'They had been so terribly efficient with each other. It had been as though his father had decided that emotion was waste. It left Carlyle with a feeling of loss; it made him deliberately perform for his father, wanting to do things that would please him. But his father had never really let him know that he had, beyond a few times when there had come an expression of intensity on his face' (332–33). Thoughts of his father are related to the pictures of skinless bodies exposing the various human organs for study, which he had seen in his father's medical books. There are no memories of a warm smile or of comforting arms. Carlyle realizes that his father had been unable to give him the love he so desperately required. They had been two people apart: 'you in your small corner and I in mine' (336).

Bly suggests that 'not seeing your father when you are small, never being with him, having a remote father, an absent father, a workaholic father, is an injury' to the development of the child which can affect him or her for life. He goes on to state that 'having a critical, judgmental father' can be even more damaging, comparing it 'to being one of Cronos' sons, whom Cronos ate,' thus, suggesting that it can amount to being swallowed up by one's parent and, hence, vanishing (31).

Carlyle's determination to make a difference in Paradise Valley may thus be directly linked to his need to 'perform for his father,' to live up to his father's expectations, and thus to ensure his very survival. His obsessive need to see Victoria succeed in a 'White' profession stems from this same desire to succeed in his father's eyes. Her achievements will be the living proof that he has succeeded in some tangible way, in a way that matters to the society to which he belongs. He is incapable of conceiving that this success may not be of any great importance to Victoria's society or to her as an individual with her own priorities and her own agenda. Hence, her disappearance and the threat that she would not prove equal to his expectations are a direct threat to his self esteem, to his very being: 'He could not tell which drove him more, his own need or hers. If he were honest with himself – probably his own. It did frighten; it was so goddam ridiculous and unheard of: that Carlyle Sinclair wasn't. You couldn't, for God's sake, deny your own existence' (323).

Carlyle's inability to admit that his growing attachment to Victoria is anything more than a purely Platonic relationship may also be linked to his father's cerebral and puritanical approach to life and love. Carnal love, according to the older Sinclair, was a secret exercise, not to be talked about; something related to Sadie Rossdance and her girls; something involving shame. With such an example in his past, how could Carlyle feel sexual passions for his 'little lamb,' Victoria? Again, what his 'little lamb' might actually need and feel is not a consideration.

It is not surprising, therefore, that Carlyle's response to Victoria's pregnancy is so violent. For him it means the shattering of all his dreams. Her 'failure,' as he sees it, signifies his failure, indeed, the failure of all her people: 'If I've failed with her – I've failed with all of them ... Victoria is one knocked-up mess! I am! The Stoneys are!' (373–74). As this statement would indicate, Victoria's 'loss of innocence' signifies, for Carlyle, a total loss of worth. Like Fyfe's prize orchid which had been 'entered' by the intruder bee and 'spoiled' for any further use (94), Victoria now is blemished. She has 'failed him! Utterly!' (381).

Carlyle's first impulse is to kill all sensations of tenderness within himself, to dispel all loving thoughts, 'admit not one hurtful memory ray of feeling' (380). This is his time of ultimate suffering, his moment of utter darkness. However, in the end, his true feelings for Victoria will not permit him to inflict further suffering on her. His determination to reject love is shattered when he sees Victoria sitting alone and abandoned at the dance. While he cannot bring himself to approach her, he cannot refuse her when she approaches him. The suffering and pain of his search for Victoria and his ultimate despair when he finds her have been powerful experiences for Carlyle which serve as a lesson that the success of all human relationships depends on genuine reciprocity: 'Man lifted bridges between himself and other men so that he could walk from his own heart and into other hearts ... How could he have forgotten that! ... Victoria had not truly failed, but he had' (385). When they leave the dance, Carlyle and Victoria walk side by side.

Later, he wonders why he had not known that he loved her; why it had taken him so long to acknowledge his love. 'His life just hadn't taught him how. It had given him the wrong commandments' (388), through care-givers who, like Aunt Pearl, believed in neatness, cleanliness, and whiteness, but not affection; who, like Mr Macky, denied even the existence of physical love; who, like his father, regarded love either as a shameful deed or as an abstraction. In an interview with David O'Rourke, Mitchell emphasizes the importance of balance in a mind-oriented world: 'You simply have to be a good balancer ... One has to, more than one does, trust the intuitive, gut, empathetic response of love, which includes the sex act.' He goes on to say that 'technology, religion, mysticism, myth won't work, but what will work ... is love. Which covers a lot of things. But – even though civilized – one has to trust the intuitive, gut, heart response' (156).

Life had taught Carlyle to erect and maintain barriers, dams that would check the flood tides of emotions so that they could be channelled into an orderly, predictable stream which would eventually be reduced to a harmless trickle. His journey through pain has, however, weakened these barriers and heightened his awareness of his own needs, paramount of which is the need to love and to be loved. Through love, which, by its very nature, suggests death and rebirth, Carlyle is enabled to break through the barriers of his past, to die to his old self, as it were, and hope for a fresh beginning.

Carlyle has emerged from the dark sterility of self-absorption within which he tended to reduce all otherness to sameness in the image of himself. He has now reached a level of understanding which leads him to reject his old values and to embrace that which is other or obect in love. Watching Ezra's little grandson playing in the water, Carlyle thinks:

> Dear little bare-bum shaman, I am here – I'm standing here. Oh, let me show you to you – I want to mirror you so you may be more nearly true! ... Trust me now. I promise you I won't destroy you with distorted image. I will not turn you into a backward person. At least I will try not to. Let's you and I conjure together. You watch me and I'll watch you and I will show you how to show me how to show you how to do our marvelous human tricks together. (389)

His new world is filled with wonder, a wonder which is fuelled by physical love now fully acknowledged: 'Black was the colour of her hair, in a dark scarf laid down over her cheek. Black was the lovely curve of her lashes. Freckles still spiced beneath her closed eyes. Look at me – look at me! No – don't wake yet, my sleeping love ...' (387). His wonder-filled love for Victoria leads Carlyle to a new vision of his surroundings which, thanks to the rebirth of the river Beulah, are now replete with signs of new life and abundance.

For Blake, it is in Beulah (the Hebrew word for 'marriage') that the relation of subject and object is transformed into the union of lover and beloved (*Fearful Symmetry* 49, 135); 'it is in Beulah that the sexual aspect of life becomes fulfilled' (*Fearful Symmetry* 196).

Carlyle's ability to accept Victoria and her unborn child in marriage shows that he is now finally able to love in the true sense of the word:

Love seeketh not Itself to please,
Nor in itself hath any care,
But for another gives its ease,
And builds a Heaven in Hell's despair.
        (Blake, 'The Clod & the Pebble')

Spring has come at last, and this time it is the real thing. Beulah Creek is overflowing, reborn at last; it had been on the point of vanishing, but no more. Nature has overcome the obstacles of man and is 'breaking free in a fresh place' (390).

NOTES

1 In her insightful Jungian study on human development, entitled *The Hero Within*, Carol Pearson describes six principal human archetypes. She charts the human journey from the original state of Innocence, which she terms the 'prefallen state of grace' (4), to the inevitable Orphan state. She sees these two primary archetypal modes as '[setting] the stage' (4) for later phases of the human being's passage through life, with the Orphan state as the inevitable first experience of disenchantment when 'Shades of the prison-house begin to close / Upon the growing Boy...' (William Wordsworth, 'Ode: Intimations of Immortality from Recollections of Early Childhood').

2 In an interview with David O'Rourke several years after the publication of *The Vanishing Point*, Mitchell depicts Beulah rather negatively as 'a dreadful place of adult people ... a nonescape' (153). These comments must, however, be read in context. Mitchell is referring, at this point, to 'those people who are now adult and civilized but think the answer lies back in trying to recapture the innocence of childhood.' Beulah, in *The Vanishing Point*, does not represent such an 'escape'; rather, it is a symbol of understanding of self and thus of the possibility of mature, adult love. For the seekers of escape, it is not the answer. But for those who, like Carlyle, have confronted the reality of their childhood experience, the 'breaking out' of the Beulah represents a new beginning.

3 It is, of course, important to realize, as Pearson suggests, that the human journey through the various archetypal patterns of behaviour is not usually

straightforward. According to Pearson, 'these heroic modes are developmental, but they actually are not experienced in linear, ever-advancing steps ... The typical hero's progression [is rather like] a cone or three-dimensional spiral, in which it is possible to move forward while frequently circling back' (13). If the individual is fortunate he or she may reach the final stage or archetypal mode of the Magician, who will be able to 'claim the universe as home, a friendly, inviting place to be, and in doing so, ... reclaim innocence' (117). Thus the circle would be completed, and the individual would actually realize his or her quest to rediscover the innate wisdom of his origin.

Quest in W.O. Mitchell's
Since Daisy Creek

CATHERINE McLAY

'Who Has Seen the Bear?' is the title Mitchell might well have chosen for his fifth published novel. For *Since Daisy Creek* explores a search or quest which arises out of a failed attempt to return to the wilderness and emerge a hero. Colin Dobbs, failed husband and father, artist *manqué* and creative writing professor, has turned to hunting to escape his mid-life crisis. But his attempt to escape from failed relationships and academic sterility to the more 'real' world of primitive ritual leads to a literal life crisis. Dobbs barely escapes death. His whole right side is scarred by the raking claws of a sow grizzly. Like Mel Gibson in *The Man without a Face*, he arouses terror in those who see him, or so he believes. Moreover, like Gibson's character, he has to look back over his whole life, face his own dark side, and resolve the conflicts, both without and within, that have brought him to this point. But the grizzly is not yet finished. For when Dobbs unwraps what is supposed to be his magnificent hide before a party of friends and colleagues, he exposes instead the hide of a small brown bear. His recourse, to take Wild Trophy World to court to recover his trophy, shows that he has not yet learned his lesson. It is only when he concedes defeat that the sow grizzly up Daisy Creek really changes his life. For she has taught him humility, charity, mercy, and the true nature of love.

In this complex and often profound novel, published when he was seventy, W.O. Mitchell has described the inner journey of a man entering the second half of life, a man who symbolically dies and who, in returning, undergoes a spiritual transformation. During this journey he must come to terms not only with his ex-wife and daughter, but also with his dead mother, his unknown father, and his own feminine or creative self. In *Since Daisy Creek*, Mitchell tells us, more fully than in any other of his fictions, what it means to be human and flawed, yet searching for grace.

The genesis of this story was a real incident which occurred some thirty years previously, an actual bear hunt which Mitchell took part in up Dolly Creek, west of High River. As Mitchell has described the experience to Peter Gzowski on *Morningside*, he joined several hunter friends but was himself armed only with a book and pencil. From his retreat, he watched a female grizzly come out of the bushes, lift up the bait, a poisoned horse carcass, with its 'garden of entrails dangling,' and walk away (Gzowski 1985).

Ten years later, Mitchell drew on this incident for his radio play, 'The Trophy,' broadcast on Sunday, 19 January 1964. This episode was the thirteenth and last of a radio series, *Foothill Fables*, which ran as a successor to the very popular *Jake and the Kid* series. Even at this point, however, Mitchell recognized that the story had the potential for something greater. At the end of the draft he sent to Morris Surdin, his musical collaborator, he penned: 'Sorry not to have given you more time on this one, Morris – for it could be the best of the series,' adding that he knew Morris would 'come through' as always, in spite of the shortness of time ('Trophy' 25–26)![1]

'The Trophy' presents the story in a more basic form than the later *Since Daisy Creek*, although it is already relatively sophisticated in its treatment. Narrated by Dr Bruce, the town doctor of Shelby (the fictional High River), it employs three time sequences: events leading up to the hunt; the consequences of the hunt; and the party to celebrate the unwrapping of the grizzly hide trophy. The central character, Donald Armstrong, in some ways resembles Mitchell himself. He shares with him a Saskatchewan boyhood and a physical weakness, a tuberculous wrist developed at age twelve, which 'denied him an athletic adolescence or later experience of war' (6–7). Unlike Mitchell, however, Donald is a real estate agent who has spent thirteen years in a search to test himself against the wilderness, 'one opportunity... [to] face violence – fear – and be a hero'(11). The grizzly bear is the perfect quarry, and Donald boasts of his 'perfect kill': 'He puffed up – his – every hair stood on electric end – I can't forget that moment forever... it was *fair* – and he nearly got me' (17–18).

Already in this story there are elements which suggest future possibilities. Donald is not permanently scarred, but he is clawed, needs extensive stitches, and spends two weeks in hospital. His guide, Peter Powderface, plays a small role but will develop into Archie Nicotine, one of Mitchell's best characterizations in *The Vanishing Point* and *Since Daisy Creek*. The crisis in 'The Trophy' occurs close to the end of the radio play, when Donald unwraps the hide, not of his magnificent grizzly, but of a small American brown bear shot by an American hunter from Minnesota. The story closes with music which Morris is invited to translate from Mitchell's notation: '*Wry comment and finale – Oh My – Oh My*' (25).

While Dr Bruce is a neutral narrator, his wife Sadie comments pointedly on the ethics, not only of using poisoned bait, but of hunting itself as a male ritual, criticisms later voiced by Dobbs's daughter Annie. There are, as well, elements of social satire. Donald's new suburban home in Meadowlark Park has risen in five years from raw prairie, yet the rhythms of the subdivision still follow the beat of the Stoney Bear Dance (3). And Donald ironically describes the businessmen as modern hunters 'hunting your commission at the Petroleum Club water hole – begging your contracts at the salt lick – business lunch' (25). Donald even proposes here that Bear was the first artist: '[Bear] clawed the cave wall and then man put his palm print there by the claw marks and that was the first painting' (24). And he suggests that the hunt, too, is an art form: 'you haven't a possible hope of ever understanding why a man might hunt ... or why Hardy wrote *Jude the Obscure* or Katherine Mansfield did *The Doll's House*' (23).

During the next eighteen years, both the passing of time and certain events and realizations contributed to the development of this amusing hunting story into a much broader and more complex work. First, the setting of the novel changed when Mitchell accepted the invitation of the University of Calgary to become writer-in-residence. In 1968, he and Merna left High River and bought a home in the city. In 1971, while he was completing *The Vanishing Point*, he told several of us in his creative writing class of a second novel which involved the substitution of one bear hide for another, and commented that it would be a study in corruption, both academic and societal. The protagonist was now a professor and the party guilty of changing the hides was the taxidermy firm. During the next twelve years, Mitchell had an opportunity to study several other campuses where he was a lecturer or writer-in-residence: the universities of Alberta and Toronto, York University, and the University of Windsor, where he spent five of the most productive years of his life. The events and situations, even the buildings of Livingstone University, are drawn from all of these as well as from Trent University, where his son Ormond was teaching.

Also during these years, the Mitchells' daughter, Willa Lynne, grew up and became an artist. She is the model for Annie, the first really strong female portrait in Mitchell's fiction.[2] As well, Mitchell came to terms with the memory of his mother, who had died in 1960, through writing *How I Spent My Summer Holidays* (Orm Mitchell, 149–50). Mitchell is thus freer in treating Dobbs's relationship with his mother, and the need to accept and forgive before he can achieve healing himself.

Finally, the experiences of Colin Dobbs are drawn from two periods in Mitchell's own life (though the novel is not autobiographical in the true sense of the word), and these make Dobbs a much richer character than Donald Armstrong of 'The Trophy.' Dobbs's situation as a failed writer draws from the period around 1960 when Mitchell had two failed novels on his hands, *The Alien* and *Roses Are Difficult Here* (finally revised and published in 1991), and no successful work to follow his classic *Who Has Seen the Wind* in thirteen years. Indeed, Dobbs is given the short story 'Roses are Difficult Here' as an 'Atlantic First,' like Mitchell's own 'The Owl and the Bens' and 'Saint Sammy' from *Who Has Seen the Wind*, to point up the comparison. While Mitchell had other successes during these years, including the *Jake and the Kid* series and several versions of *The Black Bonspiel of Wullie MacCrimmon*, he has expressed for us the pain and frustration of this period in his life in his depiction of Colin Dobbs's blocked writing. Colin's physical suffering, his sense of humilation at the demands of the body, derive from a period much closer to the revised version. At age sixty-five, Mitchell broke several vertebrae while demonstrating double flip somersaults to his grandchildren. The hospitalization and subsequent years of therapy and exercises give life to Colin's aches of the flesh and spirit after his encounter with the sow grizzly.

All of these elements combine to give *Since Daisy Creek* a breadth and depth of vision that 'The Trophy' lacks. Yet the core is still the story of the hunt. It is central to Dobbs's lost art and to his escape from his failed relationships. Colin himself links all three, admitting that his first hunt five years earlier had followed his wife Sarah's move to Victoria with Annie: 'Several times he had tried to return to his writing for surcease. It hadn't worked. He had taken up something less dangerous than marriage: bear hunting' (94). And Annie points out that the year he stopped writing was the year his marriage with her mother went 'sour': 'Why the hell were you chasing after bears in the first place! I'll tell you why! It's because you'd quit writing' (241).

Colin's escape to the primitive ritual of the hunt is similar to Donald Armstrong's in 'The Trophy,' to 'face violence – fear – and be a hero' ('Trophy' 11). It is a return to an earlier world where man was triumphant over the natural world and the male role as hunter and provider was celebrated. But in the later novel, the treatment of the hunt is more mythic. Indeed, it is antecedent to the action and the actual events are not described to us in full until a late stage when Colin is forced to relive in a waking state the horror and fear he had felt. William French's review of *Since Daisy Creek*, 'Ahab of Alberta,' points out the parallel to Melville's *Moby Dick*, where the search for the great white whale becomes an obsession which Captain Ahab cannot escape and which ultimately destroys him. Colin Dobbs is scarred like Ahab, but not destroyed. Instead, like Ishmael, he must return, an 'ancient mariner' doomed to recount his story for the rest of his life. He is not allowed to disappear into a nineteenth-century wilderness but must enter again his own society, resolve his relationships with the world, and learn to know himself. Thus the search for the bear becomes Colin's search for himself, a symbolic inner journey which he must complete to find wholeness.

One of the most significant changes in the story is the sex of the bear. The bear in 'The Trophy' was male, although Mitchell's recollection of the original incident in the 1950s identifies the bear as female (Gzowski 1985). All the great quest stories of the past which involve animals or birds have employed males, perhaps because they are the strongest or most powerful adversaries and because there is a metaphoric identity between hunter and hunted. One can cite *Moby Dick*, Faulkner's version of man versus bear in 'The Bear,' Jack London's *White Fang*, E.J. Pratt's 'The Cachalot,' and Mitchell's own gander Old Croaker in *The Kite*. Presumably after 1964, Mitchell began to consider the symbolic value of employing a sow grizzly. On a surface level, Colin has clearly rejected the females in his life: his mother, Sarah, and any successors of Sarah, in particular Liz Skeffington. When Annie was born, Colin vowed: 'She'll be better than any damn man!' (178), but Sarah complained that he was attempting to turn her into a boy by teaching her to fish and to tie flies. Her revenge was to send Annie to a ladies' college in the East, then to remove her to Victoria. Thus Colin has lost the one female that he can connect with and, as well, his own role as father. Escaping from females, Colin encountered the sow grizzly up Daisy Creek; he describes this in sexual terms, as an 'embrace,' which he likens in its after-effects to rape (5).

But the encounter with the bear is also archetypal. Colin himself is identified with the bear in the frequent references to his basement 'cave,' where he retreated from his marriage, and to the 'den' in which he proposes to display his trophy hide. Indeed, Colin is at war with a more significant female, his own anima. In 'The Stages of Life,' Carl Jung first observed certain characteristics of mid-life, including a fear of approaching the 'afternoon phases,' but also a need to develop the unexplored parts of the personality. This often took the form of a crossing-over of the sexes. Thus the male, preoccupied in the past with his achievements, his career, and his competitiveness, in his forties needs to turn to his more feminine side, to a concern for relationships and connection with others. Even his body becomes more feminine. In contrast, women turn more to their individual needs and self-fulfilment (12–18). In the novel, Colin has repeatedly chosen the masculine in his career and marriage, the competitive, the intellectual, and the rational. His creative side is blocked. It is the sow grizzly up Daisy Creek who forces him to face his feminine self, by raking her powerful claws across his right or dominant side, almost blinding his right eye, and tearing across his right chest and arm. Although he is not wounded sexually, as he assures us, he is emasculated. His right cheek will never grow hair. He is physically weak and dependent, subject to the control of others: doctors and nurses, his daughter, the department head.

Now Colin can no longer deny the body and its humiliations and live only in his mind. The pain and suffering he undergoes lead him to recognize pain and loss, both physical and mental, in others. And by disabling his right side, with its connection to the left and rational brain, the bear forces him to turn to the right or creative brain. Thus, the bear is not only a vehicle for the revenge of Nature and the feminine which he has abused; she is also a guide. Through her, he can overcome the block in his writing and attain artistic maturity.

Mitchell's choice of a university setting for *Since Daisy Creek* is also significant. The absurdity of the university scenes and the elements of fantasy and the grotesque may serve to puzzle or confuse readers. Indeed, Jamie Portman entitled his review of the novel 'Comic Flights Muddle Complexities in New Novel.' Mitchell has been prone in previous works to scenes of fantasy, such as the marvellous passage in *The Vanishing Point* where Carlyle sees a collection of lawn ornaments – bambis, dwarfs, bear cubs, and does – begin to propagate on their own until 'the entire defenceless world would be up to its arse in fluorescent flamingoes!' (*Vanishing Point* 41). But in *Since Daisy Creek*, the fantasy and satire are more integral. The corruption embraces the university, the courts, and society as a whole.

In his 'Theory of Myths,' Northrop Frye examines the phase of winter in literary works. In this phase, irony and satire predominate and these often serve as parody of romance (the *mythos* of summer). Frye differentiates between satire and irony: 'satire is militant irony: its moral norms are relatively clear, and it assumes standards against which the grotesque and absurd are measured' (*Anatomy of Criticism* 223). While anti-intellectualism is sometimes characteristic of works in this phase, an attack on ivory towers and pedantry, true anti-intellectual satire points up 'the comparative naivete of systematic thought' and is not cynical or bitter (*Anatomy* 230). Another aspect of this phase is the 'disappearance of the heroic' (228). *Since Daisy Creek* fits Frye's definitions of this phase. Colin's life is decadent, in the period of winter, as Livingstone University and the unnamed foothills city are decadent. Heroism no longer exists. In tone, the novel bears some resemblance to Swift's *Gulliver's Travels*, in particular the satire on the universities and sciences of book 3. Mitchell, too, exposes hypocrisy, ambition, pedantry, greed, and corruption in his contemporary Livingstone U.

Mitchell is obviously enjoying his lampoon. The new university president, Cal Donaldson, wears a freshman beanie, uses his influence to get his novel read, and ultimately is found to have a mail-order degree (a situation which in fact occurred at the University of Victoria). The head of Native Studies, from Toronto's affluent and Waspish Rosedale, is a Grey Owl look-alike who performs Native sweet-grass ceremonies in the university lounges. Liz Skeffington sleeps her way to an appointment as assistant professor and pursues Colin in his office across a carpet of term papers. Some of the scenes are more specifically black comedy. The fountains of Kathleen McNair College bubble up with foam, and hundreds of goldfish die from detergent as a result of student pranks. The fire alarms of Wapta Towers go off during an oral examination of a creative writing student as a result of Whyte of Native Studies burning alder shavings in a metal dish.

The university is sterile, empty, even grotesque. Colin's vision of the whole institution, expressed at his lowest point, is in fact the view that led him to attempt to return to the natural and primitive world of the hunt in the first place. His recent visit to Wild Trophy World influences his choice of metaphor:

> Sick of academe, where magpies, crows, and ravens in their black gowns hook their hoods, set their mortar-boards, then glide off and alight before that stuffed ground owl in black and gold chancellor robes, to carry off rolled and ribboned B.A.'s, M.A.'s, and Ph.D.'s in eager beaks while learned head-mounts look down on solemn ceremony. Master Bear presides, as learned moose and caribou, scholarly elk and deer and sheep and goats gather in their department herds. (136)

Colin's return to the world of romance, the heroic world where the dragon may be slain, is blocked. Mauled by the sow grizzly, and passing through a symbolic death, he is denied heroism. When, after many months in hospital and at home, he comes back to the university he cannot escape, he comes to recognize he is a different person. Standing by his office door to read his name, Dr C. Dobbs, and last year's office hours, he comments: 'Wrong term. Wrong year. It was now another Dr. C. Dobbs' (57). The anger he feels is not so much against his individual fate as it is against the human condition: 'Not against the bear and Tait and Skeffington so much as against this body he was trapped in. Mortification of the flesh wasn't what it was cracked up to be. The logical destination of stoicism had to be self-destruction, for only then could there be freedom from the tyranny of this too, too solid flesh' (75). Despite his awareness of the body, Colin is still operating from his left or rational brain, as evidenced by the quotation from *Hamlet*. He, like Hamlet, is too introspective, as underlined by his recollection, immediately following this passage, of Sarah's acid comment: 'You never look *out*! You're always looking *in*!' And he internalizes her voice: 'Anything outside yourself doesn't interest you! Anything or anybody! You are a selfish son-of-a-bitch!' (75).

Colin's real journey does not begin until half-way through the novel. Abandoned by Annie for too long at the reception for the new president, he gets disgustingly drunk, throws up at home, and has to face Annie's cold shoulder the next morning at breakfast. To escape her and also to calm himself, he decides to visit the mixed sauna on campus. His encounter there with Helen Sweeney, the exchange professor from Lausanne, and her teenage son Robin, is a turning-point in coming to terms both with his physical condition and his connection to others. When he first sees Helen and turns away from her exposed body, he shows identification and compassion: 'it had to be the first time since Daisy Creek he'd averted his face for someone else's sake' (145). Seated two levels above Helen and to her right, Colin observes the towel over her right shoulder shift to reveal the scar where her breast has been removed. Colin's move down and to the left, like Helen's to the right, is symbolic, a move away from separation. As they talk first about their humiliations and then about their scars under the signs of Ursus and Cancer, both face their own wounds and give up self-consciousness.

While Colin does not encounter Helen again, he pays tribute to her in the last words of the novel, where he tells Annie that he began to change the day he 'went into the sauna to sweat the poison out' and met a woman who helped him to get 'rid of quite a lot' (277). The meeting has an immediate effect, however, for Colin begins to talk to Annie about his early life and his own mother. Annie Dobbs died at fifty-one while Colin, Sarah, and young Annie were in England, from 'a mastectomy she never told me about' (151). After the funeral he went to visit his 'Aunt' Nell in a mental home, but she was unable to recognize him. At this point, Colin tells Annie the true story of his life: of the mother who emigrated from Ireland, became a chambermaid at the Chateau Laurier, and then a housekeeper for Aunt Nell; of the father whom no one knew – 'Some travelling pharmaceutical or dry goods or fountain pen or encyclopaedia salesman,' perhaps even the Prime Minister or the Leader of the Opposition (149). Colin admits to feeling the loss of his mother but remarks of his unknown father, 'no big deal.' When Annie asks later – 'Do you wonder about him? Who he was – what he might be like?' – Colin denies it: 'When I was a child maybe... Lots of people lose their fathers one way or another. If it's going to happen, then I guess mine was as good a way as any' (166–67). He has suppressed his anger at his mother, perhaps for depriving him of a father. But now he begins to recall his childhood fiction that his mother was not really his mother. As he recalls these memories after his meeting with Helen in the sauna, his relationship to his mother begins to heal.

It is Annie who functions as guide on Colin's inner journey. An unlikely Cordelia, she nevertheless becomes a mediator, both by forcing Colin to explore his own motivations and hopes, and by her action in interpreting him through a series of portraits, which she undertakes as an assignment for her art class. Colin, like Lear, has given away his kingdom, here the kingdom of art, and, like Lear, he is alone, physically dependent, hating his own weakness and the humiliation of his body. Colin resists the portraits, still trying to preserve appearances, but Annie retorts: 'I am not interested in your surface! I'm interested in *you* ... The guy I've built inside of me all my life! The person I don't think is scarred' (152). The surface scarring she refers to is emotional, the damage caused by his marriage and its break-up, by the hypocrisy of his teaching students that they must write 'every day, every week, every year' while not writing himself; and by his unethical hunting down of a grizzly bear for its hide. In donning Colin's old shirt, left over from the days of his refuge in his basement 'den,' Annie takes on Colin's self behind the persona. As she paints, Colin opens himself up to her, the first human being he has been able to do so with, letting her find 'her image of him inside herself. Or his – inside himself' (154). While Colin is posing 'in limbo' and Annie is absorbed in line and colour, they return to their old relationship of her childhood: 'removed from each other, yet they were quite close. The old camp-fire magic' (154).

The series of portraits which Annie paints shows a progression from an interpretation of Colin's past to a prophecy of his future. While Annie denies any conscious intent, the first portrait depicts a headless figure with its hands 'crab-clawed,' turned down over nothing. Colin realizes with a sickening sensation the significance of the pose – no typewriter, no guiding mind – a non-writer (161). Another portrait he describes as 'the last of the mole people'

(163), still living in the burrows or caves and not emerged into light. Still another, done in blobs of yellow, he repudiates, 'Jesus Christ, I haven't got jaundice!' (163).

But the final painting, of head and shoulders only, is the most striking, for it shows a Colin who could be. It is unfinished, or rather done 'as much as it ever will be.' The eyes are closed. The head is slanted down and to the right with the light shining on the left, the creative and instinctual side which Colin has so far denied. The wounded masculine side is 'simply sad in shadow' (168). This is a Colin who has reached the end of his journey, who is reconciled with others and with himself.

By this point, Colin has come to terms with his concern with appearances, he has started to heal relationships with his dead mother and his recovered daughter, and he has begun to accept his own inner self and his incompleteness. Indeed, he is even making amends to his ex-wife, for he gives Annie the Christmas present of a cheque for air fare to Vancouver Island: 'It's also a present to your mother... She probably misses you as much as I did... She needs you too. Spend New Year's with her' (189).

But the real test is yet to come. For it is at this point that Mitchell introduces the problem with which 'The Trophy' closes: the discovery of the small brown bear-hide instead of that of the magnificent plains grizzly. But now the substitution is clearly deliberate. The Christmas party that Annie has arranged to celebrate the installation of the trophy in Colin's den is destroyed before his eyes as he removes the brown paper wrapping. Colin's pride is humiliated. Donald Armstrong justified his killing of the bear, 'he's beautiful and he damn near got me – but I got him and he's mine,' and he boasted 'they don't come any bigger – more dangerous or more elusive than my grizzly' ('The Trophy' 15, 19). But the experience is transformed for Colin into something deeper – a justification of his past life and a restitution of his losses. The revelation of the small and rather insignificant brown hide takes Colin back into the nightmare of the hunt and the actual events of the bear's attack. For the first time we are given a full account of what occurred before the opening of the novel. This nightmare develops further into a judgment:

The circle dream that returned to him again and again was a new and dreadful one. Inside meant to be destroyed by suffocation; outside meant he no longer was. He had been a bastard child, an adolescent, become a teacher, an almost-writer, was now a middle-aged cripple. All of these should belong to each other and they no longer did, for he seemed to keep losing the self key and was locked out from them ... Death does not mean I end, for there was no I to die. (183–84)

This feeling of annihilation should lead to the next stage of the spiritual journey, from Thomas Carlyle's 'Everlasting No' to acceptance and ultimately the 'Everlasting Yea.' But Colin turns away from these depths, refuses to give up his pride, which has given him an identity, and demands retribution. Against the advice of Annie, of Archie Nicotine, even of his own lawyer, he determines to take Wild Trophy World to court, to expose the fraud which has exchanged his hide for that of a hunter from Minnesota. The firm has an impeccable record, established by the father of the present owner, Andrew Munro. It has provided mounted specimens for museums around the world. The substitution is clearly the work of Mr Munro's grandson, son of his own dead son. To take the case to court will ruin the firm and old Mr Munro.

While Colin decides to proceed with the trial, he also begins to consider the cost of his actions to others. The process he goes through is connected to his growing awareness of how he has repressed his need for a father, and how he has both sought and denied the father in others. The most extreme of Mitchell's fatherless protagonists, Colin has no memories of being fathered at all. In his anger at his mother, he had dreamt of a father who would be a companion, who would skate and fish with him (181), dreams that he later attempted to transfer to Annie. But even these were destroyed when, at age fifteen, he was told he was a bastard. Even his choice of occupation had been determined by the absence of a father: 'Maybe it had been inevitable that he should end up a teacher, the father he'd been denied – to others' (181).

Like Mitchell himself, Colin has had an academic mentor as a father-figure. Based on Dr F.M. Salter, Mitchell's mentor at the University of Alberta, Dr Lyon has taught Colin the writing of the great masters of English literature and has also shaped his future. For Colin, this involved taking a master's degree at the University of Toronto, a Woodrow Wilson fellowship to study in London, then a job at Queen's University and later at Livingstone, all with Dr Lyon's support. But the novel does not really explore this relationship and Dr Lyon's only real connection to the action is his contribution to the break-up of Colin's marriage to Sarah. The episode is farcical but also symbolic. Dr Lyon leaves his old, incontinent dog Polly to the care of the Dobbs while he is on sabbatical. Sarah demands that the dog sleep outside in a doghouse and she dies. Unable to bury her by the river till spring, when the ground unfreezes, Colin puts the body in Sarah's freezer, to be found one day when she is searching for meat for dinner. Like the bear, the dog is female, another contributor to his failure.

A more significant father-figure in terms of the novel is Archie Nicotine. He is Colin's guide into the wilderness, both literally and figuratively. The knowledge he passes to Colin he has learned from his own father, passed down through the tribe of Stoneys. He too contributed to the break-up of Colin's marriage, giving Colin a set of elk-hooves which Colin installed over Sarah's laundry tubs using her clothesline. In each case, Colin placed his male relationships over his relationship with his wife. But Archie is also Colin's deliverer. He saved Colin from death, dragging him out from under the grizzly body and carrying him back to civilization and medical help. He also saved Colin's trophy, skinning and preserving it and later delivering it to Wild Trophy World in contradiction to his own Native beliefs. He fails to understand Colin's desire to go to court for a bear hide, and to pay great sums to a lawyer: 'You whites go to a lot of trouble about a lot of things don't seem to be worth a lot of trouble ... You must have it in for that bear pretty bad ... The way you want that hide' (228). When Colin insists that the bear hide is his, Archie replies: 'The bear's. Just because it's dead don't make it stop belongin' to it ... You want the right hide so you can look at it and you can tell it's the one is dead and you're the one is still alive ... It is difficult for me to understand ... You white savages' (228–29).

But Archie has more to tell Colin. Before they go to trial over the bear Colin has reputedly shot, Archie sets the record straight: 'I said you didn't kill it, Dobbs. I said I did that.' And when Colin exclaims: '*You* killed her,' Archie replies with regret, 'Hey-up. I'm afraid I did' (244). This discovery should free Colin from the need for revenge, since the trophy is now not ethically his, but Archie's. His first reaction is relief and gratitude for 'an unexpected parole. From Archie,' and for absolution from the bear: 'What cruel penance he had paid since Daisy Creek ... Not a full pardon but lovely. From *her*!' (244). But he is not yet ready to accept defeat, for again this involves an annihilation of his own identity, a giving up of ego. He continues to assert his right to the grizzly hide: 'She had almost killed *him*. She had not done that to the man from Minneapolis. She had not done that to Archie. Just to Colin Dobbs. He had the real right to her hide. This false hip, pinned elbow, broken spine, clawed eye, and raddled cheek entitled him! Colin Dobbs!' (245–46).

The trial fails. Archie is the only witness of the events of the hunt and the only one who can identify the hide. It is his word against that of Frankie. Archie is not a credible witness in the eyes of the law and he refuses to play by White rules. The judge, known as Old Pisser, is alcoholic and has a short attention span. Worst of all, old Mr Munro perjures himself to protect his grandson. In exposing Archie to 'white justice,' Colin has betrayed him and to no purpose. But the damage he has done is more extensive than he knows. For Archie tells him of his vow years ago to Master Bear and Bony Spectre: if his daughter Magdalene should be cured of her pneumonia, he would give up hunting. 'Me. Inside of me. I made a deal there. I said it to myself and him. The rest of my life I won't do that no more ... He kep' his deal ... I broke it. I had to. When she was at you' (272–73). Thus Colin, in hunting his grizzly, has set Archie up to violate his promise as a father. And in placing Colin's life above his sacred vow, Archie has become Colin's father too.

The lawyer encourages Colin to appeal the trial on the basis of the missing ledger entries and old Mr Munro's obvious perjury. But Colin determines not to do so. His decision is made when he recognizes that he is guilty of betraying the father in Mr Munro. Annie has never supported Colin in his desire for a trial, in part because she has compassion for the grandfather. Before the trial, Mr Munro attempted to deflect Colin by offering his own prize grizzly trophy in place of the lost one. Colin replied, 'suppose it were you, not me – nearly gutted – had half your face ripped off – would you accept *my* offer?' And Munro answered: 'If your daughter were Frankie, would you go along with what you're asking of me?' (199). After the trial, Mr Munro faces Colin to explain: 'I had no choice,' and asks why Colin could not simply accept his offer of his own trophy: 'You should ask yourself that. Think about it, as I will think about perjuring myself today – till I die.' And then he adds: 'Please give my love to your daughter' (270–71).

Thus Colin, in going to trial, has betrayed the father in Archie, the grandfather in Mr Munro, and the father he himself might be in the eyes of Annie. He has put all these fathers at risk. In his final words to Annie, he reveals how he has changed. He recalls his visit to the sauna much earlier, where 'I got rid of quite a lot of poison,' and connects this to the trial. Before Annie, he is able to cry 'for a woman in a sauna and for a broken old man who asked me to give his love to my daughter' (277).[3]

At the end of the novel, Annie announces that she is departing for California, where she plans to study art and teach. Colin loses Annie physically, but he does not lose his newly gained fatherhood. Annie must go her way, become the artist that she needs to become. Through her visit, however, she has helped Colin to get in touch with his own emotions and also with his own artistic self. She demands that he resume writing: 'That's what you owe me. And yourself ... Cut the cute games. You going to shove that rock back up there again or aren't you?' (276). Colin promises, like Sisyphus, to persevere despite all odds, to push the rock back up the hill. He will return to his writing, not to the novel he gave up ten years before, but to a new one, perhaps a version of his own story 'since Daisy Creek.' The sow grizzly has finally taught him compassion. He has become the whole person that Annie envisioned in her final portrait.

Since Daisy Creek has not received its due from most reviewers and critics. Certainly Colin is not the most lovable of protagonists, although he is a direct descendent of Daddy Sherry in the novel *The Kite* (1962) and, even more so, in the play of the same name. The predominance of satire and black comedy may puzzle readers, as Jamie Portman suggests, but it is in keeping with Mitchell's belief that laughter and tears should alternate in literature, as in life, as Shakespeare has shown us in scenes such as the one depicting the grave-diggers in *Hamlet* (McLay 7). Nevertheless, this is a rich, complex novel which shows Mitchell, at seventy, at the height of his artistic powers. Drawing on material which had germinated for nearly thirty years, it reflects themes which Mitchell has been concerned with throughout his writing career: the search for identity which changes through childhood, adolescence, adulthood, and mid-life or after; the struggle to succeed as an artist; the need to reconcile relationships with family members, especially with the mother; the search to replace the absent father; and above all, the necessity to reconcile in oneself the masculine and feminine aspects of the personality, the intellectual and the creative, in order to find balance. In the novel, the quest for the bear becomes the quest for the self and for spiritual harmony. A classic in a very different sense than *Who Has Seen the Wind*, *Since Daisy Creek* shows us Mitchell at his very best.

NOTES

1 I am indebted to Special Collections, the University of Calgary, and in particular to Mrs Apollonia Steele and her staff for their support and assistance with my work on the Mitchell Papers, in this case, 'The Trophy.' Since the paging of the manuscript is irregular, page references here are to the foliation numbers assigned by the archives.

2 The play *The Kite* (1982) introduces a strong female character in the person of Helen Clifford, who is not the romantic heroine of the novel *The Kite* (1962), but a stronger woman who anticipates Annie in *Since Daisy Creek*. In his article 'Invading Caves,' Orm Mitchell questions the role of Annie, whom he identi-

fies as based on his sister Willa. He feels that the relationship between Colin and Annie, while very similar to that of W.O. and Willa in many ways, is treated at too superficial a level, is resolved too easily, and evades the darker aspects of any such relationship. However, he admits he is perhaps too close to the situation to appreciate the treatment of many of the father-daughter scenes in the novel (150–51).

3 Dick Harrison, in his study of *Since Daisy Creek*, sees Dobbs as 'a classic figure in western literature: the individualist male seeking to transcend his mortality through symbolic achievements and fleeing from woman as the reminder and agent of that mortality' (188). He finds the resolution 'comic but strange'; Dobbs abandons his individualism and 'accommodate[s] the demands of the self to the need to rejoin the mortal family' (190). Harrison notes Mitchell's recurring theme of the importance of family – 'Family is Mitchell's most common metaphor for community, and Dobbs has violated the bonds of family' (188). But while he observes that, as a bastard, Dobbs has been deprived of family, he does not quite make the jump to the theme of the absent father and the need to replace him which underlies all of Mitchell's fiction.

'Upstairs with Mark Twain': The Peril of Magic Lies

MICHAEL PETERMAN

W.O. Mitchell's *Ladybug, Ladybug...* (1988) is a novel with two related aims. It is at its most poignant in dramatizing the isolation of old age and what Dick Harrison calls in his review 'the experience of loss.' The novel's second goal is to call attention to the unified field of North American cultural experience; that is, to make both Americans and Canadians more aware of the interrelatedness of their particular experiences and national identities. In both cases human connection and cultural understanding are crucial ingredients in the elderly Kenneth Lyon's struggle to shape and write a biography of Mark Twain, which is his consuming project throughout the duration of the novel.

Mitchell's seventy-eight-year-old protagonist is a Canadian professor and writer who has had a great deal of American experience, both as a resident and as an interpreter of Western writers like Twain (Samuel Clemens). If Lyon's life seems, loosely, to fit Mitchell's own, the parallel is no accident, for he resembles his creator in suggestive ways. They share numerous distinctive habits, a prairie childhood, a Florida adolescence, an important mentor (the real Dr Rupert Lodge of the University of Manitoba), and a longstanding involvement in the teaching of creative writing in Canada. But unlike Mitchell, who became a member of a university creative writing department late in his career, Lyon has served out a long and distinguished academic career in the United States, first, at the state university in Buffalo, then at Michigan State. At the former institution he held the prestigious 'Mark Twain Chair' (136), and at the latter he initiated 'the first Canadian Studies program – ever – anywhere' (136). Returning to his native Canada, he founded and chaired the English department at Livingstone University, a new university located in a foothills city closely resembling Calgary. In addition, during his twenty years at Livingstone he developed an outstanding creative writing program. Finally, and most importantly, he is working on the aforementioned biography, the major opus of his career when, at the novel's outset, he is forced unwillingly into retirement.

Lyon's struggle to recast, refresh, and complete his biography is one of the primary actions of *Ladybug, Ladybug...* It is the novel's literary business, its serious cultural matter. In paralleling Clemens's life with Lyon's, Mitchell develops a 'thematic destination' for both the biography and *Ladybug, Ladybug...*, one that celebrates Clemens as 'the voice of *both* our American nations' (275). That 'destination,' which Lyon arrives at late in the novel, is not, however, an attempt to subsume Canada's vision and experience in the American juggernaut of which Twain is a part. Far from it. It seeks rather to awaken myopic American nationalists and shrinking Canadian apologists to an enlarged sense of cultural sharing and cross-fertilization. As one character observes, 'Americans are much better informed about Mexicans or Cubans than they are about Canadians' (257). Clearly, in Mitchell's view, it is time that Americans and Canadians alike begin to better understand their complex and important relationship.

In this essay I want to concentrate for the most part on the ways in which Mitchell presents his protagonist at work on the biography of Twain. The novel makes clear that Professor Lyon's vision is his message from the summit of his academic and creative writing career. However, Lyon's struggles are fraught with difficulties for the reader. The biography's 'thematic destination' risks, for instance, the banality of Canadian chauvinism. Even worse, it may seem yet another instance of Canadian sour grapes at being unfairly overlooked south of the border. While Lyon's vision, we are told, represents the wisdom of a long and thoughtful life lived close to the longest undefended border in the world, a sad but disturbing question naturally enough arises – Is anybody down there in the United States listening?

W.O. Mitchell writes from the continental attic just as Lyon works on his Clemens biography in the attic of his Western Canadian home. In 1960 Robertson Davies chose that same metaphor – 'a voice from the attic' – to characterize for American readers his distinctly Canadian perspective upon literature and writing. Canada, Davies suggested, is like the spoon that is in and out of the cup and saucer of American and British experience. The spoon readily affects cup and saucer, but has limited capacity in itself. It does serve, however, to stir things up and is most recognized when it is 'most a nuisance.' Nearly three decades later and with his own Western experience in mind, Mitchell argues that the 'upstairs' voice has more shaping power and pertinency in the new world than has previously been recognized. He carefully structures *Ladybug, Ladybug*... to emphasize the complex 'literary genealogy' (275) of the North American continent, and he stresses in his final chapters that much importance is generated by cross-fertilization, despite the fact that most contemporary Americans, so caught in the thrall of their mythology of special and exclusive New World nationhood, hear and absorb far too little, if anything at all, of what is sounded from Canada. One aim of Lyon's biography is to correct that characteristic myopia: it will alert 'You fellows down there below the forty-ninth [that you] never have been and never will be the *only* Americans on this continent' and it will 'welcome you as one of us in our new world' (275–76).

Whether Lyon's voice from the attic will actually be heard 'below the forty-ninth' is not something that *Ladybug, Ladybug*... can deal with. Marketplace results, however, confirm what the novel describes. Very few Americans have read the book since it was published in 1988. Despite its attention to Samuel Clemens and its mention of many other American writers, it has not been published in the United States. Nevertheless, its conviction and optimism provide an important perspective, even if that conviction only applies north of the border. Canada still awaits its cultural recognition in the United States even though there are many well-informed Americans and students in Canadian Studies programs in American universities like the one Lyon started at Michigan State – working in support of the very goal set out by Mitchell's fictional biographer.

Paralleling the novel's continental vision, Mitchell provides a non-literary plot line that springs from Lyon's need for rejuvenating companionship in his 'maundering' old age (84). Professor Lyon is dispossessed of his university office, and thus suddenly deprived of his daily rituals and contact with his academic cronies. Stung by the bureaucratic way in which he has been unceremoniously put out to the pasture grazed by professors *emeriti*, he is barely sustained in his loneliness by his passions for billiards, cigars, and the cultivation of flowers. Neither is he able to make much progress on the biography, despite a recent research trip to Hartford and other locales. His solution is to seek a new human connection. He places an eccentrically worded 'Help Wanted' ad for a companion / housekeeper. The applicant he selects is a struggling actress named Nadya. She comes to him not only with a five-year-old daughter named Rosemary, but also with a covert enemy, a disgruntled and psychotic graduate student from the university ominously named Charlie Slaughter.

Nadya and Rosemary soon fill the domestic void left by Lyon's wife Sarah, who had died five years earlier, and their long lost daughter Susie (named for Twain's second daughter), who disappeared at age three while Lyon was teaching at the Fine Arts Centre in the Canadian Rockies. Indeed, their presence helps to rejuvenate his writing. Nadya not only provides a sympathetic ear, but she also proves to be 'the best researcher [he has] ever had'; she devotes what little time she has left from mothering and her day job to 'tracking down [his] correspondence' and making excursions to the university library for him (105). Much like Sarah before her, she steadily encourages him to keep at the biography while indulging him in his various pleasures like playing pool and smoking cigars in the evenings. In the precocious and forthright Rosemary he finds a consolation for 'the wilderness loss of the other little one' (217).

The plotting of *Ladybug, Ladybug* ... hangs on the revenge that

Charlie Slaughter sets out to enact on Nadya. Some time shortly before the action of the novel, she had found herself in a sexually vulnerable situation with Slaughter as a result of her neighbourly kindness and initial attraction to him. Fearful of his state of mind, she had given him shelter and played along with him until he surprised her in her own bed; rather than perform the 'blow job' he demanded, she bit his penis and escaped. Coolly and deliberately, Slaughter resolves to track her down and revenge himself on her. His plan is to attack her at her most vulnerable point – by kidnapping her daughter. The plot thus builds to the moment when he is in a position to execute his plan. That moment comes when Nadya is out of town, auditioning in Minneapolis for the lead in a production of George Bernard Shaw's *Saint Joan*.

Surprisingly, given his literary and 'thematic destination' in the novel, Mitchell makes no particular connection between Shaw's play and Clemens's reverent treatment of Joan in his lesser-known *Personal Recollections of Joan of Arc* (1896). Indeed, within the novel it is as if Twain had no recognized interest in the figure of Joan. All we are told is that Nadya would make 'one hell of a Joan' (107).

Nadya leaves 'the Professor' or 'Doctor,' as she calls him, to look after Rosemary in her absence. Directed by the inner voice of his hard-minded and spiteful God, Slaughter sets himself up in a cave in the cliff-like escarpment overlooking Lyon's suburban home. Watching patiently, he has no trouble catching the absent-minded Lyon off guard. He kidnaps Rosemary and holds her prisoner in his hideaway until, acting on the prompting of his demonic inner voice, he commits suicide. Having nothing against the girl and no interest in her other than as a child he can punish in the cruel deprivative ways his mother practised on him, he leaves Rosemary alive in his hiding place, sexually unharmed but psychologically wounded by his treatment of her. As the novel ends, however, we are assured that her psychic wounds are curable, in large part because of her excellent home life.

The attempt to enter the mind of a violent psychotic male – one whose sexual appetites vary from art class exhibitionism to aggressive heterosexuality to preying upon and beating up lonely homosexuals – constitutes a difficult challenge for Mitchell. Indeed, the sudden shift from Lyon's point of view to Slaughter's, which first occurs in chapter 5, creates a shock in the novel's narrative flow. Though Mitchell clearly has in mind certain ironic parallels between his two major figures – Lyon and Slaughter are creative writers who specialize in Western subject matter; both are drawn to Nadya and serve as 'protectors' of Rosemary; both are let go, as it were, by Livingstone University; both make idiosyncratic public statements at convocation; both communicate with inner voices; and both are drawn to three as a magical number – his counterpointing of their points of view is more often problematic than illuminating. The differences between them are so great that the ironies carry little force.

In his depiction of Slaughter's mind at work, Mitchell implies a simplistic Freudian explanation of a man committed to bullying and violent acts of revenge against those who offend him. Charlie's antisocial problems are rooted in the puritanical denials of his mother and the sexual abuse he experienced at the hands of a fundamentalist minister once favoured by his parents. He also suffers from blinding headaches out of which the voice of his demonic God emerges to guide his actions. Nevertheless, his utter delight in inflicting pain, his stylized acts of vengeance, and his suicidal inclination are not convincingly rooted in these factors. Indeed, he is often so intensely attracted and alive to his sadistic pursuits that self-annihilation seems an unlikely motive in such a man. Overall, his perversity, which is as all-encompassing as it is creative, seems less a convincing psychological state than a means of driving a forceful plot. Mitchell is the kind of author who feels it necessary to explicate such a state of mind; he won't allow Slaughter simply to go unanalysed, as many suspense writers would choose to do.

While the novel's melodramatic plot drew praise from an experienced reviewer like Patricia Morley – who wrote that it has 'more raw suspense than any I have read for some time' (27) – *Ladybug, Ladybug* ... is less gripping than she suggests. Its effect is less that of a dark and lethal force threatening the narrative's sympathetic characters than of a textbook-like and predictable set of actions to be worked through in order that the important concerns of the story can attain due prominence. When Slaughter finally commits suicide by driving his motorcycle over the escarpment cliff on orders from his dark God, he provides a convenient end to that plot. His links to Lyon, Nadya, and Rosemary are tenuous at best; nothing anyone in the novel does in opposition to him affects his decisions, particularly his final and surprising act of suicide. He simply ends his plot by ending his own life; thus, despite the anxiety he has created and the psychological pain he has inflicted, his suicide allows a return to the comic order that Mitchell's vision requires.

The particularities of the Slaughter plot remind the reader that, although the masks of tragedy and comedy hang over the sofa in Lyon's study and although a fly occasionally lands on the tragic face, the author's vision is essentially comic. It is an outlook at once orderly and cozy, a view of life committed to human merit, kindredness of spirit, and the building of bridges between people, and the masks are, in fact, tilted away from each other in Lyon's office (108). So strong is Mitchell's comedic commitment that he struggles in this novel (as he does elsewhere in his fiction) to give real force to what he calls – in a literary shorthand he has evoked from *Who Has Seen the Wind* to this novel – 'the heart of darkness' (140).

Reviewing the novel with some disappointment, Jonathan Webb asked a pertinent question. Troubled by a 'rather pedestrian novel' that, despite the author's 'solid' virtues, was 'never compelling for long enough,' he wondered, 'what, after all, was Mitchell trying to get at in his exploration of the life of Clemens? The answer,' which Webb admitted he had somehow missed, 'might have made the difference between a book that is comfortably diverting and one that could have been remarkable'(24). That question goes to the book's core and reverberates the more one wrestles with its structure and development. Kenneth Lyon is writing a biography of Samuel Clemens, but he is also thinking his way through his own life, beginning with his prairie boyhood and moving outward to the New World outlook he shares with Clemens. By planting so many similarities between Lyon and himself, Mitchell also makes it clear that Lyon's autobiographical meditations are closely allied to his own, particularly those that bear upon a complex sense of a shared and informing Canadian-American 'literary geneology.' Thus, an exploration of the aspects of biography and autobiography at play in the novel are the primary focus of this essay. We need to ask ourselves what Mitchell was 'trying to get at' in his dramatization of Lyon the biographer at work.

Having been for years compared in Canada to Mark Twain both for his fiction and for his humorous stage performances, Mitchell was, perhaps inevitably, drawn to a meditation upon that connection. In the 1980s, his stature within Canada was such that he had been approached by at least one would-be biographer before he decided in the mid-1980s to designate his son Orm and daughter-in-law Barbara as his official biographers. *Ladybug, Ladybug...* contains numerous signs of Mitchell's consciousness of certain aspects of the biographical process. For instance, Lyon reminds himself early in the novel that objectivity in biography is something of a myth and that the biographer's quest for objectivity is fraught with snares and pitfalls; moreover, he realizes that at the core of the biographical exercise there is either a battle for power and voice between the biographer and his subject or an empathy, perhaps even a dialogic relationship between them, that supports the undertaking.

Early in the narrative Mitchell plants certain indicative questions in Lyon's mind. Lyon, for example, interrogates himself in the voice of his 'literary conscience': 'Hold on a minute, Lyon!' that voice cautions. 'Whose biography is this anyway?' (13). In a different context – this time concerning the act of story-telling – he answers a query from Rosemary by throwing a question back at her: 'Look – whose story is this – yours or mine?' (32). More importantly still, Lyon cautions himself with these words: 'You seem to have forgotten. Inside every biographer there's an autobiographer struggling to get out.' This repressed voice, he jokes, may not be 'quite so troublesome as that bad novelist you've got inside you, but keep your eye peeled all the same. Constantly' (14). How troublesome, we ask. Watch out for the autobiographical voice within, Mitchell seems to be saying, even as Kenneth Lyon increasingly allows that voice to influence and inform his approach. The challenge to be on guard is one the reader must be prepared to take up.

It is soon clear that *Ladybug, Ladybug...* is as much about what Lyon knows as a writer and a human being as it is about Samuel Clemens's life. In his intimate 'talks' with Clemens, Lyon finds himself taking increasing exception to the way his subject acted in his later years, especially towards family members and friends. An element of moral disapproval peeps out behind Lyon's admiration of a man who seemed so wise to so many and who, aspiring to be the 'most conspicuous person on the planet,' appeared to have so much going for himself (quoted in Kaplin, p. 381). As Lyon digs below the surface of the public Mark Twain, the showman, the man in the white Palm Beach suit, the man who made everyone laugh, he finds ways to measure the worth of his own life on the Canadian border.

Revitalized by Nadya's companionship, Lyon begins to rework his chapters about Clemens's Mississippi boyhood, and in the process taps deeply into his own childhood memories: 'For the first time since he'd been kicked out of Livingstone, he found the biography growing well, particularly when he returned to the earlier years. Sam's voice was coming to him so much clearer now, and more and more the act of writing was one of conversation with him' (44). Placing a special emphasis on talk or conversation, as if it were intrinsic to the actual writing of his text, Lyon revels in his feeling of having made a fresh start. It is the authority of his own boyhood experiences that allows him to 'trust [Clemens's] powers of observation' (45). Recalling Clemens's essay on hunting the 'deceitful turkey,' he draws on his own hunting ventures to confirm a pattern of deception among female turkey, partridge, and killdeer that verifies what Clemens reported. Lyon, however, uses that evidence to testify to something more. Working beyond Clemens, he locates in such actions the power of mother-love, and thus amplifies the theme of connectedness in *Ladybug, Ladybug...* At the same time, though he accuses Clemens of exaggerating the shooting prowess of his uncle and his boys, he also commends him for his perceptive attack on James Fenimore Cooper's literary offences: 'I won't say anything about [your own exaggerations] to Jim Cooper. Trust me. You were dead on target with him'(45). Though Cooper may have provided an inspiration for Lyon's boyhood make-believe as an Indian guide, he is in Lyon's mind no model for a serious writer. Cooper is thus assessed and dismissed, much in the spirit of Twain's own view.

Concerned a few days later that he may be growing too self-focused and thus 'drawing a bead on the wrong past,' Lyon wonders 'what possible relevance to the biography ... his own rebel and rural childhood, his own Southern adolescence, [could] have?' 'Behave, Lyon,' he cautions himself (58–59). The answer he comes up with is reassuring. The deeper he looks into Clemens's life, the more he awakens powerful personal memories that are not only important to him, but that serve as well to inform the complex way he thinks about his subject.

'Strangely now,' as he puts it, 'he found himself spending much more time on inner rather than outer research.' Though he worries that indulgence in 'recapturing personal past to inflict it upon bored victims was the well-known maundering symptom of old age' (58), he is not long in validating the shift in process and method. Has the biographer thus let loose the autobiographer Lyon warned himself about? Indeed, he has. Shortly after the arrival of Nadya and Rosemary and for reasons 'only God knew,' Lyon had experienced what he calls 'the beautiful insight.' It becomes the basis for his new commitment to dredging up his 'inner' reality: 'He saw that his own remembered feelings of delight, disappointment, impatience, grief, bitterness, rage were the true way to recognize and understand Sam Clemens, and just possibly might give life resonance to the biography he had promised Sarah decades ago.' Addressing his dead wife, he adds, 'A bonus for you, darling, not one but two: Sam's; my own' (59–60).

The 'life resonance' that Lyon craves is emotional resonance, emotion that is first of all compelling to himself and secondly important as a means of informing the biography he is writing. But while Lyon is refreshed and enthused by this 'insight,' what Mitchell seems to forget is that a biography is a serious and professional exercise that is ultimately about someone else. While a biographer needs something like a 'thematic destination' and a non-linear way to 'map' his subject, it is essential that he have his 'outer' facts correct and his 'chronological structure' in order (12). All the emotional resonance in the world can't patch over factual errors and the failure to research the 'outer life' of one's subject as thoroughly as possible.

Since the novel sets out to show what purports to be the development of a serious biography by a qualified scholar, it has as a primary condition of its representation the requirement of convincing the reader that there is capable biographical work being done. Such work is not something that any 'hard-working idiot' can do, as Lyon well knows (12). It requires what Brigadier General Mackenzie Denison rightly calls 'the necessary scholarly research' (261). Moreover, when one's subject is as well-known a personality and literary figure as Samuel Clemens, there are particular pitfalls. As Timothy Findley observed in his essay, 'Everything I Tell You Is the Truth – Except the Lies,' 'history shadows your every move, a private investigator waiting to pounce' (152). How then does the reader see Lyon as biographer? Is he a practitioner whose insights are moving him toward the completion of his major opus? Or is he a maundering, misdirected old man, more governed by illusion than insight? *Ladybug, Ladybug...* makes it very difficult to decide. Indeed, it leaves unclear, in a way that is both alarming and disconcerting, the question of Lyon's basic competence.

In terms of the shared experience of youth, the outer-inner parallel between Clemens and Lyon holds up well, except for the fact that Clemens was more a river kid than a prairie boy. To paper over that gap Mitchell calls on another American writer, Wallace Stegner, to authorize and define the special gifts of a prairie childhood. Stegner, who spent his adolescent years in Eastend, Saskatchewan, and wrote an important prairie reminiscence about those early years entitled *Wolf Willow*, was a writer whom Mitchell admired; in fact, in Mitchell's papers at the University of Calgary there is a film script that works closely with that book. In *Ladybug, Ladybug...* Lyon paraphrases him during his Convocation address. According to Stegner, 'the prairie and the foothills West should create poets' (137), and he goes on to celebrate the way in which the vast prairie landscape could stimulate imagination and awaken important realizations. Like Stegner, Lyon knows that landscape; indeed, his image of the 'dirging,' 'urging' and singing wind pointedly recall Mitchell's own classic novel of boyhood, *Who Has Seen the Wind*: 'In my young world, at a very early age, I learned I was mortal; I could die. End of Kenny Lyon. The humming, living, foothills did not give a hoot about that... When you learn you are going to die, you truly understand you are human; you have then been given a new perspective, which is very helpful in deciding what is important and what is unimportant' (138). Mitchell makes much of that perspective, even if he can't quite link it to Clemens's life in the Mississippi. Rather, Lyon shared with Clemens a 'frontier boyhood,' a New World 'perspective' that was fresh and stimulating. On their respective frontiers they learned a sharply defined sense of self and mortality, of 'being separate from all the rest of the living whole' (137–38).

Lyon's two years as a teenager in Florida further define his point of view, both by familiarizing him with American life and by awakening him to a new awareness of his Canadian point of view. Taken to St Petersburg by his mother because of his tubercular wrist (just as Mitchell himself was), Lyon quickly learns to see Americans in the complex way that typifies a Canadian vision. In particular, he learns how intrinsically different he is. That special sense of himself is galvanized when, as a student of elocution, he is required to recite the Gettysburg Address at an Independence Day celebration in a Florida park.

The sequence, which has for years been one of Mitchell's most successful humorous pieces on stage, draws on the oral tall tale tradition which he consciously shared with Clemens and which he brilliantly uses for his own purposes in this instance. Shrewdly constructed to be pertinent to young Kenny's expanding perspective, it is one of the novel's funniest episodes. Underprepared for his recitation, Kenny accidently wedges his foot in a spittoon placed on stage for an elderly, tobacco-chewing Civil War veteran. With a sense of 'the enormity' of 'perform[ing] an act of treason' in public (73), he can remember only the beginning of Lincoln's speech. However, he carries on, 'ad libb[ing] in a Lincolnesque way' (76), until he is able to recall the words of the final paragraph. To his great surprise his recitation is greeted by loud and warm applause. Feeling as a Canadian that he 'owed allegiance to the king, the beaver, and the Maple Leaf' (73), he becomes aware that most patriotic Americans have but a superficial awareness of their classic texts and learns 'a rather sad truth: everybody had heard about Lincoln's Gettysburg Address; nobody really *knew* [it]' (77).

The experience thus has a definitive place in the awakening of Lyon's border-line awareness. It prefigures the American and Canadian dimensions of his later university career and his desire to make Americans more aware of Canada's presence and importance on the North American continent. That perspective is amplified by other characters in the novel, notably Harley Alcock, the chancellor of Livingstone University, an American-born millionaire who, despite his wife's resistance, has become a lover and booster of the country where he made his fortune. 'Canadians could truly teach Americans a few things,' Alcock ruminates as he prepares his address for the convocation at which Lyon is to be made an honorary professor (123).

As the recipient of a Livingstone University honorary degree at the same convocation, the elderly Lyon finds himself thinking of the elderly Clemens – himself the recipient of many such honours – in less empathetic and more critical terms. In his acceptance speech, Lyon emphasizes the need to build bridges, to connect 'lonely human self to lonely human self,' especially through art (138): 'Death and solitude justify art, which draws human aliens together in the mortal family, uniting them against the heart of darkness. Humans must comfort each other, defend each other against the terror of being human. There must be civilized accountability to others. The coyote, the jack rabbit, the badger, the killdeer, the dragonfly do not experience alien terror; they are not accountable to each other' (140). In the light of this speech, which employs language and imagery very important to Mitchell, especially from *The Vanishing Point* on, the despair voiced by the mature Clemens is found sadly wanting.

Lyon views him as a man who succumbed in his later years to an inadequate view of life and art. Overwhelmed by his notion of the mysterious stranger (death or perhaps utter disillusion), Clemens allowed a darkened and self-pitying view of life to overtake his vision. Surprisingly, Lyon makes no allowance for certain external factors (like the effects of America's growing imperialism, its money-driven economy, and the persuasiveness of evolutionary thought) that affected Clemens's outlook. Rather, Lyon is disappointed in what he takes to be Sam's selfishness. In one of their later conversations, Lyon says, 'Well, Sam, we both knew that sooner or later this life of yours was going to turn dark; all of us can be dealt rotten cards.' In Lyon's view, Clemens took his bad cards (especially, the loss of his wife and two daughters) too personally and self-pityingly: 'You shouldn't have stained your bereavement with regret and guilt so that it would keep right on hurting.You should have mourned them more and yourself less. You held some pretty nice cards in a long run of luck: affluence, fame, friends, three daughters, and a loving and supportive wife, the best wild card of them all. You should have played them better' (153). Lyon's hindsight allows him to pity and judge the Clemens who in his later work bitterly decried human hypocrisy, politicians, Christian ministers, and 'the damned human race.' The implication is that Lyon knows better how to view life and, above all, how to honour art as a human action and response to the facts of mortality. Certainly, Lyon's views make good sense here. Given the frontier upbringing they shared, Lyon feels that Clemens should have known better what to expect from life and how to respond to it. The weight of moral authority that Mitchell grants to Lyon in such passages makes it seem clear that the biography is building a positive and informed direction.

Yet in choosing certain representative parts of Clemens's experience to define Lyon's work-in-progress, Mitchell ran risks that the novel cannot manage either to obscure or to contextualize for the reader. Several components of Clemens's life are given prominence in *Ladybug, Ladybug* ... I will consider three of them here: the

paralleling of Sam's relation with his brother Orion to the fraternal relation between Lyon and Henry; Twain's jealousy of and
nastiness toward his former mentor and friend, Bret Harte; and
the preoccupation with Twain's ancestry that Lyon develops. In
each case a reader with more than a passing interest in both Clemens and Mitchell has reason to feel disappointment in the rendering that Mitchell provides.

In delving into his own life, what Lyon dredges up often relates
to his younger brother Henry, whom he came to ignore in his later
years. Why, he wonders, had he 'let the brother ties be broken?'
(270). Yet he blames Henry for the neglect as much as himself,
apparently because he himself was unaware that Henry had
slipped from a successful legal career through three marriages to
disbarment, bankruptcy, alcholism, and finally suicide. The note
that Henry left at his death, however, serves starkly to remind
Lyon of the part he may have played in undermining his
brother's self-esteem. Though in his work as biographer Lyon is
very conscious of Clemens's brow-beating of his ineffectual older
brother Orion, he seems disinclined to accept much blame for
Henry's sad demise. It is as if, in his 'serious self-examination'
(111), he can recognize some things but not others. He whose
carelessness and absent-mindedness played a part in both the disappearance of his daughter and the kidnapping of Rosemary,
publicly advocates the building of bridges and the overcoming of
despair in the face of 'the mysterious stranger' and the fact of
human aloneness.

In fact, if one looks closely at Clemens's letters to the feckless,
forever-optimistic Orion, as Lyon does in the novel, one sees a
man who, despite all his flamboyant protestations, did not aban-
don his brother. When Lyon ponders the excessive language of a
particular Clemens letter (29 November 1888) to Orion, he thinks,
'I could have written one like this to Henry. Probably did. Several
times' (60). Yet the language Lyon himself uses – 'could have' and
'probably did' – does not promote confidence that he actually
wrote such letters. The reader is caught here, unsure of how to
evaluate what Lyon is saying, perhaps suspicious that the contrast, which Lyon wishes the reader to see in his favour, offers less

by way of justification or insight than he hopes. Still more troubling in an entirely different way, a comparison of the letter as quoted in *Ladybug, Ladybug* ... (60–61) with its text as recorded in *The Selected Letters of Mark Twain*, edited by Charles Neider (188–89), reveals numerous errors of punctuation, emphasis, and omission in Lyon's transcription. While the general sense of the letter is not altered, the imprecision of the presentation does little to promote confidence in Lyon's scholarly care. Has Mitchell meant us to see Lyon's textual errors in parallel with his treatment of Henry? It does not seem likely, since the novel itself gives the reader little obvious reason, other than old age, to doubt Lyon's scholarly reputation.

A look at Justin Kaplin's biography also reveals an interesting fraternal comparison that Lyon or Mitchell simply overlooks or chooses to ignore. The brother whose death most haunted Clemens was not Orion but his younger brother Henry. In 1858 Clemens had persuaded the quiet and bookish Henry to take a job with him on the steamboat *Pennsylvannia* where he was himself apprenticing as a pilot. Henry Clemens had been in service as a 'third clerk' for about four months when a fight occurred between Sam and another pilot named Brown over Brown's rough treatment of Henry. The result was that Sam returned home from New Orleans on another boat, arriving in Memphis two days after the *Pennsylvannia* had been destroyed there in a horrendous explosion and fire. Henry died from his burns a few days later with Clemens doing all he could at his bedside to save him. All his life, according to Kaplin, Clemens 'held himself responsible for Henry's presence' on the steamboat where he felt that he too should have been (194). His wife Livy was the only other person with whom 'he felt in entire sympathy' (91) after Henry's death.

So, too, Lyon's comments on Clemens's outspoken hostility to his old friend Bret Harte are troublesome. Calling his attitude to Harte 'shabby' and pointing to his 'jealousy,' 'vanity,' and anti-Semitism (82–83), Lyon provides further reason to find fault with Clemens's behaviour as a mature writer. He locates the source of the misunderstanding in charges of plagiarism apparently made by Harte concerning Clemens's use of oral sources in his famous tall tale, 'The Celebrated Jumping Frog of Calaveras County.' The problem is that the blow-up – and blow-up it certainly was, on Clemens's part – resulted not from a disagreement about plagiarism and frontier humour but from a play that failed on Broadway in 1877. Much taken by the theatrical possibilities of a Chinese character Harte had created in his poem 'The Heathen Chinee' and his play *Two Men of Sandy Bar*, Clemens had urged his friend, who at that point was much in need of money, to join him in co-authoring a play which would feature Harte's character, Ah Sin, in the lead role. The play, Clemens believed, would make their names and fortunes on Broadway. Harte agreed to participate and moved in with the Clemens family while the two worked together on the script. The result was what Gary Scharnhorst has called 'the most ill-fated collaboration in the history of American letters.' What was worse, 'it doomed their friendship' (29). The effort at co-writing a play on which much profit seemed to depend released in Clemens a startling vindictiveness toward his former mentor and friend.

That hostility lasted unchecked for decades. It seems that Clemens blamed Harte not only for the play's failure, but also for insulting his wife (and home), and for shamelessly and repeatedly borrowing money from him. His anger, which seemed to feed on itself, perplexed the reticent, more retiring Harte, who seldom responded to or wrote about his former friend's charges, at least directly. Their play, entitled *Ah Sin* after its central character, was performed for several months and gained some acclaim, but its failure to realize its potential seems to have set Clemens loose upon a campaign to ruin Harte's reputation. What is surprising in *Ladybug, Ladybug…* is that Lyon appears to have heard of neither *Ah Sin* nor the real source of his subject's complaints. In fact, the *Ah Sin* collaboration would have provided further evidence of Clemens's shabbiness, vanity, and racism, had Lyon, the purportedly capable researcher, but known about it. Since Margaret Duckett had in 1964 traced the strange relationship in her excellent monograph, *Mark Twain and Bret Harte*, the evidence was readily available to him. Justin Kaplin also included the story in his biography two years later.

Another factual error is found in Lyon's description of Clemens in England on the occasion of his receiving his Oxford honorary degree: 'Must have been a great day for you when you hung that Oxford scalp on your coup stick. Long time coming, that one, Bret and Howells scoring ahead of you by several years. Sweet victory all the same, with Livy and the girls cheering, though I do wonder how they felt when you started wearing the scarlet and gold gown and pancake tam all over the house, in place of your bathrobe' (106). Wonder indeed! The problem is that Clemens received that degree, which he so much coveted, in 1907. By then Livy and Susy were dead, while Jean was in a rest home and Clara was busy with her singing career. Though he was, in Kaplin's words, 'as widely celebrated a literary person as America ever produced' (381), Clemens went to England that year a very lonely man, accompanied only by a male secretary. In fact, to console himself he read aloud on shipboard from Susy's diary.

Finally, there is Lyon's strange preoccupation with a story he had heard decades earlier, an old rumour that Sam Clemens was an illegitimate child, the son of his unhappy mother, who had married on the rebound, and the peregrinating William Lyon Mackenzie, 'the red-wigged journalist firebrand, who had set and ignited the 1837 rebellion' in Upper Canada two years after Twain's birth (255). Told this tale many years earlier in Buffalo by an eccentric former Brigadier General named Mackenzie Denison, Lyon has let it lie deep in his memory until, while dredging his inner life to deepen the 'life resonance' of his biography, he becomes preoccupied by its potential, even though he had dismissed it at the time as 'something I thought was too ridiculous for words' (262).

Detecting stylistic and anecdotal similarities between Mackenzie's colonial journalism and Clemens's frontier sketches, Lyon plays with the possibility for two apparent reasons. In the first instance, both his wife Sarah and his new helpmate Nadya intuitively feel that there is something in the connection that is worth investigating in detail. Secondly, he is able to seize upon what he has long been searching for – 'the thematic destination of this biography.' 'You see,' he tells Sam, 'whether or not you had a

rebel Canadian father isn't all that important, but what is important is that your voice is the voice of *both* our American nations'
(275).

As removed from fact as the idea of illegitimacy is (Jane Clemens was in Kentucky, Tennessee, and Missouri during these
years), it allows Mitchell to make an important point. It can at
least be argued that Clemens found his writerly parentage in
Canadian sources like Judge Thomas Chandler Haliburton's Sam
Slick. Haliburton is, according to Lyon, 'the father of American
humour,' a debt that both Twain and Artemus Ward were 'decent'
enough to acknowledge in their lifetimes (275). There is, then, a
New World voice, perfected by Twain, but born in Canada, that
speaks 'to the whole world, *for* the new world' (275). With this
mapping in his imaginative possession, Lyon is apparently
empowered to complete his long-delayed biography.

Overall, then, *Ladybug, Ladybug...* suffers from an ambitious-
ness which Mitchell struggles to control the further he takes Lyon
into the precise representation of his biographical project. The
novel pursues three interrelated concerns: the business of writing
a biography of Samuel Clemens; the elderly biographer's need to
connect to Clemens as a Westerner and a human being, and to
find himself in the process; and the pursuit of a viable Canadian-
American, hence North American, connection in Clemens's writing. However, these concerns do not always mesh well and the
problem of *reading* Kenneth Lyon as a creditable biographer as he
reads Sam Clemens's life increases the further that Mitchell takes
the reader into what Lyon – and Mitchell – actually know about.
Too often what we get undermines both the protagonist and the
author.

It would be intriguing if in fact Mitchell intended the reader to
deconstruct Lyon as biographer. To be sure, there is a good deal of
playfulness in Lyon's approach to his subject and there is much
concern developed about maundering tendencies as a man in the
grip of old age. Overall, however, when it comes to scholarly
authority on Twain, the novel, does not seem to allow for that
kind of reading. Lyon is too much the Mark Twain scholar to be so
unreliable and so underprepared. He is human and thus flawed,

inclined, as an old man rampant with memory, to be (more than) a little self-preoccupied and absent-minded about things that deeply matter. Certainly, neither Nadya nor Rosemary judge him critically and they come to know him as he essentially is – a likeable, curmudgeonly old man. We are thus left with the sense that, for all his human weaknesses he is really a very good fellow, a man we can trust with many things, including Samuel Clemens's life. Too often, however, the novel inadvertently reveals that he lacks the very knowledge and skills he is supposed to possess in plenty. In particular, there is an unsettling lack of professional discipline and intellectual rigour in parts of Lyon's biographical research that is puzzling and disturbing. When Lyon worries that it is 'perilous to write such a man' (60), he speaks a far greater truth than he seems to realize. There is, regrettably, too little magic in the creative lies that *Ladybug, Ladybug...* tells about Kenneth Lyon's biography of Samuel Clemens.

NOTE

1 The author is indebted to the Special Collections of the University of Calgary Libraries for use of the Wallace Stegner filmscript by W.O. Mitchell and to Orm and Barbara Mitchell for providing material from the private papers of W.O. Mitchell that are still in the author's hands.

'Telling' Stories in
Roses Are Difficult Here

BARBARA MITCHELL

'Each unique soul in Shelby must give its special gift of momentum,' (319) concludes Matt Stanley near the end of *Roses Are Difficult Here* as he vigorously pumps, then watches his daughter's spinning top gather momentum and sing out its different sounds. The image of the spinning top suggests the variety of voices and stories that give momentum and meaning to the community of Shelby, Alberta. Stories, just like the top, can project different sounds: a 'soft hum,' a 'solemn harmony,' a savage hooting, and a 'low mourning.' Ideally all these sounds will 'blend and blur and whirl to balance' (319) and finally create the 'GLORIA CHORAL' (318). One story in particular, however, the survey of Shelby written by the visiting sociologist, Dr June Melquist, does not allow these different stories told by Shelby's citizens 'to spin in a living balance' (319). Rather, as Matt muses, Dr Melquist has 'propped' and 'supported' her own 'abstract' (319) story so that it emits no sound but is simply 'held upon its point. Dead.' Reluctantly Matt concedes that even so it 'perhaps ... stated some truths' (318), as he recognizes that it takes all kinds of storytellers, the sensitive and the poetic but also the snobbish, the cynical and the anarchic (319), to create the 'GLORIA CHORAL' of a community.

Nearly every character in this novel has some kind of story to tell. Many of the stories are public: published stories like Matt Stanley's and his Uncle Ben's editorials for *The Shelby Chinook*, and Dr June Melquist's sociological report on the town of Shelby, which appears as a 'fat paperback' (308). There are also shared oral narratives such as the tall tales of Clem Derrigan, the Senator, Ruth Stanley, and Mame Napoleon; the gossip of 'Flannel Mouth' Florence Nelligan and Millie Clocker; the satiric stories or anecdotes of Dr Harry Fitzgerald and Joe Manley; and the semi-public ambitions and fantasies such as Nettie Fitzgerald's planned and talked about local history, and Millie Clocker's 'obscene' letters (298) to the town's élite, which transform Matt and June into romance-magazine lovers. Rory Napoleon's story is the most public of all, involving the whole town. More than a told story, it is a comic fable enacted dramatically on the stage of Shelby's Main Street when his goats, transfigured by him into the élite members of Shelby society, invade the town. There are also private stories, for a remarkable number of characters (twelve in all) are given their own interior monologues. Some of these private monologues are delivered by the 'lonely and homeless ones' who, as Joe Manley says, quoting Walter de la Mare, constitute a 'host of phantom listeners' (99). Stories are as various as the flowers grown for the Annual Perennial and Annual Flower Show at the Shelby Fair.

Mitchell is concerned with the ambiguous interplay between truth and lies in communication. Aside from the fundamental problems created by language referentiality, by the gap between the word and the object, differentiating truth and fiction is made more difficult by the inescapable encoding of social and cultural ideologies into narrative, by personal biases, by the figurative use of language, and by extra-linguistic devices such as 'the quick swallow, the clucking tongue, the lifted eyebrow,' which 'coloured ... and embellished, distorting not so much out of malice as from relish in a story better told' (10). In this context the historical or sociological text is not an untroubled field of fact and truth, nor is the folktale a dismissable narrative of lies. The word 'story' itself reflects such ambiguities. From the Latin *historia*, 'story' originally referred to biblical history and legends of the saints (*OED*), and therefore privileged the historical, as opposed to the fictional, function of narrative. Today 'story' conveys more the sense of fictitiousness, or at least a subjective and personalized history that is associated with novels and short stories, with tall tales and anecdotes. Completely reversing the original meaning, 'story' is used euphemistically to refer to a lie. Embedded in the definition of 'story,' then, is the confusion of fact and fiction, of information and entertainment, and of communal and individual narratives. Mitchell uses the word 'story' fairly broadly in *Roses* to refer to newspaper stories, tall tales, gossip, fantasies, and fiction. Although Mitchell does not specifically attach the word 'story' to June Melquist's report, I will treat it as story, the type of story implied by its obsolete meaning, a factual, historical narrative.

Mitchell employs the image of mirrors and reflection to suggest the barriers to communication and the blurring of fact and fiction. Matt Stanley discovers that facts can distort the truth just as much as gossip. June Melquist's sociological report on the town 'stated some truths, but it did not mirror Shelby' (318). It slandered the town just as Millie Clocker's revengeful letters purporting an affair between June and Matt slandered them. Both kinds of story show how language can distort and destroy; both show what Mitchell calls 'the falseness of the reflection' (318). On the other hand, some stories, such as Clem Derrigan's tall tales, Matt's first-signs-of-spring exchanges in the newspaper, and Dr Harry Fitzgerald's dog stories and anecdotes about the animosity between urban and country hunters build bridges between people.

As roses are difficult, so are stories difficult to cultivate; ironically, though, the winning rose, like the 'winning' story, flourishes better under natural than forced conditions, under what Mame Napoleon describes as 'luck, the Lord, an' goat manoor' (197). At the centre of *Roses* are two major characters who tell antithetical stories, one forced, one natural. June Melquist's is a factual story about a small-town community, a sociological and statistical book-length report, 'a fat paperback, published evidently for public consumption' (308); Matt Stanley's is a personalized editorial, countering Melquist's report, written for a special edition of the *Shelby Chinook*, 'The Voice of the Foothills' (320). In writing his special editorial Matt Stanley, who, like other Mitchell heroes, is a blocked writer,[1] not only discovers his own voice, but discovers how he can represent his community and more truly become the 'Voice of the Foothills' through a blend of individuality and commonality. The spinning top image that Mitchell uses near the conclusion of *Roses* suggests that voices 'must blend and blur and whirl to balance' (319), and it is this 'living balance' between 'commonalities' (319) and individualities that Matt Stanley attempts to recognize in his final story, the special editorial celebrating the unique and positive characteristics of his community.

It is perhaps ironic that Mitchell himself is not entirely successful in discovering his own voice in this novel. *Roses*, as I will discuss below, was begun in 1957. Like his protagonist, Mitchell had returned from Toronto six years earlier hoping to find time to escape the deadlines of media writing (*Maclean's* for Mitchell, the *Star* for Matt) and write novels. Although Mitchell was finding success in other areas, such as radio drama, with his *Jake and the Kid* series, he was having difficulty writing novels. He had recently (1954) failed to get his manuscript 'The Alien,' published.[2] *Roses* seems a deliberate attempt to counter the criticisms levelled against 'The Alien' with regard to its length, its unsympathetic main character, and its dark and tragic ending. Although positive in its outlook, *Roses* does not convincingly convey, in terms of structure and character, the 'living balance' that he tried for. Denouncing the sociologist's view of 'commonalities' (319), Mitchell obviously wants to celebrate the individual; yet he fails to individuate his major characters as successfully as he portrays the community. Unlike the sociologist, who works deductively (and reductively), Mitchell and his protagonist are inductive philosophers highlighting the individual before the community; nevertheless, Mitchell's central characters lack the vital life that the portrait of the community conveys. Although not entirely successful in plot and major character development, however, this novel has remarkable secondary character studies (such as the anarchic Napoleons and the lonely Millie Clocker), some highly comic scenes or moments (the night the goats invade the town), and an intimate and sensuous capturing of the psychological and physical shape of a small-town community. However, without the story-telling motif to connect these multiple voices and plots, the novel would be unsatisfactorily fragmented.

The fact that the community is a better conceived 'character' than the main characters, Matt and Ruth Stanley and June Melquist, underlines Mitchell's thematic concern with the communal function of story-telling in this novel. First of all, Matt and June are deliberately not as compelling public story-tellers as the secondary characters, and their interior monologues do not make up for the lack of substance in their characters. Secondly, although the story-teller is important to Mitchell, it is often the reception of the tale – the community's responses – that interests him. It is community myth-making rather than individual soul-searching that takes centre stage in this novel. While most of Mitchell's novels are concerned with the rediscovery of the protagonist's creative energy (and that is still a concern in this novel, for Matt finds his own voice by the end), the main emphasis here is towards an understanding of the other side of the creative partnership, the effect of the story upon an audience. Certainly community dominates any particular individual in this book, and what dominates the community is story-telling.

Mitchell has always been interested in the complex relationship between truth and fiction. Although fundamentally a story-teller and novelist, he has worked on assignments of a more documentary nature. He has investigated and written on political and historical issues concerning the Mennonites, the Metis, and the Hutterites.[3] The ranch community west of High River, goose hunting, and a small-town rodeo have been the subjects for descriptive documentary pieces.[4] He has also written or scripted biographical profiles: one on Wallace Stegner, a well-known American writer who grew up in Saskatchewan, and another on a business executive and entrepreneur, Ron Southern, President of ATCO.[5] None of these could be described as employing the traditional archival historic approach but, rather, are a blend of historical detail and imaginative reconstruction. Behind these pieces is always a sense of bonding with his subject, a sympathy for the people and the landscape he is describing. One piece, 'What's Ahead For Billy?' about a young Stoney boy, written early on in

Mitchell's career (1943), was rejected by *Maclean's* because it was considered to have an unworkable relationship between fiction and fact. Initially, Mitchell was unwilling to rewrite and sacrifice the fictional for the factual account, but eventually he published a shortened, hybridized version of it in *Canadian Forum* (1944).[6]

Thus, Mitchell has had personal experience in the practice of writing factually, though he has always taken a 'new journalism' approach to it, believing in the subjectivity of history. In an article entitled 'Grace and Illusion: The Writer's Task' (1963) Mitchell asks, 'why didn't Galsworthy write a sociological text instead of writing the story "Quality," about the effect of an industrial age upon two old German shoemakers? ... why write a short story, why create characters, passions, successes, failures, in order to premeditate a truth? Why not clearly and simply and carefully just state the truth, just state it in a psychological treatise or in an economic tract?' (11). He had certainly considered and answered that question earlier in the *Roses* manuscript, and his answer there as it is in the article (and as it is in the published *Roses*) is that the artist is interested in 'a *human* truth' (1963, 12) by which he means that the artist is concerned with, as he says in the article, both the individual and the universal, or as he says in *Roses*, with the individual and the 'commonalities,' whereas the sociologist is only concerned with commonality. The sociologist in *Roses* generalizes, reduces, and schematizes whereas Matt, or the artist, comes to recognize, to accept, and to embody in his writing aspects of difference. Mitchell does not say in the article but does say in *Roses* that truth, for the artist, is multiple, and is as much apprehended as comprehended.

The truth-value of a story was first explored by Mitchell in 'The Liar Hunter,' published in *Maclean's* in 1945. It was rewritten as radio drama for *CBC Stage* in May 1950, and later that year turned up as a *Jake and the Kid* script, 'Is that the Truth?'[7] The story concerns the visit of a folklorist to Crocus, Saskatchewan, and his attempt to collect facts which are lies, namely folklore, or as Jake says, to write 'a new kinda hist'ry' (101). Thus, the folk story becomes re-visioned as a valuable and historical tale, not just 'utterly senseless and – immoral,' as Molly Gatenby says to Jake

(98). The folklorist explains that not only is the tall tale the unrecorded history of ordinary people, but it has a purpose: 'When [a person] exaggerates things he isn't lying really; it's a defence [against "terrible things"], the defence of exaggeration' (101). In *Roses*, Clem Derrigan, the Senator, the Napoleons, and even Ruth Stanley, are all tall-tale tellers, stretching the truth to defend themselves against 'terrible things,' whether the hard winters out on the range or being ostracized by the townspeople. June Melquist is a sophisticated liar hunter who, however, unlike the original liar hunter, never sees any truth in the tall tale which, for her, remains 'the ludicrous lie' (199). While Mitchell here (and elsewhere) sees the tall tale in its vital role of reclaiming ordinary and marginalized voices, he also explores the dangerous aspects of exaggerated tale-telling through such characters as Millie Clocker, who falls prey to romance novels. In other works he explores a deceiving and manipulating version of the tall tale, the spiels of con men such as the evangelist, Heally Richards, in *The Vanishing Point* or the medicine man, Dr Winesinger, from *Jake and the Kid* (who makes a brief, but innocuous, appearance in *Roses*).[8]

The distinction between tall tale and traditional history, the history of 'great and famous men' ('The Liar Hunter' 100), is also explored in the conflicts between the tall-tale teller, Jake Trumper, and the history teacher, Miss Henchbaw, in such stories and radio drama as 'The Golden Jubilee Citizen'[9] and 'History's Gotta Be Accurate.' In 'The Golden Jubilee Citizen,' when Miss Henchbaw tells the Kid that his essay on Jake, the hired man, is untruthful because it is filled with Jake's tall tales, the Kid retorts, 'Maybe he doesn't smoke House of Senate cigars an' eat Winnipeg goldeye three times a day an' – an' spit into gold goboons an' wipe his mush with a silk napkin – but he is the greatest livin' human bein I ever knew in my whole life!' (180). Miss Henchbaw, unlike Dr Melquist, recognizes the truth-value of the Kid's emotional account, and with a little polishing up, locating the facts among the anecdotes, she submits the Kid's essay to the *Crocus Breeze*.

Roses Are Difficult Here originally arose, then, from these various concerns about story-telling that Mitchell was exploring during the 1940s and 1950s in his short stories and his radio drama.

One particular event focused for Mitchell all these concerns about fact and fiction, about authorial responsibility and standards of judgment. In 1951 a book entitled *Next-Year Country* was published by Dr Jean Burnet, a lecturer in sociology at the University of Toronto. It purported to examine the social organization of Hanna, Alberta, a small farming community northeast of High River, where Mitchell was living at the time. Burnet's conclusion was that 'the rural community of the Hanna area has not achieved a stable adaptation to its physical and socio-economic environment' (151). Her overall presentation of Hanna is negative; she finds examples of incest, drunkenness, and cliquishness, and she finds the so-called professional class (the doctors, lawyers, and ministers) to be not only ill-qualified but unwilling to take on the leadership of the town. Town and country are hostile to one another, and there are examples of racial prejudice particularly against the German-Russian ethnic group (36). Nearly every chapter begins with a note about Hanna's 'failure' (3, 34, 121), its 'serious problems' (16), its lack of 'positive contributions' (75), its being 'severely limited' (96), and its 'inadequacies' (121). Only slight hope is held out that Hanna can be saved from complete disintegration. The book was criticized by Basil Dean of *The Calgary Herald* for its 'merciless clinical dissection of Hanna society,' and condemned by Mitchell's close friend Mrs McCorquodale, an editor of *The High River Times*, to whom Mitchell dedicates this novel. In her editorial, 'Under the Microscope,' Mrs McCorquodale calls into question the authority of Burnet's 'serious' study: 'It seems high time that someone from Alberta went down to Toronto to study manners and habits of the professional element there. If their customs and ways of thinking didn't conform to general deportment on the prairies, then of course they would have to be in the wrong. That seems to be the way it works out. They might be very curious people judged by our standards.' This is a declaration of the subjectiveness and fallibility of judgment and an argument against generalized truth. Mrs McCorquodale's Leacockian view of small town versus city perspectives ('Your standard of vision is all astray,' says the narrator in *Sunshine Sketches*, 'if you judge Mariposa by New York standards' [3]) impressed Mitchell, and Matt Stanley's opening for his final editorial (320–21) echoes Mrs McCorquodale's editorial.

Mitchell, angry about the betrayal of a small town (particularly the revelation of the name of the town and the finger pointed at easily identifiable doctors, ministers, and lawyers), wrote a *Jake and the Kid* episode entitled 'Crocus Under the Microscope.' It concerned the appearance in Crocus of Dr A.R. Campbell, a sociologist from the East. There occurs, of course, a confrontation between Jake and Dr Campbell, and Jake wins out with an emotional recollection of how the so-called unfriendly, class and race-conscious community came to his rescue when he was hailed out. Although Mitchell did not begin writing *Roses* until early 1957, about five years after 'Crocus Under the Microscope,' the incident with its devastatingly negative assessment of a small town became a significant motivation for his new book, the aim of which was to examine community life, including its darker side, but, in the end, to locate its positive functions.

To populate his small town Mitchell used characters from the middle section of 'The Alien,' the unpublished novel he had worked on between 1947 and 1954. The first mention of *Roses* is in a letter from Merna Mitchell to Macmillan on 1 April 1957 specifying 'The Alien' as the generative force for a 'new book': 'In reading through the middle unpublished portion of *The Alien* he [Mitchell] noticed that the lonely people, such as deaf Aunt Fan, Mr Oliver, and the Napoleons, could all be salvaged and worked into a new narrative involving the general theme of communication between people' (*W.O. Mitchell Papers*, MsC 19.8.16.10). These minor characters were wonderful creations, too good to be lost, and they are fundamentally unchanged from the original material in 'The Alien' manuscript. On the other hand, the major characters are largely new creations. Matt Stanley, although he borrows some of Carlyle's musings about the landscape, is a much less troubled human being, and significantly more sociable. Ruth is a version of the earlier Grace, although much more feisty, and the marriage in *Roses* is less painful and more believable than that in 'The Alien,' enduring only minor eruptions and implicitly patched up by Matt's decision to stay in Shelby.

There are a striking number of sub-plots woven into the main plot of *Roses*, with several borrowed from other *Jake and the Kid* radio episodes which employed characters from 'The Alien.' The highly successful comic scene of the invasion of the town by Rory Napoleon's goats had its genesis in an episode entitled 'Somethin's Gotta Go,' and was later published as a story called 'Patterns.' 'Scandal, Scandal, Scandal,' concerning Millie Clocker and her desperate attempt to get attention by inventing romantic gossip, is revised, with darker overtones, to suit the characters in *Roses*. The story of Lucy Candy (Mame Napoleon in *Roses*) winning the Annual Flower Show competition is borrowed from 'Nature Knows Best.' Two other *Jake* episodes were motivated more by actual events in High River and used the regular repertoire of *Jake and the Kid* characters. After a series of dog poisonings Mitchell wrote the episode 'Murder Will Out.' Transplanted to *Roses*, this episode serves to comment on the under-side of life in a seemingly 'rosy' small town. Joe Botten (Joe Bunch in *Roses*) justifies his poisoning of the dogs by pointing out that they are better treated than human beings like himself. The feud between Shelby and Maple Ridge over which area produces the first sign of spring is the plot of Mitchell's 'Documentary from the Banana Belt.' While this multitude of plots gives a realistic vitality to the community and, in many instances, reflects well the theme of individual and multiple voices, it also fragments the novel and disrupts the centrality of the major characters. Particularly the dog poisoning episode remains just that – an unintegrated episode. Some of these plots, as well as the three main characters, like the image of the top 'held upon its point. Dead' (319), have been 'propped' and 'supported' (319) rather than developed naturally.

Roses was written and then revised between January 1957 and September 1959.[10] The first version of *Roses* was sent to Macmillan and Atlantic Monthly Press (Little, Brown) in March 1958 and Atlantic rejected it in April. Revisions were completed by September 1959 and, although Macmillan was quite willing to publish this second version, the American publisher rejected it again. Mitchell, already under way on a *Jake and the Kid* television series and on *The Kite*, decided to drop *Roses* and concentrate on his new projects. When he picked up the manuscript some time in the late 1980s, he felt he could make some changes that would make it publishable. There are, in fact, few substantial changes between the revised and the published version, although some scenes are more effectively arranged.[11] He did add one new scene (120–28), the Santa Claus visit to Shelby which, while comic in its own right, is not successfully integrated into the whole; also, he expanded the characterization of Canon Midford (114–20), and he slightly, but significantly, expanded the role of Uncle Ben (7–9, 324).

Matt Stanley, the editor of the *Shelby Chinook*, inherited the newspaper from his Uncle Ben, who, in 1935, had won the Pulitzer Prize for 'DEFENSE OF FREEDOM OF THE PRESS' (7–8). When the provincial government had brought in censorship legislation Ben Trotter 'broke that law, attacking it editorially with rage and satire ... all the way to the provincial Supreme Court' (8). Uncle Ben represents the committed newspaperman, one interested in significant, provincial and ideological issues. He can, though, write satiric, local, and entertaining pieces such as 'The Sex Life of Old Mount Rundle' (56). Matt, on the other hand, seems primarily engaged in writing 'gossipy' news such as the 'Shelby Round-Up' (9), the 'First Gopher of Spring piece' (22), and obituaries for the dogs who have been poisoned (110–11). The dog obituaries, or 'stories' (135), as June rather pointedly calls them, become grounds for a debate first with June and then with Ruth about responsible journalism. Quoting Nettie Fitzgerald, one of the culturally ambitious townspeople, June suggests to Matt that his dog stories are 'evidence of ... limited horizons in Shelby,' and that he has been ignoring 'all the exciting and wonderful things of importance happening all over the world' (136). Matt defends himself, stating that his obituaries are 'important' (136), but he is obviously upset by her remarks and later tests out Ruth's response. However, when he says that he has just been 'writing sentimental slop about dear old pets' (137), Ruth disagrees vehemently. June and Ruth represent two opposing approaches to writing: factual, objective reporting versus the human interest, subjective story. Mitchell does not present any easy answers about which kind of journalism is better, although the obituaries are successful in flushing out Joe Bunch (212–14). The reporting of local items is important in knitting together a community which wants to know about 'Webb Bolton's boils, and Mrs Charlie Tait's gall bladder' (319) because, as Matt suggests in his editorial at the end of *Roses*, it is through such communication that neighbours can 'seed Melvin Parker's farm for him when he lay helpless in hospital' (321) and can show sympathy with food and flowers when someone is sick or has died. Furthermore, such seemingly trivial items as the first signs of spring are a means of expressing 'simple-as-breathing things like a man's delight in spring' (22).

However, immediately following Matt and Ruth's debate is a scene with Mr Oliver which appears to undercut Ruth's idealism. Ruth has angrily argued that June's criticism of Matt's sentimental and local concerns arises from a 'scale of life values' (138). She objects to having 'death graduated on a sociological scale' (138) that dictates that you must be less sad for dog deaths than for human deaths. But, the scene immediately following surely must undermine Ruth's assertion that there should be no scale of life values, for we are witness to Mr Oliver killing slugs, moles, and sucking insects that eat his plants and, in spite of Mitchell's detailed description of a wasp's death throes, we do not experience any great sadness. Although Mitchell may simply have wanted to draw a parallel between June and Mr Oliver, who both attempt to regulate life in an unnatural way, the scene raises questions about Ruth's judgments. Later on in his very moving monologue, Rory Napoleon reinforces the view of a 'scale of values' by asking, 'Ain't it more important to be a human than to be a horse or a dog or a goat?' (256). Thus, we are more prepared to question along with June whether or not Matt is too limited and is shirking his journalistic responsibility by ignoring more serious issues like the plight of Joe Bunch and Rory Napoleon. Matt's final editorial, which I will discuss later, illustrates his discovery of a tougher and broader kind of journalism, one that combines the best of June Melquist's sociological, fact-finding approach with his own individual talents for the sympathetic and local interest approach. Matt's confession near the beginning of the novel that 'he had followed a policy of considerate omission' (9) so that 'in the pages of the *Shelby Chinook* the people of the town and district lived blameless lives' (10) is modified by his concluding editorial.

Matt, however, has insights that June fails to understand and to employ in her writing. What Matt recognizes satirically in his first-signs-of-spring scoops is that truth is subjective and relative. After discovering that the first crocus that Magnus Benson finds was really nurtured under a cold frame rather than naturally, Matt writes, tongue-in-cheek: 'we deplore the *Mable Ridge News*' partial attitude in withholding essential facts from the reading public' (74). The Senator, Clem Derrigan, Mame and Rory Napoleon all tell stories which are versions of truth, which are partial and withhold some of the facts. At the dinner party that Ruth and Matt host for June, the Senator and Clem tell tall tales about the West. The Senator's stories are about the quasi-British society of the Western town with their dances, calling cards, afternoon musicals, and ranchers wearing dinner jackets; Clem's stories are about the uncivilized Wild West, about whisky traders, about men who carve their dentures from hickory wood, about royalty like Miss Shackerly, who is civilized in one way (the aunt of the Prince of Wales) and uncivilized in another (riding the range and exposing, unknowingly, her back end to Lord and Lady Minto). Both colonizer and colonized have their histories of the settlement of the West. In this novel, Mitchell pairs a number of versions of truth, such as the competition between Mable Ridge and Shelby over the first sign of spring, the Senator's and Clem's stories of the West, Joe Manley's and Ruth's versions of gossip (162), and June's and Matt's views of the small town, to comment on the impossibility of locating a single and certain truth.

Because of the subjectivity of truth the role of the listener becomes vital. Matt is able mentally to separate fact from fiction as he listens to these tales. He recognizes that Clem's anecdotes 'just about cancelled out the Senator's version of early Shelby' (51). There are versions of truth, and the listener must creatively and actively listen. While Matt's intent in asking June to dinner is to introduce her to people who can 'tell her about Shelby's childhood' (47), the word 'childhood' tellingly indicating the townspeople's view of community as a living, growing entity, June considers these men only 'great story-tellers' (61) who entertained her. She asks Clem at one point, 'Is it true?' and Matt comments, 'Even when both listener and teller knew he was lying, nobody probably had ever asked Clem that question before' (54). June does not know, as Matt knows, that some 'statements were true' (55) and some were exaggerated. She cannot interpret the voices of people she has only known briefly, and she does not understand the implicit contract or set of rules in place between teller and listener. Furthermore, she does not recognize that these stories impart a truth-value, if not the facts in every instance. They tell about a spirit of the West, about the character and humour of the people. June Melquist is no Miss Henchbaw who can listen creatively as these ordinary people 'tell' themselves into history.

In contrast to the tall tales, the first piece or story that June writes is devoid of personal input; it contains statistics of rainfall and temperature (102). Mitchell provides four examples of June's writing (102, 156–57, 198–99, 238–39) which illustrate her scientific approach – reporting statistics and organizing material into 'patterns' (239), a word that June repeatedly uses as she manipulates her material and people into 'the basic pattern' (157). From her interviews and encounters with characters such as the Senator and Clem or the Napoleons June generalizes: Shelby people had their 'elite' although they lived in a 'cultural wasteland,' and the humour was 'primitive,' 'mordant,' and based upon 'exaggeration and sarcasm' (309). Individual instances become patterns and general scientific truths in her study. For example, hearing of one rancher, Sam Barnes, who dislikes the town (244), June concludes in her report that the 'conflict between town and country was close to the surface' (309). Although Matt warns her to listen to the voice of the speaker, for 'Sam says things a little more strongly than he really means to' (244), she moves from the individual to the general pattern quite unthinkingly. If the story or tall tale fits her thesis, she accepts it as part of a pattern; otherwise she

dismisses the tall tales as 'ludicrous lie[s]' (199). Just as the anecdote that Dr Fitzgerald tells her about Sam Barnes dumping
refuse and garbage on the lawn of a Calgary hunter (79) becomes
evidence of the town and country split, Mame Napleon's story
that Dr Fitzgerald 'lost Mrs. Olsen her baby' (67) becomes evidence of the 'uncertain' (322) or inferior skill of professionals in
Shelby. June's writing is, as Matt discovers, 'wonderfully impersonal and cold to be so inflammatory': 'The sociological prose
was dedicated always to the use of the Latin- or Greek-derived
word, to hyphenated diad and triad terms, to intransitive and
copulative verbs, or, if unavoidably transitive, hamstrung by the
passive voice, rendered quite mindless by the absence of personal
pronouns' (308–09). Furthermore, June's story does not speak to
the audience it depicts. June believes that writing from an outside
position guarantees her an authoritative voice, whereas, paradoxically, Matt and Ruth believe that such alienation undermines
understanding. The very impersonality of her work flaws it
because, as Ruth says, she has never successfully been 'emotionally engaged' (304) with the people. June's 'patterns' or thesis
constitute a veiled and dangerous subjectivity masquerading as
fact.

June, however, is not treated entirely negatively; not only do
Matt and Mame Napoleon approve of her at first (68–70), two
measures of her acceptability, but Mitchell gives us a glimpse of
June's interior when he has June musing, after spontaneously
kissing Matt, that she has had a childhood deprived of parental
love. Her emotionless and lying mother (who tells 'sweet fictions'
about June's father [237]) is at least part of an explanation for
June's inability to express any attachment to her interviewees,
and her inability to hear stories except in black and white terms.
For Mitchell the joy and value of story-telling rests in its ambiguous nature, its telling of the truth 'in a way' (159). Some truths can
only be told through substitution and transference – of one thing
for another – through parable, tall tale, myth, and metaphor.
When Matt suggests to June that Mame Napoleon's story about
the birth of Byron on top of the ferris wheel is a partial truth, June
retorts, 'you can't tell the truth "in a way"' (159). Because

June cannot detect or accept shades of truth, versions of truth, her sociological report becomes destructive and false. As Matt says near the end of the novel, 'The survey was not true of them; perhaps it stated some truths but it did not mirror Shelby. Even when angry disenchantment had distorted his vision most, [Matt] would have known the falseness of the reflection' (318). Interestingly, Matt's own kind of reporting has been false in another way, in its omission rather than commission. Whereas June has committed errors by false interpretation, Matt has erred by omitting the harsher realities, for he has 'reflected only the best of all possible Shelbys in his paper' (11).

One of the most important aspects of story-telling is the establishment of a contract of understanding with the listener or reader. Tall tales are recognized as such by both parties, as Matt indicates: 'both listener and teller knew [Clem] was lying' (54). June's story is called 'slander' by Matt at the end of the novel and its destructiveness is compared to the insidious effect of Millie Clocker's obscene letters, sent to various townspeople, which slander Matt and June (318). Both texts use the authority of the written word and the seeming authority of fact to persuade their readers. June Melquist's report obviously conveys much more of this authority of fact, but one of the dangers of gossip is its ability to convince listeners that guesses are facts. Millie Clocker cannot differentiate guess from fact. Earlier in the novel she fabricates a story about Rory being the dog poisoner simply because she imagines he might be upset about overturned garbage cans. Ironically, it is June who stops her: 'You're just guessing about it and you're telling others about your guesses as though they were facts and you could hurt the Napoleons a great deal by doing it' (209). Millie is both victim and perpetrator, for, as a regular reader of I Confess (44) and This is True (197), she has begun to live a fictionalized life. Although Aunt Fan tries to tell her that these stories are 'anything but true to life' (35), Millie identifies herself and others with the heroes and heroines in these stories. A false contract of 'truth' is established between Millie and her fictional heroines, just as she establishes a false bond of credibility with some of the recipients of her letter. Mrs Nettie Fitzgerald argues with her husband that 'if somebody writes a letter like this there must be ... [some truth in it]' (270). While the other recipients claim not to believe the letters, they do not tell Matt and he comes to believe that 'an entire community had given the vicious act wide life' (300).

The frightening point of all this is that even Ruth does not tell Matt, believing that she is protecting him, whereas he reads or hears her action as a betrayal. Facts become lies and lies become facts when the contract with the audience is broken. Although Ruth's silence is not literally a lie, Matt *feels* 'lied' to (295), and the untold story, the story not shared, nearly undoes this relationship. In this context, Matt's deliberate action of telling Ruth about his special editorial before running it off (324) seems a significant shared story that augurs well for their relationship.

Some characters have only minor stories, but these stories prevent them from getting totally lost in the community – or the novel. Joe Manley, the school teacher, muses about being one of the 'lonely and homeless' (99). Later, in a kind of modern day parable about the prying gaze of townspeople, he explains his feeling of ostracism to Ruth: 'Living in a small town is just like taking up residence in the underwear section of the Hudson's Bay catalogue ... there's a whole group of us, and we've got that muted seriousness of pall-bearers – and we're quite ignorant that only our underwear stands between us and the eyes of the town' (162). Aunt Fan's monologues about her soundless and hunger-filled little world (277–80) are, on the other hand, sadly about the lack of attention paid to the old and lonely of the small town. If we are to believe Matt, Nettie Fitzgerald's local history project would benefit from some of June Melquist's objectivity, for, as Matt indicates, she is primarily interested in events and people of position; 'her values are snobbish – always' (134). Harry Fitzgerald's mock-sociological story about how 'dogs tell a story' about 'the change in land use and major climate variation' (78) satirizes the too-abstract and too-impersonal story that June Melquist attempts to tell. Even Daddy Sherry has a role to play, for he is used to make the point that it is by means of stories, not documented proof, that one truly proves his age and his identity. Although 'Daddy had been unsuccessful in winning over the fair board [as the oldest old-timer] by telling them how he had come West by shrieking Red River cart in '72,' almost everyone but Mr Oliver, who is 'a stickler for rules and regulations' (169) believes that he is the oldest old-timer. The stories of these secondary characters underline the function of narrative in the self-determination process, and the brilliant differences in the stories cited above (humorous anecdote, meditative monologue, satire, tall tale) exemplify Mitchell's concern with marginalized people.

The two most vivid characters who story-tell and who are on the periphery of society are Mame and Rory Napoleon. Rory is ostracized by polite society for being of mixed race (Indian, French, Basque and Scotch), for having a common-law wife, and for being the nuisance man. But perhaps what most annoys the townspeople is that Mame and Rory are natural – they have a 'casual façade' (155), an 'insouciance' (156), and they are associated with uncontrolled sexuality, having had ten children. Mitchell juxtaposes Ruth's hospital, doctor-controlled, and anaesthetized delivery with Mame's story (story of a story because the story of Byron's birth conceals another story, the story of his conception) of her natural but startling carnivalesque delivery of Byron on the top of a stopped Ferris wheel (155). In a similarly natural manner it is Mame, not Mr Oliver, who produces the winning rose at the Flower Show, and on that occasion Mame delivers her parable of how to be a winner in life: 'I don't know what makes anything beautiful ... unless it's luck, the Lord, an' goat manoor' (197). Keeping the Napoleons out of town, literally and figuratively, is a measure of keeping out naturalness, spontaneity, sexuality, earthiness – and anarchy.

As Mame says, all the townspeople do is 'pick, pick, pick' (217), but Rory gets his revenge on the townspeople when his goats invade the town and throw it into complete chaos. Rory, like Pan the shepherd-god, half goat and half man, is associated with licentiousness, with wanton behaviour, and with inciting panic. Rory's instigation of the goat invasion occurs, not so coincidentally, just before 'Millie knew she must post the letters,' for both 'loosed upon the town' (265) panic, revenge, and all repressed impulses. In his intoxicated state Rory sees the goats taking on human form; he removes the veneer of civilization from Mrs Fitzgerald and Mr Oliver, and they become the real instigators of town disunity because they have denied him a place in society. Rory's drunken story is a plea for recognition, for a place, and for a voice in the community: '"I was born human!" he shouted after Mr Oliver [the goat]. "I'll die human! I eat human! I drink human! I am human! I'm me! I'm Rory Napoleon!"' (256). The freeing of the goats becomes, not just a revenge on the townspeople, but his discovery of self and freedom. It is his answer to Mrs Fitzgerald's local history of the town's élite, which had eliminated him. His visionary story is that 'the whole world had turned into a nuisance grounds with garbage-eating goats!' (128).

The invasion of goats is a comic version of other kinds of 'darkness' (313) unloosed upon the town – the 'infection' (273) spread by Millie's poison letters and the 'flagrant invasion of ... privacy' (307) perpetrated by June Melquist's book on Shelby. Yet, as Mame says, the goat invasion 'kind of perked the town up a bit' (286), and it is paralleled with another kind of invasion of a more serious nature, the sociological report, which 'perked the town up' by drawing it together in a public meeting. The victimizers (in particular the élite who had 'picked' on the Napoleons) are now the victims. As the townspeople identify their enemy in June Melquist and her impersonal report, Rory Napoleon voices to them their own culpability: 'Maybe you got a lot more than what's comin' to you – maybe a lot of what you got *was* comin' to you' (314).

Matt completes the cleansing process when he writes his editorial denouncing June Melquist's book and detailing the positive features of his town. Defending his people, their humour, their professionalism, and their community spirit, he finishes with a space-filler, a 'tag' about a collection of dinosaur bones along the Red Deer River. But when he imagines how his Uncle Ben might have finished up, he hears him say, 'that dinosaur tag won't do' (324). He realizes that he can and must 'reach a wider audience' (324). Not only can he 'reach' a wider audience, but he recognizes that he should attempt to *reflect* more truly and more widely. Thus he adds his 'perfect tag,' the note about the Napoleons leaving town: 'The many friends of the Rory Napoleons will be sorry to hear that they have left Shelby...' (325). His reflection of Shelby now includes the marginalized, the anarchic, and the lonely ones, and his satiric remark about the 'many friends' of the Napoleons is added to imprint upon the townspeople the need for greater tolerance.

The 'tag' reminds the community that truth, standards, judgments, and stories are not impartial. They, who have sat in judgment on the Napoleons, have themselves been judged, perhaps no more unfairly than have the Napoleons. Through the multitude of stories in this novel, Mitchell has suggested that different versions of truths are generated by different points of view. He juxtaposes the Senator's stories with Clem's, Ruth's with June's, and Mame Napoleon's rose cultivation with Mr Oliver's, and so he ends the novel with dual stories – one which celebrates the town (Matt's editorial), and the other which criticizes the town for its class and race prejudices (the tag about the Napoleons). Although Matt had earlier said that Clem's stories 'just about cancelled out the Senator's version of early Shelby' (51), it is evident at the end of the novel that stories, like roses, flourish better if hybridized. The hybrid rose described earlier by Mr Oliver as having 'wild roots and tame bush' (86) only survives if both parts co-exist. Rory puts it rather bluntly in his speech to the community:

'We're leavin' you – tomorrow – for the Yukon. Maybe it ain't gonna be all razzberries an' honey there, but she can't be any worse than she's been for us here.'

He raised his hand at the mutter of protest that rose in front of him. 'All right, all right. A lot of you figger it ain't any skin off your – knuckles – where the Napoleons go. Well, it will for a while, I promise you, right until you get somebody else to haul your goddam garbage an' empty your goddam cans and pump your goddam cesspools.' (314)

His speech, his story, his words, 'all right,' subtly undercut the celebratory conclusion to Matt's editorial response: 'We are all right, Dr Melquist' (323). Until the community learns to accommodate (or hybridize) the stories of the 'lonely and homeless ones' (99) and the wild ones, 'roses [will be] difficult here' (325).

NOTES

1 Matt Stanley is not only a frustrated newspaperman but also a blocked writer who has written 'a handful of failed short stories' and has dreamed of writing 'the Great New World Novel' (9). David Lang in *The Kite* (1962) is a freelance writer for magazines and television but wants to find time to write a novel or a play (6); Colin Dobbs in *Since Daisy Creek* (1984) is a professor at Livingstone University who teaches creative writing but is unable to free himself to write the novel he wants (48); Dr Lyon in *Ladybug, Ladybug* ... (1988) is attempting to write a 'Mark Twain biography' (8).

2 Only part 3 of 'The Alien' was published, and that was in nine parts in *Maclean's* from September 1953 to January 1954.

3 W.O. Mitchell, 'Tragic Trek of the Mennonites,' *Maclean's*, 1 March 1951; 'The Riddle of Louis Riel,' *Maclean's*, 1 February 1952; 15 February 1952 [on the Metis]; 'People Who Don't Want Equality,' *Maclean's*, 3 July 1965; and 'The Strait Gate,' dir. Peter Kappele, CBC, 28 December 1964 [on the Hutterites].

4 W.O. Mitchell, 'Cow Heaven,' *Maclean's*, 15 November 1943; 'The Goose Hunt,' *Explorations: Man in the Landscape*, dir. Peter Kelly, CBC, 8 May 1963; 'A Saddle for a Stony,' writ. W.O. Mitchell, *20/20*, dir. Peter Kelly, CBC, 14 July 1963.

5 'East End Was Just the Beginning,' *Telescope*, dir. Peter Kelly, CBC, 17 November 1966 [on Stegner]; 'Ron Southern – Master-Builder,' *Telescope*, dir. Peter Kelly, CBC, 30 June 1965.

6 W.O. Mitchell, 'What's Ahead for Billy?' *The Canadian Forum*, 24 (July 1944). Mitchell employed documentary strategies, quoting exact speeches of real band members, and used statistics. However, he also used fictional strategies. The band meeting is seen through the eyes of young Billy, a fictional character, and Mitchell descriptively details sounds and sights of the meeting which go beyond the usual documentary reporting.

7 'Is That the Truth?' writ. W.O. Mitchell, *Jake and the Kid*, dir. Peter Francis, CBC, 17 October 1950. My quotations are from the reprinting of 'The Liar Hunter' in *Jake and the Kid* (1961). I have corroborated my own datings of the *Jake and the Kid* stories with the following bibliographies: Timothy James Zeman, 'An Annotated Bibliography of the Radio Drama of W.O. Mitchell in the Special Collections of the University of Calgary Libraries,' thesis, U of Alberta, 1993; Alan Yates, 'W.O. Mitchell's *Jake and the Kid*: The Canadian

Popular Radio Play as Art and Social Comment,' diss., McGill, 1979; Sheila Latham, *W.O. Mitchell: An Annotated Bibliography* (Toronto: ECW Press, 1981).

8 Orm Mitchell in 'Tall Tales in the Fiction of W.O. Mitchell' (*Canadian Literature*, No. 108 [Spring 1984]: 16–35) looks closely at 'The Liar Hunter' and follows Mitchell's exploration of the tall tale as defence through characters such as Brian and Uncle Sean in *Who Has Seen the Wind* and fantasizers such as Carlyle in *The Vanishing Point*, Saint Sammy in *Wind*, and the mad women of Mitchell's play *Back to Beulah*.

9 W.O. Mitchell, 'The Golden Jubilee Citizen,' *Maclean's*, 25 June 1955. Reprinted in *Jake and the Kid* (Macmillan, 1961), from which I take my quotations. It was also done as radio drama: dir. Esse W. Ljungh, CBC, 17 November 1955.

10 For a discussion of the genesis of *Roses* and a positive judgment on its worth – before its publication in 1990 – see Catherine McLay, 'Novels are Difficult Here: W.O. Mitchell's Unpublished Fiction,' *Essays on Canadian Writing* 37 (Spring 1989): 86–102.

11 Mitchell worked from the revised second version (1959) when he began editing for the 1990 version. It is not within the scope of this essay to comment fully on the variations in the versions. More changes were made between the first and second versions than between the second and third. For example, from the first version he removed the 'poetess' Belva Tinsley, removed or condensed some of the descriptive scenes, newspaper items and tall tales, and tightened up the narrative structure. However, the main areas of concern, plot and major character development, were not substantially altered in the last two versions.

PART II

The Drama:
Radio, Television, and Stage

Genre to Genre:
Tracing Sources through Bibliography

TIMOTHY ZEMAN

A careful reader will identify a variety of similarities within the works of an author. Most commonly, the connections are limited to stylistic comparisons. But in the case of W.O. Mitchell, the connections extend beyond the stylistic level to the transfer of plots and characters from genre to genre. For example, a plot, its characters, and other material which first appear as a short story may be transformed into a radio play, then into a stage play, and again into a television script. Occasionally, the material even reappears in novels. This pattern of transformation has been repeated regularly in Mitchell's work, most recently in the novel *The Black Bonspiel of Willie MacCrimmon* (1993). The process of tracing these transformations begins with the early stages of Mitchell's literary career.

The radio plays were and continue to be a fertile source of characters and situations both for Mitchell's later fiction and for his stage and television drama. In fact, one might argue that the *Jake and the Kid* radio plays were the training ground for much of Mitchell's work, for he has returned to them frequently enough. Four of his eleven books of published fiction owe a significant debt to the *Jake and the Kid* series. While the first collection of published short stories, *Jake and the Kid* (1961), is drawn from stories first published in magazines, and later adapted as radio scripts, the second collection of short stories, *According to Jake and the Kid* (1989), is nearly identical to the radio play episodes from which the stories take their inspiration. The novels *The Kite* and *Roses Are*

Difficult Here are very clearly based upon radio play episodes. To a lesser extent, *Who Has Seen the Wind* and *The Black Bonspiel Of Willie MacCrimmon* are connected to *Jake and the Kid* and its later companion, the *Foothill Fables* series. Still other radio plays were extended or combined to form longer stage plays and even adapted to make television screen plays.

Mitchell says that he has written as many as four hundred radio plays, the majority of them in the *Jake and the Kid* series, which aired on CBC radio from 1950 to 1956 (Mitchell interview, 31 October 1992). His success in both this popular medium, the radio play, and in more conventional literary endeavors such as novels and stage plays, is unique among Canadian authors. Within Mitchell's published work, the conversion of thematic and other material from radio drama to fiction is particularly interesting in that radio drama is 'the medium in which drama and fiction come closest to meeting' (Lewis 8). Listeners to the radio plays, like the silent readers of fiction, actively engage their imaginations to create what they hear or read; however, any serious attempt to study this relationship is frustrated by the inaccessibility of the radio play scripts.

While some of these scripts are available at Concordia University, McMaster University, and the National Archives, the largest collection is contained in the W.O. Mitchell and Morris Surdin Papers housed in the Special Collections of the University of Calgary Libraries.[1] The W.O. Mitchell Papers is a fully processed collection of the personal papers of Mitchell; the published archival inventory, *The W.O. Mitchell Papers*, lists the entire contents of the papers with comprehensive indexing. The Morris Surdin Papers is a partially processed collection of the personal papers of Morris Surdin, prolific Canadian composer and orchestral conductor for many CBC radio dramas, among other musical accomplishments.[2] The Surdin Papers are valuable because they offer a more complete collection of Mitchell radio play scripts than do the Mitchell Papers. In addition to CBC production scripts, the Surdin Papers contain the musical scores to all but a few of the episodes as well as some recordings of the radio plays.

There are three main series of radio plays represented in the

University of Calgary collection: *Jake and the Kid*, *Foothill Fables*, and *Theatre 10:30* (essentially a 1969–70 revival of earlier *Jake and the Kid* episodes). The *Jake and the Kid* episodes, by far the most popular and numerous, are all set in Crocus, Saskatchewan. The core cast of characters (and actors and actresses) is consistent throughout the six years: Jake Trumper, the Kid, Ma, Old Man Gatenby, and Repeat Godfrey. Other members of the community appear frequently enough to be recognizable from episode to episode and series to series (e.g. Mayor MacTaggart, Miss Henchbaw, Professor Noble Winesinger, poet Belva Taskey, Pete Botten, and others). *Jake and the Kid* was broadcast in six series from 27 June 1950 until 26 April 1956.

Series I: 27 June 1950 to 29 April 1951 (45 weekly episodes)
Series II: 30 September 1951 to 25 May 1952 (35 weekly episodes)
Series III: 11 January 1953 to 24 May 1953 (20 weekly episodes)
Series IV: 27 September 1953 to 18 April 1954 (30 weekly episodes)
Series V: 26 September 1954 to 19 June 1955 (39 weekly episodes)
Series VI: 29 September 1955 to 26 April 1956 (30 weekly episodes)

The *Foothill Fables* series was broadcast in two instalments from 25 December 1961 to 25 March 1962 and 27 October 1963 to 19 January 1964. They are set in the fictional Alberta foothills town of Shelby. Despite this change in locale, many characters and events from the Crocus scripts (*Jake and the Kid*) found their way into the lives of Shelby characters. For example, although the names have changed, Old John Jackson's goose hunt in a pit large enough to hold his wheelchair, the minister, the undertaker, and the doctor in 'Old Croaker' (*Foothill Fables*, 27 October 1963) is almost identical to Old Daddy Johnson's experience in 'Daddy and the Gander.' Similar parallels occur in at least four other pairs of scripts, all of which reappear in *The Kite*.

The potential topics for further research may be grouped in several ways: studies of radio play technique; connections among the radio plays themselves; connections between the radio plays and the fiction; and speculative or trans-discipline considerations.

The plot structure of the radio plays follows a common pattern.

Many of the plays focus on an experience in which either Jake or the Kid is a key participant, whether willingly or unwittingly. The plays generally open with a passage of monologue or dialogue which discusses in general terms the conflict about to be established. The opening often includes some male-biased philosophical ramblings about town life or human relations from Jake or Repeat Godfrey, the barber; this conversation is often set either in the barbershop or in Mayor MacTaggart's General Store. Then the conflict is established and played out to a climax in which Jake inevitably has a key role. A hasty dénouement is often followed by a pithy concluding statement, frequently in Jake's colourful vernacular.

The role of the local newspaper (*Crocus Breeze* in *Jake and the Kid* and *Shelby Chinook* in *Foothill Fables*) as a plot device to present information, to clarify character actions, to establish conflicts, and to act as social conscience is a technique that Mitchell pursued in his fiction with the role of journalist narrators (especially David Lang in *The Kite* and Matt Stanley in *Roses Are Difficult Here*). The technique of frequently using newspaper articles to begin or sustain a *Jake and the Kid* script is echoed in *For Art's Sake*, where sixteen separate newspaper articles are used to advance the plot.

The original Mitchell typewritten scripts were adapted at the CBC to fit the demands of production, especially the constraints of time. Some scripts were too long, and thus were split into two-part episodes. Other scripts were too short, so CBC directors had to insert parts of other plays in order to create a full half-hour episode. The Surdin collection reveals the changes which occurred from Mitchell's scripts to the CBC production scripts, changes which provide insights into the production process as well as into the adaptations which Mitchell himself later made in transforming them from radio play to fiction and other genres.

The resonances from radio play to short story to novel are particularly strong when one considers the characters and social strata of the towns in Mitchell's fictional worlds. There are characters who appear, it seems, in each of the works. For example, Repeat Godfrey, the barber in the *Jake and the Kid* radio plays, is a philosophical businessman who spends hours chatting about his latest reading to his customers. He is Milt Palmer in *Who Has Seen the Wind*, Merton Spicer in *The Kite*, and Repeat Golightly in the *Jake and the Kid* short story collection. The tall tales told by Jake are also told by the Ben and Uncle Sean of *Who Has Seen the Wind*, then again by Clem in *Roses Are Difficult Here*. Daddy Johnson of *Jake and the Kid* becomes Old John Jackson of *Foothill Fables* and Daddy Sherry of *The Kite*; Young Pete Tincher and Matthew Behind-the-Rock in *Jake and the Kid* are parallels to Young Ben and Saint Sammy in *Who Has Seen the Wind*. The strong female social leader, or as the Kid calls her, 'boss of the social herd,' appears as Elsie Abercrombie in *Jake and the Kid* and *Who Has Seen the Wind*. She appears, with changed name, as Florence Allerdyce in *Foothill Fables* and *The Kite*, and as Netty Fitzgerald in *Roses Are Difficult Here*. The consistent presence of a doctor central to town life is paralleled by the existence of a goose-hunting funeral director, usually named Ollie Pringle. Mitchell offers a range of clerics, both legitimate (Reverend Powelly in *Who Has Seen the Wind*, Canon Midford in *Roses Are Difficult Here*, Reverend Donald Finlay in *The Kite* and so on), and less than trustworthy (Elijah Stevens in *Jake and the Kid* and *Foothill Fables*, Heally Richards in *The Vanishing Point*, and Reverend Elijah Matthews in *Ladybug, Ladybug...*). The Bens in *Who Has Seen the Wind*, the Candys in *Jake and the Kid*, and the Napoleons in *Foothill Fables* and *Roses Are Difficult Here* are social outcasts who all experience arrogant treatment at the hands of the town's social élite; they also manage to exact poetically just revenge on their socially hypocritical enemies. Thus, a detailed composite social profile of Mitchell's fictional town(s) can be created from both the radio plays and the novels.

Critics have long mentioned the obvious connections between Daddy Sherry of *The Kite* and Daddy Johnson of *Jake and the Kid* or Old John Jackson of *Foothill Fables*. A careful study of the radio plays and the ways in which they are altered to become the novel should consider the evolution of such similar scripts as 'RIP' (*Jake and the Kid*, 30 March 1952) and 'Salt of the Matter' (*Foothill Fables*, 25 February 1962); as 'Daddy Johnson Travellin' Man' (*Jake and the Kid*, 15 March 1953) and 'Move Over, Magellan' (*Foothill Fables*, 11 March 1962); and how all three pairs of scripts were incorporated into Mitchell's novel *The Kite*. The process could be extended to consider the adaptations necessary for creating the stage and television versions of the same story.

Even in the later novels, resonances back to the radio plays occur. The complicating event of *Since Daisy Creek* – a man being mauled by a grizzly bear after several years of fruitless hunting – first appeared in several *Foothill Fables* episodes ('Lullaby for a Hunter,' 'Green Thumb, Red Finger,' and 'The Trophy'). Furthermore, Colin Dobbs's embarrassment at the public revelation of a diminutive brown bear skin, instead of the huge grizzly pelt which he anticipated, is the central event of 'The Trophy.' A careful study of these interconnections and of the adaptation, extension, and interweaving of radio play episodes within the novels as Mitchell shifts genres would be most fruitful.

One of the less well-known examples is the parallel between several radio scripts and *Roses Are Difficult Here*. This 1990 novel draws significantly upon five radio play episodes from *Jake and the Kid* and *Foothill Fables*; Mitchell appears to extend and weave them together to form the novel. The central plot of the novel revolves around the episode entitled 'Crocus Under the Microscope,' broadcast 24 February 1951, in which an Eastern Canadian sociologist comes to Crocus (or Shelby) to study the makeup of a small prairie town. The original version was based on an actual experience in Hanna, Alberta, in which a University of Toronto sociologist visited the town, boarding with a talkative socialite. The sociologist seemed to accept much of the socialite's information as fact and based many of her conclusions on this misleading evidence. The publication of her report scandalized the residents of Hanna, as in the scripts and novel, because the sociologist failed to preserve the anonymity of the town and attacked the narrowness of vision and accomplishment of the residents of small prairie towns. Mitchell's *Jake and the Kid* episode was an attempt at public rebuttal, and he used his characters, particularly *Crocus Breeze* editor Chet Lambertson (or Matt Stanley in the novel) to reply with dignity to the Eastern attack.

Interwoven with this central plot line is the story of lonely Millie Clocker, a former telephone operator, now receptionist at the

Shelby Chinook, whose obsession with romance magazines leads her to discredit the married man with whom she is infatuated, newspaper editor Matt Stanley. She creates a scandal by sending anonymous letters to important social figures in town, graphically describing Stanley's supposed affair with the visiting sociologist. This plot is borrowed directly from a *Jake and the Kid* episode, 'Scandal, Scandal, Scandal,' with the slight change that Crocus's Mayor MacTaggart is the target of the scandal in the radio play. Furthermore, the inclusion of two *Jake and the Kid* dog poisoning scripts, 'A Man's Best Friend' and 'Murder Will Out,' adds some colour to the novel's plot. The Napoleon (or Candy) family plays a role in the novel as well through the adaptation of a *Jake and the Kid* script 'Nature Knows Best' and its *Foothill Fables* counterpart, 'Phlox, Stocks and Hollyhocks.' Mame Napoleon (or Lucy Candy) wins the annual flower competition with a single yellow rose she has planted haphazardly beside her house, defeating and humiliating town socialites (and expert gardeners) who have traditionally dominated the competition with their scientific methods. Several other connections – the Napoleon goats in town, the comparisons between goat and human facial characteristics – reinforce the correlation between the novel and the radio plays. The connections between *Roses Are Difficult Here* and 'Crocus Under the Microscope' are worth examining at some length, for they reveal much about Mitchell's creative process.

Mitchell's return to the 'Crocus Under the Microscope' script after many years is curious considering the controversy which the episode stirred upon its airing in 1952. Perhaps Peter Francis, the successful producer and director of the first and second seasons of *Jake and the Kid*, was correct in his estimation of Mitchell: 'I have a feeling that your attitude towards stirring up trouble is a trifle casual.' The story behind this episode begins in Hanna, Alberta, in the summer of 1946, at the same time that Mitchell was finishing *Who Has Seen the Wind*.

The *Hanna Herald* welcomed 'an interesting visitor' to town on 4 July 1946:

Miss Jean Burnette [*sic*] of the staff of the University of Toronto,

who in a matter of months will be Dr. Jean Burnette Ph.D. Miss
Burnette in addition to her teaching duties at the university has
carried on extensive research work in a number of industrial areas
in the United States. Her present duties on her visit to the semi-
arid areas of South Eastern Alberta is [sic] to find out and issue a
comprehensive report on the effect of drouth on the community life
of the farm and urban people.

The brief article goes on to record that the research is carried
out jointly by the University of Toronto and the Rockefeller
Foundation, and that Burnet was to issue a report early in September 1946. A census of the prairie provinces was also being
conducted that summer, thus providing statistical data to be
included in Burnet's research.[3] The newspaper records that Burnet left Hanna for Toronto during the week prior to 5 September
1946 after having finished her research. Her stay in Hanna was
a mere two months.

This seemingly unimportant summer of 1946 took on a completely different significance five years later when, in late 1951,
the results of Burnet's research were published by the University
of Toronto Press as *Next-Year Country: A Study of Rural Social Organization in Alberta*. As might be expected, the book was received
first with curiosity, then with hostility. Alberta journalists were
alerted to the book's publication by an article in the 12 December
1951 *Calgary Herald*. In his 'All Things Considered' column, Basil
Dean comments that this book of 'less than 200 pages ... is as
explosive as anything published this year.' He goes on to quote
several passages from the book about Hanna's sex life, community leadership, hospitality, social life, and racial relations. He
summarizes: 'These extracts demonstrate that Dr. Burnet has been
something less than kind to Hanna.' Dean correctly predicts the
'wrath and indignation' of Hanna residents.

As expected, the reaction in Hanna was harsh. The 20 December 1951 issue of the *Hanna Herald* reprinted Dean's article along
with an editorial. Then, over the next three issues, letters to the
editor and reprints of editorials from other Alberta papers all
expressed contempt for Burnet's work and asserted the value and

significance of Hanna. In fact, rural Alberta seemed to take the 'attack' on Hanna as an attack on rural life in Alberta.

Of course, Mitchell was not immune to the controversy. He had friends in Hanna, used to hunt geese and ducks there, and had begun his teaching career in Castor, sixty-four kilometres due north of Hanna. This natural interest, coupled with the coverage in the *Calgary Herald* and *High River Times*, provided a fertile source for a radio play episode. And this sort of issue, according to Peter Francis, was exactly what Mitchell would enjoy writing about.

Mitchell's carbon copy typescript was sent to the CBC in Toronto for Peter Francis to prepare for airing. In Francis's correspondence with Merna Mitchell, he mentions in a letter dated 18 February 1952 his concern that the 'sociological script' is a strong piece of writing: 'I am not sure that it really belongs on *Jake and the Kid.*' He is 'a little worried' about the laws of libel and in particular wishes to know if Mitchell 'invented all the quotations from the sociologist's book, or whether he took any of them from the book in question.' Francis finishes the letter by apologizing for being so fussy, 'but the fact that the book was unfair and inaccurate would not say [*sic*] us from a suit, and if any of the quotations in the script were really from the book we'd be dead ducks.'

In order to protect the CBC and *Jake and the Kid*, Francis did make several changes to the script. For example, Mitchell's original version begins with the Kid reading from the *Crocus Breeze* about a single female sociologist (Dr Campbell) from 'a university they got' in Toronto who will do a survey of Crocus and district for a projected book 'Next Year Town.' Dr Campbell takes a sabbatical leave to do her research, made possible by the 'Rockerfeller foundation.' Peter Francis changed the potentially libelous material by switching the gender of the sociologist, changing the location of the university to simply 'eastern,' and eliminating any reference to a book title ('Crocus' 5–6).

Francis also softened the response to Dr Campbell's book in the CBC version. In the original script, Ma says 'I'm afraid it's not Crocus people who are wrong – *but Dr. Campbell. She must be terribly twisted herself to – to do a thing like that!*' The italicized portion was deleted by Francis. Furthermore, Chet Lambertson, *Cro-cus Breeze* editor, states in the original script: 'If you remember that [it is not true of our town and of our people] then this thing becomes simply what it is – a false report made out by an immature and biased person.' Francis removed the inflammatory words after 'report'; his sensitivity to issues of libel proved to be prophetic.

Peter Francis wrote apologetically to W.O. Mitchell, also on 18 February 1952:

> So far as radio goes, the sociological script is a remarkable piece of work and contains a lot of things that should be said and are well said. Whether it really belongs on *Jake and the Kid*, I am not sure. It's not particularly entertaining, it certainly isn't funny, and it is not very heart-warming either, except the final recitations at the end ... [I feel] as you must have that the things in it ought to be said and that it is drama, so in it goes, for next Sunday, Feb. 24.

The episode was broadcast during the regular *Jake and the Kid* time slot at 5:30 P.M. Sunday afternoon, Eastern Standard Time. Francis was still apologetic in a second letter to Mitchell dated 28 February, in which he wrote that he hoped Mitchell did not mind the cuts and changes to the 'sociological piece'; however, his worst fears were realized a few days later.

In his next correspondence with Mitchell, dated 29 February 1952, Francis reports that a university professor has been asking for a copy of the 'Crocus Under the Microscope' script. He also mentions that there may be a lawsuit against the CBC with heavy damages. Even if the Town of Hanna were to countersue, Francis states, 'it would be the end of Jake.' Unfortunately, copies of the letters and internal CBC memos about the threatened suits are not in the Mitchell Papers, but Francis's reactions are clearly recorded.

To compound matters for Francis, Mitchell's assurances that the supposed quotations from the fictional sociologist's book were entirely fabricated turned out to be false; Francis discovered that Mitchell's quotes bore an uncanny resemblance to quotations from *Next-Year Country* in Basil Dean's article in the *Calgary Herald*. In a letter to Mitchell dated 9 March 1952, Francis states: 'you did after all quote from Jean Burnet's book when you assured me you had not seen it (meaning in your Scottish casuistry that you had not seen it but had heard quotations from it I daresay).' In the script of the 24 February broadcast, eight pages chronicle the response of Crocus residents to Dr Campbell's book. Approximately two pages provide 'quotations' from the book and the rest records the reaction of various community members, from Ma to Chet Lambertson. The quotations from Dr Campbell's book read as follows:

JOE: (reading) – Social an' economic background of Crocus, Saskatchewan. Situated in a one-crop agricultural district – wheat and coarse grains.

MUSIC: BRIDGE THEN DOWN BG. FOR:

PETE: – a community of no discernible social pattern of grouping – no salient culture – no history or tradition...

MUSIC: BRIDGE THEN BG. FOR:

MA: It is natural that the community should look to its professional men for its leadership and it is true that this is the most highly educated group. They are neither talented nor well qualified. To some extend [sic] this may be attributed to their feeling that they cannot measure up to urban competition. In Crocus demands upon their professional skill are less; they are safe.

MUSIC: BRIDGE THEN BG. FOR:

FANNY: – who consider themselves socially superior. This group do not feel themselves subject to the puritanical code governing the rest. Setting themselves apart, they have devoted their efforts to a hedonistic life and are completely uninterested in community affairs and community government.

MUSIC: BRIDGE THEN BG. FOR:

MA: – resentment of foreign born elements in the community. These have been isolated deliberately...

MUSIC: BRIDGE THEN BG. FOR:

JAKE: – the myth of Western hospitality dies quickly in Crocus,

Saskatchewan. No effort is made to welcome newcomers to town. In one case no notice was taken for an entire week ...

MUSIC: OUT ('Crocus' 16–17)

In his review, Basil Dean had quoted five passages. Observe the similarities between Mitchell's version and two of the quotations:

> On community leadership: 'The ability of the professional men is open to question ... They are the most highly educated people in the community ... but they are not otherwise outstandingly well qualified. Some are in Hanna because they feel they cannot measure up ... to urban competition. They cling to Hanna as a "safe berth," contributing less and less to its life. Others are presumably competent but personally ill-qualified in health, appearance, or conduct. Still others are both incompetent and personally ill-qualified.'
>
> On Hanna's hospitality: 'In Hanna, little notice is taken of a newcomer for at least one week. Little effort is made to enlist new arrivals in town activities. Three months after a young professional man, his wife and his parents moved to town, both his wife and his mother complained of loneliness.'

In addition to the above examples, Basil Dean quoted a passage about racial relations in which Burnet suggests that German-Russians were 'socially isolated' by the English farmers who 'react to what seems a serious threat with heightened hostilities and more frequent assertions of superiority.' Clearly Peter Francis had reason for concern.

The libel suit might well have proceeded had it not been for the timely intervention of Oswald Hall, chair of the Department of Sociology and Anthropology at McGill University.[4] In a letter to Mitchell written on 28 February 1952, he praises *Jake and the Kid* as a 'Sunday afternoon visitor in our living-room.' Hall expresses keen interest in the 'Crocus Under the Microscope' broadcast, and clearly associates Burnet's book with the Jake episode: 'we have been concerned about this unfortunate affair ever since the book appeared in print.' He goes on to explain the 'almost universal convention that the sociologist devises some means to conceal the identity of the community he studies.' Without actually mentioning Burnet's name or book directly, Hall states:

> When some of us heard that this book had violated the rule we anticipated that there would be violent objections ... As a spokesman, for people whom I feel have been victimized in this case, you certainly let us have it – both barrels, plenty of powder ... But let me assure you that we were thoroughly alarmed and distressed at the decision of the editors and publishers to take the step they did.

As the brief tempest calmed, partly due to the quick and efficient work of Peter Francis, Hall wrote a second letter, this time to Peter Francis, in which he states:

> I hope my letter and the others will not result inevitably and inexorably in a decision to protect university disciplines from attack by such people as Mr. Mitchell. Though they are painful I welcome such attacks. Given the kinds of thick skins and the unswerving assurance of superiority that life in the academic world can bring to people, I am not sure that occasional attacks of this sort are not both desirable and necessary.
>
> In my view, what he has done is to clarify a problem that might have got kicked around clumsily for five or ten years more, and I for one feel we owe him a debt of gratitude.

Both Mitchell and Francis were vindicated. On 12 March 1952, Francis wrote to Mitchell that he was glad in retrospect that the show was written and broadcast. He affirmed to Mitchell that 'what it said needed saying,' but he also cautioned that *Jake and the Kid* was not the place for frequent personal attacks.

In addition to marked similarities between the script and Burnet's book, the reactions of editors and readers in Alberta newspapers, particularly in Calgary, Hanna, and High River, seem to have provided fruitful sources for the script as well. For example, a letter to the editor in the 28 December 1951 *Calgary Herald* from

Reginald Wright, vicar of All Saints Anglican Church in Hanna at the time, attacks Burnet's work. In what appears to be an edited version of a longer letter published in the *Hanna Herald* on 20 December 1951, Wright states that he had, by coincidence, read a manuscript of Burnet's book three years previously and felt certain that she would find no one to publish it. Wright's '16 years of commercial experience' prior to entering the ministry lead him to suggest that 'a sociologist if she were young and hadn't been around very much could write something seamy about any town if she wanted to build upon all the gossip that she listened to.' He concludes with a series of statements, each prefaced by 'J'Accuse.' In Mitchell's script, the special issue of the *Crocus Breeze* dedicated to 'answer[ing] Dr. Campbell' has 'in real big type... J'ACCUSE and I guess that's French for Look Out' ('Crocus' 16).

The opening lines of Chet Lambertson's editorial in the fictional *Crocus Breeze* are almost identical to the words of the *High River Times* editorial on 20 December 1951. Following the headline, 'Under the Microscope,' Hughena McCorquodale begins:

> It seems high time that someone from Alberta went down to Toronto to study manners and habits of the professorial element there. If their customs and ways of thinking didn't conform to general deportment on the prairies, then of course they would have to be in the wrong. That seems to be the way it works out. They might be very curious people judged by our standards.

Mitchell's script reads:

> It seems high time that some one from Saskatchewan went down to an eastern city to study manners and mores of the professorial element there. If their customs and ways of thinking didn't conform to general comportment on the prairies, then of course they would be in the wrong. We feel they must be very curious people judged by our standards. ('Crocus' 20)

In *Roses Are Difficult Here* (320), a nearly identical passage opens the editorial of the rebuttal issue of the *Shelby Chinook*.

Because the *Jake and the Kid* episode was limited to thirty minutes, Mitchell could not provide the volume of detail which a novel permits. The novel, however, contains numerous additional details which seem to confirm the common sources for both versions. The twenty-fourth chapter of *Roses Are Difficult Here* chronicles the events as Dr J.L. Melquist's book, 'published evidently for public consumption by an Eastern University Press' (308), is mentioned in 'the local city newspaper' in an article entitled 'Under the Microscope.' The novel also echoes Oswald Hall: 'The Shelby report was particularly brutal in its criticism, a most flagrant invasion of their [Shelby residents'] privacy' (307).

Furthermore, the novel echoes the accusations of editorials and letters to the editors of the newspapers of 1951 and 1952, which referred to the gossip-mongering which seemed to be at the root of the sociologist's research (whether Dr Jean Burnet, Dr Campbell, or Dr J.L. Melquist). In *Roses Are Difficult Here*, the narrator, Matt Stanley, recognizes many voices beneath the 'abstracting mist' of the sociological jargon; the most frequently recognizable is that of Flannel Mouth Florence, the town gossip (309). In the *Hanna Herald*, the editorial of 20 December 1951 questions the source of Burnet's information: 'We can visualize an interview with a common gossip, or a person utterly devoted to a life of pessimism and condemnation of the success and achievements made by others in the community.' In the *Drumheller Mail*, an editorial attacks Burnet's sources, suggesting that she 'spent the greatest part of her time listening intently to the tales of scandal mongers and apparently shunning the average members of the community.'

After describing the reactions to the sociologist's book, both the script and the novel go on, almost verbatim, to exemplify how the actual experience of Crocus/Shelby residents contradicts the 'findings' of the sociologist. Written by the editors of the local papers in the fictional works, the rebuttals describe the many deeds performed by residents of the town, defend the professional men of the community, and conclude with the affirmations 'We are all right, Dr. Melquist' (*Roses* 323) and 'If there's any soc – any these doctors down there in the east listenin' in – we're – all – right' ('Crocus' 23).

Perhaps the most typical rebuttal by a rural Albertan to the sociologists' attacks on small-town prairie life, whether in the real world of the newspapers or the fictional worlds of the script and novel, is summarized by the following poem, by a Hanna area resident, which appeared in the 10 January 1952 *Hanna Herald*:

NEXT-YEAR COUNTRY

In the homestead days when the trails were dim,
And the summers dry and the winters grim,
When we worked all year and returns were slim,
We named it 'Next-Year Country.'

Through hail and hoppers, drought and frost
With all but our faith in the country lost
The price was high, but we paid the cost,
And built this 'Next-Year Country.'

And today we view with a growing pride
The lasting towns and a countryside
Where love and peace and law abide,
In this our 'Next-Year Country.'

Now a high brow stranger comes to show
How we missed the mark and our aim was low,
We can tell her just where she can go,
For we love our 'Next-Year Country.'

While rural Albertans reiterated their self-worth, Peter Francis, in a letter to Mitchell dated 9 March, eloquently described the significance of *Jake and the Kid* for both the CBC and Canada:

The fact seems to be that *Jake and the Kid* has become such an institution and a power in the land that all this steam over the sociological piece is resulting in the program attaining not merely greater notoriety but greater eminence. I am telling you the simple truth when I say that Jake really has become something of a power in the land, and that almost anything said on the show seems to bring repercussions in high quarters – fortunately most of them favorable. I feel slightly awed at having anything to do with it. One of your beer-parlor characters makes a crack about the Liberal government, and Agriculture Minister Gardiner asks for a copy of the script – and ten thousand farmers cheer and feel that they have a voice. Stevie Kiziw's house burns down, and the film board and the Ottawa citizenship people think the cause of tolerance has advanced several notches. And so on. As I said, an invisible web of power radiates out from you in your reservation out there, and it will be a pity if you ever stop spinning it.

Mitchell has stated that he attempted to include current events in his radio play episodes, even if only incidentally. While 'Crocus Under the Microscope' illustrates more than incidental use of current events, it seems to show that, in addition to providing a portrait of small-town prairie life in both *Jake and the Kid* and *Foothill Fables*, Mitchell was also chronicling the current events of the time. From the Burnet episode to the Winnipeg floods to the royal visit and coronation to the Social Security Act to the new Canadian flag debate, Mitchell provides in his radio drama an authentic description of the prairie experience. The work of Burnet from a more academic perspective corroborates the fictional world of the radio plays and novels. While Burnet's conclusions are diametrically opposed to Mitchell's, the details she records, combined with the sources in the newspapers of the time, affirm that the fictional world of Mitchell's radio plays is firmly rooted in real prairie life of the 1950s. This may partially explain the widespread appeal and immense popularity of the plays and the loyalty of listeners across Canada during the Golden Age of radio.

The discussion of sources in Mitchell's work begins with bibliography. By providing access to the radio plays, a bibliography also indirectly leads researchers to consider still other sources for Mitchell's fiction. As the bibliography expands to include all of Mitchell's radio plays, then his stage and television drama, more and more sources and connections may be identified. Exploring the role of the radio plays in the fiction leads naturally to a detailed examination of the shift from genre to genre and to a broader understanding of Mitchell's creative process.

NOTES

1 I have compiled 'An Annotated Bibliography of the Radio Drama of W.O. Mitchell in the Special Collections of the University of Calgary Libraries' (thesis, U of Alberta, 1993). It summarizes the plays and notes the connections both among scripts and especially between scripts and the published fiction. There are 257 records, each of which is a different radio play episode; they represent 185 different radio play titles. Each play is summarized both in a paragraph and by key words, then indexed in a variety of ways in the appendices: alphabetically, chronologically, by key word, by character name, by connection to page numbers in the published fiction, by actor and actress, by director and producer, and by composer and conductor. Copies of my bibliography are available at the Univeristy of Alberta Libraries, University of Calgary Libraries, and the National Library of Canada.

2 Surdin and Mitchell worked together throughout the *Jake and the Kid* series and collaborated on such other projects as the successful musical 'Wild Rose.' Surdin composed original music for each week's radio play episode based on notes in drafts of the scripts which Mitchell sent him. Surdin also conducted the small live orchestra in the overwhelming majority of broadcasts in the *Jake and the Kid* series.

3 The 6 June 1946 issue of the *Hanna Herald* advertised the beginning of the census on 1 June and encouraged the participation of all Hanna and district residents because a census 'merits the support of each and every citizen as a patriotic duty.'

4 In a second bit of timely fan mail received by the CBC in Toronto, dated 24 February 1952, Mrs F.N. Brown of Kingston, Ontario, thanks Mitchell for the 'Crocus Under the Microscope' episode. She writes that she 'admires the simple heroism of a farmer who can work his life away waiting for "next year."'

Jake and the Kid:
Their Radiophonic Echo in W.O.
Mitchell's Literary Style and Legacy

ALAN YATES

No review or assessment of the prolific literary and dramatic output of W.O. Mitchell would be complete without serious consideration of his broadcast plays. Nor could analysis of his most recent literary output be complete without taking into consideration the important influence that his radio writings, and especially the *Jake and the Kid* series, have clearly had on his later novels. Reviewing the radio productions of the 1940s and 1950s is, however, no easy task from today's perspective.

To begin with, radio is the most ephemeral of the media and its dramatic products are even more dated than the black and white films of yesteryear. Radio drama operates on a complex code of conventions related to both the theatre and to the medium of radio. These are well documented by drama scholar and former broadcaster, Martin Esslin, but, specifically of radio plays, he claimed in a personal interview that 'decoding by a trained audience of an ambitious sound drama is as difficult and demanding as listening to a complex fugue' (1975). Yet, at best, the radio play is a fragile dramatic construct, particularly by today's standards. As the BBC's Donald McWhinnie put it in his bench-mark manual on the radio medium in the 1950s, *The Art of Radio* 'cannot be reproduced on the page, except as a pale shadow; it is as uncapturable as a half-forgotten song' (115).

Making matters more complex for the researcher is the distance that separates us from the radiophonic art of our past. This is compounded by the lesser socio-cultural role played by the medium today, and by the difficulty the present generation has in understanding how much sway radio had over the vast majority of the Canadian population in the pre-television era. In this age of over-abundant media choices, as the 'Death Star Satellite' and hundreds of video channels threaten to engulf us, it might appear far-fetched to hear that millions of Canadians were glued to CBC radio, spellbound by the hockey descriptions 'for the blind' by Foster Hewitt, or that communities across the country shared the experience of tuning in to the antics of John Drainie as Jake, the hired hand, and Billie Mae Richards as his sidekick, the Kid. The attempt to analyse the literary and cultural value of Mitch-ell's popular radio series and to explore the influence of these plays on his later novels is fraught with unusual challenges.

How do we place ourselves in the context of the so-called Golden Age of Radio Drama more than thirty years after radio has been eclipsed, first as dramatic medium, and now as fast news vehicle, by television? How do we measure the impact these shared tales had, not only upon Mitchell's literary style, but also upon Canada's very psyche and upon its popular culture?

It was perhaps because serious research into radio drama was long neglected that either too little serious attention was paid to it or it was misunderstood as a valid dramatic genre. Critics and reviewers consequently complained that Mitchell frittered too many of his most productive years away with these 'frivolous' radio tales, here today and gone on the broadcast wind tomorrow, when he should have pursued the serious artistry he demon-strated in his first novel. Had he traded financial convenience and popularity in the radio era for the chance at that Grail of writers, posterity? Some critics were concerned with the oral cultural inspiration and popular character of most of the radio scripts. Might these popular radio plays not, in insidious fashion, have resulted in his marginalization as a legitimate Canadian novelist? Might the weekly radio visits to Crocus, Saskatchewan, have con-demned Mitchell to a more folksy, anecdotal, tall tale style of humour? Might W.O. forever be type-cast by that style and might it reverberate down through his later novels and cause them to be taken less 'seriously' by literary critics and academics? In much the same fashion, one assumes, the crime of folksiness and a popularly accessible style of humour also dogged Stephen Leacock, yet his works and our fondness for Mariposa live honourably on. Who, today, denigrates Mitchell's own literary hero, Mark Twain, for such qualities?

Mitchell's prolific publications since 1981 have put the question of wasted energies completely to rest: he has earned his laurels and will no doubt achieve literary posterity. The academic respect might take longer. But what, one might ask, determines which are the 'definitive' Canadian novels: the opinions of a few academic critics or the appreciation of the vast reading public and a solid row of volumes in every book store and public library down through the decades?

Nor is there anything intrinsically wrong or artistically inferior about having created radio dramas with which an entire nation identified. The *Jake and the Kid* radio plays were a legitimate dramatic genre and an ideal vehicle upon which Mitchell could hone his writing skills, experiment with characterization and dialogue, and shape his own special style. Besides, they kept him writing and his peers working in radio during hard literary and theatrical times, and they constituted a veritable proving ground for his later novels. To appreciate the importance of these apparently simple radio plays in Mitchell's growth and development as a leading Canadian novelist, we must be sensitive to the context of the late 1940s.

The Jake and the Kid stories and characters had already been well established for readers in *Maclean's* magazine by the time Mitchell tried his hand at the radio medium. He first worked on a few radio scripts[1] for CBC *Stage* and CBC *Summer Theatre*, such as *The Devil's Instrument* directed by Andrew Allan (27 March 1949), *The Black Bonspiel of Wullie MacCrimmon* (30 July 1950), and a stand-alone Jake and the Kid story, 'The Liar Hunter' (May 1949). Then CBC programmer Harry Boyle suggested Mitchell tackle an extensive series of half-hour Jake radio scripts, as a summer replacement series based on the *Maclean's* stories to begin with, and gradually featuring original stories. Peter Francis was the first series producer and the first episode aired was 'The Oldest

Old-Timer,' on 27 June 1950. It was scheduled in the prime, family, evening slot of 5:30 to 6:00 P.M. in the pre-television years and, when television arrived, was moved to 10:00 P.M.

It should be remembered that virtually every household had a radio set in those days and that pre-television entertainment options were limited. Individuals or households gathered together by the radio, tuned in religiously to those most popular of CBC radio shows, *Jake and the Kid* and the *Hockey Night in Canada* broadcasts with Foster Hewitt. Although audience statistics for individual plays are difficult to obtain at this remove, indications of the resounding popularity of the show can be found in the correspondence in the Mitchell Papers at the University of Calgary. Further, CBC radio was the only network in the country and its audiences were vast by today's media standards, since there was no audience fragmentation across a multitude of stations and networks.

One should also remember that there was no dependable publishing industry and that there were few theatrical outlets. Those who wanted to be noticed in literary or acting circles and, especially, remunerated for their efforts, simply had no better outlet than CBC radio. On radio they not only survived, but became household names. It was the Golden Age of radio, indeed. Andrew Allan with his *CBC Stage* and *CBC Wednesday Night*, and directors such as Allan King, and in Montreal Rupert Kaplan, were carrying on theatrical traditions largely imported to Canada from Britain by such directors as Tyrone Guthrie, or were perhaps inspired by American radio directors such as Orson Welles. Len Peterson was mounting ambitious dramas and dramatized documentaries based, not upon the classics, but upon reality-based Canadian social themes.

Canadians from coast to coast recognized and identified with the characters portrayed on radio by such actors and readers as J. Frank Willis, Budd Knapp, Henry Comor, John Drainie (Jake), Tommy Tweed, Ruth Springford, Sandy Webster, and Billie Mae Richards (the Kid). Through their voices, fictional characters such as Jake and the Kid and their cronies from Crocus, Saskatchewan, became a part of popular culture and regular visitors to the living rooms of the nation.

The *Jake and the Kid* plays were not the only entertainment of their kind. There was humour to be found on the airwaves, with such shows as *The Happy Gang*, and in the themes of some lighter plays or shows, by contrast with that more 'serious' of radio drama outlets, *CBC Stage*. *Stage* tended to concentrate on more classical productions that some have unkindly described as 'canned theatre' or the 'radio reading of bedtime stories by the fireside.' It remained to *Jake and the Kid* to establish itself as one of the few series specifically and ideally designed for the radio medium. Furthermore, it was a series set in a specific region, but appealing to an entire country. The genre itself was hardly original and it was followed by other regional serials. Its model in theme and tone could easily have been the Leacock 'Mariposa' stories earlier adapted for radio by Tommy Tweed. But Mitchell and his creative team went much further than the Tweed model.

In the *CBC Stage* version of 'The Speculations of Jefferson Thorpe,' for example, Tweed used twelve pages of unrelieved narrative from the Leacock figure to tell his stories. Mitchell and his radio team moved much closer to oral culture. Combining a restrained use of skilful soliloquy with a preponderance of natural and realistic dialogue, amid an aural canvas of sound effects and music, they created entertaining and truly radiophonic plays. What was it that made them so successful in audience terms?

A particular 'chemistry' resulted from what Mitchell frequently refers to as the 'creative partnership.' In novels this 'chemistry' was between the writer and reader, but in radio plays it was among the writer, producer, cast, musicians, sound effects men, and the listening audience. It was no mean achievement to turn out these plays every week and to perform them live and without the safety net of later editing and other adjustments. It called for a strong script to begin with; for professional cast members who could extract the most from their lines; for sound effects specialists and a composer and musicians who could supply atmospheric and emotional reinforcement to the words; and for a director who could orchestrate this 'live circus' into a convincing and credible dramatic illusion. However, no amount of questioning of surviving team members and recounting of anecdotes about that weekly process could supply the framework with which to analyse this creative chemistry in less impressionistic fashion.

The interview approach threatens to sweep the researcher up in the very myths and entertaining anecdotes that surround any successful and long-running broadcast series. J.L. Styan provides a framework for the study of radio drama in his *Drama, Stage and Audience*, wherein he focuses on what he calls 'the four dramatic constituents or focal points': the author, the text of the play, its performance, and the audience to which it is addressed (9). Thus, the radio play is first approached by considering the script of the radio play as literature, subject to the same analysis and criticism as any other printed text, then analysing the play's performance in theatrical terms. One can dissect and discuss the following elements of the radio play: the genre; the script, with its particular characteristics; the author, W.O. Mitchell, his background, milieu, and literary region; the mounting of the play on the 'sound stage' by a producer/director; the interpretation by the cast; the additional levels and dimensions added by sound effects staff, composer, and musicians; the presentation of the resulting performance on the *medium* of radio; and its reception and perception by the *audience* of radio listeners and by the critics and reviewers of the day (Styan 9–14). However, the interviews with the production team members, impressionistic and anecdotal though they may have been, provided a more human dimension and insight into the creative chemistry that was achieved. They revealed a great deal about the creative and often unpredictable contributions of the team.

Mitchell himself was, we learn from various producers and cast members, extremely disorganized and unreliable. According to the first producer, the late Peter Francis, Mitchell seldom came through with scripts in time, often submitting them short or incomplete. Francis's successor, Arthur Hiller, suggested that the scripts were sometimes intentially submitted a page or two at a time, to keep everyone on edge. He tells how, when he telephoned Mitchell about having received nothing in the mail, Mitchell responded, 'Been out to the traps, eh? Found 'em empty!' Francis often had to take great liberties with Mitchell's prose, cobbling episodes together from parts of previous shows. Later *Jake* producer and actor Fred Diehl maintains that there were really only about ninety original *Jake* episodes, rather than the three hundred or so claimed, when you consider this cobbling process. Similarly, episodes that were supposed to be in one part, grew into two or more due to Mitchell's failure to resolve them. Sometimes the material never even arrived in the studio in time. Francis tells the anecdote of Mitchell driving to the Toronto studio with a late script and being further delayed by a fire in his car, started by his having absent-mindedly set his pipe down. When he left Toronto to return to High River, the production team presented him with a stopwatch, as a hint. However, all of his producers admitted that despite his disorganization, Mitchell supplied copious notes and instructions on his scripts and, when he did turn up at the studio while in Toronto, was not obtrusive but clearly enjoyed his rapport with the cast.

Nowhere was that more evident than in his complicity with John Drainie, a born raconteur, like Mitchell himself. Despite his stellar reputation, Drainie is described by both Francis and his successor, Arthur Hiller, as a shy, insecure person on first encounter, who gave the initial impression of being ill at ease and even clumsy with the script. The lines grew on him, however, and he quickly became Jake Trumper. Tempting providence in live broadcasts, Mitchell played games with Drainie, building traps into his dialogue, hoping that Drainie would 'boot' the lines. This may even have provided additional humour. One such trap was laid for Drainie, who had to react angrily to the moral objections of the ladies of the Athenians Club. Mitchell had Drainie retort: 'I don't give a damn for the whole —— clucking flock of them!' He drew a big boot on the margin with triple exclamation marks. Drainie's response is reported to have been priceless. According to Hiller, he stretched out his apoplectic pause and started to use the letter 'f,' then read the line correctly.

A staunch contributer to the 'chemistry' in the studio was Tommy Tweed, who played cantankerous Old Man Gatenby, or Gate. He also played centenarian Daddy Johnson in later episodes directed by Esse W. Ljungh. Ljungh's successor, Fred Diehl, tells how Tweed so much became the character that he could wheeze for thirty seconds between lines, and would take his false teeth out to enhance the senile effect. Diehl says this was so hilarious that the production crew were advised to avoid watching the performance through the control room window.

No child, no matter how precocious or dramatically gifted, could have done justice to the role of the Kid, as was evidenced in the screenplay of *Who Has Seen The Wind*. It fell upon a middle-aged housewife, Billie Mae Richards, to play the role of the young boy, and she sounded so much like a boy that the audience was convinced she in fact was. Nor did her voice break or grow older during an extended series, giving the radio Kid a Peter Pan quality.

Mitchell clearly knew exactly what he wanted of the production crew and gave explicit instructions to the composers, first Morris Surdin, then Lucio Agostini, to supply specific atmospheric overtures, stings, bridges, and comic effects with which to clothe the words on the page. Surdin described in an interview one such apparently obscure instruction, which reads, 'Give me Tobacco Road with one yellow rose' (1977). Knowing Mitchell, Surdin knew exactly what was required, as did the actors, for nuances of tone, and the sound effects men for subtleties of descriptive noise.

All in all, the *Jake and the Kid* plays were not simply a family series, but resulted in a creative family approach to production. Harry J. Boyle attributes much of their success to 'the nature of the production experience and to the fact that they were a professional community, despite producer changes over the years. They were a professional as well as a fictional family' (1978).

Furthermore, the team established a working 'formula' for the series. The formula was based upon a repeating pattern of characters, situations, and even of institutions. Much of the humour lay in the predictability of these responses and situations. Sometimes it lay in the unexpected breaking of those patterns. Jake, for example, was always involved as mediator or corrector, or simply became tangled because he boasted his way into a contest of some kind. The secondary characters were used to illustrate traits such as prejudice, avarice, fraud, or intransigence. Jake set these characters or situations morally straight and would take the villains down a few notches. Most of this was for the benefit of his apprentice in life, the Kid, who, like the audience in turn, could be exposed to moral or social issues or the facts of life on the prairies. That the tales were regionally set mattered little to a national audience, since the lessons learned in these modern morality plays were universal.

The various producers of the series were charged with bringing all of these elements in the *Jake* formula together in a successful blend. The pioneer, Andrew Allan, was not involved in the ongoing series but his treatment of the longer stories appears to have been more formal, with a scrupulous respect for the importance of the words and painstaking direction of the cast. The first regular series producer, Peter Francis, exploited the radiophonic qualities, shaping an integral whole and leaving the cast more to their own devices. He 'dared' to alter or improve Mitchell's scripts to make them 'work' better, and his final sound mixes were the most effective. By the time Arthur Hiller came along, the pattern had been set and he could not depart significantly from it but went along with the tradition, freely encouraging that chemistry in the studio. His successor for the final regularly scheduled series, Esse W. Ljungh, was in the Allan school, preoccupied with direction, and also with comic effect. When an attempt was made to revive the series in the late 1960s, it was produced by Fred Diehl of Calgary, who also played Jake. Diehl clearly looked up to Ljungh and, particularly from his direct involvement as a cast member, accentuated the acting element, again encouraging caricature.

The *Jake and the Kid* pattern, both structural and thematic, can be seen in most of the three-hundred-odd scripts, and two of the finer ones might be used here to illustrate the typical structure of the radio plays. In 'The Day Jake Made Her Rain' (11 July 1950), a short Jake soliloquy is used, with music in the background, to introduce the listener to the story. Jake tells a visitor to town why there is all the mud around. It was all because he had made it rain as a cure for prolonged drought. A flashback takes us to Jake and

Gate, in their usual duel of boasting, this time about their rain-making abilities. A bet ensues and Jake is cornered into a contest again. Their challenge persists for days, right up to the local fair. But Jake has cheated and hired the services of a local pilot to seed the clouds. Right in the middle of the fair, the heavens open and Jake, somewhat unscrupulously, wins his bet. The dénouement is a masterpiece of audio tapestry, even by today's standards, with Jake and Gate egging each other on, clearly audible snatches of crowd reaction and conversations, the sound of the plane seeding high above, children playing, and the triumphant atmospheric music.

In 'King of All the Country' (7 November 1954), a similar formula is used. Jake wants to take the Kid goose-hunting, but the Kid's Ma objects to such barbarism. Jake and Ma debate the issue for the Kid's benefit and Jake's argument is less than morally convincing. Despite the interdiction, Jake not only takes the Kid along for the hunt, but buys a light shotgun for him. Just as the geese alight for the taking, Ma appears, noisily calling for the Kid. She is subdued by Jake and the hunt commences. Three shots ring out and three geese fall, but Jake only shot twice. He congratulates the Kid, but it was Ma, standing there with the still-smoking shotgun. She has no explanation to offer. Was she drawn into the mystique of the hunt or did Mitchell simply push the trick ending too hard? As in the rain episode, Mitchell uses soliloquy most effectively and sets the issue up through the tension between Jake and Ma, acting it out and resolving it in efficacious manner through realistic dialogue and reinforcing sound effects and music.

As with short stories, in radio it is much more difficult to craft thirty-minute plays that both sound credible and resolve themselves satisfactorily than it is with the leisurely pace of longer dramas.

Mitchell's unusual approach to depicting the prairie life of Crocus universalized it by detailing its reality: wrestling with the geography and climate, with the gossiping and meanness of small-town life, and with the pioneer conditions which bred 'characters' and tellers of tall tales. But he did so with gentle and affectionate humour. The themes had been tackled before, but seldom in that light and rarely on radio. The epitome of prairie reflection is probably *Wolf Willow*, by the American plains writer Wallace Stegner, who spent some of his childhood on the Canadian prairies and to whom Mitchell frequently referred in interviews. But Stegner described a hostile environment in bitter prose, emphasizing the harshness and toll of human misery, and his voice is an anguished cry. The reality of life in small prairie towns is liberally described by Margaret Laurence, and researcher. Clara Thomas has extensively analysed her Manawaka writings and themes. Terry Angus has also reviewed these themes and treatments in *The Prairie Experience*. Few, if any, of the prairie writers, however, have dealt with that reality in Mitchell's fashion. Martha Ostenso and Sinclair Ross made their prairie marks, often with chilling themes, just as their American plains counterparts, Sherwood Anderson, with *Winesburg, Ohio*, and Sinclair Lewis, with *Main Street*.

Canadian prairie writers can be divided between historical romancers, such as Frederick Niven, Jane Rolyat, and Laura Goodman Salverson, whose romantic themes seldom disguised the hardships, and the prairie realists, such as Robert J.C. Stead, Martha Ostenso, and Frederick Phillip Grove, whose writings were often characterized by dire and despairing situations. Sinclair Ross perhaps moves closer to the Mitchell approach, especially with the small-town *As For Me and My House*, but his grimness is contrasted with Mitchell's optimism.

There was also some limited prairie humour, and one of the two prime examples of it was also mounted on radio. Paul Hiebert's *Sarah Binks, Songstress of Saskatchewan*, written, like *Who Has Seen The Wind*, in 1947, was also aired on CBC *Wednesday Night* the following year, but its humour was unkind and characterized by blatant satire, parody, and cynicism. Much closer to Mitchell were the stories of Ross Annett, written for the *Saturday Evening Post*. Their protagonists, Babe and Little Joe, were the Albertan counterparts of Jake and the Kid, but their tales were never turned into a popular radio series on the CBC. The Annett stories nevertheless are significant in the context of Mitchell's radio plays. As Harry Boyle points out, 'Mitchell was aware of the Annett stories, but he was the first to bring the genre to the medium of radio' (1978). Their stories, more significantly, had the same apparent source. The Babe and Little Joe stories, Boyle feels, were considerably if not wholly derived from oral and folk culture, rather than from a written one. He feels the origins of the style are to be found in Bob Edwards's Calgary *Eye Opener*. Edwards was himself one of the types of 'characters' who abound in the Mitchell stories and used to hang around the Palliser Hotel with cronies such as Pat Burns, R.B. Bennett, and Leonard W. Brockington, telling and trading tall tales. A similar group frequented the Bessborough Hotel in Saskatoon. Attracted to these gatherings were, according to Boyle, mostly 'remittance men, drifters from the South, people in fact, like Jake Trumper himself, in to work on the harvest' (1978). Mitchell, in turn, harvested their tales, styles, dialogue, anecdotes, and much of the gathering process continued and flourished on the steps of the post office in his own town of High River.

Thus, it can be suggested that Mitchell's prairie tales were doubly original, not only because they became a unique radio genre, but because they were genuinely humorous, even while dealing with serious themes and issues and the often grim reality of prairie life. This 'works' when, as Leacock suggests in his essay 'Humour As I See It,' 'humour is blended with pathos 'til the two are one and represent, as they have in every age, the mingled heritage of tears and laughter that is our lot on earth.' Leacock also reminds us in that essay that the essence of good humour is that it 'must be without harm and without malice' (139), and adds, 'nor should it convey incidentally any real picture of sorrow and suffering or death' (144). It was precisely the unrelieved humorous character of the *Jake* stories that prompted one of their early critics, Margaret Laurence herself, to suggest that they were sugarcoated, that they 'had no bite of acid to cut the sweet taste' ('A Canadian Classic?' 68–70).

However, in his genre, and abetted by the *Jake* cast, Mitchell was able to tackle the gossips, the meddlers, the meanness, discrimination, prejudice, prudery, holier-than-thou attitudes, church lady do-gooders, and other such inevitable perils of small-town prairie life, including the intrusive outsiders, such as travelling patent medicine salesmen or meddling sociologists from the East who try to put Crocus under the microscope. Unlike his literary peers, Mitchell accomplished this with wry, warm, down-to-earth humour, emphasizing the laughter that kept up the spirits of prairie-dwellers in moments of adversity. This humour also enabled an entire nation to share and laugh *with* rather than *at* the characters, characteristics, and ironies of life in prairie communities. The lessons learned by the people of Crocus, and especially by the Kid, as by their avid audience, were all essentially, as Mitchell put it, 'about the Ten Commandments and about how terribly difficult it is to be human' (1977). The Crocus characters grew and learned over the months, as did their audiences, in ways that could not have been possible with either the most penetratingly socially conscious of novels or stage plays, and were delivered, with the sweetener of humour, directly into every Canadian home.

The style and the humour of his radio genre clearly spilled over into his later novels, but it might be asked at this point whether that is a blessing or a curse; whether that very sweetener of humour and popular style may have backfired on Mitchell and resulted in his marginalization by some critics. Were the lubricant of laughter, the 'teaser' of tall tales, and the appetizer of anecdotes, laid on too heavily for the radio plays to be considered on a par with those of his more serious contemporaries in prairie literature? Had the sweet folksiness and outrageous caricature of the radio productions condemned his plays, and even their published versions, to be taken less seriously than their due? If blame is to be laid, then Mitchell has to share it with his radio team, and especially with Esse Ljungh.

He has been singled out by his peers for allowing the cast, such as Drainie and Tweed, to exploit the humour and caricature to the point where, as Peter Francis put it, 'it verged on the burlesque, the slapstick' (1978). It would seem that the scripts themselves encouraged the very factors that contributed to this problem – the blatant caricatures of Drainie and Tweed, the use of the comic aside or joke shared with the audience, the often outrageous parodies of the sound effects or musical jokes in the score.

By extension, and especially from today's perspective, one might ask whether this very style, again much exploited in his hilarious public readings or radio appearances, has found its way, obtrusively, into his later written works, in order to make them more approachable, more palatable, and more popular. In other words, do these apocryphal anecdotes, patterns of speech, quaint dialogue, and crusty old characters inspire and salt much of the material he is still mining from his 'subconscious notebook,' and serving up in his more recent published works, to negative or positive effect?

Mitchell's prolific outpouring since 1980 has dispelled forever the charge that the radio scripts somehow short-changed him and Canada. We have seen, in rapid succession: *How I Spent My Summer Holidays, Dramatic W.O. Mitchell, Since Daisy Creek, Ladybug, Ladybug ..., Roses Are Difficult Here, According to Jake and the Kid, For Art's Sake,* and most recently, *The Black Bonspiel of Willie MacCrimmon.* Yet these later works have also, in some ways, borne the imprint of his radio writings, both in characterization and in style. These resonances bounce down the years, not only in our associations with the writer, but in his very style, narrative, and dialogue. In short, their stamp is upon his very literary identity. But has that stamp made his newer works any the less valuable or original? If viewed from that 'radio roots' point of view, it can be strongly argued that the later works are marked and even permeated with material gleaned from prairie oral culture and perfected on radio. Let us review some of the commonalities and influences.

Firstly, in the area of their oral cultural style and inspiration, most of Mitchell's characters and their dialogue were 'made' for radio presentation or for public readings by W.O. His later works, like the *Jake* radio scripts, abound with the same qualities that cry out to be brought to life by someone of Drainie's calibre or to be acted out by Mitchell himself at his public readings or on the Peter Gzowski show. His characters are mostly rough-and-ready 'frontier cowboys,' young and old, who speak in terse, economi-

cal, almost telegraphic style, interspersed with outrageous anecdotes and crude, down-to-earth metaphors.

It is a style that bears many similarities to that of Mark Twain.
In *Ladybug, Ladybug...*, protagonist and almost later-day Mitchell
figure Professor Lyon is Mark Twain's biographer, and describes
Twain's style as 'colloquial, witty, unrestrained. It's a speaking
style ... He loves the anecdotal too' (266). It is, again, the 'speaking
style' of those very characters that Mitchell used to soak up in
High River and that Professor Lyon attributes in Twain's case to
similar eavesdropping sessions 'by a mining camp fire, in some
saloon or press room, or over a pocket or poker table' (82). These
characters, such as Jake, Malleable Brown, and Daddy Sherry,
speak in telegraphic bursts, drop articles, and refer to a fellow as
'he' or 'him,' but to an inanimate object or process as 'she.' Thus,
in *How I Spent My Summer Holidays*, one of the young 'characters
in training' searches for an easy way to dig their cave and says, 'If
a fellow only had a fresno and a team, he could really scoop her
out ... If a fellow could soak her good ... run her full of water –
soften her up' (44), sounding in the process like a bluffing adult,
Jake or Gate, during a boasting contest. Like Jake, later characters
use the safe sardonic or non-committal response, 'that's nice,' in
tense or ambiguous situations. Jake always responds thus with
respect to any well-meaning but impractical proposal by the
Athenians ladies, as in *Roses Are Difficult Here*. In that work, as in
such *Jake* plays as 'Cabin Fever' (25 March 1951), Clem Derrigan,
Daddy Sherry, and old man Gate almost snort the term in order to
express their scepticism of rival tall tales about the weather.

Outrageous metaphors abound and they are the same ones,
from the same oral cultural source, that are found throughout the
Jake and the Kid stories. In one single page of *How I Spent My Summer Holidays*, we rediscover: the description of a prime irritant,
which King Motherwell says was 'enough to give a gopher's ass
the heart-burn'; that the bank manager 'was tighter than a cow's
ass in fly time and wouldn't pay a dime to see a piss ant eat a bale
of hay'; and that a character 'was so stubborn, if he were to
drown, they'd have to look for his body upstream' (this latter was
also used by Mrs Napoleon in *Roses*); and that a character 'was so

mean, I wouldn't piss in his ear if his brain were on fire' (32). In his own introduction to *According to Jake and the Kid*, Mitchell uses the classic expression 'He had a wife who couldn't cook guts for a bear' (x).

Part and parcel of the oral characteristic and appeal, and a tributary of the above sayings, is the very nature of the prairie humour employed. It relies heavily upon caricature, tall tales, and gross exaggeration. The caricature bears the same qualities as the burlesque and slapstick employed in Ljungh's productions of *Jake and the Kid*. The humour appears to have its roots in the stand-up comic routines of the music hall or the pantomime, including the humorous aside to the audience. Caricature, reminiscent of Tweed's portrayal of centenarian Daddy Sherry, is most evident with the paranoid character of Grampa in *How I Spent My Summer Holidays*. He has a phobia about being sneaked up on by those 'out to get him.' The kids ultimately do get him by setting off dynamite in the backyard while he is in his favourite haven, the outhouse. The description of tracking down Grampa by following his 'saliva trail' and noting his 'expectoration rate' (43) completes the caricature and exaggeration.

Also in *Summer Holidays*, a baby born in prairie cabin style is 'squirted right out,' with the placenta landing on the floor and in danger of being eaten by the dog (119). Real prairie men chaw tobacco and the spitoon is omnipresent where they congregate; the exaggerated sound effects of wads of saliva clanging in spitoons echoes through the *Jake* productions and, in *Ladybug*, when our young hero moves to recite the Gettysburg address and steps in a spitoon which cannot be removed, he goes 'anvil chorusing' to the stage (76–77).

The height of exaggeration occurs in *Roses Are Difficult Here*, when, as in a previous *Jake* episode, 'Somethin's Gotta Go' (3 October 1950), drunken Rory Napoleon herds his goats through the Shelby town centre, creating what Mitchell describes as the 'ultimate hyperbolic chaos.' Goats, the epitome of wilful behaviour and unpredictability, wander through stores, tie up traffic, enter business establishments, and turn the town into a veritable shambles (254–64).

Tall tales, escalating in exaggeration, also abound in the later novels, and many are repeats from Jake tales. In *Roses*, we again encounter Daddy Sherry's tale of 'the blue Snow of ought-six and ought-seven,' featured in *Jake* episodes such as 'Cabin Fever' (25 March 1951), and in the novel *The Kite*. In *Since Daisy Creek*, as in such *Jake* plays as 'The Day Jake Made Her Rain' (11 July 1950), we are given descriptions of life in sod houses: 'When it rained outside for three days, it rained inside the house for five days (206). And in *Roses*, Clem Derrigan again tells Jake's tale, immortalized by Drainie in 'The Day Jake Made Her Rain,' of the aftermath of the great drought when frogs died in the sloughs, 'Kind of tragical way they died – lacka dust' (276). Just as they did for *Jake* audiences, the same old characters – Daddy Sherry, Clem Derrigan, and the Senator – tell these tales and boast of consorting with long-dead figures from Canadian history.

As in the *Jake* scripts, there is a coarseness and a crudeness to much of the humour, in both the foul language and the situations, such as the above, which will not recommend it to some teachers. Outhouse and brothel humour and coarse language abound in *How I Spent My Summer Holidays*; in *Roses*, Rory Napoleon describes the ultimate horrible chore of cleaning out a local cesspool when 'she fills up with Tregillis shit an' piss' (18); in *Ladybug*, one of the characters is described as 'pussy- as well as prick-struck' (166). In the radio scripts this aspect of Mitchell's writing was the target of the CBC's 'moral custodian,' Neil Morrison. Such novelistic details as Dr Harbottle's phalometric study could not escape censorship in the family-type radio productions of the 1950s.

Nor were coarseness, crude humour, and swearing the preserve of the cowboys, or even of the males. In *Roses*, Ben Trotter was a publisher who chewed tobacco, had 'an endless store of funny and exciting anecdotes,' and 'swore a lot too' (8). In the *Jake* stories, young boys such as the Kid emulate their coarse role models and are even egged on to cuss. The later novels go a step further, with similar behaviour by more emancipated daughters. In *Since Daisy Creek*, Professor Dobbs tries to turn his daughter into a boy who is 'just as sarcastic' and 'just as foul-mouthed' (26), and she, in turn, threatens him with 'if you cry again I'll bust your jaw' (40).

If all of the above traits are peculiar to prairie or frontier humour, or at least to Mitchell's depiction of it, what purpose does this humour serve, other than to make *Jake* radio audiences and later novel readers laugh? The point goes back to the very nature of life on the prairies and the way both Mitchell and the characters he creates deal with trials and adversity, both natural and human.

In *Roses*, the dreaded sociologist somewhat cruelly concludes that 'there is a crudity and coarseness to the quality of the inter-personal humour, which is not wit at all in the higher sense, but draws on exaggeration, the tall tale, the ludicrous lie, for its com-municative impact' (199). Dr Melquist goes on to say of Shelby that 'their humour is a primitive and mordant one, erecting its amusement always upon a foundation of exaggeration and sar-casm' (309). The humour is more generously described by the edi-tor of the local paper, *The Shelby Chinook*, as 'frontier humour' and as 'a defence against blizzard and drought and loneliness' (59). He describes it as a reflection of the odds and exaggeration of the very prairies themselves, against which 'humour is a defence,' for they are 'not half so frightening if they are made ridiculous.' And the editor suggests that such humour is ultimately a thumb at the nose to Death, rejoining that other well-trodden Mitchell theme when he says 'any man who laughs at death, laughs at his own mortality' (323).

All of the above traits of Mitchell's humour – down-to-earth dialogue, telegraphic style, caricature, exaggeration bordering on the burlesque and slapstick, outrageous metaphor, tall tales, and coarse language – were track-tested in his radio scripts. The stage voices of John Drainie and fellow cast members were probably in W.O.'s mind as he wrote the later works, accounting for an authenticity of characterization and sense of locale. Whether or not their inclusion has perpetuated his marginalization, the slap-stick elements of Mitchell's radio plays are integral elements of his novels.

The setting for the *Jake and the Kid* plays, Crocus, Saskatchewan, was, as implied by an episode of that title, a microcosm for small-town prairie life. Similarly, the later novelistic towns such as Shelby have most of the characteristics common to Crocus. They have the same small-town meanness, the same gossiping, meddling do-gooder ladies, and the same discrimination against minorities and the underprivileged. The local media, such as the weekly newspaper, can never be as fast, as cutting, or as inaccurate, as what is described in *Roses Are Difficult Here* as the 'small-town, informal reporting system.' Of the influence of the local residents, we read that 'with the quick swallow, the clucking tongue, the lifted eyebrow, they coloured and they embellished, distorting not so much out of malice as from relish in a story better told' (10). As in Crocus, where Repeat Golightly's barber shop is the place for male gossip, so in *Ladybug*, the Billiards and Barber Shop is the nerve centre of town (42).

Men and women play different roles in this respect. In *Roses*, males hold forum or court in Wing's Palm Café, while women do it 'over the back fence – the party line' (75). Gossip and interfering occur at a more stratified level when practised by the ladies of the Athenians Annual and Perennial Flower, Book, Recipe and Discussion Club, just as in Crocus.

The women of the novels are as polarized in their stereotypes as those of Crocus. Most are either authoritative or mother types in the IODE or Athenians, at one end of the scale, or loose girls from places such as Sadie Rossdance's cottages in *Summer Holidays*. Somewhere in between, and usually younger, are those aforementioned girls trying to be boys.

All 'real' men in these prairie towns hunt and fish and make no excuses for it. All 'real' men in training, who look up to the cowboys, be they Jake or King Motherwell (*Summer Holidays*), similarly spend half their time 'drownin' out gophers' or 'touchin' them off' with a twenty-two. The killing of gophers and birds or the sight of dead animals provide a young boy's introduction to mortality, the large leitmotif that threads throughout Mitchell's works. For adult males, water is sacred for crops and livestock and fishing in; for the boys, it is equally sacred for cooling off in summer. The omnipresent prairie wind was not just a recurrent theme in the *Jake* plays, but was a sound effect and music score backdrop to the situations. Its physical and psychological effects are featured again in the later novels, a backdrop and undercurrent to small-town prairie life.

One of the key commonalities between the *Jake* plays and the later novels is the recurrence of both characters and themes born and first tested in the radio scripts. Some of these reappear with little or no modification. The young boys of *Summer Holidays* had their prototypes in Crocus, as did such characters in *Roses* as centenarian Daddy Sherry; Malleable Brown, the blacksmith; Professor Noble Winesinger, the flim-flam, travelling, patent medicineman; Wullie MacCrimmon, the cobbler and demon curler; and Archie Nicotine, the noble redskin. The young boy-protagonists – Brian in *Who Has Seen the Wind* and Keith in *The Kite* – are like the Kid in that they lose their fathers when young and fall under the influence of surrogate father figures.

Recurring themes or scenarios abound. In the Shelby of *Roses*, we rediscover the serial dog poisonings and the newspaper campaign against them originally featured in the *Jake and the Kid* play 'Man's Best Friend.' In *Roses*, as in the *Jake* play 'Crocus Under the Microscope,' we again find the theme of a poison pen campaign by the editor's lovesick secretary, jealous of his attention to the female sociologist. And again in *Roses,* as in a *Jake* script entitled 'Nature Knows Best,' Mrs Napoleon achieves success in the Flower Show with a humble, dime-store rose neglected and discarded in a goat manure heap.

Finally, there is the central focus and inspiration for the *Roses* novel, the interfering sociologist from the East, Dr Melquist. Originally one of the stronger *Jake* radio scripts, 'Crocus Under the Microscope' (24 February 1952), the play is expanded to novel length with more substance and depth in *Roses*, and thus appears to have better served the purpose of restating many of the central truths tackled by Mitchell in the radio play. Here, one finds Mitchell's most forceful and moving statements about the strengths and weaknesses, qualities and cruelties of small prairie towns and their inhabitants. It is also in this scenario that he takes his most vicious aim at the pretentious experts, reminding us that in the study of humans the sociologist can apply 'statistics and abstractions and techniques and emerge still a scientific stranger' (76). He had already taken pot-shots at such experts in *Ladybug*, where he describes Dr Harbottle and his 'Phallometric Study of Erotic Preferences of Deviate and Non-deviate Males through Measurement of Changes in Penis Volume' (128–29). In *Since Daisy Creek*, he takes aim again, at the academic pecking order at Livingstone University and, later, at the travesty of justice, describing both academics (136) and lawyers (250) as black-gowned 'magpies, crows, and ravens' (136).

In conclusion, a larger case might still be made of the echoes and resonances from the radio plays to be found in the later novels. Such a study might well substantiate my view that, rather than dismissing them as a corrupting influence on his later writings, we should consider Mitchell's radio scripts as an experimental proving ground, with rapid feedback from audiences and critics alike, on which to test his writing craft and techniques. It is clear that the radio plays were beneficial to Mitchell's craft in a variety of ways. They were a legitimate use of his writing time because they both enabled him to make a living from writing and provided him with the discipline to keep his writing craft active and his 'subconscious notebook' mined for material, even in the absence of novels. The plays kept his work and name current and turned them into household words, at a time when there were few publishing opportunities or theatrical outlets, and even fewer subsidies. They were a means of giving his work a much vaster and faster audience than any book or stage play could have done.

Moreover, they probably helped him write his later novels, and their influence can be clearly found in those later works, suggesting that his exposure to the 'collective chemistry' of radio production and to the practice of public readings from his works were of definite value to his later writings. There is no doubting the influence upon him of actors such as John Drainie and Tommy Tweed, and of directors such as Andrew Allan and Esse Ljungh. It is also easy to see how his popular public readings from his works or his tall tales could become a tributary of that radio experience, sharpening his humour skills and providing an instant audience upon which to test reactions to dialogue, style, and anecdotes, before trying them out in new works. The *Jake and the Kid* stories on radio were valid in their own right and an honest use of Mitchell's time, as well as an important developmental tool in the crafting of his later novels.

Perhaps the criteria for artistic achievement in writers should resemble those for composers who wish to be taken seriously and achieve posterity – to write what they will and must, including little popular broadcast 'tone poems' but, especially, to complete nine symphonies. If judged by such criteria, then Mitchell has achieved a very respectable equivalent of novels on the library and bookstore shelves of the nation, despite and partly *because* of his oral cultural forays – those radio plays and readings. They kept him writing 'on demand' and trying out his material directly on the Canadian public. The relentless pressure of weekly radio schedules kept him disciplined enough to write during the lean years and during those years when he was busy building a family. However, they provided inspiration and training as well as discipline – a proving ground and storehouse of material for later works.

We should not look down our literary noses at the hired hand and his precocious young side-kick as they wander still through his and our years, the echoes of their voices, themes, and styles still alive more than thirty-five years after their series signed off, from Crocus, Saskatchewan, on CBC radio.

NOTE

1 All of the references to Mitchell's *Jake and the Kid* scripts and radio productions which follow are from Alan J. Yates's dissertation, 'W.O. Mitchell's *Jake and the Kid*: The Popular Radio Play as Art and Social Comment' (McGill U, 1979), available in microform from the National Library of Canada.

Whiskerbits; or, We Tried to Squeeze the Prairies into Studio One

DAVID GARDNER

In addition to radio, W.O. Mitchell's literary output has been adapted extensively for Canadian television and film. Unfortunately, these electronic productions are not as readily accessible as the printed page and so they tend to be forgotten. To some extent many of the early shows are simply victims of time: grainy, black and white products of 'steam television.' But even the later works, handsomely swathed in colour, have tended to be wrapped in controversy. The frictions and *frissons* of Mitchell's screen adventures are worth exploring.

The earliest attempt to make visual the words and imagination of W.O. Mitchell was on 9 October 1955 on the CBC TV program *Folio*. Mitchell's Faustian story, *The Black Bonspiel of Wullie MacCrimmon*, starred Frank Peddie in the title role and Lloyd Bochner as the Devil. Robert Allen directed and recalls an on-air mistake when a cameraman forgot to rotate the lens so that the scoreboard appeared right way up when it should have been upside-down for the diabolical curling match. The clumsy constraints of the live television studio were also felt in the handling of the climactic sporting event, which cried out for the flexibility of film shooting. More successful was *The Devil's Instrument*, Mitchell's melancholic study of a young Hutterite's tussle with the temptation of beauty in a shame society. David Greene brought it to the screen first (21 November 1956), again for *Folio*, and Eric Till mounted a splendid repeat production on *Festival* (5 November 1962), with Douglas Rain memorable as the haunted youth who longs to play the harmonica. It is interesting how often temptation and the devil figure in early Mitchell. Like Robertson Davies at the time, and also like Gratien Gélinas, W.O. used satirical drama to help break the puritanical grip that was holding back the burgeoning of a popular culture in Canada. He would have his most delicious triumph with *Jake and the Kid*.

Ever since the *Jake and the Kid* stories first appeared in *Maclean's* magazine (15 August 1942), Canadian producers have scrambled to adapt them for radio, film, and television. But, to date, perhaps only the CBC's famous Trans-Canada Network radio series (17 June 1950 to 1956) succeeded unequivocally. With the awakening of Canadian television and film in the 1950s and 1960s the richly drawn characters and the 'period' locales of *Jake and the Kid* had to be duplicated three-dimensionally. There was bound to be a compromise and awkwardness in the transition. Those wonderful radio voices of John Drainie and the Navy Show's [Ms] Billie Mae (Dinsmore) Richards as the perennially nameless Kid had to be given faces, bodies, and clothes to wear. (I love the story of the Boston drama academy that offered a scholarship to the lad that played the Kid. The CBC had to write back that Billie Richards wasn't available at the time because 'he' was pregnant [Kirchhoff C1].)

The National Film Board was the first to attempt to capture *Jake and the Kid* on celluloid. Sitting in their archives are two black and white, half-hour 16mm productions: *Fires of Envy* (1957), directed by Julian Biggs, and *Political Dynamite* (1958), directed by Donald Ginsberg. The latter involved the ladies of Crocus taking a stand against Sunday curling (with shades of *The Black Bonspiel of Wullie MacCrimmon*). Although my memory is dim, I recall that back then the NFB seemed much more interested in landscape than either comedy or humanity. Even earlier, in 1955, the Edmonton-born, CBC-trained, expatriate film director, Arthur Hiller, hoped to transfer the radio series to TV when he emigrated to Hollywood to work for NBC television. But this attempt at southern exposure 'didn't get off the ground' (Hiller). Currently the president of the American Academy of Motion Picture Arts and

Sciences, Arthur Hiller spent several years directing *Jake and the Kid* for CBC radio.

The first time an episode of *Jake and the Kid* appeared on television was 7 November 1957, when 'Honey and [Grass] Hoppers' was telecast live on the CBC's prestigious *Folio* series. Robert Allen directed and it starred John Drainie as Jake, Johnny Washbrook as the Kid, and featured Douglas Rain as Matthew the Hermit. In her seminal account of Canadian television, *Turn Up the Contrast*, Mary Jane Miller found special praise for Rain's 'moving portrait of a Prairie eccentric..., a combination of Moses and Noah ... launch[ing] into his own idiosyncratic version of the first chapter of Genesis' (217).

The idea of transferring more of Mitchell's *Jake and the Kid* stories from radio to television was bruited about at the CBC for the next three years (1957–60). The TV and film rights to twenty-six scripts were purchased at a cost of $1000 each and story editor Frank Lalor was assigned to adapt them for viewing. He worked with W.O. for over a year. There were hopes for a twenty to twenty-five episode series (twenty-six is usual) and all the scripts were budgeted and roughly designed. An early memo (15 April 1959) estimated that sixteen of the shows could also be done as live studio shows repeatedly utilizing basic settings.

Ron Weyman was the catalytic force that finally got the project off the ground. In a memo dated 14 January 1960, he proposed that two pilot projects be shot, one on location, entirely on film, and one on videotape in the studio. In his heart he hoped that the decision would favour film, but cost-effectiveness won out, as it has so many times. Weyman was told that 'the CBC is not in the film business' (Weyman). The compromise was a videotaped production with a few filmed inserts. Even the opening titles and closing credits would be superimposed over still photographs of a prairie farm. There may have been some original footage shot, a truck turning past a field of grain, for example, but primarily the inserts would come from the stock shot library: a library of available film shots of clouds, planes, geese flying, etc. They could be integrated into a live program by means of switching to telecine, a technical projection device familiar to newscasts, where the camera cuts away from the news commentator to a war-torn area, and then returns to the live studio. This inability to shoot live film knocked out approximately ten of the twenty-six episodes chosen. I remember especially losing 'A Deal's a Deal,' in which the Kid is thrown from his colt 'Fever' while learning to ride in the paddock. Some of the other purchased shows that were not done included 'Jake and the Medicine Man,' 'History Repeats Itself,' 'Pome Romance,' 'Water Witchery,' 'The Teacher and the Wild One,' 'Old-Fashioned Christmas' (needing snow), 'Royalty is Royalty' (needing a train), and 'The Old Grey Car' (needing a car in motion).

In a memorandum dated 9 December 1959, plans were finalized for a pilot program to be videotaped in the studio. It included the proviso that if the pilot didn't work out as the launch for a series, it could always be slotted into one of the CBC's half-hour anthology programs. The script chosen was 'Earn Money at Home,' and Ted Pope directed. It was shown 10 August 1960 on the *First Person* series. John Drainie was not available to play Jake. He was about to take his family off to Mallorca, Spain, for a four-year life-style experiment, during which he recorded *Stories with John Drainie* from London for CBC radio. The gravel-voiced, Regina-born actor, Murray Westgate, replaced him. In this pilot episode Mitchell anticipates the comedy premise behind Anthony Marriott and Alistair Foot's farce *No Sex Please, We're British*. To help the Kid buy a 'lickerish black' saddle for his colt, Jake attempts to sell 'linger-ee, ... wim-men's stuff ... in plum, puce, magenta, coral and petal pink,' with Colonel Hepner (played by comedian Dave Broadfoot) auctioning the items off on the end of his cane, to raise $40.

The pilot clicked and a series of twelve episodes was scheduled for the summer of 1961. Ron Weyman and I were asked to direct. Although we shared a co-directional credit on every episode, Ron actually handled six, I did five, and Ray Whitehouse, our executive producer, tackled the odd script out. Murray Westgate, then forty-three, was set as Jake and thirteen-year-old, crew-cut Rex Hagon joined him as the Kid. In my mind's eye I can still see Murray squinting into the sun, and hear his parched and dusty voice, while over in a corner of the rehearsal room I recollect Rex slogging away at his homework and looking up to smile. Frances Tobias, an established Little Theatre actress, won the audition to play Ma, which she did with great good humour and earthy insight. Many of the radio regulars were recruited to repeat their contributions: seasoned actors like Beth Lockerbie, Peggi Loder, Jack Mather, and Frank Perry. And the repertory company of townspeople included Alex McKee as neighbour Sam Gatenby; Robert and Margot Christie as Mayor MacTaggart and Miss Henchbaw, the teacher; Eric House as the barber, Repeat Golightly; Paul Kligman as Wayfreight Brown; with Jane Mallett, Amelia Hall, Barbara Hamilton, Sharon Acker, Hugh and Sandy Webster, James (Beam me up, Scotty) Doohan, and Ron Hartmann among the many guest stars. Nestled, too, among the supernumeraries, were many names destined for later fame, favourite performers such as Don Francks and Gordon Pinsent, and the playwright-to-be David French. These were the actors entrusted with treading the fine line between rural caricature and the '"other-worldliness" that was Mitchell's hallmark' (Whitehouse 31).

Much more problematic was the look of the show. From 1952 to about 1966, Canadian television was black and white. Although the productions were recorded on videotape for showing later, they were shot continuously, scene by scene (up to a commercial break), as if the actors were performing live on stage. For the twelve-part *Jake and the Kid* TV series, CBC Toronto's small Studio One (and only occasionally the larger Studio Seven) were literally chock-a-block with six to ten 'sets' cleverly designed by Rudi Dorn and his assistant Peter Douet. Certain settings like MacTaggart's store and Ma's sitting-room were utilized repeatedly. Others were produced as the occasion warranted. The cramped studio restricted the camera angles that could be used and the amount of movement the big one-ton cameras could make. The result was often shooting that was tight and static, and shots that were held too long. I recall Alf Gallagher as Reverend Cameron in the opening episode, 'The Day Jake Made Her Rain' (4 July 1961). Because there was no room in the studio to build a church interior, Ron Weyman couldn't intercut between the minister in the pulpit and the faces of the congregation. It meant he was stuck with a sixty-second, low angle shot of the Reverend preaching about drought conditions. Therefore, by the time you came to the scripted smile at the end, 'Let us sing Hymn #292 – There Shall Be Showers of Blessing,' the humour was not forthcoming.

What was lacking also was any exterior feeling of horizontal space. The prairie sky was a cloth cyclorama hung on tracks around the studio. We had to hope for a wrinkle-free expanse beyond the edge of a house and be careful not to shoot a seam. I've called this essay 'Whiskerbits' not only because I love the word, but because it brings back memories of trying to shoot a dialogue exchange between the Kid and Jake outside the back door. Jake, with his shirt collar rolled under, had just finished shaving, and the Kid wondered what the residue around the enamelled pan was called. The technical problem was trying to find a low camera angle that included the two actors at the wash-stand, a portion of the overhanging roof, and the 'prairie' beyond. Sometimes we used a Strand cloud-machine to project a few fleecy moving clouds on the cyclorama. And, of course, a fan could be brought in to ruffle the actors' hair, although the sound man invariably complained about getting a blast of air in the microphone. Fences were built to break up the horizon line, and laundry was hung. A few bales of hay were used to disguise the painted studio floor, and there was a clever diagonal earth ramp up to the barn door, but basically the ground was never seen because the cameras and microphone booms needed a flat surface on which to dolly smoothly. If Ma, the Kid, and Jake rode in the truck, they did so with the cab window parallel to a rear screen projection of moving scenery. If you needed a bump on the road one of the 'grips' bounced on the rear bumper.

To create some illusion of the outer world, we borrowed the technique of 'sound effects' from radio. Crickets chirped at night, while chickens clucked or cows lowed during the day. We heard the sound of a truck stopping outside a window and the honking of geese in the sky. Sometimes there were bird calls or the odd dog barking in the distance. The lonely train whistle was a standby.

There was no location shooting, at least not for me, in the *Jake and the Kid* series. And it would have been nearly impossible to introduce a filmed sequence. Because we were shooting on videotape, editing at the time was primitive. In the early years the wide two-inch videotape was cut carefully with a razor blade and spliced together just like quarter-inch audiotape. But a good edit was rare, that is a join that had no electronic sparkles showing up on the air when the tape was transmitted. Eventually, by Centennial year, filmic techniques and colour came to television, and shot-by-shot, or even micro frame-by-frame videotape editing was possible electronically. But these were not available for *Jake and the Kid*, and so the bulk of Mitchell's work that was televised in the early years was seen under the most adverse of conditions.

And there were other adventures prompted by the exigencies of *live* production versus film. For the baby contest in 'Don't Scratch That Baby,' we had six real infants in the studio, along with their mothers. Jake solves the tricky problem of awarding prizes by dividing the youngsters into classes like cattle: best beef type (for a chubby one), best team (twins), best calf (diaper class), best female, and for the grand champion, Lazarus Swifteagle, a 100 per cent (Native) Canadian baby. Mitchell makes some strong points in the script about prejudice, and it is an interesting yardstick of the times that in 1961 we had great difficulty finding Native actors to portray the Swifteagle family. It would take another twenty years before they entered the theatrical mainstream. Today they star regularly in films and television series, and have their own talent agency. Eventually we did find Allan Watanabe to play the father and hired two young Japanese children to play an older Indian boy and the baby Lazarus. However, for the final taping, Lazarus had to be carried around like a papoose inside a cradleboard strapped to his mother's back. He was not used to travelling this way and we could do nothing but endure the half hour's howling of this poor unfortunate waif not yet seduced by the glamour of appearing live on TV.

Another show involving children, and one of the most touching of the series, was 'You Gotta Teeter.' At the conclusion of a school pageant, the Kid is chosen to make a pitch on behalf of World War II Orphans. Terrified at the prospect of having to make a speech, he enlists Jake's aid. However, the Kid's pup, Sir Wilfred Laurier, is lost, and he can hardly concentrate on Jake's hilarious instructions as to how you're supposed to tuck your thumbs into your pants, and lean back and forth on rounded feet, just like the great Canadian political leaders. They kept the provinces together; 'if t'weren't for teeterin' there wouldn't be no Canada.' It's hard not to presume that Mitchell has drawn on memories of his own father as a turn-of-the-century elocutionist. But the pup has been killed on the highway and Jake has white-lied about it. The Kid has been betrayed and he hides out in the truck as 'The Story of Saskatchewan' unfolds on the Credit Union Stage. His classmates are dressed as wheat and barley sheaves, threshing-machines, and derricks. 'I am the self-propelled combine.' 'I'm crude oil and I got gas, too.' Then, as they are singing 'We Are Modern Saskatchewan,' we cut back to the parking-lot, where Jake persuades the Kid that the audience is counting on him. Flustered, the lad fumbles and forgets the speech about the orphans that we have seen him rehearse in front of Baldy the cow. Instead, he pours out his heart about his own personal loss, and what it would mean if ever he lost Ma or Jake. Unconsciously, he makes the essential point about what it means to be orphaned. The Kid triumphs and the collection plates are filled. 'Jake, I didn't even teeter hardly at all.' 'You did fine,' Jake mumbles. There is talk about another puppy and the Kid considers calling the next one Sir John A. Macdonald. 'Won't be the same, Jake.' 'It never is,' he replies. With these few brushstrokes Mitchell's half-hour encapsulates the sublime bittersweetness that suffuses his work.

There were purely comic episodes, too. In 'Prairie Lawyer' Jake wins a slander case against a goateed bully when he introduces a real goat into the courtroom for comparative purposes. In 'Love's Wild Magic,' Jane Mallett as a killer nurse cures bedridden Gatenby of self-pity when she reads him most of her collection of trashy pulp romances. Mitchell, at seventy-five, chose this story to read to an International Authors Festival in 1989. It was 'a celebration of crappy literature,' he said, 'it seemed fitting' (Kirchhoff C3). Tall tales were the theme of 'Liar Hunter,' hypnotism was central in 'Mind over Madam,' and what it feels like to be on the receiving end of charity the pointed message in 'Struck Rich.'

My favourite was 'King of All the Country.' Here Mitchell dug unexpectedly deep to explore blood-lust and the killing instinct. It's autumn and the time when Saskatchewan becomes the central flyway for all the geese in North America. The Kid sits up in bed 'all cold inside of my elbows' and holding his breath 'Like bein' waked up by a thousand dogs barkin'.' He swears he could hear their wings: 'I bet they scraped their wish-bones on the ridge of our house.' He longs to be taken on a goose hunt and own a twenty-gauge shotgun like one of the kids at school. Ma takes up the opposing viewpoint.

> MA: I don't see why men are so interested in hunting.
> JAKE: Because we are.
> MA: It coarsens a man's character. Unleashes the primitive instincts ... I'm talking of killing for fun ... Why?
> JAKE: Because they're up there ... That's why.

At dawn, thirty to fifty Canada grey honkers are circling. The decoys are ready. The Kid lies fully dressed in bed and has slept the night with his new $12 shotgun. He and Jake sneak out in stocking feet, but Ma has heard them and follows. Our studio goose pit was surrounded by wheat and water. We had a windsock over the microphone so we could rustle the grass and ripple the pond. A television monitor was hung over the heads of the crouched actors so that they could see and react to the nine stock shots of telecine geese. Ma appears and Jake roughly pulls her down. They're very close.

> JAKE: (quiet and intense). She's like your own blood whanging in your ears ... Now they're lowerin' an' fillin' the sky ... Slaughter the darlin's! [and W.O. writes that Jake utters the screech of an insane man].

A shot rings out and a bird falls. But there's a twist. It's not the Kid who has fired, but Ma.

MA: I got him. I got him. I knocked it down.

In the stunned silence that follows we realize that we are all capable of killing. And Jake says softly to the Kid, 'We're gonna be all right now.'

There weren't many reviews for the series. Only the first episode was noticed and it was not the strongest entry. Listener and letter response was generally very favourable. But, on average, I fear that many of the shows would be slow and static for today's audiences. Someone, I forget who, labelled them 'photographed radio.'

Was it Don Harron who once called our author 'woe' Mitchell? Anyway, W.O. said the scripts had been 'butchered' (Lowman 57) by reducing them to their bare plot outlines. And, indeed, many character touches, mood nuances, and 'colour' bits had been siphoned off to make room for Pillsbury baking product commercials. Whenever possible (if the episode was short at all), we went back to the radio originals and reinstated the odd speech or tiny moment, even wayward adjectives where we could.

Mitchell has called *Maclean's* magazine his father and the CBC his mother (Lowman). But while he was grateful that the Corporation never censored him (Kirchhoff), he did accuse Mother CBC of 'blackmail' when he had to pay them back $15,000 'to regain the full rights to the name and stories of *Jake and the Kid*' (Lowman).

However, some sort of truce was called, for in the decade between 1961 and 1971 there were other episodes or excerpts of *Jake and the Kid* that appeared intermittently on various CBC TV programs such as *Man in the Landscape*, *20/20*, *Telescope*, and *Magicians, Acrobats and Writers*. Director Peter Kelly was a particular champion. Ontario's educational television outlet (ETVO) also show-cased a half-dozen scripts in 1968. Then, in 1993, again for the CBC, there was a revival of interest when story editor Ann McNaughton wove several of the Jake stories into a two-hour

movie of the week. However, not only was this project abandoned but the CBC formally relinquished its long-held interests
in *Jake and the Kid*.

Two York University drama professors, Joseph Green and Ron
Singer, took up the slack, joining with W.O. Mitchell and Eric Till,
who acted as liaison, to form a new partnership called Crocus
Films. This was the catalyst for a thirteen-part, one-hour, *Jake and
the Kid* series filmed in colour for the Can West and Global TV
Network System. With Green and Singer as Executive Producers,
two Canadian production companies, Nelvana and Great North,
combined to shoot the post–World War II episodes in Leduc,
Alberta. It was seen on air beginning Saturday, 16 December 1995,
and ran until mid-March 1996. Starring in it were three prairie
performers: the lanky, low-key Edmonton actor Shaun Johnston
as a 'Jimmy Stewart' Jake; young, tow-headed Ben Campbell
from the Calgary area as the Kid; and blonde, Manitoba-born
Patti Harras as the Kid's sympathetic Mom. Another westerner,
Anne Wheeler (*Bye Bye Blues*), directed the opening episode.
While the 'big sky' production values were superb and the inter-
leafing of several radio plotlines into an hourly format worked
seamlessly, there were compromises. After fifty years, *Jake and the
Kid* finally had been realized visually, but Mitchell's wry sense of
humour was virtually eliminated and the delicious supporting
cast of sharply drawn, rural caricatures had been put through a
blender. This was bland and sugary family entertainment; gentle,
leisurely and nostalgic, but owing more to *Road to Avonlea* and *The
Waltons* than to Mitchell's salty and satiric radio series. Toronto
writer-producer Laura Phillips was the creative force behind the
series and she also penned the odd episode herself, utilizing
the Mitchell characters but originating wholly new story lines.
However, as the series 'show-runner' she found herself replaced
for its second season. There was hope for a sharper thrust in
1996–97. But, as Ron Singer commented, it is 'more of the same.'
And now, after the Alberta government killed its Motion Picture
Development program, the *Jake and the Kid* series is being
moth-balled, though another network has enquired about continuing it.

Our regrets as producer/directors in 1961 were twofold. We wished we could have worked directly with Mitchell, and that we could have got outdoors with either film or videotape to capture some authentic atmosphere.

Those wishes didn't come true for me until the spring of 1965, when I directed a one-hour version of *The Kite* for CBC's *Show of the Week* (26 April 1965). The adaptation of his 1962 second novel was done by Mitchell himself, working with story editor David Peddie (son of the distinguished actor Frank Peddie). And W.O. attended 'dry' rehearsals and sat in on the studio taping. He tried to be unobtrusive but his piercing eyes burned holes in the air and it was hard to ignore the styrofoam cup in his hand, awash with the vile chewed-tobacco juice that was the residue of his trademark affliction. We were still shooting in black and white in those days, but there was budget and facilities enough to do a little location filming. We shot a street scene in Newmarket, Ontario, and then at a nearby farm (on the Leslie side-road) the camera caught Daddy Sherry gambolling through a 'heavenly' field flying his birthday kite for the closing credits, an added pastoral image that we felt was justified by the script. The cast was strong. John Vernon (Wojeck-to-be) was the journalist and love interest. Charmion King was the widowed mother, and Leslie Barringer played Keith, her kite-making son. Again, Mitchell juxtaposed a younger figure with an older. Central, of course, was the crusty curmudgeon Daddy Sherry, the oldest man in the world, haunted by the clock and set to celebrate his 111th birthday. (He would be six years older when the television version transmogrified into a stage play, probably so that the character could continue to be older than Canada itself.) John Drainie, recently returned from Mallorca, was cast in this pivotal part and gave a marvellous first read-through. But John was frail and dying, unbeknownst to any of us, and his wife Claire phoned a day or so later to say he had to withdraw from the television show. The production was postponed a month. Jack Creley took on the mantle of age quite brilliantly and it became a favoured stage role for him, which he played in many productions across the country well into the 1980s. There was even a photo spread in *The Globe and Mail* at the time of the TV broadcast, showing the (then) forty-year-old actor's various stages of visual transformation via prosthetics (liquid latex makeup). Creley was supported by a bevy of cronies left over from *Jake and the Kid*. Eric House repeated his Repeat Golightly as chairperson for the town's birthday celebration committee, and Drew Thompson was suitably lugubrious as the purveyor of coffins and headstones. Later, the stage play would split the journalist role so that the doctor attending Daddy could now be the love interest, and a silly CBC television producer, Howard Motherwell, become the butt of Mitchell's trenchant satire of the media. Mitchell also added some raunchy, gonadal humour for the theatre piece. As William French commented, 'The passing years have made him irreverent' (French E1).

If I had a wish, it would be to see and hear W.O. himself play the part of Daddy. 'This old son of a gun is probably the most autobiographical thing I've written,' he once confessed (Adilman, 25 May 1981). There is no doubt that Bill is a seasoned platform performer, with that looping, whining, crackling voice that spins around you like a lariat, catching you and drawing you in. And Mitchell is no stranger to TV, playing Stephen Leacock opposite Patrick Watson in the *Titans* interview series and a cranky misogynist for an episode of *Road to Avonlea* (*Toronto Star* 19 October 1989).

I had the great pleasure of acting Reverend Powelly in the feature film version of *Who Has Seen the Wind*. To my knowledge *Back to Beulah* (1974), *Who Has Seen the Wind* (1976–77), and *Sacrament* (1978), were the only works (prior to the 1995 TV series) seen to advantage in colour, and utilizing the technology of film. This accident of time was hard on W.O. Mitchell in terms of camera exposure, and it is perhaps significant that the second arc of Mitchell's creativity, beginning in the mid-1970s, dates in part from the renewed attention provided by the electronic showcase.

In 1972, when the CBC dropped its option on *Who Has Seen the Wind*, director Allan King picked up the film and television rights for $11,000 (Cobb 45, Hofsess 14). Initially, it was intended that Mitchell's classic 1947 novel would be shown on the CBC in five one-hour episodes, allowing a leisurely pace that would encompass all the characters and incidents that W.O. had created. King's wife, Patricia Watson, whose screenplay of Margaret Laurence's *A Bird in the House* (1970) had recently won a Canadian Film Award, was hired to adapt the book for the camera. The new *Wind* miniseries was three years in development, and Watson relates that her relationship with Mitchell began beautifully. After she had sent the five scripts to High River, Mitchell phoned and said 'I love you, I love you, I love you ... about six times' (Watson).

However, in January 1975, when the budget for the film series reached $1.5 million, the CBC pulled the plug. Allan King decided to make a feature film instead and set about to raise approximately a million dollars ($1.13 million eventually). And Patricia Watson started afresh. The Saskatchewan government granted $300,000 in exchange for an on-site training program for thirty-three would-be film-makers and a commitment that the movie would be shot in the province. The deal was a good one. Publicity for the project was exceptional, and 85 per cent of the film's investment remained in Saskatchewan in the form of meals, accommodation, and salaries. The federal government's Canadian Film Development Corporation (CFDC) matched Saskatchewan's investment, and Famous Players and a group of private donors put up the rest. To help with distribution, Famous Players suggested adding José Ferrer to the all-Canadian cast. Mr Ferrer's scenes as the Ben were shot in a block of five days. He kept very much to himself, reading books in French between the takes. The Canadian actors included Gordon Pinsent, Chapelle Jaffe, Helen Shaver, Tom Hauff, Cedric Smith, Charmion King, Patricia Hamilton, Alexander Webster, Nan Stewart, Hugh Webster, Gerard Parks, and myself, and the film introduced local youngsters Brian Painchaud and Doug Junor as Brian and the Young Ben.

Filming for *Who Has Seen the Wind* began on 30 August 1976. By happenstance I was in the first shot. Standing in for Weyburn, Saskatchewan (Mitchell's birthplace), as it might have looked back in the mid-1930s, was the town of Arcola (sixty-five miles to the east). The main street was covered with earth and gravel to hide the asphalt, and horse-drawn carts and 'Bennett-buggies' replaced the normal traffic. The shops along the route were masked with false, Depression store fronts. But, for once, the interior of a schoolhouse was genuine, and the grain elevators, the flies, and the fields of golden wheat were real. One of the jokes on location was 'Who Has Seen the Wind-machine?' But it wasn't needed. The director of photography got lucky and the unit was rewarded with a ferocious windstorm to climax the action. Because there was limited accommodation in Arcola (population 539), the cast and crew stayed in motels in Carlyle and Kenosee Park, about fifteen miles away.

I remember especially filming the Sunday morning church service. About fifty of the local townspeople were hired as extras and fitted out in period garb for the scene. The women had their hair done up in buns or braids, and wore hats and gloves, while the men in dark-coloured suits had agreed to dust bowl haircuts, and carried caps or fedoras in their laps. As Reverend Powelly I smiled sanctimoniously at my ally, Mrs Abercrombie, in the choir; received the distasteful wad of chewing tobacco when I shook the hand of the contrite Ben (I hid it in a potted plant); made some unctuous announcements about upcoming events; and, finally, brought down the wrath of the Old Testament God after the still exploded in the basement and the liquorish vapours wafted upwards. It took a whole day to shoot the sequence, with all the coverage of the congregation being done first. (Large groups of people are always released as quickly as possible to avoid overtime). So that the church-goers could react appropriately, I delivered my lines perhaps twenty times during the morning and afternoon, either off camera, or with the camera behind my shoulder. Then, at the end of the day, when the lighting was turned around for my shots, I had to deliver all the speeches once again to an empty church. This technique is one of the joys of film-making which actors learn to live with. Members of the crew sat in to approximate the 'eye-lines' when I had specific people to address.

Patricia Watson's five-part TV script had to be drastically condensed and revamped for the new movie. In the beginning, Mitchell seemed to grant qualified approval for her first draft, but he was soon to change his mind. Certainly he had complained about the decision to telescope the six years and four seasons of the novel into a few summer months. But this had been a pragmatic choice to save money. All the children, for example, would have had to be recast at least once to make the span of six years believable, and to make the seasonal changes work the shooting time would have needed to be spread over a year or more. Costs would have doubled.

Gradually, as well, two different approaches to the story began to evolve. Watson's intention was always to be as honest as possible in realizing this well-known popular novel. This meant a screenplay that was not inventive, but a cut-and-paste collage of vignettes – all the favourite scenes and characters carefully interwoven, but, like the book, somewhat lacking a strong skeletal plot structure or central dramatic conflict. Watson's solution seemed to be to make Brian the plot. We would see the drama almost entirely through the eyes of the boy: the mystery and dry-eyed pain of losing his father; the awakening to new friendships (especially the Young Ben); the discovery of the hypocrisies of small-town life; and the final, almost mystical, introduction to the raw, God-like power of the Wind that opens his heart and triggers a catharsis of tears. It was inherent to the deeper sentiments of the novel, but perhaps a gentler, more feminine, approach.

While Allan King retained artistic control, he had assigned budgetary supervision to his executive producer Budge Crawley, a contemporary of Mitchell's, give or take a year or two, and a father-figure in Canadian film. Crawley was responsible for *The Loon's Necklace* (1948), almost everyone's first memory of greatness in Canadian film. He had worked with Mitchell back in 1955 to produce *The Face of Saskatchewan*, and, in the spring of 1976, Budge had just won an Academy Award for a feature documentary called *The Man Who Skied Down Everest*. But, at this seeming moment of triumph, Crawley was also in a personal financial bind. He was suing Universal Pictures for failing to properly promote and distribute another full-length documentary that he had invested heavily in, *Janis*, all about the late blues singer Janis Joplin. Strapped for funds, Crawley was forced to sell his Quebec studio to stay afloat, and he began to have serious doubts about *Who Has Seen the Wind* as a commercial product. He was quoted as saying he 'had reservations from the start that Mitchell's book was not focussed enough for a film treatment' and 'Pat Watson's screenplay did not change my point of view' (Cobb 45). In May, just a few months before shooting was scheduled to begin, 'Crawley flew to Calgary to ask Mitchell to do a rewrite' (Cobb 45) and Allan King promised to give it 'serious consideration' (Knelman 30). Then, on 15 June, the day Budge Crawley was to sign the completion guarantee with CFDC – an agreement which would have obliged him 'to produce up to $200,000 if the movie ran over budget' – he withdrew from the picture, leaving Allan King to scramble quickly for a new producer (Pierre Lamy). Crawley declared he 'did not want to be connected with a film that would be a commercial failure' (Cobb 45), but he didn't say that he couldn't afford to be.

Meanwhile, W.O. Mitchell wrote a massive 240-page scenario which arrived, according to Patricia Watson, a few days before the first day of shooting. Mitchell said later that the whole concept had to be changed. That was 'the nature of adaptation from one medium to another' (Adilman, 25 September 1976). And changed it was. According to King and Watson it was 'Disney-like,' full of 'slapstick' elements, 'people falling into cow flops.' There were funny scenes between the town eccentrics, but the sensitivity they had envisioned was gone. Of course, it was a rough and too-late first draft, filled with ten-page dialogue scenes of the boy talking to someone on the porch and large, rambling monologues of Saint Sammy railing against the elements. But it was not 'camera-ready,' and King had little option but to continue with his wife's carefully constructed screenplay. Mitchell was hurt and furious. He dubbed the film version 'Who Has Seen the Waltons,' and wanted his name removed from the credits. And 'he not only turned down King's offer of a small role (as Judge Mortimer) but stayed clear of the production completely' (Knelman 30). He said he would go public and he did so. Patricia Watson was devastated. She says today that 'it felt like being denounced by Santa Claus' (Watson). Allan King remains philosophic. He says he had no desire to engage in a war of words. 'If you take a poke at an icon you only hurt your hand' (King).

Clearly, the fundamental differences of approach were irreconcilable. Mitchell was now sixty-two, and his youthful novel had been penned when he was thirty-three. How had he changed over the years? It sounds as though his first instincts were to please Budge Crawley and sell more tickets, that is, make the script come alive again with comedy, perhaps in the manner of *Jake and the Kid*. Were his creative sensibilities now more in tune with the town eccentrics than the gentle glow of Brian's awakening? Was it a question of Mitchell choosing Jake over the Kid, while Watson and King preferred the Kid over the handyman?

I was caught somewhere in the middle as Reverend Powelly, and I guess I still am. My vindictive schemer was a joy to play and larger than life. At Kenosee we were able to view the 'rushes' a few days after the scenes had been shot. I received a lot of laughs from the cast and crew for my performance in the pulpit. And I remember being told quietly that I came close to upsetting the balance intended. They were right. When I saw the film overall, I noted that I had been judiciously edited down.

On 2 October 1976 shooting was over. We were all given a *Who Has Seen the Wind* T-shirt and the people of Arcola threw a super party in the community hall. Mrs Abercrombie and Reverend Powelly danced to the music of the Southern Ramblers. Fittingly, a year later the feature film had its world *première* in Arcola, at the 351-seat Princess Theatre.

The critics tended to be divided along the lines of the controversy. Urjo Kareda, writing for *Maclean's*, found Patricia Watson's script had slightly softened the rough edges of Mitchell's story and Allan King's carefully crafted film seemed over-protective (Kareda 78). The reviewer in *Take One* talked of 'how indifferently the movie has treated its source material' (McCallum 15), while Robert Martin began his *Globe and Mail* critique saying 'W.O. Mitchell was right ...: his novel ... would not make a movie as it stood ... a movie that could be retitled Who Has Seen the Book' (Martin 33). But for others, such as Les Wedman in *The Vancouver Sun*, 'Who Has Seen the Wind is undeniably the outstanding Canadian film this year and a worthy successor to Claude Jutra's *Mon Oncle Antoine*.' He loved Richard Leiterman's golden photography and found that Patricia Watson's screenplay 'retains the marvelous and colorful atmosphere of the original story' (Wedman). Peter Harcourt agreed and commented on 'the scrupulous fidelity to the original text ... Admirers of the novel may, in fact, be amazed at how little dialogue has been added. For all of Mitchell's imagery, for all the interpretive function of his prose, Patricia Watson and Allan King have found visual equivalents ... [They] have managed to convey Mitchell's sense of the invisible by moments of speechlessness ... [It] is a meditative film' (Harcourt 72, 70, 71). Clyde Gilmour found a balance, noting that 'this is a sweet-spirited and immensely likable entertainment' but it 'unfolds in a rambling and episodic fashion.' The dramatic scenes were not 'milked' enough (the funeral, Mrs Abercrombie's downfall). 'Several of its most powerful moments are too low-voltage and underplayed' (Gilmour). *Who Has Seen the Wind* went on to represent Canada abroad and won the *Prix Grand* at the Paris Film Festival, being praised for its 'sustained lyricism' (Perez, *Le Matin*). At home, the audiences flocked to see it. Budge Crawley's fears were unfounded as *Who Has Seen the Wind* became Canada's highest grossing film for 1977, running, for example, in a major Toronto cinema for an impressive three months.

Martin Knelman tried to mollify the creative disagreement by suggesting that 'it almost seemed appropriate that the filming was marred by the sort of small-town family squabble that Mitchell himself has specialized in writing about' (Knelman 30). Years later, when I was directing *The Black Bonspiel of Wullie MacCrimmon* at the Kawartha Festival in Lindsay, Ontario, Mitchell passed through and dropped into our rehearsal. We were working from the text contained in *Dramatic W.O. Mitchell* and I asked Bill if he would autograph my copy. He wrote, 'Regards to David who *never* poaches on my writer territory,' and I realized suddenly how vulnerable he was and how easily he could be hurt if his 'writer territory' was invaded. In his introduction to the play collection he contrasted the loneliness of writing novels with the collaborative process of playwrighting. Living close to Theatre Calgary has helped in the transition of so many of his television plays to the stage. But, too often, in the transference of his literary works to the screen, he was half a continent away from the creative kitchen and the collaborative process broke down. There were mail-order romances, perhaps, but too few real marriages. Mitchell rightly has complained about the loneliness of novel writing, but has not celebrated its freedoms. There are no limitations to time and space in the imagination. Crowd scenes are affordable. You can span six years and four seasons with no complaints. You only have to please yourself (and Merna) and the publisher's editor, not a collaborative committee of creative geniuses. But still, while the freedoms are diminished progressively as the literary material moves onto the stage or screen, there can be unexpected eclectic rewards. Film writers are asked to provide a blueprint but not a finished product. They are architects but not builders. They must be confident enough to allow interpretive embroidery and organic input from the actors, the director of photography, and the various film and sound editors. Eventually, they even have to give over to a new head 'writer' or image-maker, the director or producer. It is the 'poaching on the writer's territory' that the contemporary media demand.

Mitchell may have chafed under this, but even prior to the 1976 controversy he was able to come to terms with the fact that 'movie writing requires a long apprenticeship' (Adilman, 24 June 1976). *Who Has Seen the Wind* was not his first scuffle. He had taken his writing credit off *Alien Thunder*, a 1974 Mountie/Indian/murder flick starring Donald Sutherland, because 'the script was changed drastically and my work was all thrown out. I didn't even recognize it' (Adilman, 24 June 1976). And *Back to Beulah*, which Eric Till directed for CBC television in 1974, before it became a Chalmer's Award–winning stage play in 1976–77, has languished as a film property for twenty years because of dissatisfaction with the screen adaptation. Eric Till is still favoured to direct this film version-to-be, which over the years has been retitled *Four's a Crowd* and *Listen to Me*.

For me, Mitchell's most accomplished screen adaptation remains *The Devil's Instrument*, seen first back in 1956. With its large cast, twenty-eight short scenes, and multiple locations, it seems to have been structured expressly for film. When it became a theatre piece in 1977, it also fared well with those who embraced the concept of open or epic staging. In many technical ways *The Devil's Instrument* seems to be Mitchell's most modern dramatic work. But, unfortunately, he never employed this cinematic formula again.

Still, it is maddening that this great purveyor of popular culture has not had more success on celluloid. Bill Mitchell is a lover of words, a stand-up comedian whose tousled prose and cracker-barrel wit will forever evoke the covers of *Saturday Evening Post*, and an era when conversation was an art. In his later novels, Mitchell has been criticized for an over-dependence on dialogue. While this theatrical gift has meant that many of his literary works have made a happy leap from page to stage (usually via a television treatment), it has not served him as well with film. Excessive talk on screen seems fussy and curiously static because it mires the action. Films love minimalism and imagistic shapes. We are told that verbal skills emanate from the left hemisphere of the brain, while spatial aptitudes originate from the right. Perhaps the problem with projects like *Beulah* is the continued attempt to graft a left hemisphere product onto a right hemisphere medium. It suggests the need to wipe the slate clean, and write specifically and freshly for motion pictures rather than perpetuate a process of adaptation.

Screen-writers still write for the inner ear, but they do so primarily through the eye. They suggest a world of meaning with body language, an unexpected move, a look, a moody silence, a smile, and, of course, even occasionally a well turned phrase. Cinema, however, likes to see its sentences in motion rather than stopping the action with a page of fixed dialogue. You rarely hear a shower of talk in film, except in the background. If the talk is front and centre then it's 'photographed radio' and that contradiction in terms defeated many of the giants of the 1940s and 1950s who were hoping to make the transition from radio to TV.

Mitchell's sweet comic gifts were always underlined with an edge of pain. He has survived because he was not afraid to tap into the darker colours of the late twentieth century. It is our loss that more of his work has not been preserved in feature films, but we must be grateful for the prolific body of work that has been realized on radio and television over the past fifty years. And it is encouraging that a new *Jake and the Kid* series was mounted on film to celebrate his eightieth year. I wonder what kind of deal it would take to get Old Cloutie to give him at least another fifty years of creativity?

SPECIAL THANKS

To York University's Scott Library, Archives and Special Collections, where the CBC television production scripts for *Jake and the Kid* were housed.

W.O. Mitchell:
The Playwright

RICK McNAIR

Working as a theatre professional, I have met many playwrights. John Murrell, David French, Sharon Pollock, and Cecil Taylor, I met at parties. Lanford Wilson I met at a most logical place for the working playwright, the photocopy machine. W.O. Mitchell I met as he was running past me with his wife Merna reminding him, 'They are ready to start, Bill.' He was almost late for his one-man story-telling performance in a sold-out Calgary theatre.

I had been waiting for a while hoping to catch him before his performance. Since that was not to be, I went to the bar where Merna was trying to catch her breath. Her introduction of Bill set me into a professional relationship that has continued since that first meeting in 1978.

One of the qualities that makes W.O. unique is illustrated in that first meeting. Many authors read nervously from their works and often get a gentle critical evaluation by an admiring reader. The difference with W.O. is that he performs with a passion and a skill that more than one actor has publicly admired. He not only writes for the stage, but he is of the stage himself. This is why he recognizes, as any good story-teller will, that the audience shares the performance with the artists. He does not see a performance as a tablet come down from a superior being, but as a song to be sung together.

In that first meeting, with water dripping out of my ears, I asked him if he would be interested in turning the novel *The Kite* into a play. I had just taken over the position of artistic director of

Theatre Calgary, and had been reading Western Canadian literature extensively because I had the belief that a regional theatre
has to tell some of the stories of the region, or it is more like a
movie theatre telling the same stories across the country. We must
tell our stories or we soon won't have any. Theatre today is not
considered relevant, important, or even interesting to a large
number of Canadians. We have to be careful that our theatre does
not just become a high tech story-teller of other people's stories.
Theatre must be more than good for you, like an artistic cod liver
oil. It must engage you as a partner.

W.O. said he didn't know about *The Kite* idea, but he had a play
about curling that had been rejected by many theatres. I said I
would read that play if he would consider what I said. It was
agreed. The play was, of course, *The Black Bonspiel of Wullie Mac-
Crimmon*.

Sometimes we read a theatre script as if it is merely a piece of
literature. But words are only part of a play. Sharon Pollock calls
the script the 'blueprint for the production.' From that blueprint
many different houses could be built. Often I have heard directors
say that they can see how the first act of *The Black Bonspiel of Wullie MacCrimmon* will work, but they think that the second act
won't work. But if you ask the audience after they have seen a
production, they remember best the second act. That is because it
is a game that has all of the excitement of a live sporting event
combined with colourful characters and a good story. The ideas of
play and ceremony are often intertwined in the plays of W.O.
Mitchell.

After reading the play I was excited by its prospects. I met with
Guy Sprung and he agreed to direct the production. When we
met with W.O., Guy asked that the second act be fleshed out. At
the meeting which followed, Merna Mitchell had two suggestions. That original draft had Haile Selassie as the Devil. Merna
asked why the Devil was a black man when there were so many
white villains available. Her second observation was that instead
of atomic energy for the Devil's fuel, it would be more in keeping
with the period of the play if the Devil's fuel were oil. Bill differed
emphatically. Being a neophyte in my understanding of the work-

ing relationship between Merna and Bill, I thought I had come at a bad time. However, when the next draft of the play arrived the Devil was Peter Lougheed and he was dealing in oil.

The Black Bonspiel of Wullie MacCrimmon is a folk play. It is based on the Faust legend transposed to the Canadian prairies. If you travel across the prairies and see the curling rinks in every town you understand how W.O. has captured something that has an importance to many people. The play has gone from being considered a play that has 'too large a cast and it is Canadian' by one Canada Council panel to being considered 'too commercial' by another. It is now a standard play in the Canadian repertory, playing in large and small theatres all across Canada, enjoying a reputation for attracting people to theatre that are not of the usual audience. It has played in every major centre, with the exception of Toronto. The town that can't hold a decent Grey Cup celebration also has had no room for *The Black Bonspiel*. One director said that the audiences were too sophisticated for the show. The reverse is probably truer. Isn't *The Mousetrap* still running there?

The success of the Theatre Calgary production was incredible. It helped to bring the Theatre from deficit to surplus. So far, there have been four productions of the play at Theatre Calgary. One of the interesting phenomena is that people often talk with excitement about the production in the lobby during intermission, something that happens all too little with many plays.

After the success of this production, W.O. turned up at the theatre with the 'idea' that *The Kite* could be turned into a play. Noticing my smile, he said, 'You mentioned that once before didn't you?'

A novel is often turned into a poor play. One of the traps into which adaptors fall is that, being too much in love with the material, they have favourite bits that must be put in. Afraid to hurt something they admire, they often give too literal an adaptation. The second problem compounds the first. A novel is a longer piece of work than a full-length play. So if you don't cut something you will have to have a series of précis-type scenes. The play then turns into a visual *Coles Notes* which pleases nobody but the uncritical admirer. The film version of *Who Has Seen the*

Wind is an example. W.O. said two interesting things about the film in a radio interview. He said that the adaptation was too faithful to the form of the book and too sentimental. He renamed the movie 'Who Has Seen the Waltons.'

So, it was with great trepidation that I went to W.O.'s house to hear him read the first draft of the play. But hearing him read the part of Daddy Sherry, the 117-year-old rebel, I felt the power of the character live in his study. Times like that are a kind of epiphany for an artist. W.O. said that when he wrote the opening scene in the play about remembering the sights, the smells of wolf willow, and Ramrod's death, he could not help crying as he typed. He said he remembered some of his friends who had died and he understood the feelings of Daddy Sherry much more than when he wrote the novel.

Also at that meeting, he told me about some of the people who were the models for the characters in *The Kite* and other plays. He described personalities, foibles, features, and even outlandish dress that could be thought to be far too unusual to be reality based. It was interesting to learn that behind such larger-than-life characters as Repeat Golightly and the multiple Charley Browns from *The Black Bonspiel* there was the inspiration of a real person. In fact, one person in the town of High River was not too pleased when he thought he saw himself in a character.

At the *première* production of *The Kite*, it was clear that the audience was able to connect with several of the characters and to care what happened to them. Additionally, the audience appreciated the humour that came out of the characters as well as their circumstances. When W.O. came to see a run-through, it was interesting to see his reaction to the set. Designed by Terry Gunverdahl, the set was not a naturalistic creation of a prairie home. It was a semi-abstract house built of horizontal wooden stripes that grew into the clouds made in the same manner. Even the tree that Daddy Sherry swung on was constructed from strips of wood. When W.O. saw it he became very excited. As he walked around the set, he said that this was the kind of set he had meant for his work. Those who thought in terms of ultra-realism were wrong.

Later, when, because of its success, the play was invited to Toronto, Mitchell saw it again. His comments on the performance of
one of the actors was interesting in a similar way. He said that all
of the actors except for one had captured the reality of the people.
That one actor, he said, had gone from character to caricature.
Mitchell suggested that the reason why that actor strayed was
related to the lack of training and discipline in the actor's background. He said that 'going for caricature' was what an actor
often did when he had never met the people who lived in the
play.

There is a scene in *The Kite* where Dr Richardson is talking to
Keith about walking on the clouds. There can be a tendency to
give what I call a 'Hallmark Card reading' of the scene. Often
during the run I had to tell the actor to be careful to make sure
that there were lots of rocks in the clouds. W.O. would often say
the same thing.

He was very aware of his punctuation and of how it influenced
an actor's reading of the script. I remember one rehearsal when
W.O. told me to stroke out some of 'the dot dot dots' that were in
the script because the actor was following the pause indications
too carefully and hurting the rhythm of the speech. Mitchell's
performing ability could be seen in his comments on the work of
the actors in his plays.

There was another interesting phenomenon with the Theatre
Calgary production. Theatre administrators often point out that
women buy two thirds of the season-tickets. 'Make sure that
women will like the season.' In this production there were more
men than usual saying how much they liked the play. On many
occasions there was the distinct sound of men laughing, often a
rare sound in a modern theatre.

I remember in the rehearsal period of *The Kite*, W.O. was concerned about the audience's reaction to certain descriptions of the
sound of gas escaping from the lower half of a person's anatomy.
A former prime minster had his efforts in this sound production
compared to that of a brass trumpet. The audience approved, in
spite of themselves, at this bursting of pomposity. This outburst
of Greek theatre humour catalogued the emissions of several

great Canadian prime ministers. This, of course, would not be approved by the capital 'C' for culture members of the theatre establishment.

An interesting footnote to this production was that when a Broadway producer saw it, he was immediately talking up Hume Cronyn and others for an American production. He was too late because the Citadel Theatre owned the foreign rights by then.

The next project, *For Those in Peril on the Sea*, brought together many of the previous themes of W.O.'s work. There was an old man and a young boy and the idea of the journey from one generation to another. While in rehearsal, I mentioned that I particularly liked one passage in the play. W.O. started to laugh and asked me if I was sure about that. After I insisted that I was, he proceeded to point out that I had picked out the only passage in the entire play that was not his. It was a passage from *Sailing Alone around the World* by Joshua Slocum. He explained to me that Lon, the old man in the play, had read Slocum's book so often that he thought some of it had actually happened to him. It wasn't lying, it was an appropriated truth. W.O. suggested that if I liked the story so much I should read all of Slocum's book. I did, and wrote my play, *To Far Away Places*.

Unlike Daddy Sherry, the old man in *For Those in Peril on the Sea* dies at the end of the first act. At the interval, members of the audience expressed their concern about this. When they returned after the intermission, they could not accept at first the implications of the old man's empty room. Some members of the audience would not allow the old man to die. One critic questioned how a prairie writer could write a story about the sea. But as Mitchell has Margaret say in the play: 'Perhaps Lon was a little more of a romantic than the rest of us ... *Grass* sea – prairie *is* a sort of sea really' (*Dramatic W.O.* 258).

The last full-length play we worked on was *Royalty Is Royalty*, produced at the Manitoba Theatre Centre in 1987. The script came from an older version that had never had a full-scale production. Very simply, the play timed a visit of the Queen to coincide with local controversy over the rights of a First Nation family in Crocus. Sticking pins in pomposity was one of the play's central themes. The national reviews were wonderful but one of the local critics complained that the play was old news. Sometimes W.O. falls victim to critics who want the writer to be politically correct with the latest 'trend' or state-of-the-moment writing. A simple story often does not fit into this view. The ability to connect with the audience is almost a negative with some reviewers. But, it is interesting to note that some of the wonderful shows of the moment never see the light of the stage again, while the stories that are told continue to find their way to the stage. This play ran at the Manitoba Theatre Centre at the same time as Tomson Highway's *The Rez Sisters*. While reviewers failed to notice the intentional pairing, my First Nations friends all commented on how good W.O.'s story was. One said that the question of dignity was still as much a problem now as it was in the 1950s when the play was set.

It is interesting to note that *Royalty Is Royalty, The Kite*, and *The Black Bonspiel of Wullie MacCrimmon* all have the element of community and community celebration in them. They celebrate the idea of the need to come together as a group. It is therefore not surprising that when the *Black Bonspiel* toured, it was received with great enthusiasm in communities of all sizes, many of which treated the coming of the play as a form of celebration in itself.

Because of the obvious audience appeal of his plays, I was for a long time curious about why W.O. has not written more plays. One answer he gave was almost as obvious. He said that when he started there was nowhere to perform them. The most powerful theatre then was the CBC. Hence the *Jake and the Kid* series. He said that if he had been writing for the theatre he would have created many stage plays out of some of the material that was on radio. He laughed when recalling the scripts for the CBC, and talked of changing the dates at the local post office so that the scripts would appear to have been mailed out on time. The other reason he gave was less obvious. Mitchell said that as there were very few theatres at that time, writers were dependent on appealing to the tastes of a very few directors in order to get produced. He said he was not the kind of writer that John Hirsch, for example, liked. This limited the number of plays for the stage that

W.O. Mitchell wrote. It was not easy to get a play produced even if you were W.O. Mitchell. He has often said that life is like being on a ferris wheel: sometimes you're up and sometimes you're down.

One of the many pleasures of working with W.O. is the stories he tells. He has told me two fairly complete stories that he hopes someday to turn into plays or films. One was a great story about a honey dipper (related to outhouses) that gets hit by a train in full flight. The other one he described was about a married couple who go to Florida every year. It was essentially a two-character play, with the working title 'Secrets.' This was not a comedy of the type of the previous project.

W.O. writes varying kinds of plays, but they have recurring themes. His plays present stories of people who are pulled from the ordinary and placed into the extraordinary; his themes concern the continuity of life, the relations between the young and the old, the search for the father, the coming together to celebrate the unusual usual, and, of course, the sticking of pins into the pompous and the powerful. It is not surprising, then, that some critics have trouble with W.O., because they recognize him as an enemy of their vision of the theatre world. So, if you have problems with your sense of humour, please don't review W.O.'s plays. If you can't appreciate the elegance of life and death told in 'inappropriate' ways, then stay away. A joyous love of humanity runs through all of W.O.'s work.

I am saddened to think that the Canadian theatre has not been ready to accept all of the stories from W.O. Mitchell's real and imaginary worlds. But I am excited by the good productions that I have seen or have been a part of. Maybe in another country or in another time there would be a whole shelf full of his plays. But I will admit I like to read his books and travel his prairies with him in whatever artistic vehicle he creates. 'Loop the loop, you weavin' son of bitch! Keep her up there. Keep her up there forever' (*Dramatic W.O.* 214).

Acting W.O.

GUY SPRUNG

The track was heading due west, the trees giving way to the open prairie, and the transcontinental was uncoiling from the curves and inclines of the Lake Country. Inside, squashed up in a roomette, next to a dog-eared, scribbled on, read and reread draft of *Back to Beulah*, I opened *Who Has Seen the Wind* for the first time. 'To O.S. Mitchell, my father and my son,' read the dedication. A tiny jolt went through my system, the kind you park away in your memory banks until you can disassemble its meaning. I was on my way to meet the son of that father and the father of that son and the author of both book and play. He was a writer of whom, at that time, I admit shamefacedly, I knew only that I should have known him better than I did. I was to meet him in Calgary and, if he found me acceptable, I was to direct the stage première of *Back to Beulah*.

By the mid-1970s, original Canadian plays, thanks to increasing audience demand, were making it onto the stages of our larger regional theatres, where the repertoire had hitherto been confined to a slavish imitation of everything that was deemed a success in London's West End or on Broadway. Theatre Calgary, driven mainly by an intangible moral blackmail, had decided that the time was right to do a play by Calgary's most famous literary citizen – W.O. Mitchell. With his reputation in the city as a curmudgeonly Canadian Mark Twain, the fulminator of many a ribald, slightly *risqué* (for an octogenarian fundamentalist audience, in any case) tale, a presentation of a play by W.O., the theatre hoped, would score cultural brownie points.

But W.O. had been advised that Harold Baldridge, the artistic director of the theatre, was a man whose talents, though eminently suited to running American summer stock theatre, were not to be trusted with anything more demanding. He had therefore vetoed Baldridge as director. Instead, W.O. had sent a draft of the play to Bill Glassco, the artistic director of Toronto's Tarragon Theatre. Glassco didn't really like the play. Sensing instinctively that it was beyond his skills to direct, he dismissed it, off the record, as arch Canadiana.

Barging into his office at this moment, just back from England, waving a fistful of glowing British reviews and looking for work, came this abrasive Canuck director. Glassco decided he could kill two birds with one stone, getting me out of his hair and providing W.O. and Calgary with a suitable alternative. He recommended me to W.O.

So, it was the summer of 1975 and I was on my way to Calgary to get 'vetted.' After four years in London's East End, living in a squat, fighting eviction, and founding a theatre in the highly politicized world of British class struggle, how ironic that my first offer of work back home should be to stage a play by the Bard of prairie Canada.

In a conscious attempt to reacquaint myself with my neuroses about Canada, I deliberately bought a ticket to traverse the country by train. As that train rolled on across the prairie, rocking me gently inside its belly, I lay trapped in the web of a master yarn spinner. From the mundane observed minutiae, such as Brian's vision of porridge cooking being 'old men's mouths opening and closing as it boiled' (*Who Has Seen the Wind* 20), to the sublime nature of his celestial quest, *Who Has Seen the Wind* presented the world through the mind of a boy. But the strength of W.O.'s voice for me was then, and has been ever since, his characterizations. His astute and humorous human portraits, painted from the inside, are verbal Cézannes. He tells stories by creating people. His stories are the people. His drama is the characters in conflict. Plot is character revelation.

On this journey to W.O., I stopped off briefly in Winnipeg to visit my father's sister. Long-time principal of Kelvin High

School, mentor and inspiration to many young women who crossed her path, she now lay in a hospital bed, enfeebled by cancer, wig lolling on the pillow to expose her chemotherapy-induced baldness. The end, as it turned out, was only a few weeks away.

As we were attempting to converse, her lifelong female companion entered the room. Their hands met in a manifestation of dignified, unsentimental tenderness. The give and take of that moment – the strength, the need, the vulnerability, and the generosity each exhibited, one to the other – informed how I saw the three central characters in *Back to Beulah*. Rereading the draft of the script as the train continued west, Harriet became my aunt for me. Or was it vice versa?

In Calgary, over a bridge and by a river bend, a superannuated Brian from *Who Has Seen the Wind* welcomed me into his comfortable home. Still curious, still searching for God with the innocence of a four-year-old, his silver hair tousled like that of a boy waiting for a parental reprimand, reading glasses askew on his nose, his voice gravelly yet gentle, he whisked me into his unfinished greenhouse overlooking the backyard and introduced me to his jungle of orchids. A polite query as to who I was and what I had done was followed by a gentle vetting that quickly became acceptance as we sat down and talked over the script. This consisted mainly of his piling anecdote upon anecdote until this Easterner was dizzy trying to separate the embellishments from the reality. 'Merrnnna,' he would bellow to his wife off in the other room. 'What is the name of...' or, 'Who was it that said...' His snuff trailing down the front of his sweater, his hands waving from side to side, he was a compelling creation of his own imagination. His health was a worry; he was easily exhausted.

Any wisdom I might have had then about the play would have been feeble, but he nodded and listened and even occasionally bounced up and down in his chair with excitement. He had the same mustache my father had worn when I was a boy. I was pretty awed. Our work on the script might have been good work – at the time I was too inexperienced to judge. I know I would give my right arm to have those few days over again now.

Eventually, at one of the openings, my father and he met briefly. More than mere coincidence but nothing as lofty as synchronicity, it transpired that they were contemporaries at the University of Manitoba. They immediately started swapping reminiscences of professors and mutual friends. It was a little too close for comfort, and I fled their encounter.

W.O. made no secret of the fact that theatre was the summit of a mountain he was desperate to conquer. Being a 'Playwright' was a divine calling well above the mundane status of writing for *Maclean's* or even writing a novel. It was the true test of the writer's art. Perhaps this was a necessary, temporary, effusion which appeared only while he was working on plays. Who knows? Curiously, he never made any gesture to elbow himself into rehearsal. Thank God, because the directorial skills on view would have been barely worthy of his attention.

The strength of that initial production was the performances of the three central women. By happy mixture of accident and instinct I managed to make some correct casting decisions. Helen Hughes had a dictatorial hunger and becoming dignity as Harriet, so much so that she repeated the part in other productions of the same play. Maureen Fitzgerald, a large woman who carried her size with grace and humour, invested the character of Betty with a deliciously obsessive primness. Marie Mumford gave a deeply disturbing portrait of Agnes.

During the previews, the sullen staff of the theatre would mumble that they had no great hopes for the play. According to them, everyone in Calgary disliked W.O. and the box office was going to suffer. They self-righteously claimed to have put on the play out of a sense of duty. Their faces turned even more sour when the production proved a major critical and financial success. Ah, the joys of working in theatre in Canada!

The production, with the help of the touring office of the Canada Council, then played briefly in Toronto. I could see, as Mitchell stood at the end of the opening night performance, his vulnerable brown eyes sweeping the audience at the Tarragon Theatre with apprehension, how much this had meant to him, how much he had been hoping to impress the Pierre Bertons and the rest of the Toronto literati. (He will deny this.) But Toronto, then as now, was a cold and judgmental beast, and it took a few weeks before the play found its audience.

Rereading *Back to Beulah* now is a surprise. It is very close to being a major play. The precocious mixture of styles – rambunctious farce sandwiched inside serious subject matter, caricature coexisting alongside genuine people, all shoehorned into an anachronistic three act format – creates an original blend that actually works! The play is weakened only when the playwright, straying from his strong suit, takes himself a little too seriously and thinks he can revolutionize psychiatry.

The ending of the play has undergone a sea change since that first production, which concluded with Harriet alone on stage, rocking and singing her theme song, 'Amazing Grace,' the others having taken the collapsed Agnes off for help. We knew they would be coming back to get Harriet, and we knew that she was trying to sort out her own culpability in the events leading up to Agnes's breakdown. We knew, too, that the road forward for the three patients led inexorably back to the mental home, Beulah. But, after being produced in several more Canadian theatres, *Back to Beulah* acquired a new ending. In the version of the play that was published in *Dramatic W.O. Mitchell* (1982), Harriet attacks and manages to induce a breakdown in Dr Anders by using the techniques of psychiatric interrogation gone mad. It sounds like a nice idea, but it is in fact repetitive of what has already happened, gratuitous, and structurally grafted on. Like a poor man's version of *One Flew Over the Cuckoo's Nest*, the patients get to enjoy a tendentious revenge on their doctor.

Somehow I ended up with Harriet's rocker from that production. For years it followed me around in the various living rooms of my existence. The theatre carpenters had refurbished it with runners of a more gentle arc to help increase Harriet's mobility around the stage as she rocked. Off the stage, the thing was a pain. The special runners made normal rocking very awkward, their extra length making the chair a danger to life and limb. Eventually, after fourteen years of stubbed toes and bruised shins, it was 'accidentally' left behind in the course of moving. *Back to*

Beulah was good to me, however, as its moderate success helped me to get further work across the country. In the summer of 1977, I received an invitation to direct the *première* of *The Black Bonspiel of Wullie MacCrimmon* at the Arbour Theatre in Peterborough.

W.O. made a seminal gift to the early productions of *The Black Bonspiel* when he recommended we audition Hugh Webster for the title role. This wizened Scots gnome, a battle-scarred veteran of the generation of Canadian actors who had eked out a meagre living on the thin theatrical fauna of post-war Canada, was as fine an actor as ever has walked the boards in this country. He was subtle, real, honest, alive: a heightened character who played a heightened version of himself in all his work. He had also played one of the Charlie Browns in the original CBC radio series *Jake and the Kid*, which is where W.O. knew him as an actor. With his nicotine-stained fingers and tar-choked breath, Hugh would wheeze himself onto the stage and then, as if touched by some ancient Greek god of performance, metamorphose himself into the part. Nerves got to him. Opening nights were precarious, a testimony to the difficulty of carving out a niche in the Canadian public's granite philistinism. I had to sit with him in the bar, staring into his angry eyes to make sure he didn't go overboard on the libations to the gods before he went on. At such times ancient grudges bubbled up and Hugh would grumble about the scripts for *Jake and the Kid* arriving late, and either unfinished or overwritten. He got bored easily and the stage managers had to keep an eye out late in the runs to make sure he hadn't started celebrating the end of the run before it had actually arrived.

Hugh was Wullie. Looking over the play now, the stage directions constantly betray the playwright's novelistic predilections; they also conjure Hugh Webster up like magic. When O. Cloutie first enters the shoe repair shop, the directions read:

Wullie looks up from the last. He lays his hammer down. He gets up with the care and preciseness of the rheumatic and walks towards the counter. His face has a full, pursed look. His eyes still on the visitor, he lifts his hand and spits out the cargo of tacks. He places them on the counter.
WULLIE: 'Aye-he?' (*Dramatic W.O. Mitchell* 107)

I wonder if W.O. wrote Wullie with Hugh in mind?

My favourite moment was in his first scene with Reverend Pringle, when Wullie gets to intone the Presbyterian credo. Wullie has opened the pot-bellied stove that heats his little shop; he is waving around a stick of wood, just about to throw it into the stove, and the special-effect flames are roaring in sympathy:

> WULLIE: Do you believe in a three-dimensional, crackling, actually burning Hell to which we may or may not go – when our time comes... Shrieking and writhing in torment and exquisite pain...? (*Dramatic W.O. Mitchell* 112)

A first-class production of *The Black Bonspiel* would require a company of such talent that every actor, even in the smaller parts, was of Hugh Webster's class. Alas, this cast has yet to be assembled for the play. Now that we have lost Hugh (I am certain he is playing leads on celestial stages), it will be impossible to fill his shoes in the title role.

Curling on stage is a part of the magic that has helped put *The Black Bonspiel* into that canon of Canadian plays that get continually performed. Many are the technical directors of theatres across the country who have had to experiment with artificial surfaces that actually allow curling rocks to slide across the stage. Siliconed aluminum sheets, waxed and watered polyurethane, no matter how fast the surface, the actors have to be able to approximate a good shot on cue, especially in the final end. The worse the final shot, the more the actors had to cheer to distract from the bad curling.

Act 2, as handed to us for rehearsal, was clear proof that W.O. had no idea about the rules of curling, that he didn't know how many ends were normally played in a game, and that he certainly did not understand the finer points, such as how it was determined which side had last rock in any end. We had to make certain changes to the flow of the script to make it conform to the rules. After the opening in Peterborough, he looked at me with a puzzled expression: 'You changed some of act 2, you sly bugger...'

For the initial Peterborough run we adapted the place references in the text so that they had local connotations. For the subsequent production in Calgary (1979) we changed them all back. The box office success of the first Calgary run warranted a revival to coincide with the 1980 Brier which took place in Calgary that year. One of the performances was bought out by the Brier Committee. Playing to an audience of curling *aficionados* was one of those rare magical evenings of theatre. Labatt's Brewery, the new sponsors of the event, tried to get us to change the reference in the script from the Macdonald Brier (the Macdonald tobacco Lassie was the sponsor during the Depression, when the play is set) to the Labatt Brier. We declined politely.

W.O.'s play essentially bankrolled Theatre Calgary during this period and they hauled the production out in the summer of 1980 to tour Alberta as part of the official celebrations of that province's seventy-fifth anniversary. It was even revived (with some of the original cast but without the original director) after Theatre Calgary had moved into its new home in the Performing Arts Centre.

Curling is a sport not totally foreign to the Celtic progenitors of the Eastern Townships in Quebec. When I was asked by Festival Lennoxville to stage a version of the play in 1980, it seemed *de rigueur* to reconfigure O. Cloutie into a facsimile of the man who, in the eyes of anglophone Quebec, in any case, was the true devil – none other than the 'Separatist' prime minister of Quebec. Finding a québecois actor who would be prepared to accept this risky proposition was not easy; however, Jean Archambault, an actor of some stature, considerable sense of humour, and the spitting image of René Lévesque, agreed to play the part. Unfortunately, we were never to discover what reaction this little casting twist would have occasioned with the Eastern Townships audience because Richard Oozounian, the Festival's artistic director, had already given the part to another (non-québecois) actor. Naturally, as I had made a binding commitment to Jean Archambault, I felt I had to bow out of the production. No great problem for the enterprising 'Ooze,' as Oozounian is affectionately known in the theatre community; he quickly hired Rick McNair, then the artis-

tic director of Theatre Calgary, to direct the Lennoxville production. At the time we had just started rehearsals for the Alberta
tour of the play. I have never worked at a theatre where the care
and concern of the artistic director has been so in evidence as it
was once Rick McNair had been hired by Lennoxville. He
watched every move in rehearsal with flattering solicitation.

W.O. Mitchell is a fragile dramatist. There is a great deal more
than meets the eye to his writing. Lose faith in his characters and
it can appear to be pretty simplistic stuff, and can be easily
hijacked by cheap ham acting. In one of the Calgary productions,
I came back after two weeks of the run to find that the actor playing pipe-fitting Charlie Brown had invented some canine scato-
logical remnants to give himself lengthy ice cleaning business.
The audience certainly expressed its amusement, which of course
encouraged the actor to further excess. The production had
crossed an invisible boundary and become tawdry pandering.

The brevity that is the soul of wit is not the soul of good drama.
If W.O. has a fault it is that his comic caricature encapsulations,
which attempt to go deeper than mere wit, too often get sabo-
taged by brevity. Act 2 of *The Black Bonspiel*, for instance, is simply
undeveloped. Even act 1 could use a little fleshing out. It was
uncomfortable watching the actresses who had to play Annie
Brown going through the agony of trying to give reality to that
thinnest of roles. Even Dr Anders, in *Back to Beulah*, was nearly
impossible to turn into a real person on stage. Nevertheless, W.O.
deserves better than I was able to give him at the time: better dra-
maturgy, better direction, better actors, and considerably better
recognition and encouragement as a playwright. In any other
country he would have got it. In any other country we would be
on our knees worshipping this unique story teller. Not in Canada.

We don't have the equivalent of, say, an Abbey National Theatre, consecrated to dissecting our national character on stage. We
have no company of actors who, as an ensemble, have honed
their stagecraft on the tough nuggets of Canadian archetypes.

Even Macmillan, his publisher for over thirty years, could only
bring themselves to publish a cheaply edited and produced selection of his plays. The format is evidence that the printer had not

even bothered to inquire how to lay out a play on the page; the photographic reproductions are of an insultingly bad quality. Macmillan even managed to avoid what is the custom the world over when printing a piece of theatre: the list of artists involved in the *première* productions. It is the nature of the beast in Canadian Theatre. So hungry are we for plays of any quality, we gulp them down without chewing.

W.O., generous soul that he is, can never resist an invitation to tell a story, especially if it is to a fund-raising event for the theatre itself. Like all great actors, he has a divine well of energy which he seems to be able to draw upon the moment he gets in front of an audience. He has donated his genius on many evenings to worthy organizations around the country. In sharing his gifts with an audience, he was actually gifting the theatre.

I have a very clear memory of sitting in my seat mesmerized by this story-telling magus at one such evening which he donated to Theatre Calgary. One story (the exact details are gone) involved an outhouse, some boys, some dynamite, and the hired hand. His hands waving, his voice cracking, his hair dancing, he wove the three or more separate story lines together with brilliant interloping sequiturs, until they climaxed in a hilarious and inevitably explosive conclusion. This was story-telling elevated to an art form. This was great acting. We have no one else like him. The ultimate W.O. Mitchellean actor is W.O. himself.

PART III

Interviews and Recollections

W.O.

TIMOTHY FINDLEY

You never get to spend much time with W.O. – a meal's worth, perhaps, or the time it takes to have an anecdotal evening, watching him trying not to look at his watch. It's not that he doesn't like people – not that he doesn't enjoy another person's company, singly or in groups. It's just that he gets nervous if he thinks the conversation is getting too serious – that someone is going to ask him to explain his books or talk about the meaning of life. You can't expect him to give pithy answers – tie things up with bows or speak the last word. What you can ask Mitchell to do is tell you a story. This way, you can wheedle almost anything you want to know from him. Just don't let him know you're asking.

I guess it's true: there is not a better story-teller alive than William Ormond Mitchell. It is a pure, unadulterated delight to watch him wind up and go with an anecdote – rising from his place at table, eying the distance to see if his punchline is out there waiting for him – hearing him begin with his trademark hesitancy: *I shouldn't tell you this – but here it is* ... All of this is magical foreplay. Not a bad analogy. By the time the punchline is achieved, the laughter is orgasmic.

He has fed so many images into my head. The anecdotal past of my whole generation has much of Mitchell in it – the sort of anecdotage that goes with having a family – antecedents – ancestors. The voices, for instance, of John Drainie's Jake and Billie Mae Richards's Kid – real and everlasting as neighbours – someone you can visit in your mind as vividly as if they had lived up the road. The images, too, that are conjured of the prairie – which seems, at times – even in all its three-dimensional reality – to be a place invented by W.O., because he gave it shape and distance and all its smells and sounds. 'This is your prairie,' the young Brian says in *Who Has Seen the Wind*, as he watches his future self and the ghosts of all children stepping out across the wondrous landscape laid out before them under Mitchell's hand. That prairie, first encountered over forty years ago, is still my prairie, now.

We speak of Bill as 'W.O.' – which gives his name the kind of grandeur that suits him. Grandeur, that is, with a wink and a brushing away of snuff from the lapels. There ain't no guff about W.O. There ain't no guff – but there's a lot of splendour.

Let me tell you what I mean. Make a picture of an empty restaurant. Somewhere in the depths of Toronto – even deeper in the depths of winter – deepest of all in the depths of morning. Somewhere in the neighbourhood of dawning – cold and bleak and blowing. I said the restaurant is empty and I guess I lied. Out in the kitchen the cooks and one or two waiters have assembled and the cashier is picking up her first cup of coffee. She has already seated two bleary customers in a mercifully shadowed corner: me and my companion, Bill Whitehead. We have worked the whole night through, editing tapes for television. Now we will have our breakfast and go home.

Simultaneously, the coffee-revived cashier and a new customer enter the room from opposite doors. Remember that, aside from us in our darkened corner, the whole restaurant with all its multitude of empty tables is spread out before this new customer. Of course, the customer is instantly recognizable as W.O. – in spite of an all-night session with friends that more than likely involved a good deal of drinking. His famous white hair is dishevelled. His famous lapels with their famous stains from his famous snuff are turned up, perhaps against the cold. His eyes are ... well, his eyes are red. He doesn't look, to be frank, terrific. And I guess he doesn't feel terrific, either. Anyone else would seek the dark, as we had, and soothe his hangover in the quiet there. But no. This is Mitchell – W.O. And I was speaking of *splendour*.

He chooses a large round table right smack damn in the middle of the room. 'I'll sit down here,' he says. Which he does.

Food is ordered. W.O. sits desolate. He sighs. The *Globe and Mail* is spread out beside him, but his eyes cannot endure the thought of print.

Bill and I – sympathetic – ignore him. The last thing he wants, we surmise, is company. But we are wrong about this. We have forgotten his innate politeness – his genuine adoration of conversation – his need for the motor of speech. He sees us. He rises. He crosses the room. He asks that his breakfast be delivered to our table and he joins us.

Seated, without greeting, he toys with the snuff box – places some on the wrist – sniffs – dusts – and speaks.

'Did I ever tell you about the morning I was caught on the road by a blizzard and the nearest town was twenty miles off and ...'

This is what I mean by *splendour*: unforgettable – unforgotten.

One last thing to say: this, about the woman he married. Like Bill, she goes by her initials: *F.C.S.* Merna. '*F.C.S.*?' you say. 'I never heard her called F.C.S. Merna. What's it stand for...?'

Well – I'll tell you.

Whenever Bill loses his glasses – the snuff box – his fishing rod – his pen – his shoes – his mind – he calls out: *for Christ's sake, Merna! Where's my...* whatever. And there you have them: William Ormond and For Christ's Sake, Merna.

It would be unjust – it would be unthinkable not to toast them side by side. So – here's to W.O. and F.C.S. Merna: hail – but never farewell. Not ever.

Life Follows Art

FRANCES ITANI

In our home, as in the Mitchells', everything stops for story. Stories under way, stories invented and reinvented, stories that change with each telling, stories in fits and starts. It's just the way things are.

Connections between our two families began over twenty years ago, in a small lounge on the University of Alberta campus. It was 1972. I had signed up for an evening writing course with W.O. Mitchell. My son, Russell, was eighteen months old. My daughter, Sam, would be born the following August. I was completing the first of two 'night degrees' – student mothers of young babies will at once know the ineffable world into which one is catapulted by those two explosive words.

During one fall term, from September to December, I sat in that worn lounge in Edmonton, often exhausted, often connected elsewhere, and watched and listened as this teacher, this writer, beckoned to us – to me. We were a small group, no more than nine students; he was extending the invitation to the discovery of our own material.

When I think of this now, all these years later, I somehow see us perched in those frayed arm chairs, somewhat nervously leaning towards W.O. as he leaned towards us, his inimitable voice speaking of the necessity to write, 'every day, every week, every month, every year.' The unmistakable feeling that accompanies this memory is that it mattered to him that we do this; he cared. We were to sit in front of our typewriters and allow our 'findings,' our stored memories, to float to the surface. To rise to be recorded. The sights, the sounds, the smells, fragments of dialogue, emotions. The impertinences, details of lives experienced and observed; our sensuous memories become concrete. Without being judgmental about what surfaced, we would follow a strand as far as we could and set it outside ourselves no matter how irrelevant it might, at first, seem to be. Each of us has a unique stored past, he assured us, and he encouraged us to reach for the significant details of our lives.

W.O. Mitchell was inviting us to begin to explore our own territory. To allow our work to surprise us. To believe that what we had to say was important and that by tapping into those stored moments we would be making a first step towards the creation of art. It was Mitchell's Messy Method; he called it *free-fall*. Some of us went home and were able to do this and some of us were not. This probably had much to do with timing in our individual lives. Of the group, four of the nine (and there may be more) continued over the years and are full-time writers – an astonishing number given the small size of that particular class.

W.O. has occasionally expressed to me his admiration for Virginia Woolf, and as I, too, have great respect for her writings – fictional, critical, personal – we have discussed her work from time to time. It is not difficult to understand the intuitive attraction. Virginia Woolf, in 1939–40, wrote about the colour-and-sound memories of her past in 'A Sketch of the Past.' She discussed the highly sensual nature of these memories – how moments recalled could be more real than the present. She wrote:

> I can reach a state where I seem to be watching things happen as if I were there. That is, I suppose, that my memory supplies what I had forgotten, so that it seems as if it were happening independently, though I am really making it happen. In certain favourable moods, memories – what one has forgotten – come to the top. Now if this is so, is it not possible – I often wonder – that things we have felt with great intensity have an existence independent of our minds; are in fact still in existence? And if so, will it not be possible,

in time, that some device will be invented by which we can tap them? I see it – the past – as an avenue lying behind; a long ribbon of scenes, emotions. There at the end of the avenue still, are the garden and the nursery. Instead of remembering here a scene and there a sound, I shall fit a plug into the wall; and listen in to the past. (67)

This sketch by Virginia Woolf was published for the first time in 1976, in *Moments of Being*. It is of interest that Woolf and Mitchell described essentially the same process or state, and knew its importance. Each held a trusting, intuitive (and articulated) belief that one's fiction would be made richer and fuller by tapping back into individual sensuous impressions that collectively make up one's stored experience. Not that there was any confusion about this being art: the recalling had to be done without imposing structure or setting out to contrive. There *is* no invented device; only one's own solitude and concentration. W.O. knows and Virginia Woolf knew that this was a first step. That in the later stages of the creation of fiction, one event will follow another (whether the illusion moves the work backwards or forwards), that the work grows organically out of itself, that it must have thematic destination, that an overall shape has, eventually, to come down over the whole.

W.O.'s free-fall method has worked for many beginning writers across this country. He was perhaps the earliest teacher to offer this as a method for writers who had a serious desire to create fiction. The method does not work for everyone but enables some writers to set out, for their own later consideration and possibilities, raw material (life lumber, W.O. called it, in our classes) with which they might begin to build the magic lie. Now, in the 1990s one can find on shelves of bookstores books for students written by contemporary writers who have their own names for strikingly similar methods: right-brain writing, natural writing, drifting,... whatever.

To return to that dim lounge on the Edmonton campus, W.O. as teacher did not demand that we come up with finished work – not as beginners. He well knew the long slow process, the long lonely apprenticeship, and did not discourage us by emphasizing what we would soon enough find out for ourselves. He knew that one writer cannot take the creative leap for another. It was enough for some of us, at that time, to believe that what we were doing was important, that he would be honest in his response to our efforts, that we were *connected*. W.O. Mitchell is an intuitive, gifted teacher and one has only to sit with him for a few moments to realize that the art experience matters to him; the creation of art matters.

Later, during that class, while discussing possibilities suggested by our work, he talked about creating the illusion, the meaningful lie. For he never let us forget what we were after. 'Life ain't art,' he said, many a time, a gentle and truthful reminder that just because such and such happened, the fact of it did not make it art. I have had to say this to my own students. I recall, now, his voice dropping, an innocent – almost apologetic – smile as he has, over the years, responded to would-be writers.

But imagine beginning to write fiction. Taking that first creative leap. W.O. Mitchell reading – indeed, performing – one's earliest work. I try to remember those evenings in the lounge, how important they were during those few short months, how they were the beginnings of *joining the tribe*. I try to remember the discussions we had on bridging between creative partners – writer and reader – and the intimacy of that relationship; on critical judgment; on story. Always, W.O. told us stories. Reminding us that the human condition is rooted in our daily lives. I especially try to remember these things whenever I am teaching. How every connected moment helped to send one home, perhaps not to write 'every day, every week, every month, every year,' but given one's responsibilities and commitments, at the very least to keep on writing.

The above account is by no means complete. For it does not really capture how charged that room seemed, at times, to be. Nor, how W.O. could make us double over in laughter or how, by reading some moving reminiscence, he could rivet us to silence. On occasion, a guest might sit in – one evening, it was a photographer, who snapped continuously – and we would be treated to a full evening performance, that extra body being the unknowing catalyst for some excess energy W.O. would draw up.

This energy, I've observed, gathers and falls around him like some sort of broad rippling cloak. Encompassing irreverent humour, highs and lows, tiny cumulative dramas that explode into larger dramas; the sinking into the self. In the twenty-two years I have known W.O. there hasn't been a time when he has not been working on a novel, play, screenplay, or performance. Merna by his side. Merna at the other end of the phone. 'Brace yourself,' he told her not long ago. She was in Calgary and he was calling from my home in Ottawa during a hectic visit. 'Brace yourself for a verbal battering, Merna. I have a lot to tell, when I get home.'

In Toronto, October 1990, just before the *W.O. Mitchell Tribute* at Harbourfront, I told W.O. that I had never witnessed such a high-drama family (as his) in my entire life. In my journal, I wrote:

Bill has been doing TV, radio, newspaper, magazine interviews, all day, every day, since he's been here. We decide to have late dinner in the hotel, after his 7 p.m. reading.

A van takes us the two or three blocks along the water. People are streaming in to the hall. Friends of W.O. and Merna are everywhere. Bill spies a wheelchair chained beneath a stairwell and climbs in. 'There's no place to hide,' he claims, and we laugh. Merna stands apart, smoking, offering comments. Few people see him as they pass by.

Bill reads from the Art Lesson in The Vanishing Point *and a section from the new book,* Roses. *The crowd loves it. Full house. He signs books in the Book Hall for an hour after that. We return by van to the hotel. Alistair [MacLeod] is with us. We meet Willa [W.O.'s daughter] on the way – she hasn't yet written her speech for tomorrow. There are cots opened out in the bedroom, heaps of clothes, books, briefcases, homework on Einstein – Brenna [W.O.'s granddaughter] is writing a paper for school.*

Bill kicks off his shoes, lies down. There are continuous uproars about losing things, finding things, complaints about disorganization, shouts and accusations, outcries, arguments, stories, and in the midst of all –

every half-hour or so – Merna looks over at Bill and says, 'I love you,
Billy'; and he, 'I love you, too.' I start laughing and laughing. Everyone is
too tired to make any sort of decision about eating or not eating. We turn
on the TV and settle in to watch the World Series.

(Toronto, 17 October 1990)

The following week, I phoned Calgary. Bill had lost his voice,
two days after returning from Toronto. 'Just what should happen
to a writer in the middle of a book tour,' he said.

We talked about the Tribute. He's had time, now, to think about it. And he
said, 'Having you there, and Willa, and Susan, and Alistair – wasn't he
funny? – and the others, was like the experience of holding my first pub-
lished book in my hands after our copies were sent to us. That's what it
was like. Emotionally. The same kind of emotional satisfaction.' He was
whispering. His voice-loss did not prevent him from telling me a story
over the phone.

(Ottawa, 27 October 1990)

The teacher-student relationship, of course, altered as we
became friends-colleagues-family. But in 1979, I did show him
my most recent story because here in my journal is the following,
written during a visit by W.O. Our family had moved several
times since my student days in Alberta; we were hosting him at
our New Brunswick home while he was on a reading tour in the
province.

So many things keep happening ... one does not stop to wonder. And I,
recoiling when W.O. spent part of the long evening criticizing my new
story. It wasn't the story – it was the demand that I explain, be responsible
for every word. Oh yes. Does each word add up? To the central purpose?

(Oromocto, N.B., 22 June 1979)

Some time later, in P.E.I., where our family frequently vacations
and where W.O. and Merna have at times joined us, I wrote:

Bill and Merna are in Charlottetown till Tuesday. But what of his novel?

How I Spent My Summer Holidays. *He wanted me to read the manuscript so I finished it in an afternoon, evening, and morning on the verandah overlooking the sea. I think it works and has a complex level some of his other work does not. The voice is least like the voices of his other novels.*

But when I told W.O. that I'd finished it that morning, I suddenly realized how terrible vulnerability can be. For his face opened – that's the only way I can describe it. It opened so vulnerably, I could scarcely continue. Why did this surprise me? I suppose because he had been my teacher. But he was so pleased with my response. And I explained to him the way I'd felt the darker vision, the tragic quality as it came into the work and began to build, like a wave, about a third of the way. Really, I think he's accomplished something.

We were in the middle of the road when we began to discuss this. It's a miracle we weren't struck down by traffic.

(Seaview, P.E.I., 25 July 1981)

In a reminiscence of this nature, one can create only a brief impression of the overlap of the private and public man. Any illumination will be incomplete – an illusion, in fact. A friendship is just that – a friendship. By choosing to stroll down one or two avenues, one does not wander through the town.

I have not mentioned how W.O., during his visits, always had special one-on-one time with our children when they were young. How he, at various stages, nicknamed Sam, 'the human limpet,' or 'kangaroo baby.' How he taught Russell acts of magic and discussed with him methods of dealing with a bully. He went into various classrooms in various towns of the world and entertained the children's friends and teachers – talking to them about pretending and the magic lie. One night, in a tiny but crowded *Gasthaus* beneath the walls of a medieval German town, he opened the menu and pressed it to his cheekbones, peering out over the edge. He was teaching the children to be spies. We laughed till we cried at that table – Merna and I and my husband and the children – as rain poured down outside and newcomers pressed in along wooden benches while *Opa*, the Grandfather of the place, cooked our supper.

Some time later, I spoke with W.O. and Merna on the phone when they were back in Calgary. They were telling me the story of how they'd picked dandelion greens in the park across the street; how they'd brought them home and had eaten them in a salad. They'd become violently ill – they suspected from the spray. I told seven-year-old Sam this story and she looked me in the eye and said, 'Couldn't W.O. have *pretended* to eat the dandelions?'

Lately, I've noticed, as we sit around telling stories, the conversation has begun to change. No more do I hear, 'Life ain't art.' I'm hearing, 'Life follows art.' I'm not sure where this is leading; it's becoming integrated into our lives and work. In Peterborough, recently, I told W.O. and Merna about how I'd begun a short story based on what I was observing around me in Croatia, while I was living there in the summer and fall of 1993. I had begun to put a female character into the story and then, while *I* was living the experience, I wrote the ending that I imagined might happen to *her*. 'I didn't have to live the ending,' I said. 'I'd already written it – the life and the lie had become so intertangled.'

We were all laughing when W.O. nodded sagely and said, 'You see, I told you. Life follows art.'

Perhaps, I thought, perhaps fiction *is* the best way we know how to tell the truth. In this case, my writing had eclipsed my own experience.

But I'm wondering: Is W.O. writing some blueprint now – as he works on his next novel – that will leave another trail, for himself and the rest of us to follow?

Talking with W.O. Mitchell

PETER GZOWSKI

The following interview was broadcast on CBC's Morningside, *23 December 1992.*

W.O. Mitchell looked tired when I met him, and no wonder. This was last Thursday afternoon, and all week long he had been rehearsing his performance in Toronto of a kind of musical *Jake and the Kid*. A performance, by the way, that earned him and Billie Mae Richards – who came back to be the Kid to Bill Mitchell's Jake – a fifteen-minute standing ovation. As usual, too, he'd been promoting his newest novel. This one's called *For Art's Sake*, and you'll hear him read from it later on while getting ready for a very special occasion, a kind of delayed celebration (the real anniversary was in August) of fifty years of marriage to his beloved Merna. Merna is known to some Mitchell intimates as For Bleep's Sake Merna, after Bill's most frequent form of address. That celebration, as it turned out, was a lovely evening. I dropped in on it briefly on Monday night. It was in Peterborough. Now to complicate things even further last week, W.O. Mitchell has been fighting some illness lately, even though, as his friends know, it's going to have to be some illness indeed if it thinks it's going to mow him down. Anyway, we talked for a while, as we have over the years, and what follows are some moments from our conversation. They begin with a reference to one of his most recent honours: his appointment, along with a few other distinguished Canadians, to the Privy Council.

PG: Hi.

WO: Hi Peter.

PG: What do I call you now? Honourable? Right? Honourable. The Honourable W.

WO: You know, when Doug Gibson at McClelland and Stewart heard this we were over in England, and Brian Mulroney phoned me there, actually. My daughter-in-law thought it was a bloody hoax. We were in Yorkshire and it was a real shocker. We went upstairs to Orm and Barbara sitting on the bed and laughing their heads off and then Orm said, 'It figures, Bill, Queen's Privy Council. Who's more familiar with privies than you are?' That's pretty witty. Then Doug, with your same question, said 'Where does the Honourable come? Before or after?' I said 'I don't know, Doug.' 'Well,' he said, 'we know one thing for sure: it took something as dramatic as this to make an honourable guy out of you.'

PG: Has this worked? Are you honourable?

WO: Maybe.

PG: You've always been honourable in my books.

WO: I try, I try, Peter. Like you, I try.

PG: What do they give you? Do you get anything?

WO: In the way of?

PG: I don't know, a cheque or a seat?

WO: Yeah, I got a ribbon and a medal.

PG: Are you wearing it now?

WO: Yeah, and I just got a Centennial medal. It suddenly came out of the blue. As a matter of fact, I heard on the news the other day that Honest Ed got one too, so I'm in pretty good company.

PG: I think I got one of those.

WO: I didn't know what the hell am I going to do with all these things, and then Merna said, 'Hang it on your butt.'

PG: Have you got a wall somewhere with all the stuff, or a room?

WO: No, I just stash 'em away and never look at them again in a drawer somewhere. I don't remember where it is.

PG: What is your most treasured award? You're an Officer of

the Order of Canada, you have honourary degrees, you've got the Governor General's Award, you've got the Leacock Award, you've got Merna.

WO: Oh, I think the most exciting one was one of the first, when *Who Has Seen the Wind* came out. That award,[1] and because it was the first I ever received, was pretty nice. But actually, I have to make a public confession. They're labels. They don't mean all that much to me. Well, I think mainly because I once realized – I was in the bathroom, I think I was shaving and it suddenly hit me – that art is something that somebody does for its own sake, that does not involve a win/lose, victor/vanquished adversarial relationship. Like when I get asked 'What's your favourite novel you've written?' I can't answer that. Well, I do say, 'The one I'm working on now.' But it's not an Olympic event of a bronze, a silver, and a gold. These medals, singling somebody out in their relationship and their success against others, do not really mean that much to me.

PG: What do you think of living in a country that gives an award for humour?

WO: This has been embarrassing, Peter.

PG: Has it?

WO: And I really mean it. I am serious as hell. Twice, and a third time I was up. And I breathed a sigh of relief when I wasn't given the Stephen Leacock Award for the third time, though I admired him tremendously. I read him when I was in high school in Florida. It's damaging because reviewers, who are *Sturm und Drang*ers, either/or, cannot take seriously a piece of fiction that has humour in it and wit. They've never heard of Shakespeare's expression of comic relief and they think that it should be either all tragedy or all slapstick comedy: the two worst forms of writing I know. Not that it matters either. Very frequently there will be reviewers, because I made them giggle or laugh, who will say, 'This can't be a serious piece of work.' And so it has been a little discomforting getting that Stephen Leacock Award twice.

PG: Did you know him? Did you ever meet him?

WO: I never met him and I would love to have. I'll never forget when I first read him. I was in St Petersburg Senior High School in Florida, and my beloved drama and English teacher, Emily Murray, said to me one day, 'Billy, you're from Canada?' I said, 'Yes.' 'Well,' she said, 'there's a very fine Canadian writer,' and she introduced me to Stephen Leacock. So, I think I was eighteen or something when I first read him. That's only sixty years ago, and I've admired him so much over the years.

PG: Where's Mark Twain in your life?

WO: And Mark Twain.

PG: You look like Mark Twain.

WO: I've been told that.

PG: I knew him well.

WO: Yeah, he was an untidy bastard too.

PG: Leacock wasn't exactly sartorial elegance.

WO: No, but he was an academic as well. I learned to read very, very young. My father was in the last stages of what killed him in 1921 before he went to Mayo's [clinic], and one of my greatest visions is of the white sheet and that yellow foot sticking out. He taught me to read with the phonic approach of sounding out words from the Regina *Leader Post*, and the day that I pronounced Tutankhamen at the age of four he boasted all over town about his kid. Now, he was a tremendous reader and our living room, three sides were filled with stacks of books. There was where I read every single one of Mark Twain's books in hard cover. He had a whole collection of them, and that's when I fell in love with Mark Twain. Not just for his humour, but I remember loving *Tom Sawyer*. I remember being confused with *The Adventures of Huckleberry Finn* when I was six or seven or eight. And then, years later, when I did my novel *Since Daisy Creek* [sic],[2] I think, in which Mark Twain is a character (a guy's doing a biography of Mark Twain), I reread. You see what happened with Mark Twain, when my son Orm went to university and came back, for the first time I knew Twain had been given the proper respect that he deserved and that he had become hot stuff with the English departments' American literature studies in universities. So, I reread *The Adventures of Huckleberry Finn* and hurray for Sam Clemens. That is the finest, that is the great American novel. *Moby Dick* can take second place, but *The Adventures of Huckleberry Finn* is first thematically and every way, except for about the last thirty pages when for commercial reasons he drags Tom Sawyer into the thing. So, what I learned from Mark Twain – you don't generally learn from other writers but I think what was fixed very early for me – is that you write out of your own cultural and geographical context and his Hannibal in Missouri ain't too bloody different from the Saskatchewan or Alberta prairies.

PG: What's the great Canadian novel?

WO: The great Canadian novel? Well, again, because it's not a silver and a bronze and a gold, it's hard for me to say.

PG: Yeah, but you did an American one. You were bold enough to give us the great American novel.

WO: Oh, and there are others too. I mean, I'm fond of Steinbeck; Virginia Woolf is a favourite of mine.

PG: Yeah but I want the great Canadian novel.

WO: I got to tap Margaret Laurence.

PG: *Stone Angel?*

WO: I think *Stone Angel* is pretty great. I think so. As a matter of fact it's interesting to me that as Canadian novelists have come into prominence from very early, I mean very early, being Canadian back in the '40s was not a handicap. There had already been Thomas Raddall, ah...

PG: Sinclair Ross?

WO: Oh, Sinclair Ross. I read him first – something about the sign on the door[3] in *Queen's Quarterly*. But Sinclair Ross and Ralph Connor, these had already become internationally established. And what was then the case, not so much now, was publishers were interested because we were enough the same, and then they had this goofy romantic notion of penguins and Eskimos and Mounted Police and wilderness, but it was still understandable to those people south of the forty-ninth. So, in fact, it was a bit of an advantage that made Canadian writers stand out.

PG: Can I tell you a story?

WO: Yeah.

PG: I was asked to go and read or take part in the concert of a choir in a little town in Ontario. The choir was going to sing and I was to go and talk in between the songs, right?

WO: Yeah.

PG: Don't look at me like this. Oh, I should tell you how I quote you all the time when I'm making public speeches.

WO: I know you do, Peter, and I love you for it.

PG: Mostly, what I quote you on is the night you got up some place in Alberta or something and you were late in the evening and everybody had made their speech before you did and it was –

WO: No, this was in Toronto when I was on *Maclean's*.

PG: And they said, 'W.O. Mitchell will now give his address,' and you said?

WO: I said, 'My address is 350 Springdale Boulevard, and damn it, I'm going there right now.' And that was a Canadian Author's Association thing that Art Irwin made me go to and I was preceded by people who came in first, second, and third in poetry, in short story, in everything else. Yeah, that's a true one.

PG: My punch line is, W.O. Mitchell's address is High River, Alberta, I didn't know it was a Toronto address. I'll have to change my routine.

WO: It was while I was in Toronto and I was on the fiction desk at *Maclean's* and Irwin made me go there. I had already fallen out of love with the amateur association and I wasn't surprised at what happened, but I wasn't ready sitting there and listening and waiting and waiting. Then they said, we'll now have W.O. Mitchell's address. And that is exactly what I said. (I didn't behave, Peter.) I said, 'My address is Springdale Boulevard and by God I'm going there right now.'

PG: So that's not the story I'm going to tell you. This is the story. I'm supposed to sing with this choir, really *talk* with this choir, and I said I haven't got enough to say on my own in between the choir pieces, can I read you something? The young choirmaster said, 'Yeah, yeah, read something. Whatever you want. Read something Canadian.' So I said, 'I'm going to read the last page and a half of *Who Has Seen The Wind*.'

WO: I never knew that, Peter.

PG: No, no, I'm not finished yet because I remember when you read that for us on *This Country in the Morning* in the library at High River about twenty years ago. But I said, 'I can't pretend to be Bill Mitchell but the words will do it for themselves.' So, I get half way down – I'm living up in the country – and I get half way down to Toronto, to Brampton, Ontario, that's where this thing was, and oh, God, I haven't got a copy of the book with me.

WO: Oh, my God.

PG: So what will I do? So I go dashing into this young choirmaster's. He's about twenty-seven years old, a terrific guy, and I say, 'I wanted to read *Who Has Seen the Wind*, but I haven't got it with me.' He said 'Just a minute.' He went back to his house and he brought out a dog-eared copy of *Who Has Seen the Wind*. This is just a young guy – had never been to the prairies. That book was as important to him as it is to me and to hundreds and hundreds of thousands of other people and just that one moment, that one book, him bringing that out, I thought that makes it all worth it for you. Everything. I mean everything. That book is part of that guy's soul just as it is of mine. So maybe you wrote the great Canadian novel.

WO: I didn't know you had done that, Peter.

PG: Oh, I do it all the time.

WO: I'll be getting legal advice and see what I can do about plagiarism. Ha! No, thanks.

PG: That's not plagiarism, it's theft.

WO: No, I know it isn't. I'm not behaving.

PG: The new book. I'll get you to record a piece of *For Art's Sake* and we'll do that, but let me ask you. *For Art's Sake* is dedicated to Merna.

WO: Yup.

PG: I don't want to say publicly what everybody who knows you and Merna call Merna: For [Christ's] Sake Merna. The love between you two which survived for fifty years.

WO: Fifty years.

PG: And I don't know if any of the other books have been dedicated to her, but this book opens with Art remembering Irene, in his case – Art's the central character –

WO: Merna is my life model for Irene and all through the novel he talks to his dead wife and she talks back to him. I think it's probably one of the most moving sequences that I've ever written.

PG: Is that a thank you to Merna?

WO: Well you see it's my ass – pardon me, I'm in trouble – if I show Douglas Gibson, at McClelland and Stewart, a finished novel before Merna sees it. All our married life Merna has been my first editor. She could have been a leading editor for any leading publisher. It's a partnership, truly a partnership, and we read each other's minds and she says something that I've just thought of to myself. I think we're unusual and we're extremely lucky. I didn't realize that until about the time we moved into Calgary and a number of people we had known had waited until the kids grew up and they had broken up and we had no clue about that. I think it's unusual and damn lucky. I remember being very, very moved by a short piece by Greg Clark, who is a dear friend of mine, and the name of it was 'May Your First Love Be Your Last One.' It was extremely moving and it summed up the way I feel, we feel, about each other.

PG: That's nice. You once told me something else that Greg Clark told you but I can't say on the radio. It was about –

WO: Ha! No, you can say it on radio.

PG: I can't.

WO: You can't but I can. Look, I'm vulgar. So was Greg Clark. It was when I was fishing with Ralph Allen and Greg Clark up in northern Saskatchewan and, as a matter of fact, it was for Arctic grayling and I had a fly that my young son Orm had invented using mallard feathers on the side. I'm getting there, kind of off the subject.

PG: No kidding.

WO: Greg was fishing down stream from me the first time and he came up and he said 'My God. I've had six on.' I had lost count. That was what Orm nicknamed the Mitchell Killer and Greg insisted that Orm make him twenty of them for his fly collection and for the book he was going to do on flies. But anyway, while we talked as we did in the bunks that night Greg, who was quite a bit older than I was, and by this time maybe I was beginning to wonder about age and he said, 'Don't knock it, kid. From the time you were born life takes you by the end of your penis and pulls you all through, and then all of a sudden when you hit sixty, seventy, eighty, it lets go. And it's beautiful!' I said that, not you.

PG: I know. When you first told me that, the penis wasn't particularly called a penis.

WO: No, it wasn't.

PG: Never mind, Bill. That's fine. When this is on the air you and I will have seen you briefly at yours and Merna's fiftieth. It's a celebration, but the anniversary was in fact in the summer.

WO: Well, my younger son did that at the lake. We had a lot of friends at the lake but this is the real one because, Peter, we've got ten times more friends. Merna and I hang on to our friends. You're one of them, Tiff Findley is another one, June Callwood's another one, and we hang on to our friends and I'm really looking forward to touching base with all of these old buddies.

PG: Well, your friends sort of hang on to you, too, you know.

WO: Yes, they do.

PG: It's good to see you. Thank you, W.O. Mitchell. After our conversation, Bill Mitchell sat himself down in a chair and read for us.

WO: The novel *For Art's Sake*, unlike any other novel I've written, had its genesis in an actual incident that took place at the University of Calgary Art Gallery when the world's greatest collection of Albrecht Dürer prints and engravings, worth over a million dollars, was stolen, and then a series of heists went on for the next two years. That's where it started, but the novel isn't about that because now a number of artists – a poet, a painter, a sculptor, and an actor – living in an art colony owned by Arthur Ireland on the edge of an unnamed Western city. And their nearby neighbour is the hook-and-eye colony of the Hutterian brotherhood, and they're very, very fond of each other. They're both sort of brotherhoods. Near the last, after he served time in a penitentiary, Arthur has an art show. Here it is. 'The show was well underway...' [Mitchell reads from pages 262–63.]

PG: That's W.O. Mitchell reading from his novel *For Art's Sake*. *For Art's Sake* is a Douglas Gibson Book and it's published by McClelland and Stewart. That reading and the interview that preceded it were recorded last week in our studios here in Toronto.

NOTES

1   The IODE Echoes Committee Literary Prize was awarded to Mitchell in 1948.
2   The novel in question is *Ladybug, Ladybug ...*
3   'The Painted Door,' by Sinclair Ross, first appeared in *Queen's Quarterly* 46 (Summer 1939): 145–68.

Works Cited

Adilman, Sid. 'Established Novelist Dives into Movie Scripts.' *Toronto Star* 24 June 1976: E10.
- 'Mitchell Tired of Complainers.' *Toronto Star* 11 Nov. 1982: D3.
- 'Prairie Classics Headed for TV.' *Toronto Star* 26 Jan. 1994: D2.
- 'Prairie Novelist at 62 Works Harder Than Ever.' *Toronto Star* 25 Sept. 1976: H3.
- 'Tireless W.O. Mitchell Has Writing Jobs Galore.' *Toronto Star* 25 May 1981: D3.
Allen, Robert. Telephone interview (David Gardner). 26 Jan. 1994.
Angus, Terry. *The Prairie Experience.* Toronto: Macmillan, 1975.
'Around Town.' *Hanna Herald* 5 Sept. 1946: 6.
Atlantic Monthly Press. Editorial report. 15 April 1953. Atlantic Monthly Press Archive. New York, NY.
Atwood, Margaret. *Survival: A Thematic Guide to Canadian Literature.* Toronto: Anansi, 1972.
'Author, Author.' *Toronto Star* 19 Oct. 1989: C1.
Barclay, Patricia. 'Regionalism and the Writer: A Talk with W.O. Mitchell.' *Canadian Literature* 14 (Autumn 1962): 53–56.
Bly, Robert. *Iron John.* New York: Vintage Books, 1992.
Boyle, Harry J. Personal interview (Alan Yates). Ottawa, Aug. 1978.
Burnet, Jean. *Next-Year Country: A Study of Rural Social Organization in Alberta.* Toronto: U of Toronto P, 1951.
Cameron, Donald. 'Sea Caves and Creative Partners.' *Conversations with Canadian Novelists.* Part 2. Toronto: Macmillan, 1973. 48–63.
Chevrefils, Marlys, Sandra Mortensen, Apollonia Steele, and Jean Tener, comps. and eds. *The W.O. Mitchell Papers: An Inventory of the Archive at the University of Calgary Libraries.* Canadian Archival Inventory Series: Literary Papers 2. Calgary: U of Calgary P, 1986.

Clark, Charles A. 'Under the Microscope.' Editorial. *High River Times* 21 Dec. 1951: 2.

Clemens, Cyril. 'Unpublished Recollections.' *Mark Twain Quarterly* 4 (Summer–Fall 1941): 20, 23.

Clemens, Samuel. *Personal Recollections of Joan of Arc.* New York: Harper, 1896.

– *The Selected Letters of Mark Twain.* Ed. Charles Neider. New York: Harper and Row, 1982.

Cobb, David. 'Day of the Gopher.' *Maclean's* 1 Nov. 1976: 42–55.

Corneau, Guy. *Absent Fathers, Lost Sons: The Search for Masculine Identity.* Boston: Shambhala, 1991.

Cowan, Hugh and Gabriel Kampf. '*Acta* Interviews W.O. Mitchell.' *Acta Victoriana* 92, 2 (April 1974): 15–26.

Danylchuk, Jack. 'Mitchell.' *Albertan* [Calgary] 13 Feb. 1965: 16.

Davies, Robertson. *A Voice from the Attic.* Toronto: McClelland and Stewart, 1960.

Dean, Basil. 'All Things Considered.' *Calgary Herald* 12 Dec. 1951: 4.

DeVoto, Bernard. *Mark Twain's America.* Boston: Little, Brown, 1932.

Diehl, Fred. Personal interview (Alan Yates). Calgary, Oct. 1977.

'Dr. Burnet Missed Important Points.' Editorial. *Drumheller Mail* qtd. in *Hanna Herald* 3 Jan. 1952: 2.

Duckett, Margaret. *Mark Twain and Bret Harte.* Norman, Oklahoma: U of Oklahoma P, 1964.

'Eastern Visitor Seeks Story on Drouth Areas.' *Hanna Herald* 4 July 1946: 1.

Esslin, Martin. *An Anatomy of Drama.* London: T. Smith, 1976.

– Personal interview (Alan Yates). Montreal, Aug. 1975.

Findley, Timothy. 'Everything I Tell You Is the Truth – Except the Lies.' *Journal of Canadian Studies* 31 (Summer 1996): 154–65.

Francis, Peter. Letter to Merna Mitchell. 18 Feb. 1952. W.O. Mitchell Papers. MsC 19.7.10.19. U of Calgary Libraries, Calgary.

– Letter to W.O. Mitchell. 18 Feb. 1952. W.O. Mitchell Papers. MsC 19.7.10.20. U of Calgary Libraries, Calgary.

– Letter to W.O. Mitchell. 25 Feb. 1952. W.O. Mitchell Papers. MsC 19.7.10.21.a&b. U of Calgary Libraries, Calgary.

– Letter to W.O. Mitchell. 29 Feb. 1952. W.O. Mitchell Papers. MsC 19.7.10.22.a&b. U of Calgary Libraries, Calgary.

– Letter to W.O. Mitchell. 9 Mar. 1952. W.O. Mitchell Papers. MsC 19.7.10.24.a. U of Calgary Libraries, Calgary.

– Letter to W.O. Mitchell. 12 Mar. 1952. W.O. Mitchell Papers. MsC. 19.7.10.26. a. U of Calgary Libraries, Calgary.

– Personal interview (Alan Yates). Ottawa, Mar. 1978.

French, William. 'Ahab of Alberta.' Rev. of *Since Daisy Creek*. *Globe and Mail* 27 Oct. 1984: 17.

– 'Mitchell Returns to Raunchy Style.' *Globe and Mail* 22 Oct. 1981: E1.

Frye, Northrop. *Anatomy of Criticism: Four Essays*. Princeton, NJ: Princeton UP, 1957.

– *Fearful Symmetry: A Study of William Blake*. Princeton, NJ: Princeton UP, 1947.

Gilmour, Clyde. '*Who Has Seen the Wind* a Likeable Movie.' *Toronto Star* 7 Nov. 1977: D7.

Green, Joseph. Telephone interview (David Gardner). 30 Jan. 1994.

Gzowski, Peter. 'Interview with W.O. Mitchell.' *Morningside*. CBC Radio. Toronto. Oct 1984.

– 'One Hour in High River, Alberta.' *Peter Gzowski's Book about This Country in the Morning*. Edmonton: Hurtig, 1974. 18–25.

Hall, Oswald. Letter to Peter Francis. 14 Mar. 1952. W.O. Mitchell Papers. MsC 19.7.10.27. U of Calgary Libraries, Calgary.

– Letter to W.O. Mitchell. 28 Feb. 1952. W.O. Mitchell Papers. MsC 19.7.10.25. U of Calgary Libraries, Calgary.

Harcourt, Peter. 'Allan King: Filmmaker.' *Take Two: A Tribute to Film in Canada*. Ed. Seth Feldman. Toronto: Irwin, 1984. 69–79.

Harrison, Dick. 'A Tale of Mortality and Isolation.' *Alberta Report* 7 Nov. 1988: 35.

– *Unnamed Country: The Struggle for a Canadian Prairie Fiction*. Edmonton: U of Alberta P, 1977.

– 'W.O. Mitchell (1914–).' *Canadian Writers and Their Works*. Fiction Series. Vol. 4. Ed. Robert Lecker, Jack David, and Ellen Quigley. Toronto: ECW, 1991. 141–208.

Hiller, Arthur. Personal interview – tape exchange (Alan Yates). Montreal-Los Angeles, Aug. 1977.

– Telephone interview (David Gardner). 2 Mar. 1994.

Hofsess, John. 'Hard Faith for Hard Times.' *Canadian Magazine* 25 Dec. 1976: 11–15.

'In the Editor's Confidence.' *Maclean's* 15 Aug. 1942: 2.

James, F. 'Next Year Country.' *Hanna Herald* 10 Jan. 1952: 2.

Jung, Carl G. 'The States of a Life.' *The Portable Jung*. Ed. Joseph Campbell. 1971. Harmondsworth, Eng.: Penguin, 1980.

Kaplin, Justin. *Mr. Clemens and Mark Twain: A Biography*. New York: Simon and Schuster, 1966.

Kareda, Urjo. 'Films: The Bumper Crop.' *Maclean's* 19 Sept. 1977: 76–79.

Keith, W.J. *Canadian Literature in English*. New York: Longman, 1985.

– 'W.O. Mitchell.' *A Sense of Style: Studies in the Art of Fiction in English-Speaking Canada*. Toronto: ECW, 1989. 61–76.

King, Allan. Telephone interview (David Gardner). 27 Jan. 1994, 6 Mar. 1994.

Kirchhoff, H.J. 'Mitchell's Messy Method: A Canlit Cornerstone.' *Globe and Mail* 21 Oct. 1989: C1, C3.

Kizuk, R. Alexander. 'The Father's No and the Mother's Yes: Psychological Intertexts in Davies' *What's Bred in the Bone* and Atwood's *The Handmaid's Tale.' Atlantis* 14, 2 (Spring 1989): 1–10.

Knelman, Martin. 'A Night at the Pictures in Arcola.' *Saturday Night* 92 (Sept. 1977): 27–30.

Kolodny, Annette. 'Turning the Lens on "The Panther Captivity": A Feminist Exercise in Practical Criticism.' *Critical Inquiry* 8, 2 (1981): 329–45.

Kreisel, Henry. 'The Prairie: A State of Mind.' *Contexts of Canadian Criticism*. Ed. Eli Mandel. Chicago UP, 1971. 254–66.

Kristeva, Julia. *Powers of Horror*. Trans. Leon S. Roudiez. New York: Columbia UP, 1982.

Kroetsch, Robert. 'A Conversation with Margaret Laurence.' In *Creation*. Ed. Robert Kroetsch. Toronto: New Press, 1970. 53–63.

– *Gone Indian*. Toronto: New Press, 1973.

– *The Studhorse Man*. Toronto: Macmillan, 1969.

Kurelek, William. *Kurelek's Canada*. Toronto: Pagurian Press, 1975.

– *A Prairie Boy's Summer*. Montreal: Tundra Books, 1975.

– *A Prairie Boy's Winter*. Montreal: Tundra Books, 1973.

– *Someone With Me: The Autobiography of William Kurelek*. Toronto: McClelland and Stewart, 1980.

– *William Kurelek: A Retrospective*. Edmonton Art Gallery, 20 Sept.–20 Oct. 1970. Edmonton: Edmonton Art Gallery, 1970.

Kurelek, William, and Joan Murray. *Kurelek's Vision of Canada*. Oshawa: Robert McLaughlin Gallery, 1982; Edmonton: Hurtig, 1983.

Lacan, Jacques. *Écrits: A Selection*. Trans. Alan Sheridan. New York: Norton, 1977.

Lane, Christopher. 'Queer, Query? Identity, Opacity, and the Elaboration of Desire.' Paper presented at QueerSites conference, U of Toronto. May 1993.

Latham, Sheila. 'W.O. Mitchell: An Annotated Bibliography.' *Annotated Bibliography of Canada's Major Authors*. Vol. 3. Ed. Robert Lecker and Jack David. Downsview, Ont: ECW, 1981. 323–64.

Laurence, Margaret. 'A Canadian Classic?' *Canadian Literature* 11 (Winter 1962): 68–70.

Leacock, Stephen. 'Humour, As I See It.' *Feast of Stephen: An Anthology of Some of the Less Familiar Writings of Stephen Leacock*. Ed. Robertson Davies. Toronto: McClelland and Stewart, 1970.

– *Sunshine Sketches of a Little Town*. Toronto: Bell and Cockburn, 1912.

Leslie, Susan. 'Moments with Mitchell.' *Vancouver Sun* 9 Nov. 1973: A36.

Lewis, Peter, ed. *Radio Drama*. London: Longman, 1981.

Lowman, Ron. 'Author of "Jake and the Kid" Isn't Smoking Because ... Chawin' Tastes Good.' *Toronto Star* 10 Apr. 1965: 57.

McCallum, Gary J. 'Who Has Seen the Wind.' *Take One* 6 (May 1978): 15–16.

McCorquodale, Hughena. 'The Stoney Indians Petition Federal Government for Land Suited to New Skill.' *High River Times* 21 Oct. 1943: 1, 5.

– 'Stoneys Hold Pow Wow On Easter Monday to Renew Prayer to Govt. For Land.' *High River* Times 13 Apr. 1944: 1.

– 'Eden Valley Sold to Dept. Indian Affairs.' *High River Times* 14 Oct. 1948: 1.

– 'Eden Valley Operating as Stoney Sub Reserve.' *High River Times* 8 Sept. 1949: 1.

– Letter to W.O. Mitchell. 3 Nov. 1943. W.O. Mitchell Papers. MsC 19.3.1.34. U of Calgary Libraries, Calgary.

– 'Under the Microscope.' Editorial. *High River Times* 21 Dec. 1951: 2.

McLay, Catherine. 'According to W.O.: An Interview with W.O. Mitchell.' *Working Title* 2, 2 (Fall/Winter 1991): 6–8.

– 'Crocus, Saskatchewan: A Country of the Mind.' *Journal of Popular Culture* 14 (1980): 333–49.

– 'Novels are Difficult Here: W.O. Mitchell's Unpublished Fiction.' *Essays on Canadian Writing* 37 (Spring 1989): 86–102.

McWhinnie, Donald. *The Art of Radio*. London: Faber and Faber, 1959.

Martin, Robert. 'Who Has Seen the Wind: Mitchell's Tale of the Prairies Looks Wonderful but Does Not a Movie Make.' *Globe and Mail* 5 Nov. 1977: 33.

Miller, Mary Jane. *Turn Up the Contrast: CBC Television Drama Since 1952*. Vancouver: U of British Columbia P and CBC Enterprises, 1987.

Mitchell, Barbara. 'The Long and the Short of It: Two Versions of *Who Has Seen the Wind*.' *Canadian Literature* 119 (Winter 1988): 8–22.

Mitchell, Orm. 'Invading Caves: Autobiography and W.O. Mitchell's *How I Spent My Summer Holidays*.' *Reflections: Autobiography and Literature*. Ed. K.P. Stich. Ottawa: U of Ottawa P, 1988. 142–52.

– 'Tall Tales in the Fiction of W.O. Mitchell.' *Canadian Literature* 108 (Spring 1984): 16–35.

Mitchell, W.O. *According to Jake and the Kid: A Collection of New Stories*. Toronto: McClelland and Stewart, 1989.

– 'The Alien.' Manuscript. Mitchell family private collection.

– 'The Alien.' Notes and manuscripts. W.O. Mitchell Papers. MsC 19.12.4–7. U of Calgary Libraries, Calgary.

– 'The Alien.' *Maclean's* 15 Sept. 1953–15 Jan. 1954.

- *Back to Beulah. The Play's the Thing.* Dir. Eric Till. CBC Television. Toronto. 21 Mar. 1974.
- 'Billy Was a Stoney.' Partial Manuscript. W.O. Mitchell Papers. MsC 19.18.10. U of Calgary Libraries, Calgary.
- *The Black Bonspiel of Willie MacCrimmon.* Toronto: McClelland and Stewart, 1993.
- *The Black Bonspiel of Wullie MacCrimmon. CBC Stage.* Dir. Andrew Allan. CBC Radio. Toronto. 25 Feb. 1951.
- *The Black Bonspiel of Wullie MacCrimmon. Folio.* Dir. Robert Allen. CBC Television. 9 Oct. 1955. Reproduced. *Playdate.* Dir. Melwyn Breen. CBC Television. Toronto. 7 Mar. 1962.
- 'The Black Bonspiel of Wullie MacCrimmon.' *The Curler* 1, 6 (Dec. 1964): 14–21.
- *The Black Bonspiel of Wullie MacCrimmon.* Calgary: Frontier Books, 1964.
- 'But As Yesterday.' *Queen's Quarterly* 49 (Summer 1942): 132–38.
- 'Catharsis.' Manuscript. Mitchell family private collection.
- 'Cow Heaven.' *Maclean's* 15 Nov. 1943: 9, 63–65, 67.
- 'Crocus Under the Microscope.' *Jake and the Kid.* Dir. Peter Francis. CBC Radio. Toronto. 24 Feb. 1952.
- 'Crocus Under the Microscope.' Typescript. W.O. Mitchell Papers. MsC 19.25.7.1. U of Calgary Libraries, Calgary.
- 'Crocus Under the Microscope.' Production script. Morris Surdin Papers. B101.12. U of Calgary Libraries, Calgary.
- 'The Day Jake Made Her Rain.' *Jake and the Kid.* Dir. Ronald Weyman. CBC Television. Toronto. 14 July 1961.
- *The Devil's Instrument. Folio.* Dir. David Greene. CBC Television. Toronto. 21 Nov. 1956. Reproduced. *Festival.* Dir. Eric Till. CBC Television. Toronto. 5 Nov. 1962.
- 'Documentary from the Banana Belt.' *Jake and the Kid.* Dir. Esse W. Ljungh. CBC Radio. Toronto. 17 Apr. 1955.
- 'Don't Scratch That Baby.' *Jake and the Kid.* Dir. David Gardner. CBC Television. Toronto. 1 Aug. 1961.
- *Dramatic W.O. Mitchell.* Toronto: Macmillan, 1982.
- 'Earn Money at Home.' *First Person Series.* Dir. Ted Pope. CBC Television. Toronto. 10 Aug. 1960.
- 'East End Was Just the Beginning.' *Telescope.* Dir. Peter Kelly. CBC Television. Toronto. 17 Nov. 1966.
- 'Elbow Room.' *Maclean's* 15 Sept. 1942: 18–20, 39.
- *Face of Saskatchewan.* Dir. Budge Crawley. Crawley Films, 1955.
- *Fires of Envy.* Dir. Julian Biggs. National Film Board of Canada, 1957.

- *For Art's Sake.* Toronto: McClelland and Stewart, 1992.
- *Free-fall: An Anthology of the Writing Division.* Banff: Banff Centre, 1975.
- 'The Golden Jubilee Citizen.' *Maclean's* 25 June 1955: 32–34, 46–48, 50, 52–53. Rpt. in *Jake and the Kid.* Toronto: Macmillan, 1961. 172–84.
- 'The Golden Jubilee Citizen.' *Jake and the Kid.* Dir. Esse W. Ljungh. CBC Radio. Toronto. 17 Nov. 1955.
- 'The Goose Hunt.' *Explorations: Man in the Landscape.* Dir. Peter Kelly. CBC Television. Toronto. 8 May 1963.
- 'Grace and Illusion: The Writer's Task.' *The English Teacher* 3, 2 (1963): 5–15.
- 'Honey and Hoppers.' *Folio.* Dir. Robert Allen. CBC Television. Toronto. 7 Nov. 1957.
- 'How Crocus Got Its Seaway.' *Maclean's* 20 June 1959: 16–17, 55–56, 58–60.
- *How I Spent My Summer Holidays.* Toronto: Macmillan, 1981.
- 'Is That the Truth?' *Jake and the Kid.* Dir. Peter Francis. CBC Radio. Toronto. 17 Oct. 1950.
- *Jake and the Kid.* Toronto: Macmillan, 1961.
- 'King of All the Country.' *Jake and the Kid.* Dir. David Gardner. CBC Television. Toronto. 19 Sept. 1961.
- *The Kite.* Toronto: Macmillan, 1962.
- 'The Kite.' *Show of the Week.* Dir. David Gardner. CBC Television. Toronto. 26 Apr. 1965.
- *Ladybug, Ladybug ...* Toronto: McClelland and Stewart, 1988.
- 'The Liar Hunter.' *Maclean's* 15 Aug. 1945: 16–17.
- 'The Liar Hunter.' *CBC Stage.* Dir. Andrew Allan. CBC Radio. Toronto. 21 May 1950.
- 'The Liar Hunter.' *Jake and the Kid.* Dir. Ronald Weyman. CBC Television. Toronto. 29 Aug. 1961.
- 'Love's Wild Magic.' *Jake and the Kid.* Dir. David Gardner. CBC Television. Toronto. 12 Sept. 1961.
- 'History's Gotta Be Accurate.' *Jake and the Kid.* Dir. Peter Francis. CBC Radio. Toronto. 3 Feb. 1952.
- Letters to Dudley Cloud. 7 Apr. 1947, 23 July 1950, 28 Dec. 1950, 22 July 1952, 2 Mar 1953. Atlantic Monthly Press Archive. New York, NY.
- Letter to Ernest Buckler. 27 Dec. 1949. Thomas Fisher Rare Book Library, U of Toronto, Toronto.
- Letters to John Gray. 23 Oct. 1952, 3 Mar 1953, 23 May 1953, 5 Feb 1954. Macmillan Archive, McMaster U, Hamilton.
- Letter to Orm and Barbara Mitchell. 10 Dec. 1967. Private collection.

- Letter to F.M. Salter. 21 Sept. 1948. W.O. Mitchell Papers. MsC 19.11.6.11. U of Calgary Libraries, Calgary.
- 'Mind over Madam.' *Jake and the Kid*. Dir. Ronald Weyman. CBC Television. Toronto. 22 Aug. 1961.
- 'Murder Will Out.' *Jake and the Kid*. Dir. Esse W. Ljungh. CBC Radio. Toronto. 7 Mar. 1954.
- 'Nature Knows Best.' *Jake and the Kid*. Dir. Arthur Hiller. CBC Radio. Toronto. 10 May 1953.
- 'The Owl and the Bens.' *Atlantic Monthly* 175 (Apr. 1945): 79–83.
- 'Panacea for Panhandlers.' *'Toba. Manitoba Arts Quarterly* 1 (Nov. 1933): 21–23; (Feb. 1934): 24–25, 28; (March 1934): 20–21.
- 'Patterns.' *Ten for Wednesday Night*. Ed. Robert Weaver. Toronto: McClelland and Stewart, 1961. 59–74.
- 'People Who Don't Want Equality.' *Maclean's* 3 July 1965: 9–12, 33.
- Personal interview (Alan Yates). Nov. 1977.
- Personal interviews (Orm Mitchell). Dec. 1981–Jan. 1982, 26 Dec. 1985, 27 Dec. 1986. Private collection.
- Personal interview (Timothy Zeman). 31 Oct. 1992.
- *Political Dynamite*. Dir. Donald Ginsberg. National Film Board of Canada, 1958.
- 'Prairie Lawyer.' *Jake and the Kid*. Dir. David Gardner. CBC Television. Toronto. 5 Sept. 1961.
- 'The Riddle of Louis Riel.' *Maclean's* 1 Feb. 1952: 7–9, 43, 45; 15 Feb. 1952: 12–13, 41–42, 44–45.
- 'Ron Southern – Master-Builder.' *Telescope*. Dir. Peter Kelly. CBC Television. Toronto. 30 June 1965.
- *Roses Are Difficult Here*. Toronto: McClelland and Stewart, 1990.
- 'Royalty Is Royalty.' *Jake and the Kid*. Dir. Peter Francis. CBC Radio. Toronto. 18 Nov. 1951.
- 'A Saddle for a Stony.' *20/20*. Dir. Peter Kelly. CBC Television. Toronto. 14 July 1963.
- 'Scandal, Scandal, Scandal.' *Jake and the Kid*. Dir. Arthur Hiller. CBC Radio. Toronto. 3 May 1953.
- *Since Daisy Creek*. Toronto: Macmillan, 1984.
- 'Somethin's Gotta Go.' *Jake and the Kid*. Dir. Peter Francis. CBC Radio. Toronto. 3 Oct. 1950.
- 'The Strait Gate.' Dir. Peter Kappele. CBC Radio. Toronto. 28 Dec. 1964.
- 'Struck Rich!' *Jake and the Kid*. Dir. Ronald Weyman. CBC Television. Toronto. 8 Aug. 1961.
- 'Tragic Trek of the Mennonites.' *Maclean's* 1 Mar. 1951: 7–9, 54.

– 'The Trophy.' Typescript. W.O. Mitchell Papers. MsC 19.35.18. U of Calgary Libraries, Calgary.

– *The Vanishing Point*. Toronto: Macmillan, 1973.

– 'What's Ahead for Billy?' *Canadian Forum* 24 (July 1944): 84–86.

– *Who Has Seen the Wind*. Toronto: Seal, 1982; Toronto: Stoddart, 1993. (Note: Citations to *Who Has Seen the Wind* are from the easily accessible 1982 Seal edition and its 1993 Macmillan/Stoddart reprints, unless stated otherwise. Mitchell's first novel was published in 1947 in two editions: a longer Canadian edition by Macmillan of Canada, and a shorter American edition by Little, Brown. For more information about the differences between the two editions, see Barbara Mitchell's 'The Long and the Short of It: Two Versions of *Who Has Seen the Wind*.'

– *Who Has Seen the Wind*. Ill. William Kurelek. Toronto: Macmillan, 1976.

– *Who Has Seen the Wind*. Ill. William Kurelek. Toronto: McClelland and Stewart, 1991.

– 'You Gotta Teeter.' *Maclean's*, 15 Aug. 1942: 8–10, 29–30.

– 'You Gotta Teeter.' *Jake and the Kid*. Dir. David Gardner. CBC Television. Toronto. 25 July 1961.

Morley, Patricia. *Kurelek: A Biography*. Toronto: Macmillan, 1986.

Morley, Patricia. 'Sweetness and Light with Black Edges.' *Books in Canada* 18 (Jan./Feb. 1989): 27.

Morton, W.L. 'Seeing an Unliterary Landscape.' *Mosaic* 3 (Spring 1970): 1–10.

Moss, John. *A Reader's Guide to the Canadian Novel*. 2nd ed. Toronto: McClelland and Stewart, 1987.

Newton, Ron. 'Kurelek Exhibit Strikes Chord with City Viewers.' *Edmonton Journal* 14 Nov. 1977: B1.

O'Rourke, David. 'An Interview with W.O. Mitchell.' *Essays on Canadian Writing* 20 (1980–81): 149–59.

Paglia, Camille. *Sexual Personae: Art and Decadence from Nefertiti to Emily Dickinson*. New York: Vintage, 1990.

Paine, Albert Bigelow. *Mark Twain: A Biography. The Personal and Literary Life of Samuel Langhorne Clemens*. 3 vols. New York: Harper and Brothers, 1912.

Pearson, Carol. *The Hero Within*. San Francisco: Harper and Row, 1986.

Perez, Michel. *Le Matin* [Paris]. Quoted in a *Who Has Seen the Wind* advertisement: *Toronto Star* 10 Nov. 1977: F3.

Peterman, Michael. 'W.O. Mitchell.' *Profiles in Canadian Literature*. Vol. 2. Ed. Jeffrey M. Heath. Toronto: Dundurn, 1980. 9–16.

Portman, Jamie. 'Comic Flights Muddle Complexities in New Novel.' Rev. of *Since Daisy Creek*. *Calgary Herald* 17 Nov. 1984: F1.

Ricou, Laurence. *Everyday Magic: Child Languages in Canadian Literature*. Vancouver: U of British Columbia P, 1987.

– 'Notes on Language and Learning in *Who Has Seen the Wind*.' *Canadian Children's Literature* 10 (1987–88): 3–17.

– *Vertical Man/Horizontal World: Man and Landscape in Canadian Prairie Fiction*. Vancouver: U of British Columbia P, 1973.

Robertson, Heather. 'W.O. Mitchell: Pain beneath the Laughter.' *Saturday Night* 89 (January 1974): 31–32.

Ross, Sinclair. *As For Me and My House*. Toronto: McClelland and Stewart, 1957.

– 'The Painted Door.' *Queen's Quarterly* 46 (Summer 1939): 145–68. Rpt. in *The Lamp at Noon and Other Stories*. Toronto: McClelland and Stewart, 1968. 99–118.

Salter, F.M. Letter to Dudley Cloud. 29 Aug. 1944. Atlantic Monthly Press Archive. New York, NY.

Scharnhorst, Gary. 'The Bret Harte–Mark Twain Feud: An Inside Narrative.' *Mark Twain Journal* 31 (Spring 1993): 29–32.

Sedgwick, Eve Kososky. *Between Men: English Literature and Male Homosocial Desire*. New York: Columbia UP, 1985.

– *Epistemology of the Closet*. Berkeley: U of California P, 1990.

Shelley, Percy Bysshe. 'Adonais,' *Alastor*, and 'Mont Blanc.' *Shelley's Poetry and Prose*. Sel. and ed. D.H. Reiman and S.B. Powers. New York: W.W. Norton, 1977.

Singer, Ron. Telephone interview (David Gardner). 2 Feb. 1994 and 4 Apr. 1996.

Slocum, Joshua. *Sailing Alone around the World*. New York: Dover, 1956.

Smith, Henry Nash and William M. Gibson, eds. *Mark Twain–Howells Letters*. Cambridge, MA: Harvard UP, 1960.

'Some of Today's Developers Have the Sensitivity of Fascist Book Burners.' *Canadian Heritage* (Dec. 1980): 29.

'The Speculations of Jefferson Thorpe.' *CBC Stage*. Writ. Stephen Leacock. Adapt. and dir. Tommy Tweed for the *Mariposa* series. CBC Radio. Toronto. Summer 1949.

Stegner, Wallace. *Wolf Willow: A History, A Story and a Memory of the Last Plains Frontier*. New York: Viking Press, 1963.

Styan, J.L. *Drama, Stage, and Audience*. London: Cambridge UP, 1975.

Suleri, Sara. *The Rhetoric of English India*. Chicago: U of Chicago P, 1992.

Surdin, Morris. Personal interview (Alan Yates). Nov. 1977.

Sybesma-Ironside, Jetske. 'Through a Glass Darkly: William Kurelek's Picture Books.' *Canadian Children's Literature* 39/40 (1985): 8–20.

Tallman, Warren. 'Wolf in the Snow.' *Contexts of Canadian Criticism*. Ed. Eli Mandel. Chicago: U of Chicago P, 1971.

Thomas, Clara. *The Manawaka World of Margaret Laurence*. Toronto: McClelland and Stewart, 1975.

Till, Eric. Telephone interview (David Gardner). 2 Dec. 1993.

Trilling, Lionel. *The Liberal Imagination*. New York: Viking Press, 1942.

Varble, Rachel M. *Jane Clemens: The Story of Mark Twain's Mother*. Garden City, NY: Doubleday, 1964.

'W.O. Mitchell and the Magic Lie.' *Toronto Star* 21 Oct. 1989: J12.

Watson, Patricia. Telephone interview (David Gardner). 9 Feb. 1994.

Webb, Jonathan. 'A Cozy Little Thriller from W.O.' *Quill & Quire* 55 (Feb. 1989): 24.

Weyman, Ron. Telephone interview (David Gardner). 2 Feb. 1994.

Whitehouse, Raymond. 'It Took Him Three Years But "Jake" Reaches TV.' *Toronto Star* 30 June 1961: 31.

Who Has Seen the Wind. Dir. Allan King. Souris River Films, 1977.

Woolf, Virginia. 'A Sketch of the Past.' *Moments of Being*. Ed. Jeanne Schulkind. Sussex: Sussex UP, 1976. 61–137.

Wright, Reginald. Letter. *Calgary Herald* 28 Dec. 1951: 4.

Yates, Alan J. 'W.O. Mitchell's *Jake and The Kid*: The Popular Radio Play as Art and Social Comment.' Diss. McGill U, 1979.

Zeman, Timothy J. 'An Annotated Bibliography of the Radio Drama of W.O. Mitchell in the Special Collections of the University of Calgary Libraries.' Thesis. U of Alberta, 1993.

Contributors

TIMOTHY FINDLEY is a novelist, playwright, and television and screen writer. Among his eight novels, two plays, two short story collections, and one non-fiction book, his most recent are *Inside Memory: Pages from a Writer's Workbook* (1990), *Headhunter* (1993), *The Trials of Ezra Pound* (1995), *The Piano Man's Daughter* (1995), and *You Went Away* (1996).

DAVID GARDNER is a professional stage and television actor, a writer, and a teacher with a doctorate in Canadian theatre. An Honorary Member of the Association for Canadian Theatre Research for distinguished service to theatre in Canada, his many publications include his recent chapter on variety entertainments in Ontario for *Later Stages* (1997).

TERRY GOLDIE teaches English at York University. He is the author of *Fear and Temptation: The Image of the Indigene in Canadian, Australian and New Zealand Literatures* (1989) and co-editor of *An Anthology of Canadian Native Literature in English* (1992). He is currently researching a book on gender and national personae in Canadian, Australian, and New Zealand literatures.

PETER GZOWSKI is a journalist and the popular host of CBC *Morningside*; he has edited five books based on the *Morningside* series and two books based on his earlier CBC radio series, *This Country in the Morning*. His many other books range from his profile of Gretzky's Oilers, *The Game of Our Lives* (1981) to his *Selected Columns from Canadian Living* (1993).

DICK HARRISON is a retired English professor from the University of Alberta and is the author of *Unnamed Country: The Struggle for a Canadian Prairie Fiction* (1977), *W.O. Mitchell* (1991), and *Intimations of Mortality: Introducing W.O. Mitchell's 'Who Has Seen the Wind'* (1993).

FRANCES ITANI is the two-time winner of the Tilden (CBC) Canadian Literary Award, 1995 and 1996, for her short stories. She has published three collections of stories, three books of poetry, and a children's book. Her latest book is *Man Without Face* (1994). She has taught creative writing at several universities and at the Banff Centre for the Arts.

W.J. KEITH is Emeritus Professor of English, University College, University of Toronto. His recent publications include *Canadian Literature in English* (1985); *A Sense of Style* (1989), with a chapter on Mitchell; *An Independent Stance* (1991); *Literary Images of Ontario* (1992); and a volume of poems, *Echoes in Silence* (1992).

R. ALEXANDER KIZUK teaches English at the University of Lethbridge, has published a book of poetry *Microphones* (1987) and many articles on Canadian literature.

DAVID LATHAM teaches English at York University and is the editor of *The Journal of Pre-Raphaelite Studies*. His recent books include *An Annotated Critical Bibliography of William Morris* (with S. Latham, 1991) and an edition of Morris's *Poems by the Way* (1994).

SHEILA LATHAM is a librarian with a Ph.D. dissertation entitled 'The Social Production of W.O. Mitchell's Texts: A Bibliographical Study.' Her books include *W.O. Mitchell: An Annotated Bibliography* (1981); *An Annotated Critical Bibliography of William Morris* (with D. Latham, 1991); and *Library Services for Off-Campus and Distance Education* (1991).

CATHERINE McLAY, a retired English professor from the University of Calgary, is a writer and painter who has published many articles on Mitchell, including the 'Biocritical Essay' for the *W.O. Mitchell Papers* (1986). Her current work-in-progress is *In Place*, a study of Mitchell's fiction and drama.

RICK McNAIR is a playwright, story-teller, and theatre director who has served as Artistic Director of Theatre Calgary and the Manitoba Theatre Centre and founded the Winnipeg Fringe Festival. Two of his many plays are *The Frank Slide* (1980) and *To Far Away Places* (1986).

BARBARA MITCHELL teaches English at Trent University and is co-authoring with O.S. Mitchell a biography of W.O. Mitchell. She recently received a Ph.D. from the University of Leeds, with a thesis entitled 'The Biographical Process:

Writing the Lives of Charlotte Brontë.' She has published articles on Mitchell, Sinclair Ross, Elizabeth Gaskell, and Winifred Gérin.

O.S. MITCHELL teaches English at Trent University and is co-authoring with Barbara Mitchell a biography of W.O. Mitchell. He has published articles on William Blake, William Faulkner, W.O. Mitchell, documentary film, and biography.

MICHAEL PETERMAN teaches English at Trent University. His books include *Susanna Moodie: Letters of a Lifetime* (1985), *Robertson Davies* (1986), *Forest and Other Gleanings: The Fugitive Writings of Catharine Parr Traill* (1994), and *'I Bless You in My Heart': Selected Correspondence of Catharine Parr Traill* (1996).

THERESIA M. QUIGLEY teaches English and Canadian comparative literature at the Université de Moncton. She is the author of two collections of poetry, *Mid-Life Poems* (1988) and *A Journey of Circles* (1993), and *The Child Hero in the Canadian Novel* (1991).

GUY SPRUNG is a theatre director who founded the Half Moon Theatre in England (1971–75), and served as Artistic Director of the Toronto Free Theatre (1982–87), of the Vancouver Playhouse (1987–88), and of Canadian Stage Co. (1988–90). He is the author of *Hot Ice: Shakespeare in Moscow: A Director's Diary* (with Rita Much, 1991).

MURIEL WHITAKER is Professor Emerita of English, University of Alberta, and has written and edited several books, including *Pernilla in the Perilous Forest* (1978), *Great Canadian Animal Stories* (1978), *The Legends of King Arthur in Art* (1990), and *Sovereign Lady: Essays on Women in Middle English Literature* (1995).

ALAN J. YATES has a Ph.D. in Communications from McGill University and is now retired after working in newspapers and broadcasting, mostly at the CBC, for over thirty-five years.

TIMOTHY ZEMAN is a teacher in Beaumont, Alberta. In 1993 he completed a thesis entitled 'An Annotated Bibliography of the Radio Drama of W.O. Mitchell in the Special Collections of the University of Calgary Libraries.'

Index of Works by Mitchell